Following
Josh

Following Josh

We founded f/64 Publishing to promote crisp, clear storytelling that captures those details essential to understanding a subject. Like making a photographic exposure at f/64, this takes time and strategy…and can result in breathtaking work. The company is also named partly in honor of the association of photographers co-founded by Ansel Adams: Group f.64.

f/64 Publishing
197 Pine St. Suite 34 | Portland, ME 04102 USA
www.f64publishing.com
www.followingjosh.com

1. Travel – Essays & Travelogues
2. Travel – Special Interest – Adventure
3. Biography & Autobiography – Personal Memoir

ISBN 13: 978-0-9831858-1-9
Written and published in the USA

For Herb and Bill,
Who saw the world before me,
And told me it was good.

Also by Dave Norman

501 Paintball Tips, Tricks, and Tactics

A Small Town Celebration

White River Junctions

Contents

Josh
Seoul, South Korea
3 August 2007

Preface

My flight climbs out of St. Louis rising twenty, fifty, ninety feet towards the morning sun. Banking over Illinois, the window frames my hometown. The wing points down at the old high school, old church, old neighborhood, these things that are new to the kids who replace me.

I once leaned over the railing on a bridge above a crevasse, trying to feel that "potential energy" you read about in textbooks. I felt only the breeze. But I feel something here, in seat 34A, tumbling into a grand adventure.

My old life recedes in the jet wash, my new one lying far over the horizon—at the end of a journey across Asia and Europe by train. I'll land in Seoul, where an old friend will meet me at the airport. The journey we're beginning together ends separately—for him, back home in St. Louis. I'm off to make a new life in New York City. We're booked on the Trans Mongolian and Trans Siberian railroads, from Beijing to Warsaw along 8,500 miles of track—certainly the scenic route from St. Louis to New York. Who knows how much farther we'll go before it's over. Life isn't a destination, after all, but a journey.

So here we go.

* * * * *

I met Josh Vise in a high school play many years ago. Funny and adventuresome, he was easy to like. Taller and thinner than me, with lighter hair and very different style, there is no mistaking us for kin—rather, we became brothers of a different sort.

Josh took a college semester in Thailand. His parents threw

a welcome home party, filling the house with friends and family and pictures. Josh wandered among them, subdued by more than jetlag; watching him from across the room, he acted like just another guest waiting to greet someone important who was due any moment—anonymous at his own party.

He pulled me aside. "I tell 'em a story," he said, "and pretty early on, they can't relate. They just don't—they can't—know what I'm talking about. So they stare at me politely. I mean, what's the point? I'm just gonna listen to them. That'll make everyone more comfortable."

He went back to Thailand for another semester, then back again. He spent this past year teaching English in Korea. I've been working in New Hampshire. Our in-person friendship became internet based. We compare notes on new places and routines, on daytrips, on politics and headlines... These days our interaction— perhaps our friendship—seems predicated on entertaining each other. We haven't had a beer in person in forever.

We have a history, but not much of a present.

When he meets me in Seoul, he'll be more than a dialogue window; we won't be able to turn our computers off and walk away. It's like that point in a long distance relationship where you move in together, except we aren't lovers. Each week we'll move in, together, to a whole new country.

For him, our journey leads from Korea back to his old room in his parents' basement and—hopefully—a new start. Living abroad, he said, is fun, but with its challenges; teaching is a job, it pays the bills, and he likes it, but...something is missing. He's ready to get on with life, if not entirely sure how.

I never asked him what he was looking for over there, or if he was running away from something. Most people don't move to Asia on a lark. When he wrote home, he talked about beaches and bars and the freedom of a good exchange rate. It was interesting, but topical.

Some people "find themselves" in college, or by moving away from home, or by backpacking across Europe. Sometimes it's a junket, sometimes a pilgrimage; some people try harder than others. I mentioned that to Josh, that this might be the coming of age adventure, the Odyssey, he needs before he can wash ashore as an enlightened adult. He laughed at me. I laughed at me. I raised a toast of morning coffee; he raised a midnight beer and logged off.

But maybe there's something to that; maybe he needs a flourish to close this chapter and begin a new one.

I certainly do.

* * * * *

I had a nice apartment in New Hampshire, a part time radio job, the run of a comfortable town and a fresh Master's degree heavy with promise—heaven for a bachelor. I mixed adventure into an otherwise quiet life—hitchhiking to Mississippi to report on Hurricane Katrina, flying to Malaysia to write about sports, couch-surfing across England... I revel in learning about the places I go from the people I meet. I read about countries while wandering through the land itself—adventure, for me, is about learning as much as doing.

Then I struck up a long distance relationship with a woman rooted in New York City. My friends graduated and moved away. I don't deal well with change like this. Suddenly my nice little life felt lonely; I'm not sure which changed more, my circumstances or me, but it's clearly time to move on—to a career, a marriage, a big city, whatever we tell ourselves comes next.

But first, I want a fitting farewell to that life...a chance to see something new, learn something strange, have an adventure—everything a bachelor party should be. I sold everything I could, donated the rest, and drove back to the Midwest to visit my family as a way of honoring the past before chasing the future.

So this is the story of rediscovering a friendship and taking on the world; honoring life's changes and celebrating new tomorrows. Meeting new people. Trying new things, and seeing what fits.

Or so I hope. These are my thoughts from thirty thousand feet, airplane pointed west now, towards the first stop: Seoul, South Korea.

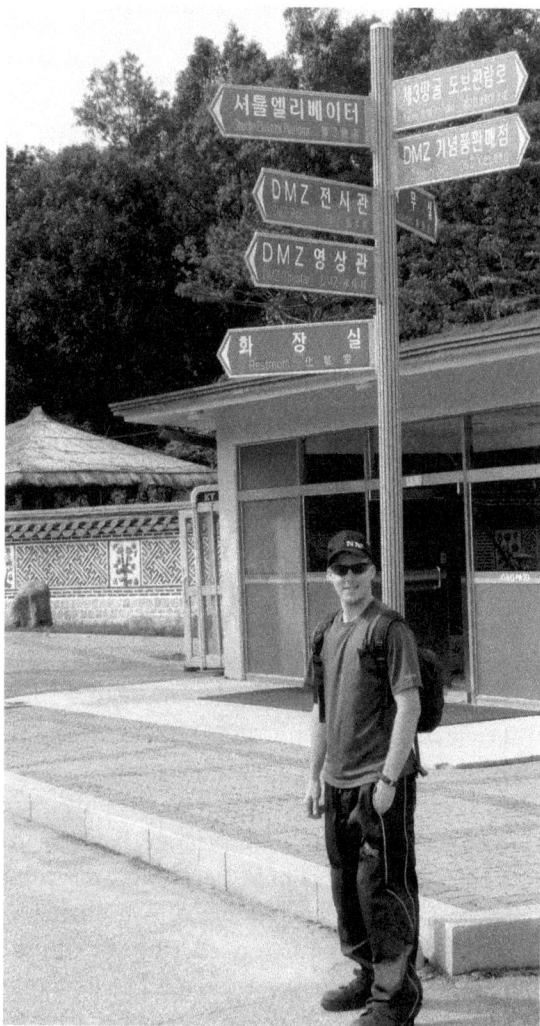

The Author
Demilitarized Zone, South Korea
5 August 2007
Photo by Josh Vise

Seoul, Korea

Tourists don't know where they've been.
Travelers don't know where they're going.

—Paul Theroux

Won in my pocket and crime on my mind... Ten bucks a night... Chewing the bulgogi... Josh goes shooting... Chill, Mellow Yellow... Own Flippin' Program...

Josh is a tall, rail-thin millionaire with bundles of Korean Won in every pocket. "Do me a favor?" he asks at the airport. "Change this into USD. You'll have to fill out a form..." This morning he cashed out his Korean savings account, filled out the form, changed ten bucks shy of the tax-free limit and hopped a train to Seoul with a year's pay crammed into his pockets.

He slips me a million Won—about seven hundred bucks—which I change with a sly grin, telling the girl in the currency booth that I'm on the next flight home. I give Josh the green American bills, a little money laundering to set the tone. He leads me to a bus and we're off.

Incheon International Airport sits on a man-made island in Kyonggi-man Bay, across the Yellow Sea from China. Some civil engineer looked west from Seoul and thought I can put an airport on that sandbar. Or maybe his boss told him to do it, so he passed the buck to the junior engineers and a thousand laborers. March into that swamp and build me an airport.

"Ne!"—yes!

There's no room in Seoul for the thing. Engineers knew how to bulk up shoals to make oil storage facilities, so it was just a matter of time and bug spray to put in the airport. Incheon is pretty cool—lots of glass, shiny metal. These are the things you remember at the far end of a trans-Pacific flight.

Our bus takes the long bridge over tidal marsh and coastal swampland that looks the way Washington DC probably did in the 1600s. "How's Seoul?" I ask.

"Oh it's great," he says in a high-pitched voice that hasn't changed much in the years I've known him.

"You still look the same, man," I say. "Maybe skinnier."

"You've gained weight!" he jokes. Josh looks elegantly emaciated whether or not he works out, so he usually doesn't;

anyone looks fat by comparison.

"Voice hasn't changed either, man."

"Yeah, I've got the voice of a twelve year old." But with an adult's range and fullness—exactly halfway between a kid and an adult. It fits. Adults don't chuck it all and wander the earth unemployed, but neither do kids. That grey area between school and whatever comes next can stretch on as long as it has to.

"But can a twelve year old," Josh continues, "do this?" He puts his nose on his shoulder and makes an elephant noise, flopping his arm like a trunk. It's pretty good; I'd be scared if I was a peanut. "The kids love it. They call me 'Joshua Teacher.' You know, I kinda like kids. I can relate."

"They're your people."

"My people?"

"I don't know…" and truth is, I don't. He'd sent me self-pictures taken at arm's length, aimed down so he stands freakishly tall over a ring of kindergartners hugging his leg. It was an artifact from a different world, where my younger friend is the adult—a teacher, no less. I feel like a teenager who keeps waking up in a late-twenty-something body. I bust his chops a little, "Did you tell 'em the elephant call is a traditional American greeting? Man, I weep for the future."

"No…" he says, dragging it out, furrowing his brows, in a—teacherly, not a "Josh"—kind of way. I'm back in that old friendship we had—the way I knew how to talk to Josh.

I've got some catching up to do.

Ten bucks a night…

The bus drops us off at a subway station and disappears into the madding traffic. We descend the fluorescent-lit entryway to a thoroughly modern platform. This city reminds me of the cleaner, neon-flashier parts of New York; to be fair, most cities remind me of New York, which is architectural chicken—everything tastes kind of like it.

For a moment I feel tall and strong, something of a bush league giant with aspirations. I worked out for the last few months, figuring I ought to be able to carry my frame and day packs—my only luggage—for three miles at a healthy pace...just in case. You never know.

He carries no pack this evening, having already established himself at the hostel. He wears a black t-shirt and jeans, and I brought him a pair of black combat boots that match mine—waterproof, sturdy, good for keeping your socks dry while hiking through who-knows-what. Bobbing that subway dance, heads and shoulders lagging just behind the train car wobbles, he smiles with the goofy, unselfconscious grin of a man who refuses to take life seriously. Working abroad, sink or swim, has strengthened that smile. Many things change, but some things shouldn't.

"I feel like a giant," I tell him, my English turning a few eyes nervously towards us (and then away quickly). I'm eye level with their hat brims; with the pack, I weigh as much as any two of them. I'm Paul Bunyan in a pine forest. "Then I look at you."

"Ha!" he laughs. "You'll get used to it."

I follow him into the neon shadows and throngs of people schooling like fish. Asia is full of people, and neon. And little shops. Each little shop has its own sign, Korean letters taunting me—the same symbols appear over and over, so that the whole tableau would make sense if I could just figure out the basics. I point to one, and Josh sounds it out phonetically, giving me a quick Korean reading lesson that goes mostly over my head. I'm struck by the way that someone I grew up with, who is younger than me no less, can know such things that I don't. So I just listen.

The characters on these signs come from the 1400s, when Sejong the Great ordered that Korea should have its own written language, something more than their mishmash of ancient Chinese and Japanese characters. Sejong had artists create distinctly Korean characters to represent their spoken sounds, taking that final step to a unique Korean language. Now there are nineteen consonants and twenty one vowels that are generally combined into twenty four sounds, analogous to letters in our alphabet.

Memorize the symbols and what they sound like together, then read left to right like we do—Josh is a quick study at it, though going from sounds to meaning is way more complicated. I see the patterns, but can't make sense of them; the most important signs, thankfully, have English subtitles.

"Coffee." "Lunch." "Stop." The road signs come in familiar shapes and colors, but with Korean letters and occasional subtitles. This is important when crossing the street, where the difference between survival and dismemberment—not just death, I mean actual dismemberment—is waiting for the right sign or crosswalk signal…then waiting one second longer.

Seoul traffic is orderly, though dense and fast and dangerous. Drivers push the red lights, but usually don't blow wantonly through them. Cross while the light's green, and you're burger; wait for the red, let the last daredevil through, and you have relatively good odds. They also drive on the American side, having never been under British rule, which helps—I instinctively look left when stepping off a curb. In Seoul, that means I'm looking at actual threats to my safety. In former British colonies like India or Malaysia, I'd see the taillights of the car ahead of the one that's going to kill me.

These are important comforts when you're jetlagged—the little things, far from home.

Josh booked us seven nights at Windroad Guesthouse. I haven't stayed in a hostel before, but don't expect much for the price—this dim-lit alley, the dingy 7-Eleven, and the festering dumpsters seem fitting. A corrugated metal door on a heavy steel frame groans and shudders, a cat shrieking in chorus. Inside the walled off grounds, we go up some concrete stairs with crumbling edges and down a long outside balcony, up to the last door. He jiggles it open without a key. We take off our shoes, and I survey our quarters: six bunks in a little room on the left, and two right there in the hallway; a washing machine, with a black and white cloth fedora—a stylized jazz hat for yuppies—crowning a forgotten pile of lost t-shirts from many continents; and a bathroom around the corner.

Asian bathrooms take some getting used to. This one has a Western-style toilet, as opposed to the porcelain square with an oval hole like elsewhere; there's a small trashcan (don't flush the paper), a curious plastic housing over the toilet paper roll, a communal pair of pink rubber flip-flops and a shower wand on the wall. Lock the door. Turn the water on…it's freezing cold. I'm used to a giant water heater quietly burning propane day and night somewhere in the bowels of the building, hot water just a few seconds away.

Not here.

The water heater is built right into the wall in this shower/sink/toilet-cell. Turn it on, pick a temperature between "City Water Main" cold and "Sort Of" warm, and away you go, hosing down your body and everything else in range, including your towel—there's no good place to hang it, except on the hook outside the door. The sink has only one knob, dispensing only one temperature, which must chill your bones in winter.

But it's a hot summer day now, August 3rd, and my framepack is stowed under my prison mattress. Our room has a fan, yellow linoleum floors that aren't glued down—the bubbles remind me of slowly boiling curry, except they don't pop—and the entryway is two inches lower than the main floor. So is the bathroom, but that's for drainage.

The lowered entryway is a Korean custom, and great for stubbing American toes in the dark. It provides a little place to kick off your dirty shoes, a custom taken seriously. This is a good country for loafers; my combat boots are comfortable, but with such long laces trussed up tight, they're a royal pain to take on and off, and on, and…off…and…

The office on the ground floor is open when the surly teenage manager wants it to be open, and the refrigerator in the adjoining "social room" hasn't been cleaned in months. It's an archeological treasure, if you're into that sort of thing and don't have any sense of smell. Opening the door clears everyone out of the room, a trick Josh says he relishes.

Then there's the blood smeared on the wall, where sated mosquitoes met their gruesome end.

You get what you pay for.

Chewing the bulgogi...

We spend the day talking, walking, getting caught in a cloudburst and laughing like fools in the rain. By evening we've run out of old friends to talk about, and twice been through my account of changes back home: gas has gone up. Tim Irwin got married. Hardee's burned down. They lowered the highway speed limit...our hometown, changing without us. We trade memories like currency.

With the past exhausted so quickly, we embrace the present. He treats me to dinner, playing my host to Korea, ordering bulgogi: "Korean BBQ," with shiitake mushrooms and onions, carrots and bean sprouts. Our waitress uses a pair of scissors to cut a chicken breast, bone and all, into strips that fall on the pan recessed into our table. She turns a knob and propane bursts with a whoosh down by our knees, dinner just moments away.

"Think you'll come back to Korea?" I ask.

"Maybe," he says, in a carefully wistful way that is loath to discount anything from his life. "But I've got some stuff I want to do in St. Louis, some videography. I wrote a script I need to work on, so many things, you know?" The waitress brings our Hite beer, which is unremarkable—a watery lager better suited to dank fraternity basements than meal-pairing. "I could teach college here, I was offered a position."

"Joshua Professor?"

"It could be fun. I'd meet some new people, and it would pay better than the hogwon," the term for a language academy like his recent employer.

"Are you happy here?" I mean it as a bomb-dropping question, requiring a life-changing answer.

"Yeah, it's a cool place," he says offhandedly. Then he pours me a glass of water with both hands on the bottle—a Korean sign of respect that means nothing to Americans, though we're the only ones at the table. "But so was Thailand. Asia's pretty neat, you know? I mean, Asia—who do we know who really spends time here?"

If I want to see people who look like me and speak English

well, I can go to Europe. The Far East, though… Josh and I are attracted to Asia because it's so incredibly different. Here they eat things you'll never find on American menus; the languages are written and spoken in completely different ways from Western tongues; the incense-filled shrines are impossibly mysterious. Asia is completely foreign to the American Midwest of our youth… and holds all the romance of true adventure.

Even the mundane things, to a Korean anyway, are hopelessly novel to me…like bulgogi, and holding the water bottle with both hands. We talk while each bite cools between chopsticks, savoring the dinner and this chance to reconnect. This is my week, he says, to get my body adjusted to the time zone and Asian cuisine—to dodgy hostels and living out of a framepack. He's forgotten that I've travelled quite a bit, although not quite like him—Josh is one of those rare souls who truly embraces his freedom to shake hands with the world.

He planned our next month of adventure; all I can offer him tonight are stories from our past. It's good enough for this evening.

Josh goes shooting…

We stuffed our pockets with glossy tourist flyers for shows and tours and food, food, food with ads like neon signs pulsing eat, eat, eat. One of them has a bull's-eye. The advert reads "Learn art of Pistol Shoot!" Josh thinks it'll be fun; I target shoot all the time as a form of meditation—high-velocity yoga. I don't feel compelled to do it here, but Josh is excited; perhaps he wants to give me something familiar in this foreign place, an appreciated courtesy. Target shooting is an upper class leisure sport in Korea, where ammo is expensive and licenses are hard to come by—it appeals by conspicuous consumption.

The Won-flush millionaire is gung-ho.

The range is on the fourth floor of a tall building, an exceedingly odd place for a shooting gallery. They're set up like a golf pro shop, only instead of clubs and balls, they sell bullets and earplugs. An overly-enthusiastic instructor shakes our hands and walks us to a table; his uniform makes him look like a police officer from a low budget comedy film. There's a book on the table with laminated pages featuring dramatic photos of different pistols and their rental fees, with a column for ammunition costs. I see why it's elitist—no one in their right mind, even the most gun-starved expat, can afford this.

Josh orders the .50AE Desert Eagle and ten bullets—for a good day's wages. The instructor smiles and asks what I'd like to shoot. "No thanks," I say. "Too expensive."

How about revolver? No.

Smaller one? No.

Nothing? Right.

Ho-kay!

He ignores me and helps Josh into a bulletproof vest. Unless they plan to exchange fire, this is utterly pointless. They walk into the range, on the other side of bullet proof glass, where another instructor brings in the Desert Eagle. It's a massive piece of Israeli engineering, a gas-operated, magazine-fed semi-automatic with a barrel wide enough to stick your thumb inside. It's one of those pistols that well-heeled collectors buy because they can; the firearm equivalent of compensating for a personal deficiency with a fancy sports car with such power that you're quietly thankful for the speed limits.

The instructor clips the trigger guard into a box on a taught cable running sideways across the range—now Josh can't turn the muzzle more than a few degrees off target. So much for...for... whatever dubious intentions they thwarted.

And so much for the experience. You shoot a fifty to feel the recoil; to feel your arms go numb holding up a five pound gun. Target shooting is fun because it's hard. Hook the pistol to a cable?

Lame.

He loads the magazine, chambers the first round, and I spare a thought for the office on the other end of the backstop. I wonder what they think, the insurance salesmen or bankers or whoever works over there, knowing that tourists get their jollies firing jacketed hollow points at their wall.

Aim. Fire.

Pooft.

Guns make lots of different noises. Pooft is not usually a good one. It jams. The instructor fixes it. Josh aims, squeezes, pooft.

Sub-velocity loads. Josh paid for the sex and adrenaline of shooting a mad dog hand cannon; to work with their steel-and-rubber backstop, they loaded custom rounds to have a tenth the power the gun's designed for, like revving a Ferrari up to twelve miles an hour. Pooft.

Bullet proof vest?

Pooft.

Cable retention system?

Pooft.

One…hand…clapping…

One hour. Ten bullets. Sixty dollars. Josh folds his target into his pocket with a smile.

This is how the trip starts—not with a bang, but a pooft.

Chill, Mellow Yellow…

We're back from drinks at a basement bar, back from hearing a band play for only us on this Sunday night. Back, to a blacked-out stranger on the bunk above mine in the hostel at the end of my wits. There's a puddle of something soaked into his sheet. "I'm gonna say that's soda," Josh says.

It's yellow.

"It's Mellow Yellow. Go to bed."

We wake up to the drunk man screaming. He thrashes around, punching the wall, kicking the bed frame.

"Chill, Mellow Yellow," Josh pleads in the darkness. More screaming, cursing, punching. "Hey! Mellow Yellow! Chill the fuck out!"

Ten bucks a night.

Own Flippin' Program…

A few days in, the bustling capital city is stressing me out, and it's only the first of five capitals on the schedule Josh set. He proved good with logistics, our dream taking shape under his direction, so I let him run with it. I prefer to travel by my wits, drawn to the countryside and places where life slows down to the pace of tea brewing in stoneware pots—I can somehow find these havens if I can just wander within range. It makes planning pointless and counterproductive—you can't schedule a whim, or indulge a whim on a schedule.

So I trusted Josh with the details and my credit card and now we have tickets clear to Warsaw with hostels booked along the way. I appreciate that, but it means we're on a tour of the biggest cities in Central Asia…not exactly my scene. I plan to wander a fair bit, following my fancies.

"I think we should tell each other where we're going," Josh said. "For safety, you know, and so we can go together if we want to see the same things."

With no hard feelings, I added, if an invitation is declined. "Exactly."

I invoked that rule this afternoon, setting off on OFP—my Own Flippin' Program, the civilian-legal version of a Marine Corps epithet that fits me to a tee. I'm wandering the quieter parts of Namsan Park to get away from the crowds and neon and flickering LCD billboards; Josh is exploring Changdeokgung Palace, alone with his camera, for similar reasons.

Though Josh is an urbanite, Seoul can get a little big for him—he boycotted it for months before working up the courage to visit. Then he came during the Chinese New Year, expecting the city to be packed; it was vacant. "Koreans go home to celebrate with their families," he told me. "A lot of them moved in from outside the city, so they went home and Seoul wasn't crowded at all."

The folks who remained were in high spirits. They met in parks to play games, have picnics… I think of cities in terms of towering glass and giant steel and the anonymity of crowds, where the sheer number of people ought to make getting to know any of

11

them impossible. But that weekend in Seoul, Josh said, he found a refreshing sort of community…and here in a city he thought too big even for him, he saw life on a human scale.

"I watched this girl skip rope," he said. "About seven years old, maybe. Her parents swung the rope, and she jumped at the wrong time. Got whacked right in the face, started crying… So her dad hugged her and kissed her head, and then made her get back in there. Made her keep jumping rope, crying the whole time. It was…it was the funniest, most macabre thing I've seen here."

Now he likes Seoul in small doses—the secret gardens, ninety cent subway rides, and the nightlife. He likes good views from tall buildings, bar hopping, and late-night cafés, all of which abound. Wherever he goes, Josh makes friends with strangers and follows them like tour guides. With other tourists as a filter, he sees the best places that several people can find…then he moves on, lathers, rinses, and repeats. In these ways, he is much wiser and more adaptable than I—when not wandering the countryside, I roam the streets and avoid white people and pretend I'm the first Anglo in Asia. It's random, unfocused and somewhat deluded, but works for me.

"You're always welcome to join me," he said, "but yeah, no hard feelings." We agreed, and word is bond.

Glorious People's Coal Mine... Disrespecting the yellow line...

I wake up early, my body on American Samoa time as it catches up westbound to this time zone. Josh is out cold, sleeping with grim determination. Mellow Yellow is splayed diagonally across his bunk, arm and leg dangling limp over the edge like tentacles.

I sneak out of the room, strap on my boots, and walk to the bakery at the end of our alley. The counter girl speaks self-conscious English, beaming with a schoolgirl's smile as I navigate the bins. "Try the bungeoppang," she urges, pointing to a small waffle in the unappealing shape of a fish; red bean paste is pressed in the middle, like blood, and I wonder if it has little pastry bones, too. I politely decline.

Korean pastries are more filling than ours, probably from the fiber in the bean paste they use like we use frosting. I grab a few round pastries, one with a semisweet black paste, another with fried poppy seeds in brown paste. "Very good choice," she says slowly, my smile sending her eyes nervously down to the cash drawer. She hands me my change in her right hand, left hand touching her right elbow—a custom I'll adopt from here on.

With some mini bananas from a street vendor, the tiny fruit adorably delicious, I'm set for a power breakfast in motion. There's no time for a proper Korean meal, and along our alley, nowhere to find it.

Locals might wake up to a hot bowl of tofu or mushrooms in clear broth; perhaps with tofu strips served sweet, white rice, boiled potatoes, fruit—lychees, bananas, pears—and kimchee, the universal Korean side dish. It's paired with pork and chicken, lunch and dinner, soups and salads, and even breakfast—spicy, fermented cabbage to get you going in the morning.

Back at the hostel, Josh is awake; we walk to a main street to get picked up for a tour of the 38th Parallel.

We're heading for the Demilitarized Zone, that swath of border about two and a half miles wide and just over a hundred fifty miles long that separates Kim Il-Sung's experiment from

South Korea. Kim Jong-Il, Il-Sung's son and the current "Glorious Leader" of North Korea, keeps firing dud rockets into the Bay of Japan and making crazy threats. The nuttier he gets, the better a spokesman he becomes for the South Korean readiness campaign.

The DMZ is the most heavily defended border in the world, and if either country breaks through, they'll release all sorts of fiery hell. The Korean War got costly and unpopular, and their stalemate probably got a little bit boring for the major players; there was an armistice, but it's important to note that the war never officially ended.

Our tour bus is a little portable city hurrying us through dense forests and clean country air. We're packed in tight, breathing recirculated Seoul smog, shut in from bushes and trees. I press my hand on the window, towards the hot day outside; the glass feels cold from the air-conditioner. Josh watches the land flatten into farm fields, then rice paddies as we near a small river. There is a guard station on a bridge, just a regular concrete bridge that could be anywhere, but it's not—it's on one of the main roads from the capital to the DMZ. An armed guard checks the license plate and the driver's paperwork, and waves us past his hut. We drive under a large highway sign which is mounted to a duct three feet thick.

Which is packed with explosives.

The bridges leading to the DMZ are rated for heavy military vehicles—troop transports, bulldozers, tanks. They're wired to blow on a commander's orders, any minute of any day, to slow down invaders. I wonder how many explosives we drive over, how the wires weave around rebar in the concrete. The North has not attacked since 1953, not really. But the threat is there and must be taken seriously, a specter the South Korean government tries hard to keep in everyone's mind.

South Korea has a conscript Army, refreshed by eighteen year old men who serve for two years before college or starting their careers. They perform disaster relief and community service and train for a defensive ground war. There is only one threat they worry about: orders from Pyongyang that would unleash the red hordes across the DMZ and into their homeland.

The Line of Military Control runs through the middle of the no-man's-land. When nits get picked, this is the line that matters—it runs through several border checkpoints and miles of wilderness. The Imjin River does not respect it, flowing where it wishes and where it has for years. The river becomes an estuary where it joins the Yellow Sea, serving as a freshwater highway into South Korea; turn left around the mainland, go upstream again on the northwest-flowing Han and in a few minutes your yacht—or gunboat—is right there in downtown Seoul. The South Korean banks of this and every river flowing in from the north are traced with miles of reinforced fencing and razor wire, and camouflage-painted guard shacks with M249 Squad Automatic Weapons on swivel mounts, their muzzles pointed north.

Josh is among the first off the bus at Dorasan Station, black t-shirt flopping loose. He takes a few pictures, pointing his camera at the northernmost train station on the Gyeongui Line. We're just shy of the southern edge of the DMZ. Before World War II, this was just another section of track; now it's the terminus for most northbound trains. The exceptions are once-daily freighters that haul raw materials north and bring back finished goods, which seems incredibly bizarre in context. The tracks are mined, probably on both sides of the DMZ—just in case.

Inside, we pose for pictures with a teenage Korean guard. Josh looks at the paintings, a series of oils on canvas that celebrate this outpost. This is the last calm, quiet train station we're going to visit; there are no cars on the tracks. The only people inside are guards and tourists who come to feel the emptiness of a grand station on a closed border. We stamp our passports with a novelty stamp that has two doves soaring high and free over barbed wire and railroad tracks. It's a meaningless stamp for a passport, but a hopeful piece of art—a counterbalance to the "readiness campaign."

Two generations of Koreans have grown up knowing only this constant state of peacetime readiness—which is preferable to the war their grandparents remember. We have no concept of war in our homeland, and no concept of looming danger. I watched the end of our Cold War on a television wheeled into my elementary school classroom. So far as I've known, life has been beer and skittles ever since. Our military is voluntary; my biggest fears growing up were acne and girls.

That's probably the same with Korean kids, but they also have the low-murmur of readiness in case…in case…

In case ten thousand North Korean soldiers march under the DMZ in the opening hour of a desperate attack. I'm looking across a parking lot now at their military's attempt at a tourist attraction, a glass and metal structure with a small museum and gift shop, and a long, steep ramp into the ground. This is the "3rd Invasion Tunnel Visitor's Center," a place where anyone can take a look at what the nefarious Main Enemy is up to.

The problem with a cold war is that it's hard to photograph, and without photographs, it's hard to get people excited. Our Cold War with Russia was prosecuted with spies and diplomats; soldiers and missiles were pawns and rooks in a giant game of chess that was fun to photograph, but were never used for much.

When you see the flash, duck—and cover!

Drama. Fear. Take those old newsreels, shown in my parents' classrooms, and pair them with frightening pictures of Russian military parades around Red Square—that keeps people interested…but only for so long. Then you wonder, really…who's going to nuke Boise? The threat may be real, but doesn't seem terribly personal.

Enter Korea: lull the populace to sleep with a few decades of peace and complacency, and they're soft and flabby when the red hordes come calling. The South Korean generals know this. So it's really important to the South Korean military to keep those murmurs humming, to conscript teenagers when their bodies are strong and their minds are malleable, and instill in them the fear and passion that make good soldiers. You sleep safe in bed because rough men stand ready in the night to visit extreme violence on your enemies, or words to that effect—it's the meaning that matters, and the meaning is central to this monument.

The South Korean government needed something to raise that ugly specter of looming destruction, to keep the people ready…

This "Invasion Tunnel" was practically a gift from the North.

In 1975, a North Korean defector helped the South Koreans detect a tunnel bored under the DMZ an hour and a half northeast of Seoul. There they had it—proof of maniacs in the dark, proof the threat was still real.

In the years since, South Korea found—and closed—three more invasion tunnels. Were they the setup for a simultaneous, subterranean invasion? Repeated attempts at the same failed idea?

The DMZ is full of video cameras and expensive sensing equipment…and old pipes driven straight down, filled with water, and loosely capped. That's how they discovered one of the latter invasion tunnels—shockwaves from the dynamite made the water spurt up like a geyser.

On this tour we get to walk through part of the First Invasion Tunnel, a six-foot-round tunnel three quarters of a mile long. I take a picture of a green-painted cyclone fence around the parking lot, with its little red sign—"mines!"—and follow Josh into the visitor's center.

They issue us yellow construction helmets and lockers, cameras being strictly prohibited just about everywhere in the DMZ—they like to think there is a real threat from spies, that one of us might send cell phone camera images of…tourist spots…to Pyongyang where they figure in Kim Jong-Il's sick machinations. They use the tunnel to justify this paranoia, but it feels hollow. The really important things are well hidden, I'm sure.

A tour guide blocks my path, angrily pointing at the camera tucked under my arm—foiled.

The tunnel floor is slick and there are puddles where condensation dripped down from above; the air is cool and my breathing, heavy. Cave temperatures stay in the low sixties all year long, and today it's a nice change from summer heat. In the southern wall, pointed into South Korea, are narrow holes bored horizontally where miners planned to pack more explosives. They were detected somewhere between the drilling and the blasting, these holes remaining as monument to their aspirations. The walls are painted black.

Seoul confronted Pyongyang, exposing the incursion to the UN and world media. The North painted the walls black in the last few feet, took photos, and admitted to the tunnel.

To their coal mining tunnel, anyway. Far from South Korea, of course—look at these photos, guys, c'mon…that's coal, isn't it?

I pat the paint and laugh.

Disrespecting the yellow line…

"Dude, don't do that." Click.

"Don't do what?" Click.

Josh rolls his eyes and walks off, back across the wide yellow line painted on the concrete here at the Dora Observation Center. The concrete building has a lecture hall inside with a plaster relief map of the Dorasan region of the DMZ. We listened to a lecture from government officials on the history of regional conflicts, the South Korean hopes for reunification, and a description of North Korea's "Gaeseong Village" in the valley below.

"Their south-facing windows are painted black," the lecturer said. "You see world tallest flagpole in Panmunjeom Village, few kilometer farther." The North Korean flag it holds weighs six hundred pounds; more when it's raining. Then he barked, "No take photo past yellow line!"

I'm past the yellow line, leaning against a low concrete wall, camera tucked nonchalantly under my arm. Back there, you can't see anything interesting.

Click.

My camera silently captures hurricane-angle shots of North Korean farmland. The buildings are uninhabited for the most part, and probably full of transmitters and listening stations. The façades and farmers are just for show; it's a "cultural village" you can't visit, something of a life size diorama of the North Korean utopian ideal, dressed up and animated for the tourists at Dora Observation Center. It's the first propaganda village I've ever seen, and it creeps me out.

Click.

On our side is the South Korean response: the "Freedom

Village." Directly opposite Gaeseong, and no more convincing, it looks downright tacky. I wonder if their north-facing windows are blacked-out...

For all the talk of imminent threat and doom, for the tunnel tour and the barbed wire fences and guard posts, it's surprisingly...tranquil. And verdant. And almost kitschy, as if the observation post and guards and thick yellow line are recreations of something far away in a much scarier place. The modern DMZ, being undeveloped and unmolested, is an accidental sanctuary for rare birds and animals.

Not quite the Cold War spook show I expected.

* * * * *

Heading back to Seoul, we transfer buses at "Peace Land," a hokey children's amusement park near the stunted root of a bridge that used to span the river. The parking lot is full of families and school groups, alive with carefree voices in many languages.

The tacky "Peace Land" sign belongs to an era of even less certain peace that tried so much harder to seem happy; the rides are now rundown, like rusting people-traps designed by a deranged cartoon mouse.

"If the North attacks," our tour guide says as we get off the bus, "this park will be destroyed in the first five minutes." But it hasn't been in fifty years, and try though I might, I just can't imagine tanks ripping through "Peace Land." I'd really like to, but I can't.

So we watch children play in a fountain, and take a few minutes to walk around a Confucian temple with its giant "Peace Bell." This is where older Koreans come each year to pay respects to their ancestors buried up north, as they can't cross the border to visit the graves. It's a serene place, with a good view. There's an old man sitting here in a brown vest, staring vacantly north and back through time.

The land of Budweiser... Soju and the acid reflux of doom...

I'm in the thick of it now, my body almost adjusted to the time zone. We're having drinks on the top floor of the 63 Building, the tallest in Seoul. From up here the city is a patchwork of white and yellow streetlights, rows of identical apartment buildings and long black lines, just exactly the way a circuit board looks from high above. Massive office buildings have alternating darkened and lighted windows like chessboards; neon signs grow sideways and giant, flickering billboards bring television outside...pure Asia. I watch the lights, drinking Budweiser—that world famous St. Louis beer—and listening to the Korean Children's Yodeling Choir perform behind us. They're wearing lederhosen, singing in pitch-perfect Austrian accents. I can't explain this.

I ask Josh where he considers home.

"Columbia." He was born in St. Louis and moved, very young, across the Mississippi River to the suburb I'm from. He contracted viral wanderlust on a student exchange trip to Germany back in 2000, and after studying in Thailand, sent his passport in for extra pages to hold all the stamps and visas. He keeps it in a belly pouch that has the locker room smell of mildew and old sweat.

I was in Germany on the same program in 2000; we spent a teenage night drinking excellent Licher beer and dreaming of travels to come. Seven years hence, here we are, sucking down Budweiser in Seoul, listening to Korean children yodel.

"This beer tastes horrible," I complain. "Like horse piss, like every Budweiser I've ever had. I was hoping, since we're in a different country, this would be different too, but..."

"Quiet, you," he jokes. "It's on me, what'er you complaining about?" He had a college apartment just a stone's throw from Budweiser's World Headquarters in St. Louis. I woke up on his couch once, the brown morning-after-drinking taste blending terribly with the smells of the brewery down the street in a perfect storm of nausea and regret. On the far side of the planet now, he bought a round for us that tastes like home. Budweiser is the most consistent beer in the world, a line repeated with creepy word-for-word similarity by several brewmasters I know. There's nothing like it, they say. Everywhere you go…a little taste of St. Louis.

I look out the window at the reflection of this bar, my doppelganger drinking resiewduB out in thin air, and ask myself what I'm looking for on the road; why I love travel the way I do. Josh asks a businessman when the aquarium in the basement closes, and they chat about everything and nothing in particular.

A Malaysian friend of mine, a painter in Malacca, spent three years hitchhiking around the world. Tham Siew Inn was young, single, and done with the highest schooling he could afford; so are we. He hit the road to find inspiration, he told me—to meet people and see places beyond Malaysia. Tham is proud of his country, and fond of his home; he wasn't abandoning anything, just taking some time to check out what lies over the next hill. His painting of two Nepali girls in a gold-cast Himalayan morning hung in my old apartment.

Tham and I talked about the way that traveling gives me a deeper appreciation for my own country; how by seeing other ways of living, I can better structure my own life, and explain why I live as I do. He smiled, nodded, and invited me to dine with his family.

I like the places I've lived; I haven't left any of them with hard feelings, just excitement for what might come next. Maybe I keep traveling because I haven't seen enough yet to be satisfied; there are customs I haven't tried, food I haven't eaten. I haven't seen it all, not by a long shot. I'm going to check a few more boxes on this trip—it might be my last really good chance. A married guy ought to work as much as he can for his family…right?

That makes this a full-bore sprint around the world in my last, best hope to do it all.

* * * * *

As he leaves the bar, Josh's new friend shakes my hand, touching his right elbow with his left hand, and lowering his head and eyes in a little bow. I mimic, passing the peace—literally. He says "ahn nyong hee ga se yo," meaning something like "go in peace," and then stumbles awkwardly towards the bathroom.

We don't bow back home, and it offends me to say "sir" and "ma'am." But here in Seoul, it's different. I bow when I enter temples, and when I say "thank you." I doff my boots, untying them, retying them, even when there would be no reason to do so back home—because I'm not.

Cross country skiing works those little muscles on the side of your leg, the ones you don't normally use; traveling somewhere truly foreign does the same thing for your mind. Just entering a room is different, with the shoe-doffing and sometimes a bow. The courtesies come naturally here, and I like them. They feel genuine, ancient. Even if it's just a façade, we should be so lucky to have pleasantries for pretense.

Back home, I react to the same things in the same ways, day after day, and that became who I am. But in completely new surroundings, I can be anyone I want as I feel my way through the customs. Travel lets me character-act, and the locals get a kick out of helping.

Traveling, we routinely wake up in different places; maybe we can wake up as different people. Nothing from our past is here to box us in.

Except each other.

* * * * *

Watching the crowds, I catch a man's eye—just a glance between two strangers looking around a room in boredom. I smile politely; he jerks his face away.

"Man, don't do that," Josh says. I'm surprised he noticed. "It's rude."

"What, does he think I'm flirting or something?"

"No. You smile at babies and kids here, but no one smiles at strangers—it's like you think they're a child or something." Maybe he just looked away like anyone else might have.

Koreans don't smile in public much; this is easily mistaken for hostility, which is sometimes the case—older Koreans, from many accounts I've read, can be quite racist and xenophobic...

even about their neighbors. I haven't encountered that yet, at least not that I've noticed. But Japan's occupation within their lifetime weighs heavily, and European colonists were in Asia within their lifetimes. They have good precedent to fear non-Koreans in their homeland, even if I don't feel like I pose any particular threat myself.

Josh is careful to explain that their hard, blank countenances are usually nothing personal—just a cultural thing. "But it makes it really hard to meet people," he confides, though he seems to have little problem doing so. "You know your coworkers, the regulars at a bar maybe, but that's about it." Prearranged dates are still popular outside Seoul, I read.

But keeping that blank face on the sidewalk, in this bar, anywhere I'm out with people, just seems…unfriendly. Maybe it's worse to smile at strangers here, but I'm going to keep doing it—I'm from the Midwest. We smile at strangers…and we're stubborn. Josh rolls his eyes.

"It's friendly," I argue. "I'm not Korean. I think it's cool when someone greets me anyeh…ayneh…

"An yung ha say oh."

"…however you say it. They seem to think it's cool when I greet them my way. Not that guy, but other people have smiled back. Lots of 'em. It's a cultural exchange."

"It's insulting," he scoffs, protective of a culture not his.

Other adjustments are easier—Hite Beer tastes beer-like, and the pastries taste vaguely pastry-like. But coffee—that's a tough one. I can buy it fresh-brewed at coffee shops, like anywhere else, but when I pick up a cup at a corner shop, or a restaurant, or a bank lobby—anywhere I'd find an old steel tank percolating in America—I get boiled water and a plastic tube of coffee crystals, powdered "creamer," and sugar. Dump. Mix.

Enjoy?

Josh likes Korean food: kimchi and mushroom soups, pork with leeks, bulgogi…chicken satay, fruit smoothies, veggie smoothies, fruit and veggie smoothies…all good stuff, by and large. We've tried a lot and barely scratched the surface, walking under dangling forests of neon signs, through crowds of stone-faced Koreans, past Starbucks. My grandpa eats KFC on Sundays; Colonel Sanders is everywhere in Seoul. Budweiser is ubiquitous. Strange connections like these wrap around the world, little strings tied at one end to St. Louis, at the other, to the beer in Josh's hand, tugging him back home the long way around the planet.

Josh is going home to the land of Budweiser, to his family and his old room in their basement. I'm on my way to New York, to get married and make a new home. The city glistens below us. The yodeling children sing "Edelweiss."

Home is where the heart is, as the old saw goes. You have to leave it someday to understand and appreciate it. The surprise, I'm told, is finding that home is not always back where you left it—that time moves on, and that sometimes "home" does, too.

It's a wonderful night in Korea.

Soju and the acid reflux of doom...

We're standing outside the 7-Eleven in the alley by our hostel, the street glistening from August rain as summer heat cooks the dumpsters like fetid stewpots. My shirt clings uncomfortably in the stifling humidity, and the hostel's rusty gate shrieks and howls behind us like it's in pain—or in heat. This is the perfect time and place for soju.

"Don't breathe when you drink it," Josh says, handing me a small green bottle containing the bastard child of rice wine and mineral spirits—each bottle should come with a cardboard box under an overpass. It smells worse than the dumpsters, with enough alcohol in the fumes to knock a horse sideways. The taste is of spoiled turpentine on fire. I want to spit it out along with its memory, but would never live that down, so I choke back two horrible gulps.

"Feisty, ain't it?"

"It tastes like burning." Josh takes the bottle and drinks half. I have no idea how his stomach lining survived his year in Korea. I remember the near-empty bottle of Tums in his backpack; maybe it didn't.

"You get used to it."
Thank God I'm not in Korea long enough.

Trusting the soup... Thunder drumming... When dinner hurts so good... Goodbye, Mellow Yellow...

Mushroom soup—it's the best food I've had in Korea. I was hungry in the art district, wandering through galleries showing Korean artists' very best and one displaying children's work; in some cases the difference was little more than the price.

I walked the length of a gallery-lined street, taking in a few displays and a dramatic sculpture installation, then wandered off in a light rain. Hungry, I decided to "adventure food," a process whereby I stand in front of different restaurants until one feels right. The rules to adventure fooding are simple: no chain restaurants, and nowhere I've been before. It's more dramatic in America, where this brings me to restaurants I've passed by for years, or never otherwise would have found. Abroad...it's almost too easy, which makes that right feeling all the more important.

With nothing appealing on the main drag, I took a right turn down a narrow side street, passed by another gallery—too much art for one morning—a small hotel (with prices far, far higher than our hostel), a Confucian temple, and there it was: a soup shop. A bowl of soup made with tap water nearly killed me years ago in Kathmandu—I've avoided soup in Asia since—but this soup shop feels right. Their banner glistens in the rain, the pictures of soup enticing me like sirens. I take a table by the window to people-watch, but see only a parade of brightly colored umbrellas floating past.

The menu is in Korean with English subtitles and a picture of the food beside the price. The better restaurants have high-quality photos of perfectly prepared meals; budget places have happy-snap pictures worked into a menu created on a word processor. The better the grammar, the better the photos, the higher the price; these things have little to do with how the food tastes. Many of the mom-and-pop-shops I've tried are as good as fancy places with gleaming brass and dark wooden tables. A rare few of each are terrible. They serve a mélange of traditional Korean food and modern dishes, with plenty of mystery meat Josh assured me is only occasionally dog. I'm getting used to bones in everything, and whole fish floating in broth.

One soup picture has a fish, too large for the bowl, tail sticking up from the spicy red broth on the left, eye staring up at me from the right. I choose the mushroom soup.

First my waitress brings the kimche, the translucent yellow cabbage stained red with peppers and spices. Then she brings the soybean sprouts in a darker sauce, then leeks, each side in its own porcelain dish, and a pitcher of filtered water—which is not conspicuously consumed as a luxury here, as it is back home. Bottled water in Korea, as in much of the world, is a matter of public health. The city cleans its water to a washing standard, but doesn't waste chemicals and money making it completely potable when most of it will be flushed or drained anyway; for drinking, there is bottled water.

Then she brings a large bowl she holds in both hands. The steam is thick and smells amazing. She sets down a pair of stainless steel chopsticks and an Asian soup spoon that is like a trough with a bowl at the end; she smiles hopefully, bows, and walks back to the kitchen.

A few stringy "golden needle" mushrooms float in the soup, with flat-pressed leeks and little oil bubbles. I stir, raising some ginger from the bottom along with shiitake mushrooms, matsutake and oyster mushrooms, and four or five more types I've never seen before. The broth is thick and the steam roils across the surface like fog.

It tastes amazing.

If I learned my lesson in Kathmandu, I would not have come to this soup shop at all; though once bitten, I try not to shy away from real treasures. Other lessons, like being told not to brush your teeth with tap water (which is alright here, but a terrible idea in many other countries), are better translated into rules. There is no substitute for experience, though. Sometimes it comes down to luck, which I was born into, and instinct, which I trust a little more every day.

Thunder drumming...

"I wanna do something cultural," Josh said. "And something social, and something entertaining, everywhere we go." That's his three step plan for victory; it sounds great, and it should give him a good standard to compare the stops along our way. My plan adds and spend as much time outside as possible.

I walked Changdeokgung Palace in the rain, saw Namsan Park, and now I've spent the day in art galleries. It's time for something...louder. Enter the traditional drumming performance at the Seoul Arts Center, just a few blocks from the soup shop. Josh met me at the stairs coming up from the subway, and with an hour to spare, we paid way too much for coffee in a little upstairs shop with black and white photos from New York in the fifties. We were the only customers; with five-dollar-a-cup coffee, it's no wonder.

Cross the street, thread the traffic, and now we're passing through a little sculpture garden leading to the Center. The performance is in the basement, and dapper Koreans mingle with well-dressed foreigners in the foyer—if the locals like it, you know it's good...and probably authentic. Locals don't do tourist things in their own town, and definitely don't support gimmicky or demeaning art—a valid concern when you follow tourist pamphlets around.

On each seat is a little spinning drum—the kind with beads on strings attached to a double-sided drumhead, itself on a stick that you spin between your flattened palms so the beads whirl around and strike the drum. I had one as a kid and for a moment—a glorious moment—spin it between my hands with sparkly-eyed glee. Josh looks at me strangely, but turns his drum in his hand so the beads strike it once...just to make sure it works, of course. Just so he doesn't feel left out.

The show starts with an English-spoken history of drumming in Korea, then reaches deep into the history books—just shy of the appendices—to evoke the first sounds on the peninsula. Then come dancing and drumming, fire and music, performers thumping out the story of the Korean people. There are wars and epic loves, dragons and a cabaret of historic emotions. Thunder drumming now, they beat a rhythmic frenzy and stop—giving way to the longing of a lone drummer thumping slowly on a darkened stage.

I really want to play my own little drum, and here at the end our chance arrives. The audience explodes in high-pitched tink-tink-tinks. We're swept away in the noise, each out-spinning the other and loath to quit as the number ends, as the history on stage catches up to the present and seems now to have led inexorably through love and loss and war and hope to…to a room full of people spinning toy drums in the dark.

It's not all blood and glory on the leading edge of the spear.

When dinner hurts so good…

I don't know how these things happen, but they do, and I'm glad. We're doffing our boots on the landing outside an apartment. We took a train, a bus, and ten minutes walking to get here, led by a Brooklyn girl Josh met at our hostel. They both taught English in hogwans, and story swapping led to our invitation. It's her last night in town, and a Korean friend of hers is throwing a farewell barbecue. We're leaving in the morning, too—farewells are the theme tonight. We didn't bring anything to offer—a faux paus back home—but it doesn't seem such a big deal. The dinner is hosted by the friend's parents, and despite our ages we are the kids for whom the adults expect to provide. It will be our turn someday; karma is an investment.

A middle-aged woman opens the door and the Brooklyn girl greets her in pitch-perfect Korean—no trace of Brooklyn until she switches back to English with us. We're welcomed into a living room with a large velvet painting traced with blinking Christmas lights. This is home for the parents and two children, these six rooms, and there is no clutter. I wonder how they manage, where they put all their…stuff. But this, I'm told, is normal—Korean families just don't accumulate the sort of detritus that clogs our homes.

She leads us back outside, up the stairwell, and then out

onto the roof, where her husband sits cross legged on a raised platform—a sort of Korean picnic table. There's a small charcoal grill beside him, and a row of plastic baggies full of meat and sauces. The roof is set up like a garden, with potted tomato and pepper plants and a trellis overhead. A hill rises steeply behind us, large neon signs flickering over the crest. To the southwest is a pulsing blue neon cross over a white Lutheran Church hemmed in by concrete-frame apartments. It looks as out of place here as a Confucian temple in the Midwest, but faith does not abide political boundaries.

Our traditional dinner kicks off with Hite beer and sprouts, soy sauce and kimche served from a white plastic bucket. We pass the kimche first to the mother and her two daughters, the hosts; such is polite in nearly every culture. The father is too busy grilling chicken thighs and passing food around to take anything for himself.

The chicken was marinated in a plum sauce with chili peppers and tastes fantastic. I say as much, and the father smiles his generic smile of uncomprehending gratitude; we don't understand each other but are trying, and laughing, and that counts for a lot. I rub my belly and he gives me more. Too much. A glorious excess… and we're just beginning.

Between the pork and the beef courses, mouth bee-stung with chilies, I hit that crazy stride where the spice hurts too good to stop. I compliment the hostess on her vegetable plants, and ask if the little green fruits on one are zucchini. She shakes her head and tells me its Korean name.

Come again?

"Not ready yet," she continues, pausing. "You want try tomato?" The cherry tomatoes fattening on the vine are perfectly ripe. They taste amazing. Josh takes one, this is so good, he says, thank you! and bows with his hands folded—an automatic gesture.

"Fantastic," I say, a word I use too much. "That was great!" Then I clasp my hands prayer-style and bow. Her family smiles.

"Food okay?" the mother asks. Excellent! I say. I love the spicy food!

"Oh," she says, brown eyes widening with pride and mischief.

"You want try chili?"

"Absolutely!" She holds her arm out, shaking her hand in the direction of the chili plant; it's impolite to point with your index fingers, so Asians point with their thumbs. To say go ahead, she curls her fingertips and then pushes them out, up, quickly, like scraping crumbs from an invisible table. It's the same gesture my grandmother uses to say "shoo, go away!" Tonight it means please, eat my spiciest peppers!

There's a rule with peppers: spiciness is inversely related to size. Take your average bell pepper: they're big, and don't have capsaicin, the chemical that burns your mouth. Now consider the Thai chili, like the ones on this bush. They're tiny, like a little red ceramic miniature of themselves...and they could knock the teeth right out of a bear.

I love them.

I take a few of the ripest chilies and offer them around the table, but no one joins me—eight pairs of eyes just stare, twinkling. Expectant. I eat one, and it's really, really good. Very spicy. The perfect crunch, where you can feel the pepper buckle and snap between your teeth. The seeds are small and soft and pop as I chew them. They will ferment these peppers with cabbage, vinegar, and spices to make kimche, or use them to spice green beans; they're added to soups, cut up and laid on grilled fish, mixed into marinades...they're a staple of East Asian cuisine.

And they're very, very hot.

One of the Korean sisters hands me a Hite, which I decline—alcohol makes the burning worse. Her friend hands me a small green bottle of soju.

Schadenfreude—pleasure at someone else's pain. It's a German word for something universal. Everyone has a laugh.

Especially me.

Goodbye, Mellow Yellow...

It's one in the morning and I'm tired, loopy, sated. My body has finally caught up to this time zone. China is going to be harder; more people, more grit and dirt-life-authenticity. Communism.

Beijing—a shock to the senses. I hear that you can see the smog hang like a cloud from a hundred miles out. I've gotta be rested, be fit and ready. I've been getting up when my body thinks it's morning, letting my body catch up to the time zone by degrees. In my exhaustion and the rain I missed much of the city, but in Changdeokgung Palace I ran my hands along walls laid by men who are now remembered only in the chips and nicks they left in the brick.

Seoul is a nice place, and cleaner than I expected—our hostel notwithstanding—but the coffee is bad and I still don't like kimche. As a metropolis, it's a substitute for any other chicken-flavored city at this longitude. The constant threat of a North Korean attack is an interesting backdrop to progress and development and school kids with bright yellow Pokémon backpacks, but I don't have any desire to linger here. It's time to move on, and feels like it.

We have the hostel nearly to ourselves now on a weeknight, and the surly teenager working the front desk is asleep on the floor in his office. I pack my bag, rescuing the forlorn jazz hat from the pile of dusty laundry. "Is it me?" I ask, striking a pose. Josh grumbles something noncommittal, the way he probably should. We check the laundry, brush our teeth with bottled water and fall asleep. We'll soon be rid of the pallid walls and bubbling linoleum floor and Mellow Yellow splayed across his bunk.

As my father says, sleep fast—morning's comin'.

Top: **Made in China, indeed**

Bottom: **Water seller on the Great Wall**

Great Wall, China
13 August, 2007

Beijing, China

"Imagine that you've built a bonfire of telephone poles—the ones dripping with creosote—and throw in a fax machine, photo copier, some asbestos stacking chairs and a roasting chicken... Turn a corner and thwack!—different items are thrown into the flames: a load of running shoes, four thousand plastic bags, hog carcasses, and a Dumpster of barber shop floor sweepings."

—Douglas Copeland on Beijing's air quality

Like a needle in a hutong… Chinese ghosts can't jump… No sign of General Tso…

China, Monday, August 13th, 8pm. I'm sitting in a wheelchair at the People's University Hospital, hooked into three IV bottles and a bag of brown liquid. Yan Ying, my friend, interpreter, and heroine, just humiliated me at another game of Super Tic Tac Toe played on the back of a hospital form. In just under twelve hours I need to be on a train bound for Mongolia. I owe 400 Yuan to a motorcycle biker in a leather jacket and chains, the People's Agriculture Bank of China doesn't take my ATM card—my PIN number is one digit too long—and I haven't eaten since breakfast. The IV drips away my last night in the People's Republic.

This is how my time in Beijing ends. Yan Ying gets up to fetch some tissues, leaving me alone to think about how it began…

* * * * *

We arrive Wednesday afternoon on an Air China flight—that's the airline you read about every now and again whose planes are grounded in Europe for failing basic inspections. Who knows if there is truth to the rumors and pictures on the internet, but the result was our very real apprehension and frantic prayer at every bump.

The brand-new Beijing International Airport, built on occasion of next year's Olympics, uses glass and steel like the primate house at a zoo—the high ceilings and glass walls make it feel expansive, while shunting groups on isolated, narrow courses. The freedom of expanse is imaginary. Uniformed guards stand at attention, pokerfaced representatives of Chinese authority. I'm not sure who's observing and who's on display. Communism hides its mortal fears behind grand architecture and bulletproof glass.

Visas stamped and on our way, we choke on our first breaths of polluted Beijing air as we contemplate a row of buses. Their placards and signs are loaded with Mandarin characters, and there are sheets of paper taped to the front windows that have English transliterations. We read them aloud, trying to match their sounds to that of instructions in our little black books. Josh and I carry these identical mini-notebooks, a creation of his that organizes our train schedule and hostel reservations. On one page Josh wrote directions from stations to the hostels; on the facing page, he pasted the same in the native language, copied from the hostels' websites. We can read one, point strangers and cabbies to the other, and presumably get where we're going.

Josh thinks of things like this, clever little details far beyond the credit he's given back home—back where people haven't seen him in too long. Whatever growing up you do away from home doesn't count with those you leave behind—their last impressions hang in suspended animation. I mentioned these notebooks in an email. "Well," my father responded, "that's a good thing at least," like this clever resource was a happy accident. Those are the impressions Josh is going back to, in a town where he plans to begin life as an adult.

Finding your way in Beijing is difficult at best, but it'll be easier after 2008—crews are busy replacing the all-Chinese signs with shiny new green and white ones, black and white ones, blue and white ones, with English words nearly as large as the Chinese characters. The Olympics are coming, and they're putting on their best face for the world. This is a transition period in China's politics, they say, and also in its aesthetics: English on signs and billboards in a country formerly closed to the West. Many big highway signs are up, with conflicting spellings of the same street names, while most of the shops and restaurants remain complete mysteries behind their Mandarin. It's impossibly exotic, and romantic when you realize they're imperiled by the translation fervor.

Our directions are straightforward enough: take this particular bus to one particular stop, wind our way through a maze-like hutong, and bam: there will be a heavy, wooden, red-painted door on the right. But the bus driver clears out his coach a few stops early, leaving us to the tiny maps pasted in our notebooks. They show two square blocks. We're somewhere in the rest of China's second largest city.

That's a problem…

Our hostel is just off Xi Si, down Liuhe Hutong. We look around at the red signs with white characters posted on building corners. They don't match our directions. "I think it's this way," Josh says, taking the lead. We're on equal footing now, in mutually foreign territory. I might as well follow him—I don't have any better idea, and we're too proud to ask for directions just yet.

Ten minutes later we're lost even worse; trial-and-error navigation in Beijing is like playing "Battleship" in a cornfield.

"Zhangzizhong Street, and Tuanjiehu Avenue?"

"Miss…"

Chinese ghosts can't jump…

We show the page for Templeside Hostel to a cabbie and are on our way.

There are tens of thousands of people gathered in and around Tiananmen Square. We drive slowly through thick traffic, the Square on our left, the giant painting of Chairman Mao hung on the Forbidden City wall to our right. There are people everywhere, lined up half a dozen abreast and thousands deep on the sidewalks, filling every open space…orderly.

Beijing is one of the most densely populated cities on earth, so I'm not sure if these crowds are special or par for the course.

"The big dinosaur model is a good landmark," the directions say, and there it is across the street. We pay thirty Yuan, a little over four dollars, for the ten minute ride. Two bucks each—a rip-off by local standards, but well worth the time and misery avoided. Wandering Beijing is going to be fun, but not with a full framepack, hungry, lost, and homeless—some stories are better lived by others.

Our hostel is somewhere in this hutong, a quarter of a city block worth of space divided haphazardly into tiny apartments, hidden gardens, and countless rooms by a complicated series of meandering walls—like living in a maze, but with fewer minotaurs. Straight thoroughfares cut through the hutongs, and every kilometer there's a main street connecting on a grid system. There are no signs that advertise what, or who, you'll find down any given alley…the locals just know, and the foreigners don't need to—we're supposed to stay in the big hotels and shop at the government-run souvenir stores.

A foul-smelling public restroom stands where our hutong meets the street; inside, some poor soul sells roast chicken by the stalls. Our alley leads past a small shop with miss-matched commercial refrigerators selling bottled water. Red doors hang at somewhat regular intervals, but there are few signs, and all are in Chinese. The alley meanders left, right, stretches for awhile, turns again…with doors, but no windows, and no sign of what's on the other side. The walls are smooth concrete, grimy down low, their tops adorned with narrow tile roofs or horizontal clay tubes. The maze may end abruptly around any corner; it feels like it stretches all the way north to Mongolia. I don't feel safe, but not for the natty Chinese men shuffling bleary-eyed through the hutong—it's just my reaction to being caged in.

We find the hostel door, which is heavy and iron-reinforced as if a remnant of feudal raids. I notice the security camera; Josh finds the doorbell. We have our priorities. An electric lock buzzes and the door swings open. Behind us: dust, grime, grey concrete walls.

"Watch the doorjamb," Josh says as I trip over a well-scuffed concrete bumper across the doorway.

"That's inconvenient," I mutter, composing myself.

"Especially if you're a ghost," he says, taking a look around a surprisingly clean, bright-painted, cheerful anteroom. It opens into an airy courtyard with bushes and vines and tables. "When you die, they tie your feet together." I listen, taking my bearings, while he shrugs his backpack off in a corner. "They totally believe in ghosts, so they have those jambs all over the place to keep the spirits out of their homes."

"Ghosts can't jump?"

"Not with their feet tied together."

A pleasant-smiling teenage girl in a black skirt emerges from the office, brushing aside a curtain of seashells on string. Her name is Yan Ying. She welcomes us "home."

No sign of General Tso...

We're drinking cheap Dali beer in the garden. A television squawks on a rolling cart, flickering images of a gala in Tiananmen—the "one year until the Beijing Olympics" celebration. The hutong rumbles with concussions from a firework barrage that lights the clouds above, rendered live in miniature on the television before us. There are more of them on TV than overhead; I'd be suspicious if I wasn't so hungry.

Dinner time.

The hutong walls trace ancient property lines; the rooms they form are parsed out by the government. The walls enclose all sorts of spaces; one door is propped open, revealing a narrow alley I would have to shuffle through sideways, with doors opening up on it and a little gutter running along one side. Another door opens directly into a room with four bunk beds crammed in the space of an American child's bedroom. Cement, dust, and mud cling to pants hung from the top bunks; a pair of nunchukas dangles from a metal footboard. This is home for eight construction workers who make less than ten dollars US a day. They use that foul public bathroom near the main street.

Some of the doors open on courtyards shared by multiple families, each with their own room (or two, if they're lucky) that fronts the courtyard. This is how our hostel is laid out; elsewhere in the hutong, each hostel room (which sleeps eight in bunk beds) would house a family of three in a little community cell. How Templeside Hostel can afford—or was granted—so much space is a complete mystery.

This alley has a curious feature: bright red and white steel exercise equipment. It's dark now and no one is using it at the moment, so I climb on. Here's one with two pedals, a leg-swinging contraption—the Glorious People's Public Exercise equivalent of a Nordictrack.

Another resembles a lat-pull resistance machine, with a small chunk of concrete on the far end for weight. The most striking device is a massage machine of some sort, consisting of a hard plastic chair with two black plastic drums. Each spinning drum is covered with rounded bumps—roll your arms over it, or bend forward, and massage whatever you like. I will see how each afternoon they're crowded with elderly Chinese men and women enjoying the sunshine and a workout in the alley.

We turn left on Xisi South Street for a short walk to a restaurant with a large green sign. I have no idea what it's properly called, but the transliterated name is "Hui Feng Jiao Zi Lou," which I suppose says it all; the food pictured on the menu in the window looks fantastic. There's a gaggle of foreigners from our hostel inside, and we join them.

"Dude," one of them says, leaning back in a brown wooden chair, "too...much...food. The dumplings are amazing." The restaurant looks like a stripped-bare Cracker Barrel, but instead of Americana nailed to the walls, it's decorated with paper dragons and red banners. The food looks like the finer Chinese I've seen in America, though the famous General Tso's Chicken is nowhere in sight.

Their pictorial menu is a fascinating study of transliteration and good intentions gone horribly, horribly wrong. Each page is loaded with pictures of wonderful-looking food, with the Chinese in red characters beneath the photos and English in small letters below that. My mouth waters for "The Lu oil ear silk." I'm smitten with "White Water Sheep Head," but simply dumbfounded by "The sauce elbow spend." Other highlights include "The sugar-treated preserves small," with its astoundingly deft hyphen, and the pop existentialism in "The sugar vinegar in the mind the."

For the faint of heart, there is the "Lemon Ou slice," or, simply: fruit salad.

It's all too tempting—especially the ethereal "five fragrant cloud beans"—but before we can order, we're invited to scarf down their leftovers. "This one's really spicy," someone warns. There are whole red chili peppers in brown sauce with chicken chunks (bone-in, of course) and mushrooms. "Be careful." They'd barely touched it.

It's fantastic, and a perfect complement to the pork dumplings, mushroom dumplings, green beans in fish sauce, and other treats left in steel serving dishes over long-extinguished heating candles. A waitress asks for our order—at least I presume that's what she asks. We don't need anything more, the leftovers are wonderful and the price—free—is right. We share a look, Josh and I, and order a dozen pork dumplings out of freeloader's conscience.

All in, this is the best Chinese food I've ever had. She brings us beer and our new friends tell us where to go and what to see as the last of the fireworks burst overhead.

Welcome to Beijing.

Great Firewall of China... The sumptuous smell of savings... "Adventure" is another word for outdoor butcher shops... Chunky coffee and spiked fruit... Tourist Green Berets... Retain your right to walk away... Haggling makes my soul hurt...

My Hotmail won't open. I'm in the little internet room at our hostel, on the faster of the two ancient computers, attempting to write home...but the email account that worked yesterday doesn't work today. The BBC website is also inaccessible, and I can't open Wikipedia, but Yahoo works alright and gives me enough search query results to suggest—merely to suggest—the internet isn't broken. I type in "Chinese censorship" and it returns no results.

I'm getting nowhere by ramming this computer against the "Great Firewall of China." That's the slang term for the censorship campaign conducted by the State Council Information Service (SCIS). Or specifically, by the SCIS, local police departments, local Internet Service Providers (ISPs), the Ministry of Public Security (MPS), and other bureaucratic and law enforcement agencies. Everyone with a finger on the power levers in China wants a piece of the action, as if blocking a website is the chance they need to justify their existence.

Sites that I know to work, simply...don't. I get a generic error page, and nothing more. The censors rather zealously block sites containing any criticism of the Chinese government, pro-Democracy sites, rights advocacy sites, and many foreign media sites...and social networking sites where teenagers talk about music and their crushes. They limit their citizens' ability to get news outside of the state-run media services. Like those glass walls in the airport, they want to maintain the appearance of freedom and access while keeping their citizens contained and isolated within China, and within their own communities, to keep social agitators from exacerbating regional, ethnic, or political differences.

Especially the political differences—no one knows the inner workings of social revolutions like those governments built from them. They aggressively limit the rights and opportunities their forebears used, lest that revolution be replaced by another. It takes one to know one, basically, and the paranoia is usually justified.

There are other reasons to limit their citizens' ability to congregate online, report on local affairs, and otherwise connect across great distances without state mediation. China has great cultural diversity, and like everywhere else in the world, their different ethnic groups don't get along ideally. It's easy to foment racial and ethnic hatred online, as we know from our comparatively unrestricted internet—half-literate hate sites are as easily found and accessed as the New York Times. It's an important recruitment and re-education tool for hate-mongers and dissidents and everyone else looking for a flock to lead or join. The government uses force to keep the peace in their far-flung provinces, while they try to keep a lid on the propagation of hate-speech and misinformation online.

The Great Firewall of China keeps the citizens from accessing much of the outside world—to keep their hearts and minds in, as much as to keep the world's views out. This keeps citizens on their strict diet of carefully managed propaganda, and inhibits citizen-journalists from contradicting government reports. They don't want anyone taking their country to task for anything, other than the carefully rendered "reports" from Xinhua News Agency, their state-run media-come-image service. Cut the people off from the world, and they will never know what sort of alternate ways of living, working, and thinking are out there. Cut the world off from the people, and the only "news" the global community gets is filtered through censors that act like corporate branding specialists.

The college-aged hostel workers say they're aware of the censorship, but aren't terribly bothered by the idea. They're well fed, clothed, and healthy, and genuinely appreciate these things without feeling cheated out of freedoms they've never had.

But given all those layers of local and bureaucratic control, the censorship is comically slapdash—Hotmail worked yesterday, but not today; Western sites work fine on computers in certain cities some days and not at all on others…or never in some places.

Perhaps there is a greater, sinister scheme of information control high up in their government...but probably not.

People add content to existing websites every minute, and new sites pop up by the hundreds in every imaginable language. That's a nightmare for the largest, best-trained censors to even monitor...and the task of blocking that content is handled by regional ISPs influenced by dozens of agencies with their own directives and rules. It's an Orwellian ordeal, but without Big Brother's success.

The result is more aggravation—and fear—than if the system worked perfectly. Dissidents and hackers might get caught their first time, or not for years, with no way of calculating their actual risk. With predictable adversaries, even the tough ones, you can model their behavior, adapt to their strategies, and calculate your risk. The genius of Chinese censorship might just be in its maddening unreliability.

In general, it works like this: the highest ranking officials in the MPS make a master list of the sites they don't want their citizens accessing—sites that are critical of the Chinese government, talk about political dissent, document their human rights abuses... Then they distribute this list to ISPs, along with notes on the sorts of things they don't want on other sites that aren't specifically blocked yet.

Thus, most foreign news sites are filtered, or blocked entirely. If you blog about your cat and one day write something critical of China, your site will be blocked if, and when, they find it. But if you visit a cat owner's chat room hosted on a Chinese server and post something negative about the Chinese government, your post will simply vanish. Why?

Because there are computer cops who spend all day madly hunting the internet with search engines and complicated software. In America, the people who spend all day on forums getting offended are unemployed and unwashed and living in their parents' basements, afraid of girls and the sun. In China, they're internet cops.

But the local police have a say in the matter, too, if they want one; they may or may not ever see the MPS's master list, but if they see something they don't like, it's within their power to get very nasty with the local ISP until the site is taken down (if possible) or blocked (more likely). They can order the ISP to trace the computer that created the site, and if it's in China, everyone at the corresponding street address disappears.

Then there is the SCIS with their lists and tastes, and all the other agencies…

Someone, somewhere, decided that today is "Block Hotmail Day," so I can't forward jokes to my mom. Humbug.

Time for a long walk through Beijing…

The sumptuous smell of savings…

Up Xi Si South Street, Josh and I pass the "Land of Restaurant." It looks more expensive than we care for, selecting instead a Chinese chain food place with lunch specials under two bucks American. We order bowls of noodles in clear broth with what I think will be chicken. The tables have a small, two sided menu with pictures of various identical looking broths with slight variations—leeks, chicken, pork, beef, egg…enough variety to keep Josh entertained for many more budget-friendly meals.

"This place is nice," he says, talking himself into the idea. It has all the charm of a Jack in the Box, except that it's in Beijing, which automatically makes it exotic and interesting the way a Jack in the Box in St. Louis would be to our waitress. "I think I'll come back here."

"The dumpling place is pretty good," I counter.

"Yeah, but this is half the price." Josh has a point…but the difference is only two dollars, and maybe a good deal of quality. We'll see in a minute. "You wanna see the Forbidden City today?"

I'd rather wander aimlessly around the city until impossibly lost, then try to find my way back. "I was going to have an adventure."

"Where?"

"I have no idea."

"You're welcome to come…"

"Thanks," I say, "but I'm going to get good and lost for

awhile." I'd like to get his take on Beijing, but am in the mood to see those parts that aren't dressed up for tourists.

"I like this city," he says. "It's a little more…I don't know, Asian. Like Thailand, less hyper-modern than Seoul."

"Much less westernized…"

"Could be it." The less English spoken, the more exotic the adventure; that's threatened somewhat by the Olympics, for Beijing at least, but we're just in time.

Lunch arrives: thin-sliced chicken with some gristle and bone, with half a hardboiled egg atop a pile of glass noodles (a delicate, translucent rice noodle) mounded under the broth like a sandbar. I add crushed red pepper flakes, and lunch is good without being great. Josh gushes a bit over his, trying to hype up the enjoyment for his own benefit. My hostel bed costs 40 Yuan a night, about six bucks, which includes breakfast in the courtyard; we pay 7 Yuan an hour, honor system, for the internet, and there's a laundry service we don't need yet. If we spend two bucks on lunch, three bucks on dinner, that makes about fifteen dollars a day. I'd like to come in under twenty bucks, so that leaves five dollars for seventy-cent-a-liter Dali beer, which is more than I need to have a good time.

I'd rather buy better food.

"Adventure" is another word for outdoor butcher shops…

Josh is back at the hostel, getting ready for the Forbidden City; I have the Chinese world at my boot-tips, Xi Si South underfoot—it's a main road through the four concentric highway circles around Beijing. Tiananmen Square, with the Forbidden City across the street, is the geographic and tourist-interest center of town…and behind me as I walk away to the north.

The shops are homogeneous; this section is dedicated to motor scooter parts, with store after store selling the same products. Everyone of some means has a motor scooter; the most successful have cars, and absolutely everyone has a bicycle. The city is too large to get by without some sort of transportation, and for special days or bad weather, there are buses and the new subway system linked to the tired old lines beneath the city. Watching the traffic is a fascinating study in Chinese life, which I would indulge more if I could take my eyes from the uneven sidewalk without tripping. I attract enough attention just being white around here, without also falling on my face.

The very outermost portions of the street are for bicycles and scooters. When a scooter overtakes a bicycle, they swerve into an open spot in the flowing traffic, and remain there as long as they must before dodging back to the curb to avoid being crushed. The next layer in towards the middle is for small cars, which generally leave the very middle of the road to trucks bounding in either direction. The centerline painted on the asphalt is merely a suggestion.

Pickup trucks hauling fruit and dusty burlap sacks drive south to market; vans with long black and white license plates head north with machinery parts and merchandise. Construction is everywhere, old steel scaffolding holding up worn planks, bamboo used where they ran out of steel braces. Sand and sawdust drizzle down as crews cut through facades and reframe windows. The smoggy air is alive with putt-puttering scooters, squeaking bicycles, and metal grinders.

The city is getting a facelift for the Olympics, and for many businesses, this means finishing construction before the summer of 2008—before the tourists get here. There is talk that all nonessential construction will be banned leading up to the Olympics, to improve air quality and ease congestion on the streets and sidewalks (the scaffolds get in the way). The impetus to spiffy up the city trickles down into the hutongs—there is fresh grey paint on many walls, and one of the girls working at the hostel told me of the public image campaigns urging citizens to mend their walls and buildings and fix broken roofs…all in the name of national pride and celebration.

I'm sure Beijing always swarmed with people carrying bags and pushing barrows, fixing and building and scurrying, but the sense around me seems a little extra eager, extra proud. Our waitress at the chain restaurant went out of her way to exercise the little English she knew; we smiled and laughed with her. There are new highway signs, and a campaign to replace the hokey Engrish (like "It is Ancient to Pack Photo") with proper English.

That'll be sad.

Part of the fun here is hunting things down, trying them out, figuring out what you're going to get if you order "Domestic Life Beef Immerses Cabbage" (never mind the menu's photo). China is for the Chinese, and their signs are for them; that there are English subtitles and attempts at explanation are wonderful, but it's not the local language so I don't expect it. It's campy to see strange and shocking phrases on t-shirts, like "BREASTS" across the appropriate area, and to get wonderfully befuddled by the local signage. It's part of the experience.

Like a strip tease, the Engrish shows you just enough to hint at something alluring without spoiling the surprise.

But back to the homogenous-business-district-thing—why do nearly-identical stores choose to open right beside each other? Maybe they have no choice in the matter; it's a form of commercial organization I don't put past the government, and a street lined with identical shops, selling identical products, is a comparison shopper's dream...but can't be good for business. The scooter parts stores far behind now, I'm walking through a music instrument district—shop after shop selling identical guitars displayed in nearly identical ways under different signs. No prices are displayed, of course—like so many places in Asia, prices are set based on what the salesman thinks you'll pay regardless of a product's wholesale cost—so you'll have to negotiate for the Fender knockoff from the "Weifang Yangsen Boyun Musical Instrument Co."

Down on the corner I see four camera stores right there next to each other, two on each side of the street. There's a fifth just a little farther down, as if struggling to catch up.

I'm in the market for a good DSLR camera. Unlike the instrument stores, the camera stores have opening bids posted next to most of their wares. 13,000 Yuan ($2,000) for a Nikon D200?

Not on your life.

I ask for a better price, and he comes down immediately to $1,800…the actual opening bid on the camera. From here it's up to me to dicker and bargain down to a respectable price. Thing is: I don't know what that price is in this market, and I don't buy unless I know the market rate…or, I'm desperate.

I'm not desperate, so I thank him for his time and move on, half a block east to the entrance for another hutong. I pass a stack of red bricks and a woman sewing shirts with a foot-pedal machine. Near her sits an old man in an open-front shirt, fingers to the corner of his mouth like he wants to be smoking. I'm not sure why he isn't, though the air quality—and today is a good day, I hear—is roughly equivalent to any basement poker room in the nineteen twenties.

The World Health Organization has standards for these things, and Beijing violates every single one like it's something to be proud of. The confluence of dust storms from the outlying deserts, construction effluent, virtually unregulated vehicle pollution, and industrial air pollution from cities upwind of Beijing, make the air up to five times worse than the WHO's limit.

So really, there's no need to smoke, but it would give him something to do while he sits surrounded by large grasshoppers in bamboo cages. The bugs are about two inches long—huge by my standards—and are a mesmerizing green color with yellow highlights. Apparently children buy them for pets, and tame them by carefully removing them from the cage and holding them with two hands until they quit squirming around. If they do it often enough, eventually the grasshopper gets used to the idea and doesn't fight it.

Even though they're made somewhere down the street, Chinese kids don't seem to have PlayStations, so I guess this is what they do between school, chores, and work. It seems every Chinese kid works, somewhere, for at least a few hours a week. They lean against their mothers' fruit juice stands; I see them hanging clothes on lines when I peek through propped-open doors; a boy, no more than eight years old, watches me from behind the counter of his father's butcher stall.

Here we are, this boy and I separated by a plywood table stacked with bleeding pigs' heads. I can buy the pork by the centigram, or I can walk away, but I'll never be able to forget the row of bleeding heads and the blank look on the boy's face as he watches me. Maybe he's considering opening bids should I ask for a price; maybe he's thinking about Pokémon. I can't read his face; it's the face that watches me from a dozen stalls in this hutong, and a dozen shops on the avenues. It haunts me.

Chunky coffee and spiky fruit...

I buy chicken satay from a teenager grilling over charcoal. The bamboo skewers run through serpentine strips of mystery fowl, laid across steel-mesh that was scrounged from a construction site and flame-sterilized.

Satay is one of the safest street foods you can eat. Tasty and ubiquitous, it's cooked on propane grills on the backs of motorbikes, charcoal grills like this one, and served in some of the better restaurants. Mostly you find it at "hawker stalls," carts with coolers and stoves that vendors roll into the shade and use to cook up all sorts of things. They get their name from the cooks who "hawk" their wares, sometimes calling out to passers-by. I don't usually have problems with hawker stall food, in part because I only eat from the ones where I see locals cued up—they know the local standards and come back for a reason.

The fire in the charcoal pit or under the wok sterilizes the cooking surface so it doesn't really matter what the metal was before someone turned it into a grill. Even if the meat isn't refrigerated—this kid grilling in an alley doesn't worry much about that—there's no problem as long as it's reasonably fresh and thoroughly cooked. The locals know, so I trust their lead.

But street food doesn't always do it for me, like a giant steel pot of boiled silkworm pupae back in Korea; when I don't trust the various chunks and sauces, I find a fruit stand and get exotic—rambutan, leechies, jackfruit... I pick fruit that has an inedible peel as a barrier between the flesh and the fertilizer, the workers' hands, the delivery truck, and the other people pawing it before I get there. Bananas are fantastic; coconuts are great when hacked open and served with a straw; dragon fruit, especially the red flesh kind, are divine.

Dragon fruit? Indeed.

If fire-breathing Chinese dragons hatched from produce, what would the fruit look like? Reddish pink with scales growing up and away from the body and trailing into a gentle, bright green spike. It's a ferocious looking fruit that feels leathery and solid. Trace down one side with a knife or pull at one of the scales and you can peel the skin, revealing either dark red or bright white flesh…and hundreds of little black seeds that crunch and pop when you chew them. They taste like kiwi, but less tart, with divine flavors that make them worth the trouble to find.

Not that they're much trouble to find here. Steady supplies come in from Thailand, Malaysia, and the warmer parts of China. I'm looking for them now, walking down the sidewalk on a wide avenue, open to distractions…such as the narrow toy store right here. It follows the classic Chinese godown style of narrow facade and deep interior. The walls are covered with stuffed animals and hats, pink headbands and baubles for young girls; a saleswoman rushes over and smiles at me, somewhat shocked to see a man—a foreigner, no less—inspecting the children's toys. I smile back and say, slowly, politely, howdy.

"Nihow," she says, bowing slightly.

I have this crazy idea to buy a stuffed animal for my fiancée and use it as a prop through which to photographically explore and artistically engage the journey ahead…which is to say that on the other side of the world I'm sort of lonely and want a cuddly toy, and think it'll be fun to take touristy pictures of it in strange places. Later, I can give it to my fiancée as a souvenir. The walls are full of knockoff Pokémon figures and other characters from Asian cartoons, and one lone little purplish-reddish teddy bear with the sweetest face.

Perfect. For her, I mean. Naturally…

But 18Yuan on the price sticker? I offer five. It's for my wife, I say, since she speaks a little English. She would like your store. No.

I'll pay ten Yuan, then, and no more.

No.

Eighteen it is; some prices are fixed…but I had to try.

The bear and I duck into a trendy-looking coffee shop designed to bleed money from teenagers. My body is going through withdrawal from lack of sugar-laden, caffeine-infused Korean instant coffee, and that's not good. Even the bear knows that, and his head's full of cotton.

The menu has only a few pictures and the English isn't terribly clear, so I point to a photo of a tall glass with a brown murky liquid. I watch the people schooling past outside, the middle-aged women and teenagers out for an errand or on their way somewhere more exciting. The coffee is tepid, well sugared, and tastes fantastic; I'm thrown off by the neon green straw, though, which is roughly the diameter of a drainage pipe and capable of slurping up the entire drink in no time at all. It's a hot day out and I like sitting here, so I nurse it just…slowly…enough…

…to suck a giant ball of something chewy through the enormous straw. I stop short, eyes wide, tongue carefully probing the object. It's soft. Kind of sweet. Squishes a bit, with a mild chocolaty flavor. I have no idea what it is.

But there are a lot more of them. They're like toffee, but not; like especially soft chocolates, but…not. The bear has no opinion on this, but I think they're wonderful.

Fruit, though—that's what I really need this afternoon, after a lunch of noodles in broth, meat on a stick, sugary coffee and mystery orbs. I'm on my way very, very circuitously towards Tiananmen Square, and have no problem with the afternoon getting on while I amble around elsewhere; it's been there for a long time and will be there tomorrow. My fruit-lust is of the moment, a now-thing, and a young woman in a black and white striped tank top just pointed me down a side street, around a corner, and through a loading door.

Pay dirt—a farmer's market, like the fruit section of a grocery store spread out on old tables inside a warehouse with impossibly high ceilings and nothing in the air between hats and roof but August humidity. Old women tend baskets and ancient scales with needles bent one way, then another and back like lightning bolts that roughly point at zero. They weigh Chinese pears, apples, persimmons, oranges and exotic fruits. A basket full of spiky red things catches my eye because the fruits look like gumballs from the sweetgum trees back home—those hard, brown, terrible seeds that are hell on bare feet.

These are rambutans, and the spikes don't hurt. I pick one up carefully, trying to figure out how to eat the blasted thing, when an old woman waddles over with an urgent smile. She plucks it from my fingers, looks at me—a kind, grandmotherly look—and before I see how she does it has the husk half off what looks like a naked white grape. Holding the furry bottom half she hands it to me, gesturing that I eat it.

Delicious—like the best parts of a plum and a grape holed up in a terrifying shell. There's a pit in the middle and, anticipating my quandary, she fakes like she's spitting onto the warehouse floor. Nearer the city center there's a small army of uniformed people wandering around with pockets full of tissues; they rush into action when they hear the dreadful hoick of someone about to fire a load of nose-filtered smog onto the sidewalk in the local custom. Their job: to hand them a tissue and admonish them, politely, not to spit in public—the Olympics are coming.

Where are they now?

I have my dragon fruit and a kilo of rambutans in plastic bags clipped to my belt with a carabiner; the bear has his own bag, clipped behind the fruit, to keep my hands free to take pictures and fish money out of the hidden pocket in my pants. I try to be polite about retrieving it—who wants money that just came from somewhere elbow-deep in some guy's trousers?—but the harder I make it to access my wallet, the safer it is. I wear my passport on a neck pouch slung under one arm and tucked into my pants, deep out of sight, so it doesn't print under my t-shirt. Everywhere I go I have enough money to take care of the basics: transportation across town, food, cheap bribes, what have you. Never too much in one spot, though, so I can turn empty pockets out and plead poverty as necessary.

I'm ready for anything, and love exploring it alone.

Dave Norman

Tourist Green Berets…

Ruggedize: to make something stronger and more averse to breaking; to improve utility and performance under adverse conditions. I am ruggedized.

I went to Nepal years ago to trek the Himalayas, having never heard the term before but finding the word "trekking" impossibly romantic. As is often the case, I was completely oblivious to the world beyond my experiences. Our guide sent a packing list with the suggestion to buy our back-country gear from Army surplus stores, so I took it to Uncle Sam's and loaded up on mismatched paraphernalia. Our first day in the back-country, everyone suited up in matching North Face and Mountain Hardware outfits; I looked like a general from a made-up country in a Marx Brothers movie. It was embarrassing, but my gear worked as well as anything and held up better than some of theirs. Image notwithstanding, I was happy.

Since then, I've had little problem eschewing fashion for function, and I appreciate that extra margin of security that comes with over-preparedness. I wear black hemp pants that are quick-drying, abrasion resistant, flame-retardant, protect my legs from sunburn, expand with hidden Velcro gussets to accommodate my changing midsection, and have a pick-proof hidden pocket I sewed into the back. Jeans would do, and work for Josh, but I value the extra utility these offer.

That's the theme of how I dress and pack for the road—utmost utility for whatever challenges come my way, because you don't find many North Face outlets in Siberia. My framepack at the hostel is rugged but light, the frame wrapped in fifteen feet of parachute cord that serves as laundry line or extra rope for the hammock or…

There are several pieces of equipment I never leave the hostel without, which have served me well so far: a large folding knife, 100-lumen flashlight with crenelated bezel, and these waterproof, chemical-resistant boots. It's broad daylight now, but might well get dark before I get back—the flashlight keeps my feet out of potholes and helps me see the people and dogs standing motionless in dark corners. They're harmless, but if not, the crenelated bezel is designed to inflict some rather nasty deterrent.

Josh makes fun of my "assault flashlight." I find comfort in having it, and relief in not needing it.

My folding knife is another comfort. I can't figure out how the old lady popped that rambutan open, but every few minutes I duck into a corner and discretely carve the shell off another fruit. With the knife I can cut rope and snacks, open blister-packs of batteries and pry the tops off bottles; that it would make short work of an attacker is surprisingly far down my list of concerns. Of the many places I've expected to find danger—indeed, been told for years were fraught with bandits and peril—most turned out to be safer than equitable places in America.

I travel with two Nalgene water bottles, and presently have one clipped to my belt—a belt which is rated to hold over 1,000 pounds and works as an emergency tow strap. Nalgene bottles are virtually indestructible things that keep fresh water handy or, if caught in the rain or on a river cruise, keep paper and small electronics dry. I don't forget them like I might lose a disposable bottle, and they're strong enough for backcountry travel.

This is the gear I consider essential for extended tourism in developing countries—even though we're scheduled through major, modern cities. Some things I value for their comfort more than congruity.

"That's completely over the top," Josh said when he first saw the gear spread across my bunk in Korea; I was doing a quick inventory while we were alone. "This isn't an action movie, dude."

Beyond clean underwear and fresh socks, Josh brought a tiny thermos for tea; he gave me one too. It looks like an artillery shell and something rattles inside when I shake it. He wears those combat boots I brought him, borrows my knife gladly, and is thankful for my flashlight in night darkened hutongs. I'm all too happy to oblige. We both tried on the jazz hat, modeling it for each other and in the mirror; it works much better for him—more urban chic, less lost-trekker.

Now it lives in his pack and on his head, and so our dichotomy goes: the city mouse and the country mouse, kitted out and geared up each to our own fancies…and comfortable in the same environment.

Retain your right to walk away…

My wandering tour has turned into a shopping spree—teddy bear, hawker food, fruit stalls, and now I need a polarizing filter for my camera.

Need?

Yes—need. When the wind parts the smog just right the sky is a brilliant shade of Caribbean blue, with the warmth of a cloudless summer day playing across reds and blues and greens on temples and tiles. A polarizing filter will be like putting sunglasses on my camera, darkening the sky just so, punching up the contrast, taking the yellow haze out of the air…all without Photoshop.

Besides, I'm in China, where all manner of camera gear is made; the prices here should be the cheapest on the planet. Knockoffs abound, but if it works the same and costs less, who cares…

I would prefer a small camera store crammed with boxes and cameras jumbled atop each other in the displays, with the ordered sort of clutter that can only be searched by the shop owner—the kind of place that has everything I need, such treasures the likes of which I have never seen, and seems to stay open by volume rather than margin. Instead of this sort of place, I wander into a gleaming, high-ceiling shop with the latest Nikons and Canons on shelves devoid of price tags.

I point to the filter I need, and the saleswoman's opening offer is one hundred twenty dollars; she shows me the figure on a calculator to circumvent our language barrier.

One twenty US? No, this is worth—cover up a decimal point—twelve. It probably cost the store five; it's an off-brand, and I can buy those all day long on eBay for twenty bucks… which doesn't help me on the road. I'm about to violate my own rule: don't go into a negotiation committed to buying. Retain your right to walk away. But tomorrow we're going to the Great Wall, and wouldn't it be neat to play with a new filter while shooting a Wonder of the World?

One hundred, she counters, laughing at my figure. Twenty, I say, and things get serious. Like the picture disappears as you shake an Etch-a-Sketch, her face drains to an emotionless blank. This is her business face, that inscrutable one that brokers no friendship and betrays no confidence. Clearly she has high hopes for this sale, but I won't go quietly into that raw deal. Twenty.

One hundred, she repeats with more than mere bullishness. Around the edge is a patina of condescension, the way a petty tyrant enjoys harassing you for his own amusement.

Twenty, I snarl, dragging the word through the air. My face must show my quick-rising anger, to her amusement more than fright.

At this point, I should give up, but that competitive thrill I get at auctions has me lured into the bidding war—I'm going to beat her, I think. I'm going to win.

Which of course is impossible. At the end of every auction you win, you've paid more than anyone else was willing to…how can that be victory?

We agree on fifty dollars—the budget for two and a half days on the road. She grimaces a little as she rings me up, turns her back, and walks away down the long row of overpriced lenses.

We both just lost…

我們都剛剛失去…

Dammit!

該死!

Haggling makes my soul hurt…

Beer time. We're eating rambutans and drinking Dali; they don't go together well, but it's a fine bachelor dessert. Josh tells me about the Forbidden City, what history of it he can remember, and how much he liked it; also, how it was mobbed with people, but that's alright. When I found him, he was holding court with a half-dozen scraggly travelers, speaking slowly in their one common language. He is quick to make acquaintances; he excuses himself to drink with me.

I tell him about the hutongs and the farmer's market, the cheerful fruit lady and how all humanity drained from the camera saleswoman's face when our haggling got serious—how that was the same poker face worn by the eight year old kid with the severed pigs' heads, the old man with the crickets…

"Yeah, that's the way it is," he says. "It's just a game." His flippant dismissal gets my smoldering anger burning again.

It is a game, but I don't like the rules. The fruit woman was polite and chummy with the prices fixed, written right there on a cardboard sign. Why can't more things be so straightforward? With haggling, the interaction is totally different, and what some see as a sport I consider a snake pit. It's not about price, so much as competition, and I don't want to vie against stacked odds for consumer goods. When it gets serious, the sales folks shut down the ways they show their essential humanity; it's like arguing with a robot programmed never to lose.

…just the way they want it.

"Of course," Josh says, "it's just a game. So what?"

"So, I don't want to pay more than I have to, and I don't like getting shafted by double standards."

"Then here's what you do," his voice firm like a teacher's. "Figure how much you're willing to spend, then don't spend more." He lifts his beer and sits back in his chair, the matter settled as far as he cares. It's simple logic, after all; but it misses my point entirely. "If you get it, hey, great, whatever. If not, you're not out anything. I mean, what do you really need?"

"A polarizing filter."

"Pffft. You can get those all day long on eBay."

There are things about haggling that I simply don't like, and then there are things that anger me on a much deeper level—like prices that fluctuate independent of value, and having to stay on guard every time I buy something. It galls me to think that for the same item, two people could pay wildly different prices. Even if somehow I end up getting the better deal, I'm still offended by the nature of the thing—this is one of my moral absolutes; at least it is when I'm getting screwed.

We had two standards in America for a long time, with different prices for different people; different water fountains and bathrooms, too, until we put an end to that garbage. Now I pay as much as the next guy; there's dickering for big things, like houses and cars, but it's not an everyday nuisance and I like to think—right or wrong—that floating prices back home are mediated, for the most part, by the goods' inherent value...not the seller's assessment of my intelligence and money, or their bias about my race—I don't like it when my race plays against me. It's a lesson I would be wise to remember.

A Malay friends call this the "white-man discount": the 1000% inflation of prices because white tourists in general, and Americans in particular, are considered rich.

There's also an intrinsically Chinese convention at play here in Beijing called "face." The phrase "to save face" comes from the idea that respect is more important than price. Consider my filter—say it cost the store a dollar. Her goal was to get me to pay fifty dollars for it, not because the filter is worth fifty dollars, but because that's what she thinks an American will spend. Perhaps that's what some of the other saleswomen have gotten out of other tourists. She'll start the bidding exorbitantly high—as if fifty wasn't bad enough—and then let me dicker her down to just above her goal price.

Then it gets personal...and nasty.

If she gets her price, or more, she's happy, and after the transaction I might find a true emotion in her smile; I have before. The salespeople always smile after the transaction, but if you look closely, sometimes you can read anger or glee, depending.

But say that I know fifty bucks is too much, and—without being a jerk about it—hold firm to a much lower price. Now I've put her in an awkward position. If she loses the sale or closes too low, she loses face...and in coming down too much there is a tacit admission that she tried to gouge me.

Settling around her comfort zone lets her close the deal on her terms—to save face. But if I close higher than her goal, then she has gained something important; a Chinese friend in Malaysia, who owns a small business, calls this gaining the advantage.

Both parties can walk away happily, though, if the buyer's comfort range and the seller's comfort range overlap and they close within it. Close below the seller's comfort zone, or above the buyer's comfort, and someone loses face...a poignant form of embarrassment always taken personally.

I won't pay fifty bucks for something I think wholesales for five—I'm from the land of Wal-Mart, where we're inculcated to believe that prices should be as near to wholesale as nature allows. But wholesale price has little to do with the game...and I take it personally when someone tries to rip me off.

When I hold fast to reasonable figures, things often get awkward; if they complete the sale, it's with forced politeness underscored by unmistakable angst—silent, terrifying taxi rides jerking madly through traffic, fruit dropped hard into bags so it bruises... I've gained the advantage, somewhat, but it brings me no joy. An hour later, I'll still wonder if I could have closed for less if only...or somewhere else...or... I can't win when I haggle; I can easily get screwed, and the best I can reasonably hope for is a final price where we each feel equally cheated.

Great options, right?

"You're taking it way too seriously," Josh says, finishing his liter of Dali and opening another. He keeps his eyes on his beer and away from me. "What is it, a couple here, a couple bucks there?"

Every twenty five dollars is another day riding this crazy trip around the world...and isn't he the guy eating cheap fast food to save money?

I can't understand how he's so Zen about the whole thing—the camera shop lady tried to steal two and a half days from my journey, and it's not an isolated incident. Except Josh is not so much Zen, as conflict-avoidant. He's yinning my yang, or something like that, and the more he backs off the angrier I get—like baiting a Rottweiler.

I've never seen Josh on a good tear—never seen him in the throes of righteous rage, and this... This is probably the first time he's seen it in me. No wonder he's drinking so fast, so passive-aggressively Zen to my fury. All I want is a little noncommittal sympathy.

So I switch gears and ruminate out loud on the best trick I've found for haggling—maybe in here he can find something to agree with, and come back to my side. I should have used the trick today—it works in Malaysia and Thailand—but it slipped my mind.

I ask two different sets of people—hostel workers and other travelers—what they pay for the basics. How much is a cab across town? A kilo of bananas, a beer, jeans…? I bracket my goal between these prices, trying to do better than my fellow gringos but not expecting to do as well as the locals.

Then I open the bidding before they can offer their starting price, so whatever they set as their goal, they can quickly readjust; they can't come down from a hundred Yuan to five without losing a lot of face, but if I open at five Yuan, we can dance our way to fifteen and call it a deal. It puts me out slightly, but it saves the interaction; it might even lower the price a bit. At least, it sets a neutral tone from which we can build a civil interaction.

It still riles me that two different people would pay two outrageously different prices…but my high horse is exhausted and I've turned back to my beer, eyes closed against the purple twilight. Where'd all that come from? I'm not usually so quick to anger, except when I'm getting sick, and I feel fine.

"Better now?" Josh asks.

Yeah.

"There's a concert at this club these guys told me about. A punk rock club."

There's some irony for you—counter culture music in the pride of Communist China. Hell yeah.

"Meet you here in five," he says, wandering off to get extra beer money.

Take the Red Line… Four feet nothin' and screaming in the dark… Chairman Mao was a punk rocker… The Budweiser of food…

It's a short walk to the subway station, down a staircase reminiscent of the whitewashed cinderblock halls of my grade school—if the grade school had been filled with Chinese moving in urgent clumps past signs exhorting them not to spit on the floor. Josh has the directions, a glossy tourist map with a dot in a circle drawn by a girl at the hostel. She told him D-22 is one of the critical venues on the Beijing punk scene. He invited her, but she couldn't come; that she is cute had surprisingly little to do with his invitation. Josh personally invited everyone at the hostel, as is his way; some were interested, but none are following us past the ticketing window and onto the platform.

The Beijing subway embodies Chinese values in building, government, and progress. This platform is newly refinished for the Olympic crowds next summer, with bright white light playing off clean concrete walls. There are yellow lines on the platform to suggest you shouldn't stand too close, should you be able to move backwards at all through the crowd packed solidly up to the edge. There are no performers like on platforms back home; no guerrilla marketing posters, either—just "no spitting" signs, propaganda and a giant subway map. The trains aren't new but they aren't old, being in good repair and of basic design—midway between New York grunge and Tokyo modernism.

Trains are incessant, arriving and departing every few minutes, identical cars moving in identical directions, disgorging and swallowing identical herds; I get the feeling that any train could vanish with all souls aboard and another would be along unaffected, disgorging and swallowing more souls from the endless crush flowing in through the hallways. Indeed, Chinese disappear every day with neither trace nor ripple.

It works, this subway line; it's not the nicest system, but it's functional, and any part or person or group could disappear and the work would go on unchanged. The rear echelon is promoted to the edge of the platform every few minutes, replenished from the hallways; even the people are replaceable.

Which is abhorrent, despite being exactly the case; the grand Communist dream is universal equality, a constant push forwards not one step back! that waits for no one and stops for nothing... least of all the vagaries of individuals doing their own things. Individualism means differences, and differences mean inequality, and inequality creates the oppression the Little Red Book rails so hard against. Follow it far enough up the line, though, away from the brilliant lights on the platform and up through the darkened tunnels, and you find that all potential for beauty and horror, good and evil, comes from the same place.

The essence of human nature is that we are full of energy waiting to go in some direction, any direction, a thousand directions between a thousand people. Sometimes it goes well and sometimes it goes badly and most of us take more or less the same sort of journey. We can mostly agree on many things but we are essentially different, and that is beautiful. It enables stunning success and dismal failure in a balance we try hard to skew...but not as hard as the Chinese.

To tuck their bell curve near enough to the center that oppression and other downsides of inequality fall off the end, they've lost as well the very best parts of freedom. Squeeze the people together in the middle and you channel their energy right where you want it, into business and development, taking over the world with quiet persistence and unlimited energy. But oh, the cost. Let the masses know of the wonder outside their channel, farther out on the bell curve and beyond their station, and they may doubt and balk and impede the flow until the whole thing bursts like an aneurysm.

The differences between people are interesting, and the most obvious things lacking on this subway. The Beijing locals dress and carry themselves similarly, work and play and ride bicycles in similar groups of similar people, stand together here like interchangeable parts of a stage set... The Marine Corps hardly does a better job with groupthink and human-standardization than I've seen with these normal people.

It's hard to move a herd of individuals anywhere together; but if they're fed and clothed and having fun wandering around on their own, what's lost? I value freedom for its own sake, perhaps because that's all I've known and been taught. Our free country leaves that bell curve well enough alone, at the same time creating potential for both success and failure.

That's how I like it—letting individuals do our own things lets us take these crazy, indirect vectors through life, all moving in generally the same direction but in whatever fashion we feel inclined. Artists and writers take us right off that bell curve and lift us higher than the madding herd to see our crazy, squiggly paths in context. When we dive back into the madness we take with us some idea what it's like outside our channel—and what other goals there are, in places we may never have thought of trying to reach.

Each trip outside the pack helps us see the struggle differently; each weave and dodge between dream and reality stokes that glorious alive feeling, because life is freedom and discovery and music you've never heard before—thinking outside our narrow channel even if we're happy with the herd's direction.

The very opposite is the Chinese subway—there is no individualism here. We're all going to the same places in the same order at the same speed. You get there, yes, and you're surrounded by many nice people along the way, but your only say in the matter is to stay on or get off where allowed. Theirs is an entire culture surrounded with clean, impenetrable walls that keep the rest of the world out and the masses focused in one direction. The trains arrive. The people board. Then the system whisks them off in the same direction, group after group, hour after hour, any hundred souls dispensable because the flow will never stop, and never stray from these polished rails.

But the internet is here. The Olympics are coming. The world is watching. The rails are polished, but there are so many more hands on the wheel now.

Four feet nothin' and screaming in the dark...

"Are you student?" the doorman asks with a rising voice, the way you teach interrogative tone in classrooms. We pay 30 Yuan each, the full cover price—which could be anything, we don't know any better—and walk into D-22. It's a high-class dive bar, the kind that's grungy from effort rather than decay.

"Carlsberg," Josh orders. Twenty Yuan.

"Dali." Fifteen.

The venue is a rectangle with the stage in the back right corner, a path leading left around it to the bathrooms and a staircase to the balcony. There are a few tables in front, this bar in the opposite corner with tall stools that swivel so you can lean nonchalantly against the railing with a beer in your hand and the world at your feet. Knots of teenagers tighten conspiratorially, someone telling a joke, and then explode outwards and upwards in fits of high pitched laughter.

While the grey race marches past outside like time, in here we're forgotten, out of the way, a little dot far outside the bell curve and everyone looks the part but me. Josh wears the jazz hat and oversized, mirrored sunglasses even though we're inside; a black t-shirt, jeans, black boots that pass for punk fashion in here. He's a leather jacket shy of Bob Dylan, a clean-cut Johnny Rotten before his break. Leaning against the bar, chatting up the bartender, he could be a singer waiting to go on or a columnist for Rolling Stone or anyone else hip and with it; with my rumpled t-shirt and two week stubble, I'm on my way to looking homeless.

The knots tighten, titter, explode, swelling and contracting and welcoming friends. They wear black leather jackets and black and white horizontal striped shirts, fishnet stockings, safety pins through their clothes and ears. Pink hair. Green hair. A mohawk dyed in leopard print with a matching faux fur jacket despite the night being far too hot for it.

One punk smells of sweat-soaked leather, not at all appealing, and that's an important part of the image—another sense engaged with that warm beer in the morning, sweat-damp smoky smell that tells you he's living the dream. He is the leader of a pack of friends and only when he's done do they move past the bar to the stairs and up, up to the balcony to hold court on plush velvet loveseats.

I have no idea what they were saying, but they sure looked punk saying it.

The bands aren't ready yet, so we're listening to a steady stream of The Clash and Sex Pistols piped in from a CD player next to the Chinese whiskey. "A Canadian guy owns the place," Josh says. "Go figure."

"How's a foreigner own a business in Beijing?"

"Who knows?" and we agree that it's an incongruity of the modern world, a head-scratcher we can share. Such feelings are conveyed in a look.

"Let's check the upstairs," I say. The pack has conquered the loveseats, leaving some tables and chairs by the railing. There's a dumbwaiter with a bucket, pad and pencil in the bottom, that lowers down to the bartender. Along with a fantastic view of the band, I have direct access to booze and a chair if I get tired of standing. Perfect.

Josh goes down for another round and to stand in front of the speakers among the punks now pushing the tables back to claim their floor space. I don't talk at shows—it's too hard to hear and I don't like the way my throat feels after a night of yelling—so this spot, with the dumbwaiter and personal space, is perfect. I'm not big on crowds; I observe them, preferably from somewhere up high and out of the way, with a cold beer and the option to join if I like—which makes being an outsider a choice, and downright comfortable.

This is where Beijing's outcasts go to find their masses; where the rebels find their own kind in torn clothes and leather and safety pins. Fluorescent hair that stands out across Tiananmen blends in. It may feel noble, but it must be downright lonely to marginalize yourself in China; here they recharge and touch base in a sanctuary full of friends.

Many of the Beijing punks stand out on the street, even when they're dressed for work or just to fit in for the day—their hair, piercings, or tattoos give them away. Across the spectrum are the guards outside the Forbidden City, the rail-thin policemen in clean and well-pressed uniforms, the very face of the establishment. In between are women in tank tops and dresses, men in khaki or grey pants or, occasionally, jeans; everyone has brown eyes and coal black hair. Everyone has a job, and those who don't, busy themselves with something, so every street tableau is an image of work or transit towards work, progress in feet kicking up the dust so it settles its blessing on everyone.

But not here outside the channel, in a bar some crazy Canuck drove clear off the bell curve—it's youth culture on the skids. Boys and girls who suspect there's something between ancient songs and Chinese Mega Pop, who might not know what else is out there, but feel in their hearts and loins that there must be some other way to live—some other goal than the government's money in the government's housing and working for the rice that strengthened their parents to work. This isn't a place they come to find answers so much as to recharge their strength for the journey against the herd. The guitars are alive now and the music explodes out of nowhere with a woman screaming into the microphone just ahead of the drums.

The underground seemingly comes out of nowhere, too, unless you're paying attention and see that beneath the surface is a generation who knows they're missing something and are going to find it if they have to invent it themselves. They suspect their country is a box with thick and opaque walls, their state run schools guiding them towards state sanctioned lives with the state mandated one child limit and how it's all an artificial imposition on…what's that thing?

Human nature.

Let's stretch this idea of live reporting in a book to the sonic level. She's four feet tall in red stiletto heels and fishnets black against pale skin. Percussion snarls and crashes like a bulldozer ramming the Berlin Wall, guitars cheering it on while she screams with the people's anguish unleashed. It's loud, it's noisy, her father would hate it and so would mine; we're the same age, but she's taming demons on stage that I have never felt in my life and don't want to. This is performance; this is what makes a punk show different from a recital, and Josh is in the thick of it down on the floor moshing away with the audience. They're chest-high to him and giving him hell, throwing shoulders and shoving and he gives it all right back in perfect time to the music and the drumming fury.

Josh did this all the time back home. There's a club at the edge of East St. Louis, one of those bars in one of those places you really just shouldn't ever go, where he rolls in the grit swept out of the city's clean streets. They are his people, the ones marginalized by choice or fate or God knows what, who sit down to have a beer together and stare out across the Mississippi at a twinkling world they just don't get. He's on his way back there—to that club, and to find a job in that sparkling city beyond it. To have them both; to have it all.

Tonight, though, he doesn't want to be anywhere else—he's found his people. I raise my beer high over the seething, sweating, spitting masses in this forgotten shadow, and salute them.

Chairman Mao was a punk rocker...

Why do these punks, and Josh and I—the youth of our next generation—lust so for change itself? We want to save the world, yes, and fix its problems, certainly, but we've only lived long enough to see one system and its flaws. Travelers are lucky, and might see a whole new way of living...but we are the exception, enlightened by the blessings of travel. In any event, a few more decades will bring a sea change or two and show that every system has its problems...and how the answers often pose problems themselves.

But the allure of change is strong, coming from the promise of something different—something plucked from the infinity of possibilities and pulled down to replace the finite structures that we call broken. Different ways and norms must necessarily be free of the problems we've seen, of course. Chairman Mao would have been a punk rocker; for that matter, so too would George Washington and Joseph Stalin.

The angsty teenagers' eternal question: why don't those who have seen the most, join the Youth and Beauty Brigade in overthrowing the dominant paradigm to start fresh with something new?

Perhaps because those who lived through major change know that every system has its problems; that nothing is perfect; that different things are flawed in different ways, and sometimes the imperfection you know feels safer than the imperfection you don't. Change the paradigm and you change the problems, which is sometimes very important, but has produced very few lasting solutions.

And while struggling to fix the new problems, our children will grow up seeing only them and longing for…change, and the false hope of problem-free living.

Though Chinese communism is far more relaxed than the Khmer Rouge flavor, it is still a totalitarian regime. So the energy bubbles among the Chinese youth, looking for somewhere out of sight to run amok; to run through crowds and soak through t-shirts, hoping to find its own kind and redouble its strength. It will run wild until someone harnesses that energy and focuses them to bring a new paradigm to life. Then it will build—build towards some new hope, a new paradigm if that's what it takes.

It's worked before.

This bar is one meeting place, this room enclosing a sweat-soaked and hungry generation; this is where they gather, and someday, may organize. With free time and energy, disenchantment and naiveté, they are the fomenters of the next revolution. I'm shocked the Chinese government, headquartered just down the street, hasn't shuttered D-22.

Maybe it will. Then the seeds will scatter and things will really get interesting.

The Budweiser of food…

I've had too much to drink, and at that, not nearly so much as Josh. We're going to see the Great Wall in the morning, and I need to be in top condition—fit. Fed. Healthy. I stopped drinking during the second band of the three that pounded our ears into submission, and that was a long time ago, but something else has taken hold of me. Maybe exhaustion; maybe the day's exercise and terrible air set me up for a grand fall in that punk bar with its poor ventilation and hundreds of glowing cigarettes. Indoor smoking—not a cultural experience I value.

We're walking down the street, Josh in the lead, urging me to keep up. His legs are longer, and he has more vim and vigor for some reason—we're both nocturnal, but clearly I've met my match. "Let's get some food," he says, "c'mon. They might close."

But they're not closed, because even in Beijing McDonald's stays open twenty four hours a day.

"I'm not going in there," I slur. "I'm not doing that to my body."

"The subway's that way," he says, pointing down an empty street with long shadows between amber lights, the darkness concealing who-knows-what. "Or you can eat with me."

Bugger.

He orders a Big Mac, which is a Big Mac in every McDonald's in every country except, perhaps, India, and he orders the meal deal which comes with a Coke and fries, like in every country including India, diving face first into waxed-paper American comfort food deep in the People's Republic.

"Nothing for me, thanks," I say to the cashier. It's three in the morning and the cashier couldn't care less.

"Bullshit!" Josh blurts, "You're having a McRib. Value Meal!"

"No."

"McRib Value Meal," he orders. "Pay the man." I had enough trouble finding a McRib sandwich when I wanted one, back years ago when I snuck off to McDonald's alone under cover of darkness, so guilty and sneaky I hoped I would not even catch myself. It's amazing to find one here, but it's every McRib I've ever had; every Coke I've ever tasted. Every McDonald's french-fry I've ever dipped in sweet 'n sour sauce.

McDonald's—the Budweiser of food.

"I can't believe," I mumble through a drunken mouth stuffed with pork and sauce, "I'm eating this shit."

"You're lovin' it," he says, and we laugh so hard we nearly vomit.

The Great Staircase of China… "What-re!..." This is not worth dying For… Enemy of my friend…

Friday morning, 0620, we're on the road to Simatai, a section of the Great Wall—they don't add "of China" here—about seventy five miles from Beijing. This section is supposed to be much less crowded than the "touristy" part closer to town. The drive, in a private van arranged with our hostel for 220 Yuan each, takes us past a grocery store to stock up on lunch and water; I grab a half kilo of grapes and several liters of water, the day already hot and my Nalgene bottles empty.

"Hready?" our driver asks with that curious h many Chinese pronounce in words that start with r.

It's another half hour to a formal welcome center at the start of our section-hike. We buy our park passes and wander past a few vendors charging too much for Great Wall –related paraphernalia. I'm wearing a long sleeve shirt to guard against the brutal August sun, carrying my camera bag and plenty of water. I'm an experienced hiker, and have comfortable boots. It's less than eight miles. Hoorah. We set off, the history as thick as the humidity.

The Great Wall got going in the 8th Century BC, with three states—Yan, Qi, and Zhao—creating their own walls of wooden troughs filled with dirt and rocks and left to bake in the sun. In these pre-cannon days, this was sufficient. When the states were united under the Qin Dynasty, emperor Qin Shi Huang had the walls between his states destroyed, and the walls separating them from the northern territories expanded and united. Construction continued into the Fifth Century BC, with ever more complicated methods. Those wooden troughs were augmented with cut and shaped stonework, and ultimately, bricks. Guard towers went up over time.

Successive dynasties repaired and improved the wall, extending it east towards the Shanhai Pass and a few meters into the Bo Hai Sea (over towards Korea) and west towards the Jiayuguan Pass north of the Tibetan Plateau. But it was the Ming Dynasty, from the mid 1300s to the mid 1600s, that developed and polished what we think of as the Great Wall of China. After a nasty mid-fourteen-hundreds military loss to the Oirats—nomads from the western reaches of modern Mongolia and China—they improved and extended the wall. It became a crux of their campaign to keep nomadic tribes from Mongolia and northwestern territories away from the center of their empire...

...and away from Beijing, the historic capital of Chinese culture.

The Great Wall's protection allowed the Ming Dynasty the peace and prosperity to develop things like the Forbidden City within Beijing, the largest navy to that point in Chinese history, and rural mail delivery (for important people). Most of the interesting, romantic and opulent things associated with the Ming Dynasty were made possible because their land was secure—protected from constant destruction in large part by the Great Wall.

But then one man screwed it all up: Wu Sangui. He was in control of a gate that came under attack by the Manchu Army. For reasons that are fun to speculate on, he just opened the door and let them in.

The Manchus swept across northeastern China like an Asian version of General Sherman's March to the Sea. They sacked Beijing and established their own dynasty: the Qing Dynasty that lasted from 1644 until World War I.

The Manchus didn't have too much use for the Great Wall—well within their territory it didn't serve a defensive role anymore and was abandoned accordingly. But with the advent of tourism, many of the sections have been restored. Hiking the whole thing, which takes three to four months of daily effort and navigating constant problems, permits, and bribes, is a badge of honor for some peculiarly hardcore hikers.

We'll invest most of the day in doing only ten kilometers. The hills are steep, like miniature mountains. The wall runs along their crest, taking advantage of the highland. The Great Wall averages about sixteen feet wide, about twenty five feet tall, and has a guard post every few hundred meters—usually on the summit of a jagged hilltop. Many of the sections are crenellated so defenders can shoot arrows or pour sewage pots down on attackers, while protected by the merlons against incoming arrows.

Their basic plan of defense consisted of a guard in a guard shack to detect Mongols as they approach the wall. He lights a signal fire with thick black smoke (the light matters at night, the smoke in daytime) that alerts other guards, who send the distress signal via fires or runners to the nearest garrison. Around one million soldiers guarded the wall in the glory days of the Ming Dynasty, spread out between garrisons and guard shacks along its length.

The top of the wall is wide and road-like so messengers can sprint along it, and soldiers can deploy swiftly across it to the site of attack...and maneuver much more easily than the Mongols.

So how does a twenty five foot tall wall in the middle of nowhere keep out a determined, experienced horde of Genghis Khan's best warriors?

The answer lies in the topography—the wall stretches across these steep, densely-forested hills. Don't believe the cartoons where the Mongol horde rides across a flat desert to attack a lonely wall...

Horses can't ascend these hills, and bushwhacking to the wall would wear down the heartiest infantry. Then, with only what weapons and siege tools they hand-carried uphill through the undergrowth, they would have to scale a sheer rock face taller than two standing men.

With their vantage point atop the towers, atop a wall, atop a hill, the guards could see the Mongols approach with plenty of warning. Even if taken by surprise, they had a distinct defensive advantage.

The wall is known for its grandeur, the stunning accomplishment and terrible cost in human lives from the labor that built it, and—erroneously—for being "the only man-made structure visible from space." That rumor was promulgated by the Chinese decades ago, before any astronauts cared to look for it. Then an astronaut did look for it, and sure enough: it is not visible from space...though at night you can see space from it.

Millions of Chinese worked on the wall—prisoners, hired

laborers, children… They lived on cabbage and rice, and not much of it; they died from exhaustion and starvation, too much work and too many accidents. This is their tombstone, these millions of Chinese who died so their wall might protect their country—whether they chose to sacrifice themselves for it or not.

I run my hand along the wall. Here and there are stone staircases leading down to the ground on either side; I'm sure the stairs leading to the Mongol side were much later additions. I follow along the wall, running my fingers over the stones, and feel every crack, every chip, every nick. Each one holds a word, a voice, in the story of the Great Wall: of the people who died for its protection. Of a wonder of the world; of the glory of emperors who never toiled a day to build it. No, this isn't for the emperors and their court; this is a monument to the Chinese—to their ingenuity and sacrifice and their hopes for peace. For billions of Chinese through untold generations, this has been an awesome symbol of national pride.

And for millions of their ancestors, it is a four thousand mile long headstone.

Another mis-assumption the wall quickly dispels is that the top is a long, level foot-highway. This section of the wall is more of a staircase than a street. If I'm not climbing up at a healthy angle, I'm scrambling down the steep stone stairs; they have probably been replaced sometime in the last two and a half millennia, though they certainly look original.

Most of the wall—here, at least—is original. It was built using shaped rocks for the foundation and bricks for the rest, filling the middle with earth and stone and bones—little labor was spared to inter the dead elsewhere, and the bones of many are thought to be interred within.

These materials last very well, though weather has dulled the decorative images once carved in many places. The Mongols couldn't destroy the wall, nor could weather and time, nature's most reliable erasers. I can't really comprehend eternity, or even 2,500 years worth of it; I'm a twenty-something, and one-hundred-times-my-lifespan is incomprehensible. Therefore, I say with conviction that this wall has been here forever, and will be here forever, and if the Earth dies screaming, the only things left will be cockroaches, asbestos, and the Great Wall of China.

"What-re!"

It's ironic, the Great Wall. It was built to keep the Mongols out. Now it employs them.

Though this stretch is less popular with tourists, there are elderly Mongols and Chinese shilling water and t-shirts at astonishing prices...

...every ten meters. It's been four kilometers now and I'm down to one liter of water and half the bag of grapes. I'm wearing dark glasses and a grey boonie hat to keep the sun off my face and neck, and my gusseted shirt breathes well. I've done everything to hide from the sun and stay hydrated, but it's clear my water won't hold out.

The hustlers and touts are counting on it.

"You buy what-re?" they say, some more demanding than others. "Ten Yuan!"—ten times the going rate in town. "Buy shirt!" others demand, "twenty Yuan!" Here, five kilometers from the nearest running water, in the midst of one of humanity's greatest human-rights-violations-cum-accomplishments, I'm surrounded and hassled at every shady area by the very people the wall was built to keep out.

When we walk too slowly, the touts follow step by step; stop, and they thrust a t-shirt in front of my face, blocking the view I'm slowly dying for. I look tired; several of them promise "I know shorter way!"

There is no shorter way from one end to the other; that's not how this topography works. If in the throes of exhaustion you fall for their lie, they take you down dangerously steep hills which you won't have the energy to climb again. Then they take you to their tents in tiny nomad clusters where they shill more t-shirts, trinkets, and overpriced water. You realize the ruse but it's too late—you're down an impossibly steep hill, out of sight and earshot, out of water, out of energy, behind schedule, and lost alone in the wilderness...except for the tout, who demands money to set you right again.

Nice guys, eh? And it's nearly impossible to get a decent Great Wall photo without them holding up a t-shirt somewhere in the frame.

We stop for photos at a pile of debris near a crumbling guard tower, and sit down in the shade to eat the last of the grapes. A gaggle of old women and one younger one approach carrying shopping bags—curious out here. But they aren't thrusting water at us, aren't holding t-shirts, and I think maybe—just maybe—they're tourists of some sort...like us. That they've come to appreciate this wonder. We move closer to the wall, welcoming them into our coveted patch of shade. I offer my grapes, and one old woman takes a few. I introduce myself—as James Dawson, the Canadian I play on all my travels. She doesn't speak English, but smiles and nods and says something in Chinese.

Then she nods to the younger girl. "Daughter," she says. Then, "very nice. You like?"

My look of complete and utter betrayal makes her cock her head and reach into her bag for a "Greet Wal China" shirt. "Buy t-shirt?"

This is not worth dying for...

I'm out of water; out of grapes. I have no idea how much farther it is to the end of our hike. Josh is in the lead, his legs longer than mine and moving faster. I trained for this sort of thing, I'm an outdoorsman...how is he doing so well? My internal monologue is evil and I'm taking the wrong kind of joy at holding up my hand and barking no! at the touts. He shows his irritation at them—and probably me—with contrasting silence, forging on with stone-set eyes. Just before he walked on ahead, I indulged an epic tirade against the touts' disgrace of my peace and quiet and the somber beauty of the Great Wall.

The wall is beautiful. It's a Wonder of the World for more than its architecture—it stands in company of the pyramids for splendor, awe, and marvel. But I can't appreciate it with these constant intrusions.

Stuck in Beijing, I yearned for clean air. Trees. Clear skies and nature; a respite from cars and horns and people and bikes and…the Great Wall should be the silent cathedral I need.

It's so close…

What-re? T-shirt! Know shorter way! What-re? What-re!

…but so far away.

After two weeks in throbbing Asian crowds, all I want is peace and nature and a moment's silence.

Buy what-re!

Josh walks on ahead, my vitriol too caustic. I'm glad for the space, but like the rearmost sled dog, I'm infuriated by the sight of his flank retreating in the distance, leaving me to face the touts alone.

Anger…

This is a shady spot—a large guard tower that, by some miracle, is tout-free. I check the ceilings; no cameras. I check the cracks and corners for wires; nothing. I'm sure there has to be a video camera somewhere; back home there'd be two. Here, there don't seem to be any. I strip completely naked to cool off, and streak a section of the Great Wall. This is one of my proudest moments—running naked across a Wonder of the World. For a moment I'm free and happy and lost in celebration, the very antithesis of a minute ago.

Wild mood swings…

I put my clothes back on, though there's no real reason—call it paranoia of authority, though I haven't seen any authority figures (or cameras) on the wall. The last thing I want is to get thrown into a Chinese prison for public indecency; who knows what would happen, but it certainly wouldn't be good.

The wall climbs up, up, up again. Another kilometer on the Great Staircase of China…

* * * * *

I just walked down some stairs on the interior side. The Great Wall here leads up some badly crumbling steps to a decrepit guard tower; on the backside the stairs are worn down so far the wall is a deadly ramp to a debris field at the bottom. I walk on a trail between the wall and a steep drop into a verdant crevasse. Bending down to tie my boot, my stomach twists in a violent knot.

Abdominal cramps....

This is how I felt several years ago when I gave myself heatstroke during a paintball tournament. I won—so at least it was worth it, right?—then drove myself to the hospital in a gauzy haze. They admitted me immediately and I passed out, waking the next morning hooked into machines. I stayed in bed for three days. That's not an option here, as my brain makes the silent switch to pure animal survival. Once you have heatstroke, your body is never quite the same—you're at increased risk of getting it again, and again if the second time doesn't kill you. Here in the wilderness, the wall the only road for miles, I put one foot ahead of the other and take a wry look at things—upon the wall, someone wrote in black marker "Made in China."

No one ever died while laughing, did they?

* * * * *

My head reels, eyes needing a moment to focus when I move my head, my brain taking another moment to make sense of the image. I buy two bottles of water, the touts more aggressive than ever because they recognize my desperate look. They know the signs of heatstroke, and they're attracted to it like vultures. That's why they carry packs of water so far out here, spending days sleeping on the wall, eating cold rice and shitting right here on the bricks. Not even off the side, though they do that, too—no, right in the middle of the path so you see it, so you have to walk around it and are offended by it the way they seem offended by foreigners being here. Racism and xenophobia are alive and well in China. It's in the touts' eyes here; it's in how the price goes up the worse I look. They smile the crooked grin of payday loan sharks.

They've got me. They're circling; raven black hair, sharp noses, waiting to peck out my eyes.

I'm dizzy; I'm sitting down now. They're surrounding me. I'm up again, off again, escaping.

There is no shortage of malice on the Great Wall. My catharsis, my enjoyment of a Wonder of the World, is blocked and mocked and turned against me. The August heat makes their shit piles smell terrible. Even the flies stay in the shade.

I've stopped sweating. This is not worth dying for.

These notes will sound horrible from my reading chair in New York, with the tap water and air conditioning. It can't be that bad, I'll say, I was just caught up. Dickens wrote something about beginning to forgive a place the moment you leave. But I'm writing this in the shade after threatening an old Mongol woman because it is that bad. I'm writing it down as it happens so I don't forget, so I don't lose the moment and smooth the edges and draw the sort of pulp-sentimentality that comes with distance and that pressure to tell a happy story; to make it all seem okay.

Because sometimes it's not.

My fiancée says I'm a nice guy, but I really, really want to hurt these people. The Chinese government wouldn't care. There are no police out here. These Mongols are non-entities to the establishment; no one would even find the bodies…except the tout ten meters ahead, and the tout ten meters behind.

Josh is far ahead of me, and not the fighting type anyway. I'm alone and surrounded. Whatever I start, they'll finish; I can take the first three, but not the next five, or ten, or twenty. They'll rip me apart until there's nothing left out here where there's no one to find my body anyway.

Why haven't they attacked yet? It's coming; I know it's coming…

Heatstroke ruins your manners. It scrambles your brain.

* * * * *

It's almost over. I'm standing outside a tall, square guard tower looking down on a river feeding into the Mandarin Duck Lake. There's a resort in the valley ahead, a narrow trail leading down from the far ridge to the buildings and parking lot. That must be where the van will pick us up… there's only one kilometer to go, and it's mostly downhill.

But there's that reservoir in the way, and the slime-green

river feeding it. The Great Wall does not cross the river; this guard tower stands opposite another, each built right up against the water's edge. From here, archers could control a narrow point in the river.

Which doesn't do me any good for crossing it. For that, I need the cable-slung suspension bridge farther down this canyon. A trail leads up the other side, from the bridge to the wall again, whereby the Great Wall climbs from the water's edge up over the crest and out of sight. The trail down to the resort joins near the summit... Down...up...down...but it's alright, because there, in sight, is my destination.

I share this tower with a man methodically working a hammer and picks on a piece of polished granite clamped to an easel. He's settled in under an umbrella, chiseling images of the wall into rock. There's a little sign—200 Yuan—that tells me his etchings are for sale. Fed up as I am with touts, I enjoy watching him; he greets me politely, turns back to work, and leaves me alone to watch or leave as I see fit. The basic courtesy is a splash of cool water, and for the first time I see someone other than a tourist taking the Great Wall seriously.

I linger a few minutes, marveling at his skill, and trying to think of some witty connection between this rock worker and those who built the wall; my brain is fried, though, so I can't.

The suspension bridge leads me across the river and straight to an old man in a dusty uniform who demands payment for having crossed the bridge. He wants 10 Yuan. Everyone today wants 10 Yuan. He seems official, the kind of person who might be missed eventually, so instead of indulging my impulse I dicker him down to 5 Yuan and amble off.

That's my top speed now: amble. It would be "shuffle," but the bricks in the path are too uneven and if I fall I'm never getting up. The path here leads to stairs along the wall that go up, and up, higher than I care to tilt my head; the journey of a thousand touts keeps plugging along with another one every ten meters, though it must be too hot—or I look too hostile—for them to bother me. A gaggle of women with armloads of t-shirts sit on the steps in the shade. We exchange hateful glares. They don't get up. I move on.

Half an hour later, praise Jesus, I'm starting my final descent to the valley. I come to a platform with a zip line strung down to a restaurant on the side of the reservoir and ask how much? 50 Yuan, they say, and I think that's too much. Besides, these are the last few hundred meters of my Great Wall trek, they're all downhill, and that old pride is welling inside me. Of course I can make it. I've come this far. I'm not weak...definitely not weak.

So I don't need an overpriced zip line over a reservoir in northern China.

Maybe someday I'll regret that decision—someday when I'm sitting in my reading chair with the tap water and the air conditioning, thinking how I could really go for a zip line; yeah, that sounds fun...

Enemy of my friend...

We're on the way back, halfway into the two hour drive. I peed once today, right on the Great Wall, marking my territory like a dog; Josh hasn't peed at all, he says.

Except now he must, and can't—we're in the outermost reaches of heavy Beijing traffic.

"Pull over, man," he exhorts the driver, who doesn't speak English. None of us speak Chinese. "Man, I've gotta pee!" His voice is the perfect pitch, invoking that eternal chorus of kids trapped in their parents' cars.

"Pee in this," I say, handing him an empty two liter jug.

"What? No."Then to the driver again, "hey, I've gotta use the bathroom—bath...room...Toilet?"

"Water closet?" someone offers in that curiously too-loud tone used universally on people who hear fine but just don't speak your language.

There's a red light ahead and he slows with this clump of traffic. Josh's malady is funny because it isn't happening to me, and anyway, something's going to give. No one ever died from having to pee; it hurts way out of proportion to its danger, so that his discomfort is hilarious.

The van stops. Now's our chance. I rip open the door and jump out, Josh following me onto the road's shoulder. Our driver goes insane, honking and yelling and waving at us, releasing the brake and rolling forwards towards the next car as if he's going to leave us behind. The light turns green.

Maybe he will.

Pants unzipped but nothing further, Josh jumps in and I dive right behind as we pick up speed. Slam the door. "Dude, what the fuck!" I yell at the driver, enraged by heat exhaustion and his callous attitude towards Josh; these extreme emotions feel like being drunk, and only anger makes sense. The enemy of my friend is my enemy, and I feel too horrible to hold it back. "Seriously you fu..." I continue in a blue streak.

Josh laughs from the absurdity of it all as we get back up to highway speed. I hand him the jug again.

He looks around. Someone says "it's alright man, just do whatcha gotta do." Someone else agrees. He climbs over the seats to the last row and turns his back to the windshield.

Nothing.

"Come on man, you can do it!" I say.

"I can't with people watching." And of course we're watching, but we promise we're not. "Seriously man, I can't do this under pressure." I do my first nice thing since offering my grapes to the tout—I turn my back and promise I'm not looking. I'd do anything for Josh if he really needed it; especially if it's such a simple favor as looking away while he pees into a jug in a tour van.

But it's no good. Despite his cringing pain, Josh can't make it happen. So I do what any good friend would— I get out my camera, turn on the flash, and fill the van with lightning.

"Seriously Dave, not cool!"

It wasn't going to happen anyway. The enemy of my friend is sometimes me.

Why it's not good to look as bad as your passport photo... My racist lunch... Down in Flames... The biker who saves my life...

They've surrounded me and I know this is it. I've gone as far as they'll let me and I'll die right now, right here, picked savagely apart by rusty knives with curved blades and quartered under an empty sky with not a single cloud for witness. You can't fight the tides and the wall has been breached, overrun, all hope lost and a new day breaks without me. My rage is swallowed by the trees and forgotten with all the screams of men before me, culled and butchered and left to rot. But I'll take them with me, by God, my knife against theirs, killing the biggest son of a bitch in a final act of noble defiance. Bring it...

I wake up cold and soaking, twisted helpless in my sheets. I'm surrounded, though not by barbarians—just people sleeping peacefully in cold metal beds with clean white sheets, the only sound the fan, the only threat... There is no threat. I'm safe, but I feel absolutely horrible.

Josh went back to D-22 last night. I remember him asking if I'd like to come; no thanks. I don't feel well. Have fun though.

"Alright," he'd said, and I didn't see him again; there he is, passed out diagonally across his bed, hand dangling over the edge. I couldn't stop drinking bottled water, had no appetite; I went to bed early, and now I'm up early, the sun just warming the curtains for another humid day. I slowly disentangle from the sheets—it was quite the struggle that got me so tied up—pull them over me, and go back to sleep.

Ten o'clock and I'm awake again, alone in the room. I get dressed and glance in the mirror—I look pale and hollow. Anyone who looks like their passport photo is not fit for travel. Breakfast waits for me, cold, under a fly screen. Josh asks if I'm feeling alright.

"I feel horrible."

"You look horrible."

"Then it fits, doesn't it?" I snap—too early for this kind of anger, but it's not anger; it's that sort of attitude that wells from the sick depths of deep discomfort. A lot of people get mopy and pathetic when they're sick; I get hostile. I have no idea why—it's just always been that way. "I'll be fine."

"Go drinking without me?"

No. The Great Wall kicked me hard and I'm still down, the count long over and the crowd gone home.

"I'm going to the temple today," he says. "Come with?"

"Going to stay here and recover."

"Don't get sick on me."

"I have Cipro..." I don't travel without Cipro. I pop one after breakfast and sit in a wicker chair in the shade, watching a kitten lick itself.

It's a beautiful morning turned strange with this foul distemper, and truth is, I'd love to go with him. I ought to see our hostel's eponymous temple. But I'd like even more to sit alone and heal by myself, conserving my energy to rebuild my body.

I'm torn. It's my last day in Beijing; I should see something. Sitting here feels like I'm cheating myself. I should...see the Forbidden City. I should...have an adventure. That's what you do when you're young and restless, right? Test the breeze and follow the wind, especially when you're not in the mood. A little adventure—just what I need to snap out of it.

I leave ten minutes after Josh, tripping over the threshold on my way into the hutong.

My racist lunch...

Tiananmen Square is cleaned up from the festival, the scaffolding and stages, chairs and banners all gone without a trace. Museums and government offices line the square, forming a stoic backdrop for military reviews and nationalist demonstrations. At the north end is the giant, ten times larger than life, portrait of Chairman Mao. He's dead and gone and the top echelon running his utopia—who aren't even supposed to exist in pure Communism—embraces capitalism and keep its spoils for themselves.

There's not much to do in Tiananmen, once you've survived

the traffic rushing around each side, seen the monument in the middle, snapped a picture of the Chairman… How many people each year take that same picture, of Mao smiling over the shoulder of a guard?

I'm not in a Forbidden City kind of mood, so I consult a glossy tourist map and head south towards the Temple of Heaven. It's lunchtime—time for adventure food. I take a small staircase into a nondescript building, past two menus all in Chinese without a scrap of English anywhere. Eureka! The heart of Beijing, where no other white man has ever dined! I'm Marco Polo, I'm Columbus.

I'm hungry.

The woman at the head of the stairs looks at me hard, like I'm a criminal in an orange jumpsuit; I feel like crap and haven't shaved since the trip began, but otherwise I'm presentable. She'd like to toss me out on my backside, though, her look saying everything as she leads me in stony silence to a table far from the windows.

There's a family a few tables over, children crawling up laps and sliding down the other side, a grandfatherly man laughing huk huk huk and spooning large chunks of pork and pineapple onto his plate. Their lunch spread looks amazing; my hunger doubles. Time slips by alone as a waitress bustles back and forth around their table, ignoring mine. At length a different waitress approaches with a smile so forced it seems as if she knows she'll die tonight and can't think of a better way to spend her final hours than working in a dive on an obscure side street.

Or maybe it's just me.

I point—with my thumb, the polite way—to the spread on the other table, then point vaguely at my all-Chinese menu, trying to indicate just give me some of that. I smile, bow, and thank her in English because I still can't pronounce the Chinese words. More time passes and the family, old man and children and everyone at their leisure, is completely gone before my lunch arrives.

Rather, my plate of deep-fried miniature shrimp arrives. Whole shrimp—shell and legs and antennae and all. A whole mound of them, each too small to do anything with.

"Rice?" she spits in English as if the word were a hot coal searing her tongue. Yeah.

I fumble to pull the fried shell off a shrimp, investing a minute in mangling the poor thing's corpse before giving up; maybe I should eat them whole.

Which proves unwise, and I'm definitely not eating another one…much less a disgusting mound of whole, deep fried baby shrimp. My rice arrives: a sticky mound of plain, boiled white rice.

Then I notice the chef standing in the service doorway, staring at me with his arms folded across his chest. The waitstaff, hunkered behind the cash register, sneer and stare at me. That old sick feeling comes back, the one that says I need to knock out as many of them as I can before the inevitable. As hungry and sick as I am I realize with lightning-clarity how stupid it would be to do anything other than stand, slowly walk to the register, pay my bill, and walk away without a word.

It's the worst lunch I've had in my life—I was the loathsome, unclean "other," made to suffer for their empowerment, and there was absolutely nothing I could do about it.

Down in flames…

My Temple of Heaven notes are sketchy, the weird ramblings of a man with a fever wandering against his better judgment through a park in the dead middle of a Beijing summer. Some excerpts:

"Student?" Yes! "ID?" No…but… "No but! Pay full price!"

Red walls not faded with time; south of the heart of Beijing; north of the diaphragm—what would be the diaphragm? Air too thick to breathe—have to be pretty big.

Wailing wall. One in Israel; Gaza? This one talks—curved design; scream and wail and the sound "disappears," actually channeled around, someone else hears it. Cacophony of agony; actual effect: cacophony of kids screaming while parents stand in shade by pagoda.

Out of water; three liters. Peed once. Danger sign?

Extensive grounds. Want to check it out on Google Earth. Is

that blocked?

Giant pagoda; beautiful; green roof tiles look like jade; blue roof tiles look like sky at twilight.

Respite from Beijing street noise, walls keep it out; no respite from bad air. Can't breathe; sit down in Pagoda, on floor, no chairs.

Old people show special reverence; young people show exhaustion, follow kids, who've stolen their energy. Woman so old she might be able to tell me what was here before this Qing temple; doesn't speak English; curses…

Coughing; can't stop…

Tennis courts? I must have left the temple. Where am I?

Back in the temple. More pagodas. Beautiful architecture; look up terms. Real gold? Looks like it.

"No cameras." Must be discrete. How many Chinese tourists are secret police? Havana: one of every four. China? Unknown.

Can't stay in crowd; can't breathe. Gotta sit. Take cab home? Sit first.

Taking cab. Too expensive. Not spending 30 Yuan—four dollars? Five? Walking.

Tiananmen at night—thousands of people. Flying kites. Long tails, little boxes. Candles. Flickering. Lights on strings. Can't take it all in; try. Fail.

Arrive at hostel…

"Dude, you look horrible." We're back where we started.

"I need to find a doctor."

"Sleep it off, we gotta be on the Trans Mongolian in the morning."

I just stumbled back across the threshold and it's clear—I'm going down, in fever and flames.

The biker who saves my life…

The staff is concerned now, and I'm sitting in the wicker chair, watching the same cat still licking itself, as Yan Ying explains where the doctors are. She's cute—the girl Josh invited to D-22. I think she went with him last night…what's that about doctors?

"…hundred meters, on light."

"On light?"

"No, on light. Not left, light."

"Right…"

I try to stand up but can only hover, quivering, my legs barely working. There's no way I'm making it and she knows it, pushing me lightly back into the chair and scurrying off. When she comes back she introduces a twenty-something man in a leather jacket, ripped pants, with the authentic kind of grunge that says this guy fixes his own motorcycle and races it for money on darkened streets. I have no idea if that's even possible in Beijing, but he exudes the kind of terrible cool that suggests, yes, there are many things that happen in this town which shouldn't, and he does most of them. But he's going to play the hero now, the man of the hour; to impress Yan Ying? There is goodness in his heart, I can see it in his eyes and the way he helps me out of the chair.

The biker thing is apt; he's the guy who gives night tours around Beijing by motorcycle. For a hundred Yuan you can ride in his sidecar; he doesn't speak English, so don't expect narration. Maybe that's a good thing, to let the Orient keep its mysteries and let you close your eyes in peace and feel the wind on your face, imagining that you're flying.

It's easy to imagine. It's warm out but I'm freezing, tucked into the sidecar under a blanket as we whip through Beijing traffic, sometimes on the right side of the road, sometimes on the wrong side, Yan Ying riding on the seat behind him, holding modestly onto his jacket; I'm sure he'd like her to lean forwards and wrap her hands around his chest, to whisper into the wind whipping past his ears. He's a hero and deserves the girl, and I hope she's only modest in public.

We pull into a hospital parking lot where I get out, lurching automatically towards the big front doors. The biker speaks to a guard, then calls me over, waving me back into the sidecar. "No open," Yan Ying translates. "Go other place." How can a hospital not be open?

I don't get out at the second hospital, and it's just as well. The third time's my charm: the People's University Hospital, where Yan Ying leads me around the back of the main building by following signs I could never read. The emergency department has heavy translucent plastic straps for an outside door—the kind that supermarkets use between the retail floor and the stockrooms. I guess it keeps out the mosquitoes.

We check in at the desk, and I hand them my passport, my health insurance card, my credit card; I would hand them anything else they asked for, no questions, just action, whatever it takes to shake off the headache and fever and the nausea that crept on so slowly I don't remember it starting and can't remember a time without it.

They give back everything but the passport, jotting notes onto a sheet full of Chinese characters and boxes they check one, two, three. Yan Ying interprets as I give my symptoms, and then we sit. My vitals are taken in a small room with surprisingly dirty walls. A gleaming stainless steel tray with individually sealed syringes are an antiseptic counterpoint to the grungy floor; she drops her hair scrunchy, regards it with pity, and leaves it there. I try to pick it up for her, but she grabs my wrist and shakes her head. What really must be clean, is, but nothing more. I'm diagnosed; my chart is filled; I'm urged out of the room and pointed towards a small window. For a moment my heart sinks, terrible thoughts of being discharged without a pill, without a hope.

"Pay first," she says. Oh. It'll be three hundred eighty Yuan; being my last night in town, I'm broke. The hospital ATM doesn't take my card—paranoid about security, I have a long pin number, and it accepts all but the last digit. The next ATM is no help, either, nor the third; Yan Ying finds the biker, and from a leather pouch on his belt he pulls four pink 100 Yuan bills.

She teaches me "Super Tic Tac Toe," where you make five across on a giant grid, and thoroughly humiliates me in every single game as my body absorbs bag after bag of saline and antibiotics. My immune system crashed. Every bug in my body, every foreign microbe I breathed or ate or drank, went nuts in my lawless bloodstream. 104 degree fever, the paperwork says; I shouldn't even be conscious. They saved my life.

Yan Ying is the kindest person I've met in China, just barely pulling ahead of the biker, and she restores my fever-addled faith in human decency. I owe her; I try to give her my change, the last Yuan I have to my name but she giggles and says "no, this is my job." Her job is to work the desk at the hostel; she is a saint, but she doesn't know that word and I can't think of an equivalent. Are there Buddhist saints? Confucian?

I only know this one.

* * * * *

"Where've you been?" Josh missed the whole episode, drinking merrily in the courtyard with new friends. "You look worse. I didn't think that was possible."

"I need four hundred Yuan."

"Hit the ATM." I explain that we've tried, none take my card, I owe a week's wages to a biker and value my kneecaps... Josh thinks for a moment, looking away and then back. "I'm not bailing you out again."

I'm appalled at his callousness, but should consider that he could be as wrapped up in his adventure as I am in mine, and genuinely surprised at how ill I've become on the sidelines of his grand tour. I get ornery and hostile when I'm sick, as if I could drive the illness out by being disagreeable, and that can't be pleasant to be around; maybe I shouldn't hold his rebuff against him. But in this moment it feels like he's buying me off, from complaining or troubling him ever again. Misperceptions are as powerful as everything else we feel.

I lurch slowly across the courtyard to the biker who sits eating watermelon with Yan Ying. I thank him profusely—no need to translate—and give him exactly what I owe him. Yan Ying dismissed my attempt to give her a tip; I don't want to offend him by offering money for his kindness and trust; can a tip cancel the virtue of a good deed? I want to do something for him, though I'm too tired and nervous to think of anything.

He accepts the money without counting it, smiles, holds my gaze a moment and turns back to his watermelon. I'll regret not slipping him an extra hundred Yuan, only fifteen bucks, for the rest of my life.

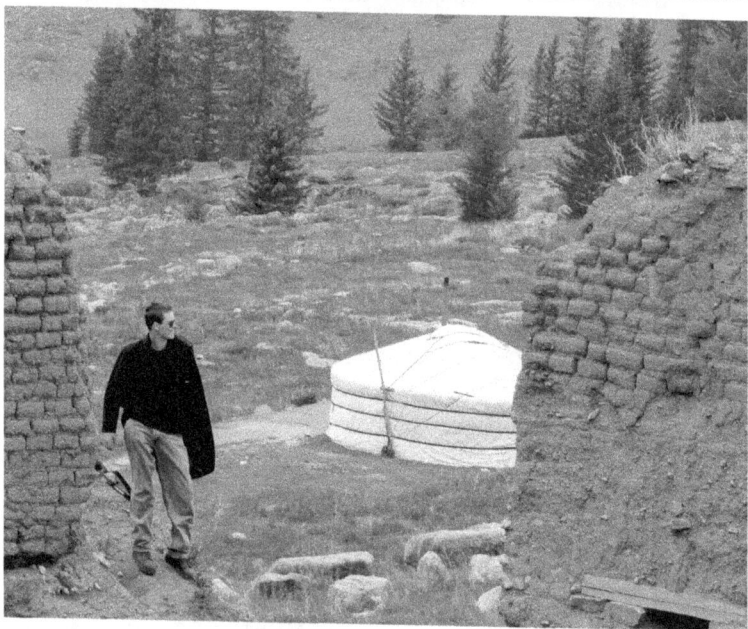

Top: **Prayer wheels at Gandantegchinleng Khiid, Ulan Bator**

Bottom: **Josh on the ruins of Manzushir Khiid, near Zuunmod**

Mongolia
18 August, 2007

Ulan Bator, Mongolia

I have found out that there ain't no surer way to find out whether you like people or hate them than to travel with them.

—Mark Twain

No one speaks English and everything is broken.

—Tom Waits

Trans Mongolian yaya's…Christina the German girl… The Zen of carrying on…That old Josh magic…

The morning is brown and everything is covered in a gritty film of Gobi Desert dust. My hand shakes across the page as I cough-write-cough on this top bunk in our lurching train car. The desert is harsh and unfarmable, arid, textured with Asian tumbleweed and yellow-stalked grasses that rise in defiant clumps bent double by the wind. There is a marathon every year in the Gobi, not because it's scenic—which it is, in a peculiar way—but because it's harsh and unforgiving and a great place to sweat out the toxins breathed in Beijing. The wind is wicked when it wants to be, nothing stopping it from whipping the parched earth into roiling dust storms—dry, paint-destroying, skin abrading storms that erode man's creations back down into the earth we came from.

The vast, open land is not empty; on the Chinese side of the border behind us were strange villages with mud walls and crumbling red tile roofs. Half-dressed and filthy children stood hollow-eyed at the gates as our train rolled past, staring at us, at this moving picture gallery of foreigners coming from nowhere and returning back to it the long way. A large factory with great tanks and pipes makes giant white clouds from issue from its standpipes; there is a little town next door for the workers.

We sway our way north along the Trans Mongolian Railroad, trying to figure out why these tiny villages are out here; what they're doing. The children probably wonder where we came from, where we're going; don't they know there's nothing in either direction, that the world ends where the rails meet the sky?

I learned a new word last night: bogey. It's a pet name for Humphrey Bogart, and action movie slang for an enemy fighter jet; apparently it also means the undercarriage of a railcar. We were herded off the train, processed through customs—our hundred dollar Chinese visas canceled so we can't go back if we don't like Mongolia—and deposited in a waiting area with a snack shop selling foil pack potato chips and soda and Mongol vodka with

Genghis Khan's face on the label.

Appetizing...

I waited outside on the platform as crews jacked our railcars up on ten foot tall hydraulic lifts, then used a small locomotive to roll the undercarriages away. Another rolled new undercarriages in place, with a wider wheelbase for the Russian-gauge rails between there and Poland. They swapped the bogeys on our car, then the next section of cars, and the next, a quarter mile parade of dark green cars with Chinese stars and Russian lettering.

Bogeys. Indeed.

In Beijing I felt like death; I felt like shit the next morning, and now I only feel like crap, each softening of language an important milestone in my recovery. Speakers on the platform filled the Mongol twilight with Frank Sinatra; feverish though I was, I clearly heard the Chairman of the Board singing My Way. "I planned, each charted course," I sang into the night without a care for modesty or harmony, "each careful step, on the byway. But more, much more than this, I did it my way." The other passengers, tired from a full day on the rails, stared at me with disingenuous half-interest like the way you watch a three-legged dog slip across an icy sidewalk.

Huh. Isn't that special.

I've been admitted to hospitals on three continents, taken by car (illness, USA), speeding ambulance (traumatic injury, Germany), and a dangerously weaving motorcycle (heatstroke, China). It's no wonder my friends worry for me, and my parents have me insured like a Rembrandt—if I croak before thirty, their investment in premiums will beat the stock market ten to one.

I can identify with Sinatra's song; by the time we're done, Josh and I will have exhausted our charted courses, run clear out of careful steps, and loved and laughed and cried...and done it all our own ways. We may have bitten off more than we can chew, and Yan Ying stood with me as I faced what sure felt like the final curtain, but here we are on the steel road north to Siberia with our little black books and prescription medication and a weaponized flashlight.

It's all so amusing...

Christina the German girl…

Christina is a German girl, a thirty-something, never-married wanderer. She's the kind of person you read about and think isn't that nice, a life so free, and if you're in a bad mood, might wonder pointedly what she thinks she's doing, traipsing all over creation with no job and no plans, abandoning all her responsibilities back home… Truth is, she doesn't have any responsibilities back anywhere, and in the homecoming sense, isn't on her way to anywhere, either—an existential place afforded by carefully orchestrated freedom and her savings from a good job. It's quintessentially…European? No, it's quintessentially… young? No…

What is it, exactly?

She stands just shorter than me, which isn't saying too much, has blonde hair that frames her face but doesn't trouble her bare shoulders, and laugh-lines that foreshadow her sweet and easy smile. She lived in Shanghai for many years, working, saving, waiting for her boyfriend to propose…but he hasn't in seven years and her bare ring finger is bitter towards him now. Maybe she'll make her own move, she says, a move he might not like, but he had his chance; anyway, she has plenty of time to think things over. She's on her way by rail from Shanghai back to Germany. Her favorite Chinese furniture and souvenirs are on their way by ship, her old apartment is tended and paid for by sublet renters, and her boyfriend is working in Berlin already—part of that world that goes on without us and always will.

So what do you do when you're unemployed and unmarried, no rent to pay and no possessions to anchor you to one place, not much to go home to and no desire to stay behind? You hop a train to Mongolia and chat with the lanky American in the black t-shirt and jazz hat, and go back to his compartment to meet his friend, the writer.

The Zen of carrying on…

The Trans Mongolian Railroad connects Beijing with Irkutsk,

Russia. The compartments sleep four people like a prison cell in an old movie. There is no front or back to the cars, and at each end there's a little room with a door to a clamorous space leading into the next car's anteroom. Then there's a door into a long hallway, either on the left or the right side of the car depending on which end faces forwards.

There's a bathroom to one side, and it takes a bit of getting used to—when you push the pedal at the base of the toilet a flap flips down and you can see the railroad ties flicker past. Whatever was in the bowl becomes a greasy smear on the tracks.

Next come the passenger compartments, eight of them per car, with a samovar at one end. From here you can draw boiling hot water for tea or instant coffee. The bathroom sinks have running water, but I don't want to drink that. There are stewards on the trains; we don't see them much. They collect our tickets, deliver our blankets, and otherwise leave us alone.

Our compartment has a sliding door and a table in front of the window; it folds up against the wall and latches in place, blocking the window but affording more room. There are two bunks on each side, one knee-height with a sturdy metal enclosure below, the other chin-height and held aloft with chains. The lower one encloses the secure storage space—we loaded it with our most valuable possessions. Whoever sits or sleeps on the bed becomes a human lock. Josh can't sit up on that bottom bunk unless he folds the top bunk against the wall, which then makes for a nice compartment where four roommates can sit around the table playing cards and drinking vodka.

We read. Josh picked up a copy of "Mr. Nice," a poorly reproduced black-market paperback about a British drug smuggler. I love a good smuggler story, but this is an autobiography with the thesis "I'm a scoundrel, but loveable." No, he's not.

I read "Escape from Colditz," the story of a German POW camp for captured officers and escape artists, written by the former commandant—also about smuggling and narrow escapes and High Adventure, but written by a gentleman whose motivation seems to be no worse than committing good stories to paper while he's able.

"Feeling better?" Josh asks me over the top of his book. I've been lying on my stomach watching the world through the window, and haven't coughed or made any other noise in awhile; maybe he thought I was dead.

"A bit, yeah."

"You look better, man. I hope you're going to be alright."

"Do I have another option?"

"I've never seen you like this." Come again? "Just being honest here, you've been pretty down. I mean, just enjoy the ride, man…" My body crashed while he was having a good time; these things happen. My illness was the brutal opposite to his health and spirit, making me feel even worse by comparison. When you're sick, you don't want to be surrounded by other sick people…but having the very image of vim and vigor dancing circles around you is hard in its own way.

I am, of course, disappointed in myself—the first one sick. I trained for this; aren't we outdoorsy people supposed to be indestructible? I don't mind weakness in others so much as I loathe it in myself, and apparently that's showing.

So I'm lying here with my book closed, watching a complex and ancient country fade behind me without really understanding much about it; without even staying on my feet for the full round. I'm embarrassed and wistful, with a bit of resentment that he didn't see how sick I was, and envious—not jealous, there's no malice—that he could flow so gracefully through Beijing without the touts getting him down or running afoul of racist cooks or having his ATM card rejected at a hospital…

He's probably just better at not letting things like that get him down; it's a kind of Zen I should quietly work on.

"Don't die on me," he says. "I can't handle the paperwork."

"Paperwork, hell. You'd sell my body by the pound for dog food." He looks genuinely confused, on the edge of being hurt, when I flash a sly grin and we share the kind of laugh that touches off a coughing fit.

"Lunchtime, man," he says. "Join me in the dining car?"

Imagine a nineteen eighties Denny's restaurant on the bleak side of a forgotten highway, and arrange its tables in parallel lines with an aisle down the middle. That's about the look and feel of the dining car…but with even more smoke and surly drunks. It holds no intrinsic interest.

"Sure," I say in a heartbeat, seeing in his eyes an invitation to a reconciliation of sorts—one that admits no wrong, but invites all who are willing to join together and renew their bond in purpose.

That old Josh magic…

We blow through a tiny railway station, horn blaring, and wave to a teenage girl clutching a baby. She waves its tiny hand back at us. This is all the interaction they get with foreigners; I wonder if she has ever seen a globe. What does she know beyond her communal farm in the middle of nowhere? What will she teach that child when it grows up and asks what lies across the plains?

I know nothing about them, about their lives under this sun that cracks their land; my glimpse of life in their hutong is fleeting: crumbling walls, old motorbikes, piles of garbage, scattered and asymmetric burial mounds with tall black headstones…a glimpse at life and death in a hutong whose walls work both ways. We pass as strangers, and leave them far behind.

We have been watching the windows like children transfixed by a television movie with no commercials. I lay on my top berth, pointing my camera out the window like a sniper, watching intently and waiting for just the right shot—a chemical plant in the middle of nowhere that explains the haze on the horizons; got it. A flock of sheep, missed. An old man riding a horse-drawn motorcycle…blurry. The Golden Hour's evening light is gone now as the world disappears into sleep.

Our accommodations are "second class hard," as inexpensive as it gets on trains from capital to capital—Beijing to Ulan Bator. First class passengers get a private room with their own shower in wood-paneled cabins. Riffraff like us get packed into these five-by-six, four-sleeper cabins. There are cheaper fares on the Trans Siberian line to the north, but with those tickets all you get is access to a large room with bunks and a lot of milling, drunken, surly strangers (or so we've read)…so we have tickets to ride "second class hard" from Beijing all the way to Warsaw with layovers a few days at a time in places that sounded interesting and exotic a few months ago; they haven't lost their allure at all, but in our conversations about them, in flipping ahead in the little black books, we've developed a sort of pre-familiarity with the idea of Irkutsk, the notion of Moscow…

We have this cabin to ourselves—very lucky—so we have room for a social life. The upper bunks store bags we need frequently, and we invite new friends over for drinks. Christina is a frequent guest, as are two recent college graduates from Ohio who Josh befriended in the dining car after I left.

I feel a sense of community on this train, if only the sort among people mashed together by circumstance. As I recover, I'm having a good time talking to Australian retirees, Swiss school teachers, Canadian college students, and the like—but never as easily or freely as Josh. Drinks and decent food in the dining car bring us a bit closer—it's the communion of strangers, where the same boring questions (where are you from, where are you going) bring exciting, fresh answers. We can be as honest with these strangers as we like because we'll never see them again.

Josh is particularly adept with social graces, easily making friends—in part because he's a foreigner to them, and therefore, automatically interesting. In Korea he met two students on their way home from a semester in Japan; they hung around in the background of our DMZ tour. In Beijing he met Toronto Peter, Michelle, the owner of D-22…single-serving friends he appreciates, promises to write, then leaves cleanly behind.

He has the innate grace of a socialite, but would never, ever let such a title stick—it has all the wrong connotations for him. " 'Socialite,' nah, that makes me sound like high society or something," he said in a rambling, slow paced conversation earlier. With little else to do, we have the luxury of lying about, filling the room with words and ideas at our leisure. " 'Sociable,' maybe that's it, I don't know. I just like people."

He might not stay in touch, but he'll enjoy the time he has and genuinely doesn't care if being easy-going by itself is a virtue. Like a fish swims, he doesn't know any other way and can't imagine a reason to change.

The graduates stop by frequently. One is a skinny, dopey looking guy with a weasely look that makes me dislike him immediately. The other is his character foil, a short, fat, hirsute guy with a Codeine smile. They're American; I came on this trip to experience everything foreign, so combined with the whole weasel thing, I have no interest in them. Josh, though, could be their best friend right now.

While I lie on my top bunk content to read and doze, he talks as a form of recreation—the old Josh magic, perplexingly simple, devastatingly effective. They compare notes on China and swap Mongol hearsay, tell stories about people I don't know in places I haven't been, then adjourn to the dining car for more of the same.

Which brings me to this brown morning, where the wind whipping o'er the desert brings a bit of Mongolia inside the hallway, our compartment, my lungs…we're three hours outside of Ulan Bator, and breakfast time has come to Car Number 7.

The Notion of Mongolia...Idre's Glass Menagerie... Wall-O-Liquor...Our Domestic Routine...

Mongolia is a hard place, full of hard people. The winters are extremely cold, getting down around -30 Celsius. The summers are dry, except when monsoon rain from southern Asia blows north and deluges the land, most of which runs off the hard earth into seasonal streams and swollen rivers. Much of Mongolia is steppe, a gently rolling topography covered with scrub grasses and land unsuitable for any serious farming—it looks like every painting you've ever seen of Mongol Steppe, and the ground cover is as lush and sustaining as that paint on dry canvas. There are small clusters of coniferous trees, and free range herds of sheep, goats, horses, and cows. The rest of the country is covered by desert (mainly the Gobi) or mountains, neither of which is conducive to agriculture.

Nomads followed the seasons across the landscape, in search of pasture land and water, food and shelter from the incessant wind. They lived in yurts, a larger version of the North American teepee; imagine a big, circular tent with a conical roof open at the top, supported all around by a light wooden framework. They could remove the yurt's leather, cloth or canvas shell, collapse their wooden framework, and travel around the countryside in carts drawn by service animals. With their worldly possessions on their backs or strapped to beasts of burden, the nomads moved in families organized into tribes. Many still live this basic way, something akin to our Amish in Pennsylvania.

This notion of "Mongolia" as a country is new, far newer than many countries; even the notion of "Mongol People" is an invention of the last nine hundred years. Before then, the nomads were of either the Borjigin tribe, or the Olkhunut, the Kyrgyz people, or the Kerait Tribe, or...

Mongolia, between Siberia to the north and the Chinese dynasties to the south, was sparsely populated with decentralized nomadic groups. With scarce resources and no economy, a warrior tradition arose on the plains—supplies could be looted, and warriors were needed to defend their tribes' wealth. Then a boy was born under auspicious circumstances, raised by a single mother after his father (a powerful tribal leader) was killed, earned a reputation as a shrewd negotiator and fearless warrior… and rose to power as Genghis Khan.

He gained influence by uniting many of the tribes, and in so doing, quelling the feuds between them and turning their time and energy towards expanding the empire. It was a masterful redirection of the energy and angst within their warrior culture, turning their arrows and spears outwards on the world at large. They pushed south against the Qing Dynasty (the Manchurians), and west through modern Kazahkstan, extending their empire all the way across Asia to the Middle East.

United by the struggle, the nomadic tribes became "Mongols" as we refer to them today, and as they refer to each other in general; proud ties still exist to their ancestral tribes, but even among those who still wander, most are quick to identify themselves first as Children of Genghis Khan and parse their specific lineage from there.

Records indicate Genghis rode as far west as Egypt, placing him in North Africa…quite the commute for a guy on horseback. His empire expanded based on sound military principles that now seem obvious and trite, but were cutting edge in his day. In the 1200s, long before war colleges and doctoral theses on adversarial reasoning, Ghengis thought it prudent to study his opponents before attacking; to gather as much information about their arms and supplies, leadership and motivation, as possible; then, to incorporate siege tactics from the Chinese, infantry techniques and equipment from the Arabs, and even civil engineering—his armies could divert rivers to cut off water supplies, quickly weakening a town's will and ability to resist. Thus his empire expanded at the point of a spear, as per human nature's unfortunate custom.

Ghengis did not live to see the Mongol Empire's full greatness; he died in 1227, whereupon his empire was divided between his sons and grandchildren. They continued these campaigns and held enough land, for enough time, to claim the record of the largest (in landmass) empire in the history of the world. They should have received a trophy, or a plaque, or something, to hang in their yurts...but oh well.

Their empire didn't last, as in the 1300s a thousand groups in a thousand places started reclaiming their autonomy. The Mongol empire shrank back over time to their ancestral land between Siberia and China, where we think of "Mongolia" today.

In the 1600s, nomadic Buddhist monks established a movable yurt village between the Tuul and Selbe rivers, on a popular route south towards Beijing. More than ten thousand monks lived in this drifting community that eventually outgrew its portability and settled where we find Ulan Bator today. Known by various names in various languages, the yurt city displayed Genghis's well-known tolerance of different religions.

With religious tolerance comes an implicit ethnic tolerance, the two being intrinsically linked throughout recorded history. This is one of Ghengis's most enduring—if not also endearing—legacies, and allowed Muslim merchants and Shamanist nomads, Christian missionaries and a tiny group of Jews, to coexist in the city founded by Tibetan Buddhists. Nomads came and went with the seasons, putting down their yurts where there was room, picking them up when they felt it time to move on. Many stayed.

The city developed around an enlarged version of the Mongol hutong, like we saw in China. Mongols build fences around their yurt villages, to keep animals in or out, or—in conflicted areas—build stronger walls designed as defense against marauders. Families live in yurts inside these walls, and fences go up between yurts as villages sprawl. Extrapolate that, and you find the maze-like hutongs in Beijing, where they used clay, brick, and concrete; leather houses were shunned in favor of more durable construction for permanent settlements.

Homeward-oriented after their heyday of empire building, the Mongols herded and wandered their homeland through a succession of dynasties that descended from the fragments of Genghis's empire, several developing into more or less autonomous states with their unique rivalries and rich histories that are better suited to more thorough accounts. What matters more to the Mongolia we're riding through is the interplay of

Mongol independence and Soviet influence at the dissolution of the Qing Dynasty in the early 1900s…and the idea that Mongolia gambled on communism, and lost.

Mongolia was a territory of the Qing Dynasty up until 1911, when a meeting of Mongol leaders convened to declare their country autonomous and take over its governance. Though a vast territory, it was (and remains) a sparsely populated country lacking the sort of infrastructure necessary for wholesale control or subjugation. Thus, the independence declared met with problems more verbal than military, a state of anarchy nowhere near as exciting as I'd like to imagine.

Picture a family tending their flock on the steppe. It's Monday, and they're on land claimed by the Qing Dynasty. Now it's Wednesday, and leaders they've never met say that the existing Chinese garrisons off in a village somewhere are interlopers because now Mongolia is autonomous. Spiffy.

Now it's Friday, and the Russians—who are they, exactly?—show support for Mongolia's autonomy as a political move to insulate themselves from the devolving stability in China. Think the family watching their goats chew the weeds was really affected? Or cared? But it was anarchy, it was exciting, it was…life as usual for rural Mongols, which is to say, most of the country's few million scattered people.

But big things were happening somewhere—in Urga, that village along the Tuul that would ultimately become Ulan Bator, where our train is headed now. Mongol nobles met with Russian and Chinese officials in 1914, where they declared Mongolia as autonomous but technically a part of China. How's that work?

In short, it didn't, and some ranking muckity-mucks on the Mongol side turned their land over to full Chinese authority—again—in 1919, whereupon their sitting leader, Bogd Khan, was promptly arrested and subject to all sorts of unsavory treatment. It's safe to assume he was singularly pissed off.

This whole debacle was a golden opportunity for the Russian agitator Baron Ungern von Sternberg, a "White Russian" (meaning west-of-the-Urals European, rather than east-of-the-Urals Asian) who made a hobby of the old ultra-violence. He swooped out of the north ala Genghis Khan himself, sacked the city, killed its Jews for unknown (but historically pervasive) reasons, freed Bogd Khan, and reinstated him to power...no doubt with aspirations of wealth and glory for his efforts.

Fat lot of good that did him: the Russian Red Army was on his heels, augmented by a horde of communist-leaning Mongols mustered by Damdin Sükhbaatar. The Baron was killed, footnoted, and forgotten, and the communists took over Mongolia with full Russian support. Urga was renamed "Ulan Bator," after Sükhbaatar, from whence its name has derived more spellings than you might care to read. For simplicity's sake, I'm going with Ulan Bator.

Thus is my understanding of Mongol history, which will shape my pursuit of the true Mongolia this week. I learn, understand, and enjoy history the most when I can experience it, try out new food and customs and pass out drunk inside the very story itself. I can't learn much in only a week wandering the capital...but I want to experience as much as I can—to taste it, to ride a horse across the steppe like Mongols have for millennia, to eat goat and sleep in a yurt and imagine that my dominion includes more than just my backpack. It's an ancient dream—one Ghengis realized from a leather hut right here on the steppe.

Idre's Glass Menagerie...

Our train coasts into the railway station, slowing, until the locomotive stops. Bang, as the Number 1 first class car slams into it—clang, the Number 2. Bang, screech, clang, on down the line until our car hits Number 6 and gets slammed by Number 8. This is how trains stop. Josh sleeps right through it.

We're travelers, battle tested, time hardened backpackers with scars and stories and about two weeks' experience on this journey. You may scoff, but I can't see you, because I'm elbowing my way through a horde of bearded Mongol men in track jackets and cheap Chinese shirts saying teksi? in such ways that I fear for my life. No "teksi," and please quit grabbing my framepack... We know just where we're going: Idre's Guest House, Building 22,

Zanabazaryn Street.

And where's that? "This way," Josh says, leading me past a low wooden building with a hundred years' worth of railroad dust in its grain. Christina falls in behind, homeless for the moment and intrigued by the cost of our hostel: four dollars a night.

As Josh met her on the train, she met another German girl—Juliana—who, having no reservations or better ideas, follows Christina as she follows me as I follow Josh...a multi-national line of ducklings following our leader.

This is Teeverchdyn Street, a wide street along the western side of Ulan Bator, paralleling the railroad tracks south towards the main part of town...such that there is a main part of Ulan Bator, a city incorporated from yurts and hutongs and then paved over and partially developed with concrete buildings by the Russians. The locals speak Mongol, an ancient language passed down as an oral tradition long before it was committed to writing; they have their written language, a vertically oriented system of curves, lines, and the occasional dot. Cyrillic transliterations of Mongol words are prevalent, holdovers ever since they sidled up so cozily with Russia.

So their street signs are all in Cyrillic...great. Even if I could remember the street name "Zanabazaryn" without looking at my little black book, we can't read Cyrillic. We can get a feel, though, and emboldened by our previous adventures, spurred by our aversion to the touts at the station, we press on undaunted. The little black book has walking instructions in meters, which are roughly analogous to yards, and which most normal people base on their stride; Josh has a longer stride than mine, but neither is tied to the metric scale. Oh well. I'm still under the weather enough to follow without protest, or input, so we have a go at the old trial-and-error.

Ulan Bator looks like the Soviet version of the OK Corral. The streets are paved below several inches of dust, their crust broken in jagged potholes, the sidewalks only sometimes flat. They're travelled by hard people with hard stares, eyes fixed like gun sights, grimacing to keep the world at bay. I've not seen anything like it; nomads are supposed to be hospitable, caring for strangers and fellow wandering souls…but these people aren't nomads anymore. They live here in ugly concrete buildings with the smoke-belching Russian vans and broken Ladas too stubborn to quit running, broken glass and litter everywhere—and yes, that is vomit on the sidewalk. Maybe their hard stares and muzzled aggression are what happens to free spirits when they're caged in a city.

And I'm moving to New York?

A few traffic lights and stop signs assert themselves stoically on the motorized chaos, mere suggestions of the sort of courtesy I don't find on the streets. On our left are Soviet barracks-style apartment houses, five-story-proof that The Glorious People's Ready Mix Concrete is useful for more than crappy roads—it can also make crappy buildings. How do you hang a picture on a concrete wall? And what sort of picture should a Mongol frame and hang when they move to Ulan Bator…a picture of yurts that remind them of how they're trapped in concrete?

There is a sort of rugged, haunting beauty on the steppe—maybe they'd hang a picture of that, of a yurt on a grassy plane that rolls uphill to infinity. How many ghosts still ride that range tending sheep long devoured, hearty souls too hard to die, too wild to live in a world like this?

We've gone too far; or not far enough. Anyway the little black book says we're close, so we do what any proud American man would never do back home: we walk to a gas station and ask for directions.

"Idre's Guesthouse?" Josh asks, offering the book. The attendant, a boy in filthy flip flops (on these streets, with the moldering garbage and rusty debris? Really?), stares at the page with hollow eyes, then stares at Josh with a jailer's look of pity and dismissal. "Idre's?"

He mimics the sound, ee-drays, then points and grumbles.

"Up that way?" Josh translates, "and to the right?" mimicking the gestures.

Grumph.

"Thanks." Josh puts his hands together and bows just slightly, lowering his eyes; I flash my best country boy, aw-shucks smile, watching him suspiciously the whole time. I'm on guard, my fever-addled hackles raised by a sense of looming danger. It's an instinct and it's unstoppable, and perhaps I'll come to understand why—on a bright and sunny morning at the threshold of discovery—I feel like a lamb in a wolf's lair.

Zanabazaryn Street, with Idre's on the left side, connects Teeverchdyn Street with a main thoroughfare through Ulan Bator, which is to say that it's comparatively quiet while hemmed in by vehicular madness—blaring horns and rust streak past in each direction. Am I current on tetanus shots? On the way up the street to Idre's is a minibus station in a grocery store parking lot. Minibuses are the first-class versions of big buses, in that they sometimes have air conditioning, make fewer stops, have slightly better suspensions, and go more places; they also cost more, but not much if you think in US dollars. This is how city folks get out to the country, to Gorkhi-Terelj National Park, and the outlying towns to visit the rest of their ancient families.

Walking up the street, guesthouse sign in sight, we pass an outdoor pool table leaned-over by teenage boys with broken cue sticks. They're taking the game very seriously, playing the swells and cants like it's a red rectangular putting green. I've never seen a pool table outside before; it clearly doesn't want to be out here, sun-bleached varnish peeling from the wood, felt moldy and torn, but here it is on the sidewalk and here it lives, one leg shimmed with a broken brick.

Idre's has a glassed-in sitting room along the sidewalk. A tall Mongol girl with broad shoulders and a nice body sweeps glass off a couch, dusty breeze tugging at her hair from a fist-shaped hole in the window. She looks up at our knocking, her face a stern mask of irritation that—with eye contact—immediately cracks into the most surprising smile I've ever seen. Such a shift, such a smile, and all…for Josh. We vowed not to shave on this trip; while I look like I woke up under a bridge, he still has the baby face of a young man who needs an older woman to show him the ropes. It works well to win girls' trust.

Or maybe she's just being nice. Her name is Golan; she lets us in and immediately double-locks the door behind us.

We take our shoes off just past the broken glass, and Golan shows us the internet computers (a thousand Tugrik an hour, honor system), the kitchenette, the drinking water machine (all we can drink, free), the living room with the big screen TV and old VHS player with Chuck Norris and Jackie Chan movies and Chinese dramas, the bedroom with eight bunks around a window crossed by thick steel bars... It's home, and it's four bucks a night, the best deal on the journey.

"You know a good place to eat?" Josh asks, and she gives a few options with basic directions. "Cool, yeah, so you wanna come with us?" That old Josh Magic, by which he means nothing...and everything.

Wall-O-Liquor

The needle sinks into the groove and the now-familiar song starts again—time to find a grocery store and see what fruit they have, their bottled water (just in case), tour their liquor and meat sections...basic housekeeping, and you can learn a lot about a new place by their liquor and meat sections. We go through the motions of settling into Ulan Bator, finding comfort in the pattern.

This grocery store, just down the main thoroughfare from Idre's, has a baked goods area with a decent selection, plenty of boxed goods like crackers and juices in waxed paper cartons, puffed flour junk foods, a small fruit selection, and basic sausages and cheeses. The butcher doesn't speak English, I don't read Cyrillic, so I have no idea if that's goat sausage or blood sausage or what animals were involved... Mongolia is a hard place for those with dietary restrictions—medical or religious or personal. I'm not usually picky, but here it seems prudent.

Religiously, Mongolia is a Tibetan Buddhist country, fifty percent to ninety four percent Buddhist, depending on where you get your information...and on how you label a Buddhist. There are clear steps and sacraments involved in "becoming" Christian or Muslim (two other religions represented in Mongolia, though not widely), but not in Buddhism. While monks in red cloth anchor one end of the spectrum, the term "Buddhist" can apply to anyone who claims it.

Ardent Buddhists are vegetarians, which must be tough in Mongolia. The limited "vegetarian" foods pre-packaged in this grocery store come from China, with dubious truth to the bilingual packaging, or from Russia with esoteric symbols I can't differentiate from Cyrillic. This would be a big deal in other parts of Asia, especially in Indonesia and Malaysia with their dense Muslim populations. Even in America I can find a range of symbols from religious authorities certifying different things Kosher or Hallal or "organic" (the new foodie religion).

Not here. I could order the black sausage, or the red sausage, or settle for a dehydrated "Cup-o-Soup," with no clue what's actually in any of it. I wander past the giant wall-o-liquor, which they're not supposed to sell to anyone under eighteen. I'm not convinced this law is enforced. It's barely ten in the morning on a regular weekday, and I've already seen stumbling-drunk teenagers fighting each other...and fighting to stay upright.

Judging by the street tableaux and all the liquor bottles, there are few better things to do in Ulan Bator than get hammered at will. There are at least a dozen different brands of vodka, all in one flavor: clear and strong. The American craze for flavored hard alcohol is completely absent—here, you only find the pure stuff, straight from the copper condenser pipes of some distillery in a warehouse down by the train station. Simple. Straightforward. Tastes like lightning and hits you just as hard and quick.

Cheap, too. I can buy a bottle of Chenggis Wodka—dig the spelling, baby—for four thousand tugrik.

Four thousand tugrik!? That's about three bucks, as at the moment a dollar US buys twelve hundred tugrik—dig the exchange rate, baby; groovy... That's another holdover from the extensive Soviet influence over the "Mongol People's Republic," the systems collapsing together in gasping heaps of concrete dust in the early nineteen nineties.

Chenggis is one of the umpteen spellings I've seen of their hero's name—I've also found "Genghis Qan," "Jenghis Khan," Chinggis Xaan," and my favorite, the Cyrillic transliteration of the Mongol pronunciation, "Чингис Хаан." I found most of these on bottles of vodka (or "wodka" or something in Cyrillic I presume is equivalent). The others, I've picked up from statues and street signs on my way here. If the various spellings indicate anything, perhaps it's the importance of a legible signature.

Never mind that Mongol, as a language, has its own written system of lines and curves that doesn't decode uniformly into an alphabetic system; if you get caught up on details like that and can't laugh at little things, like five spellings of one man's name on different bottles of the same bathtub hooch, then you probably lack the defense mechanisms necessary to deal with waking up to broken windows in a Post-Soviet slum.

Aye, but I'm getting ahead of myself...

Our common languages... Rolling bones... All that glitters is broken glass... Where "To Serve and Protect" has no traction... Broken window theories... The real James Dawson...

Josh went out last night with the graduates he met on the train. He partied like a rock star and barely beat the sunrise home. Now it's lunchtime, and he's back from the grocery store with a cup of dehydrated noodles. "Save a little money here," he says, "and I can eat a little better later."

The beer in this city is unremarkable, but what the hooch lacks in quality it makes up for in quantity, a virtue Josh avails himself of at budget-destroying pace. This city is a big downer, but...I can't help scoffing at the notion of eating bad food to save money, the morning after spending four nights' budget on booze.

Which of course I don't mention.

The German girls, Christina and Juliana, are off in search of their staple foods: bread, cheese, and sausage, which they'll find easily enough. So I'm sitting here after breakfast, alone with my breadcrumbs and fried egg when Golan sits down to chat—one of the fringe benefits, she says, of working in the hostel. She's in her late teens, but looks much older. Her father is well educated, and her family has means enough to send her to college, a rarity for any Mongol...much less a girl in their strong patriarchal society.

Rather than expensive English lessons, she works here to pick up the language. English is the official language of business and aviation, and of travelers on back roads and dusty paths; the only language Europeans, Indians, and Asians have in common is the English they pick up in school and from the television—it's how Golan talks to Germans, Chinese, and Italians. Everywhere I go, those who I really hope speak English—waitresses, salesmen, ticket agents—do. It makes travel incredibly easy...but when I want to try a little local dialect, I'm usually answered in English. They want to practice a foreign language, too, and I feel just a little left out.

Golan is very good with her English, especially for a girl

from a tiny village on the steppe. Her father worked for the government, but not anymore, so she lives with friends and has no family any longer in Ulan Bator—which she says is a little frightening, a little daunting, being a girl in this kind of place with no backup. Idre's, she says, is a safe haven between semesters, and a living language laboratory.

She asks about the ring on my right hand, one I've worn for a long time. Many Europeans wear wedding bands on their right hands, and I can tell she's not interested in me in that way. She's interested in the custom, and hearing what I have to tell her about Americans.

So we talk about marriage, and why she is single: it's hard to find a man with a good job, she says, who respects her and treats her well, is not an alcoholic, and is still single. Hearing her talk and looking around the streets, those standards are prohibitively high in Ulan Bator. Her romantic ideals are inspired by the movies she's watched—American and European films, where men are demonstratively affectionate and try (usually too hard) to earn the girl's favor and graces. She likes that idea. She also requires in a mate that he do at least as much, professionally and around the home, as she does.

Which would be hard for any man to keep up with, as Golan is studying to be a doctor. Her town has no physician, so sick people are left to their family's care and traditional practices that are unrelated to modern medical knowledge. Many women give birth at home, sometimes with midwives (almost always a family member), sometimes without. Mother and child both usually survive, and hospitalization is rare and financially devastating.

My fiancée will be a doctor soon, I say, and then I explain her interest in combining Western scientific medicine with Eastern traditional medicine. Golan is taken by the idea; she has faith in acupuncture, but doesn't yet know much about it…just that there are ways her ancestors healed themselves that don't have much to do with textbooks. She would also like to get the best of several approaches to medicine, and bring them back to her village on the steppe.

If she was writing a medical school application letter, it's right about now that she would talk about her dying grandmother or friend with leukemia or some other heartache sales pitch that takes your emotional investment and sours it with melodrama. In just about any other conversation with cute girls in poor countries, this is where she would ask for money.

Not Golan—she's sincere, and just enjoying a real conversation for its recreational benefits. She has heady idealism, but in her demeanor I get the sense that it might just work out for this one. And it's so incredibly refreshing not to have a sales pitch coming, not to be fed some line. In her interests and nobility, I'm reminded of the woman I'm coming home to.

Rolling bones...

Golan dumps a small leather pouch onto the breakfast table, spilling a number of oddly shaped bones. They're used in a game she calls "Shagai," which has been the Mongol game for centuries. Children play it for fun; adults, to pass cold grey days in their yurts. Men gamble on it, and shamans use it to tell fortunes.

The game consists of four ankle bones from either sheep or goats. The bones are scraped, bleached, dried, and sometimes painted. They are about an inch long, as wide as they are thick (which isn't very), and gently curved on each end—like rock-hard packing peanuts. With a lot of imagination, each side looks like either a horse (like the knight piece in chess), goat, sheep (with two horns), or camel (lying down). The sides have meaning in fortune telling; like dice, the side facing up is the one that matters. I shake the four of them and roll them out on the table. Three goats and a lamb—that's bad, she says; but it was just a practice roll, and anyway, the fortune telling only has as much power as you allow it.

Shagai bones used in fortune telling are normally prayed over by a lama. Four horses is about the best throw you can wish for; four goats, nearly the worst. "Not good for business," is my fortune; the question was about romance.

So they pray a question, roll the bones, and read the fortune. When that gets old, they can play the game version of Shagai.

Children, old men, and entire families gather around tables or the bare ground, taking as many pieces as they can hold and dropping them on the flat playing surface. The goal is to spot two pieces that are showing the same side up, and then flick one into the other without hitting any other piece.

Ricochet one off a contrasting piece, or simply miss the target, and the turn is over; get a hit, and take one of the two bones off the board. But look around first—the two pieces have probably tumbled, showing new sides. If one now matches another piece, leave it and take the other. Like playing marbles, the point is to acquire as many pieces each round as possible.

The pieces—the real, hand-processed bones—smell faintly of meat and old cigarettes from years of playing. Some players paint the sides with fingernail polish, so sheep are always red, horses are blue, etc. That helps, especially for newcomers like me. Over the years, nervous fingers and too many collisions wear the polish from the flat places, leaving it in cracks and nicks like antiquing.

Unlike playing marbles, you give the pieces back after the game, so one set can stay in a family indefinitely.

There are other versions, like "horse racing," where everyone gets a bone as a marker, which advances one length for each "horse" that turns up when they throw the rest of the bones. Another variant is like jacks—throw one up, sweep up as many as you can, and get that many points if you can catch the falling bone too.

When you move your possessions seasonally across the steppe, you learn to live simply. Shagai bones don't take up much space, are easy to replace, and last forever. Among nomads who pack light and revere their history, it's especially meaningful to have this old game they can play with their grandfathers' Shagai pieces. It connects the generations…and gives them something to do during long, cold days on the barren steppe.

Golan's pieces aren't for sale, and she won't give them up—these are family heirlooms, a sacred connection to her heritage. I can buy a set, she says, of plastic pieces with the animals clearly carved in the sides…or find a set of authentic bones on the black-market.

We play a few games, chatting about college and hopes and dreams. She lowers her guard a little, and then no further, confiding the same secrets she probably tells a lot of other travelers. When I leave, I'll take these memories with me, far away and out of her life, so she tells me things she might not tell a friend she sees every day.

I finally win a game, an unexpected turn in a losing streak, so she smiles and leaves me alone on a high note.

All that glitters is broken glass...

Ulan Bator glistens in the sunlight, but all that glitters is not gold—it's broken glass. I've been walking for several hours, just meandering, getting good and lost and found again, counting the broken windows up to twenty, down to zero, up again... Some buildings are abandoned, but not many; most harbor some sort of life, if only squatters who stretch sheets across windows to keep the sun out and arrest what objects are thrown through the glass.

There are drunk men on the sidewalks at all hours; they're especially aggressive when in packs, and worse after dark. But even in the mornings, those Mongols not working in the tiny shops and restaurants, in the department store, grilling shish kebabs on long rectangular charcoal grills, those Mongols not embracing the free market economy, are reeling drunk through the streets like their fathers. I carry my camera slung across my chest, arm pinning it against my ribs, guarded against snatch-thieves and scooter bandits (there are surprisingly few scooters here—too many potholes, too little money). I have never before felt so threatened while merely walking down the street.

I'm wearing sunglasses and a black hat pulled low, thankful for the sturdy boots that crunch the broken glass, knife ready in my pocket, hackles up, senses keened, the Tourist Green Beret deep behind enemy lines...

That sounds over the top. It'll read like such a farce from a comfy chair in six months' time, when I read this over in a civilized place...but it's how I feel and how I think right now and I laugh a little at the sheer absurdity of this invention, this reaction to an environment I couldn't imagine without being here.

I think of Josh, with his easy smile, his unassuming presence, his narrow minded focus on being open minded. He's the pre-September 11th American. He's not naïve; no, he's pre-jaded, unmolested by the sort of trauma that closed one era and rather dramatically started this new one. I travel with my knife and flashlight, on guard against scams and pickpockets, hopeful to make friends and embrace the world but cautious, very cautious… I'm post-9/11. Not so cautious that I miss much, I hope; in fact, the security afforded by my gear and mindset gives me the courage to wander the streets at night. To strike out as now, alone and unafraid in a very unfriendly place.

You miss 100% of the opportunities you don't take…

…but you need the freedom to take them on your own terms.

I read the US State Department Travel Advisories. I go to strange places despite their warnings, ignoring the fear propaganda, taking from them a basic idea of the problems to be aware of—specific diseases and scams, mainly. Josh dismisses the Travel Advisories entirely, and wanders home intoxicated and alone through Ulan Bator as easily as he did through Cambodian slums and a number of other interesting places in out-of-the-way countries. I wonder why he does it; it's clearly not a good idea. But he's that kind of person who bad things just don't happen to, the kind of person who lives like Teflon—problems just don't stick to him.

And he knows it.

For all my exercise beforehand and planning and gear, I'm the one who wound up in a Chinese hospital…while Josh made friends with strangers over drinks. I don't wish our fates reversed, but it's aggravating that we didn't both fare well.

Josh gets by on a smile and the essential good nature of our world. I prefer research, gut-instinct, and gear. At the least, these little concessions to my paranoia are comforting.

He is definitely from the pre-9/11 time—before box cutters were used to decapitate good people doing their jobs, before Richard Reid made us take off our shoes for airport security, before most of us knew the word "jihad"…before anyone my age had seen our flag burned in foreign streets on live television. In the long-dragging years of our "War on Terror," our pre-9/11 childhood seems so innocent. The towers came down right in our late teens, right as we were forming our world views. Baby Boomers said here we go again. People my age asked now what?

Some of us joined the military; others grabbed backpacks and flew off into the world like kids have for ages. We coped by joining the fight, or joining the peace, each side recruited by countless groups and clubs and armies. I signed up for the Marine Corps. Josh signed up to study in Thailand. Both are valid.

My father is a Marine—"was" might be the better word, but once a Marine, always a Marine, they say. His time in-service ran out before Vietnam, so he got a job and went to college—a veteran surrounded by the peace movement. He agreed philosophically, he said, that war is terrible and violence abhorrent; their views diverged, though, where mine diverge from Josh's: if violence is coming for me anyway, I want to engage it, destroy it, and do so before it comes ashore in my country.

Would Vietnam's political upheaval have threatened the US? I don't know much about that. But men my age serve in the Middle East now because they don't want any chance of the answer coming to call at home; many consider that it did on September 11th. So do I, so for that and other reasons, I signed up.

We've talked about this in passing, Josh and I; he has no aspirations towards the military, though for about a day he considered their money for college. He's too independently minded, too averse to taking orders and disinclined towards violence on someone else's behalf. "Go to interesting places," he liked that, "meet interesting people," he's game, "and kill them!" Whoops—not Josh; not in any way.

I was promptly discharged for preexisting medical reasons, and though disheartened, I got over it; the Marines are the "Few and the Proud" because they don't take everyone, and I'm part of the refuse. Oh well—I believe there's merit in trying.

The experience was indicative, though, of my mindset, which is why I think of it here on the streets of Ulan Bator. I want to know the dangers out there, prepare myself for them, and pray they never come while staying fit and ready in case they do. I believe in informed, equipped defense, as a mindset and as a guiding principle for loading a framepack—pickpocket-proof pants for places with pickpockets. Flashlight for places with unreliable electricity.

Josh has this fatalistic ideology that he'll survive the little things and probably can't stop the big ones anyway, so he drinks a toast to come-what-may and gets on with life. I admire his élan; several times he's borrowed my knife.

Broken Window Theories

As a white man with clean clothes, sturdy shoes, and a nice camera on these dusty, broken streets, I must be the poster child for conspicuous consumption—like the tuxedoed guy in New Yorker cartoons, polishing his monocle in the Bronx. The few women on the sidewalks glance at me like an exotic animal. I watch the shadows overtaking me on the sidewalk for any change of speed or direction; everything about my surroundings suggests danger for dandies.

I wonder how Ulan Bator will ever get from here, the land of broken glass and the world's worst alcoholism, to something more befitting a nation's capital. It'll take a lot, and probably won't get there in my lifetime—especially since I don't see anyone doing a thing about it.

There was a popular idea in the nineties called the "Broken Window Theory." It pertained to crime and image control, revolving around the idea that a broken window, left broken, sends the message that petty crime is tolerated—that things like broken windows aren't worth fixing, and by extension, small things aren't worth protecting. Then someone ups the ante with graffiti that isn't painted over, which begets more graffiti that is used to claim turf that stokes gang tension that turns to blood vendettas and soon everyone and their grandmas are mainlining heroin and firing machineguns.

Rata tat tat…

The solution, so that theory goes, is to fix the windows and incarcerate the petty criminals and send a message. Then, swollen with community pride (and bereft juvenile delinquents), life may continue towards white-picket-fence glory. Police Chief Howard Safir and Mayor Rudy Giuliani put that theory to work in cleaning up New York City, and the city changed so much they hit the talk show circuit.

Then the book Freakonomics pretty well eviscerated that theory, making a fantastic argument that a greater force was in play: the next wave of juveniles who would have been breaking the windows and spray painting the walls and knocking over old ladies were of the first generation born post-Roe v. Wade, and thus, were sans many colleagues who were aborted rather than born to parents who didn't want them. It was a controversial stance that made the authors' names into epithets, earning them praise and condemnation and accolades and death threats.

So which was it, or how much of each mixed in together? Ulan Bator is a world away, but a perfect place to try one of the theories anew. I honestly wonder which would work better, and what that knowledge could mean to the rest of the world.

Lock up the kids? Keep the accidents from being born? Maybe something else? Probably, some combination. This is a perfect testing ground, but I don't see anyone trying—just apathy.

We may never know.

Where "To Serve and Protect" has no traction…

I've adopted the Mongolian Stare, my brow furrowed beneath the crushing weight of this broken city. I stare out the window, face twisted, looking for problems instead of relief, and finding plenty. If the problems are with me, I don't see them; I'm looking outwards instead of within.

Why hasn't anyone fixed up this town? Why have the hard-staring, hard-drinking, unemployed men stumbling through the streets not freed themselves from this place? Lobsters in a bucket can't escape—they always pull each other down. Aren't we smarter than lobsters?

The hostel's computer is archaic, like so much of Ulan Bator, but it connected to my email and that is success in a town starved for it. Far across the steppe, across Eurasia and half the world, an email from me just arrived on my best friend's computer. It's midnight there, where Jake Jurmain is probably asleep in his cubical. It fits that my invitation should arrive during the witching hour; that my plea for him to drop everything and meet up with us on short notice should arrive in the dark dead of night like so many bad ideas. I need to reach out to someone, as if I could download comfort from half a world away, but have nothing else to say; Mongolia is here. Wish you were beautiful. Join us?

We pay for the internet by the hour, but I ignore the honor system log sheet; Ulan Bator engenders petty crime. No one will catch me; no one seems to care about rules and order at all, making me hostile towards the few rules there are. This terrible mood comes with the Mongolian Stare, encouraging the sort of contemptible behavior I normally despise.

But my crime isn't hurting anyone, and it's not wasting anything. Not like the brown fist driving through the windowpane in the foyer. Smash!

I jump out of my chair, turning, reaching for the knife in my pocket, not as quick to my feet as Idre. He leaps from his office, crosses the entryway in a single bound, and is out the front door before my hand reaches my pocket. Shouts ring out in the street as the last glass falls from the jagged edge, the knife in my hand useless because the action is outside. Blood traces the jagged hole in the window. Golan sprints outside to help her boss.

I freeze in a moment of awe, I processing the scuffle outside with the yelling and the hot dirty smells coming in through the jagged hole in the glass—detached, the camera observing the car wreck. Idre is in the middle of it, the business owner pushed too far by three busted windows in as many days; he's not going to take it anymore. The police have done nothing and each broken window is a few nights' rent stolen from his pocket. He's trying hard to rise above the squalor and rubble from the fall of communism, but plenty of hands reach up to pull him down.

A man lurches through the entryway, arm twisted behind his

back, Idre's arm around his throat. Idre throws the man on the floor. I put the knife away and grab my camera, pop a flash and then another, making the man on the floor go crazy. He flounders in blood and glass. Josh appears beside me, telling me to put the camera away, his hands balled in fists. He's not a fighter, but in these confused moments no one knows what's coming next.

Idre kneels on the vandal's back, pinning him to the floor, bleeding, while Golan calls the police. The vandal is in his thirties—far too old for this kind of juvenile delinquency. He's drunk and it's not even eleven in the morning. Disgraceful...

A few moments of awkward staring later, an officer wanders in through the front door. His radio doesn't work. He knows nothing of the situation, having merely followed the shouting. The cop is dressed like a soldier, but with a badge instead of chevrons. He talks to Idre, still kneeling on the drunk's back, and after several minutes is still the only officer on the scene; backup never arrives, and but for luck, he would not have, either. I wonder how long we would have stared at that man screaming and bleeding and writhing, waiting on police who would never come.

I laugh at him under my breath, because I can't reconcile the words "police officer" with the guy in that costume. "To serve and protect" is an American idea with no traction here. Is this what became of the vast communist police state, their cops and spies and goons and interrogation cells? Some kid in a uniform with a radio that doesn't work walks in off a broken sidewalk following the shouts of a drunk who is pinned to the floor in a pile of broken glass by a dweeb who's sick of it all...who then says there's nothing anyone can do? Are we each so truly on our own, Idre and the drunk, Josh and me, and the cop with no backup?

Is this a kind of freedom, or a kind of madness?

"He is poor, he cannot pay for the window," the cop says. "Let him go." Aren't there jails, restitution programs, any consequences in this broken place? "There is nothing to do," the cop reiterates. "I cannot arrest him. Let him go." Idre gets off the man's back and with a few terrible words on the side, shoves him through the door and into the morning trailing blood and broken glass.

Just another Tuesday in Ulan Bator.

The real James Dawson…

Back in the real world I write for sports magazines and newspapers, a few websites, and manuscripts that nobody reads. We all have our dreams and idiosyncrasies and hustles. One of mine is using pen names for competing publications, so I can write about the same event in four magazines and spin one experience into several paychecks. It's nice work if you can get it, and I've worked for years to get it. My main alias: James Dawson, a narrator with the wit I wish I had in real life, and the scathing insight and charisma I need to tell some of the better stories. I have other personas with their own diction and bent, so in our media niche four talking, arguing, competing voices are all me—but only the editors know that, and they seem to get as big a kick out of the experiment as I do.

It's nice to get outside of yourself once in awhile, to try on different perspectives and care—actually care—about things that otherwise wouldn't interest you a wit. Try writing about the same thing…four times…and staying fresh, new, hip, relevant, feature-worthy each time. You have to pay attention to all sorts of minutia, hear all kinds of stories, take all kinds of notes and talk to people you love and hate and would never otherwise speak with, so each voice is satisfied that, yes, they have enough material to tell the story uniquely.

James Dawson: he's me, when I'm not. I took this trip in part to get away from niche sports writing for awhile, away from those voices who live in my head. So far, it's worked pretty well.

I want to write my fiancée, tell her of these things I've seen, share these things I feel, find some comfort in her kindness and compassion—her ability to forgive anyone of nearly anything and see the best in a situation. I aspire to be worthy of her grace, and learn from her how to let that which does not matter, truly slide—a phrase I borrow from Chuck Palahniuk that perfectly sums the élan she and Josh both have. I love it in her, while it drives me nuts in Josh—maybe because of the way he can put on his mirrored sunglasses to keep at bay the things that get me down. Maybe that's a naïve view of the man. He's inscrutable behind those glasses.

I open the webpage for Hotmail and find someone's login already filled out: jdawson380.

James Dawson? Has that voice inside me, clambering to tell these stories in his own voice, beaten me to the computer? Of course not...but this is too strange to ignore. I dash to the common area, where a tall man in a striped shirt stirs instant coffee into hot water. He's the only person in the room I don't recognize. "James?"

"Yes?"

"James Dawson?"

"Yeah..."

"Get back in my head where you belong!"

He backs away, slowly, knuckles turning white around his mug.

"I left you in St. Louis!" I bellow, strange relief pouring out. "I left you back there, I didn't forget you, I left you. I don't need you, I don't want you right now, you're not me dammit!" Sometimes it feels good to lose your mind, like a little vacation through sound and fury.

But it confuses the hell out of people, so then I laugh and smile and walk towards him to shake hands. "James, James, James," I coo, shaking my head. There are some crazy people in hostels, and when everyone else seems normal, it's probably you. It's comforting, in a way, to define an extreme—at least you know where you stand.

"You alright, chap?" he asks defensively. Great, I think, the little voice in my head is British in real life.

Which is fine, because he's not James Dawson. He's just... James Dawson, the British guy on holiday in Mongolia. He probably has no idea that I've been assuming his name for years and killing him in strange and creative ways in mounds of unpublished fiction. If he did, it might do all sorts of horrible things to his mind.

So I smooth the situation and shake his hand, the moment

passes, and the others turn back to the television and their microwaved soups. I tell Josh to get my camera.

"I need a picture here with my alter ego," I say.

James Dawson is too confused to resist.

Ride like the stiff breeze... The horse nudger... Authentic meals included... Warts on Easter Island... Roughin' it... Nectar of the gods... Left to our own devices...

"God, I hate this city," Josh says, watching out the minivan window as we roll through dusty streets hard-scowled by idle Mongols. "Don't they have anything better to do?"

"We'll be out of it soon," I say, shoulders squeezed towards my heart by Josh on my right and Christina on my left. We're in the back of a mini-bus bound for Zuunmod, a town somewhere outside Ulan Bator. Juliana rides a row in front of us, on our way to go horseback riding across the steppe.

Really, that's all Josh had to say: hey, wanna ride horses across Mongolia? and everyone was immediately onboard. It only got better when I heard it costs thirty bucks including transportation and food. Christina, Juliana and I paid a little extra to spend a night in a yurt; Josh took a pass, preferring a clean, soft bed in town to come-what-may in a leather hut with nomads.

Pansy.

"This place is like East St. Louis," he says, taking in a sprawling, rusting, chemical-cloud-spewing factory of some sort surrounded by corroded sheet metal fencing. "That is, if it had a renaissance and then collapsed under the sheer irony of ever being a good place to live."

"You ought to write that one down."

"Maybe I will," and then he stares straight ahead, at the back of the driver's seat to keep the cityscape out of sight for awhile. He's an urbanite, but doesn't go for decay.

"Have you ridden before?" Christina asks by way of changing the subject, or maybe to find a friend in a bleak moment.

"I used to ride professionally," I say. "Roped and wrangled, you know, all that stuff. Open range," she's going for it, "six gun on my hip. Held up a bank in Reno once." Not anymore though. "All Americans are cowboys, don't ya know?"

"I rode once," she says, "many years ago."

"When you were a kid?"

"Ja."

127

Revisiting childhood things and trying them out again, seeing if they still fit—seeing what's worth carrying into the future. Maybe that's what we're all up to on this journey. That, and riding Genghis Khan –style across his old stomping grounds for the sheer thrill of it.

The horse nudger...

Zuunmod is the way you'd imagine a western boomtown fifty years after the gold ran out: not a miner or tourist in sight—just knocked-together buildings held up by will and bailing twine. The better buildings are stucco-finished with red tile roofs, and most structures are spread apart as if waiting for some miraculous undergrowth to sprout in the open areas. Instead there are rows of pallets here, trenches there, holes lined with earthen berms... There are a few yurt clusters around the two lane highway leading into town, but no yurts in the downtown—just a few concrete apartment buildings, plywood homes, shop fronts with Cyrillic signs and windows opaque with dust glowing in the morning light. There's a school somewhere to the left, drawing children slowly through the streets, over the potholes and around the horse dung, like reluctant iron filings to a magnet.

A leather-skinned man with a thick black mustache, close-buzzed hair, silver wedding ring, saddle-worn jeans and old leather boots walks up to meet us here in a small parking lot. He is a real Mongol cowboy, a horse wrangler who works seasonally taking tourists for rides and then, when it's cold, tending his animals and his family's small herd of cows and sheep. Askaa is his name, and he's friends with Idre, who gets a commission for every tourist he sends this way. It's a nice package—arrangements we can make at the hostel, including transportation and an optional overnight with Askaa's mother in her yurt just beyond town, including meals, for one fee. I packed a bottle of Chenggis Wodka as a yurt-warming present.

Askaa went urban some years ago, he says, to start this business. His wife and three daughters live in a house in town that reminds me of the one my cousin built for himself in the hills of southern Ohio, beyond the reach of building inspectors. The floors are bare plywood, an old iron stove in the kitchen heats that part of the house, a small gas burning stove heats meals, and there's a family table with chairs enough for the family and one more person, someone who might come along some day or never.

I meet my horse, De'art, who Askaa tells me is three years old. He has magnificent red hair, a close-cropped mane like a teenage rebel's Mohawk, and a steel bit pulling his lips back in a perpetual smile. He stands with the other horses, tethered to a telephone pole, Mongol saddle over a blanket on his back. This saddle has a leather seat with high ridges in front and back to keep me from sliding off, and narrow padding that lets my legs wrap tightly around his ribs. The stirrups are cast aluminum, circular, dangling from the saddle on canvas straps. I wear no spurs, and Askaa tells me that with a good Mongol horse, you don't need them.

De'art is part of the Tarpan subspecies descended from the last truly wild horses in the world: the Przewalski's Horse. There are tiny bands of them still roaming the steppe, mating with the sort-of-domesticated Mongol Horses to produce impure bloodlines that, as far as I'm concerned, make fine, wild animals. Even the domesticated horses are allowed to roam free until needed, at which point whoever needs them rides across the steppe to find, rope, and return the desired number. There's nowhere to escape on the steppe—it's too open to hide, and their general freedom makes working occasionally not such a bad thing, so they don't resist too fiercely when Askaa recognizes his brand on their flank, slips a rope around their neck, and leads them back to town.

De'art is stocky with short legs that make him look like the low rider version of a brown horse—about twelve hands tall, in the parlance. He bears Askaa's brand, a backwards S with a curved underline, and his domestication shows in his calm demeanor wearing a wooden saddle over a thick wool blanket while surrounded by strangers. He seems a gentle beast, patient and kind, or maybe just bored—maybe staring off into space, eyes glassed over, he's thinking about being on the steppe again and everything he'd do there: run to the left. Maybe run to the right. Eat something and then sleep…or sleep, and then eat something.

Such decisions…

Askaa shows us how the blankets keep the wooden saddles from digging into their backs, how the reins attach to bits in their mouths so that we can turn them in the direction we want to go, that our feet go here and our other hand goes there and then we're riding and it's just that easy. He speaks passable English, so long as his needle stays in the well worn groove—instructions, explanations, the sorts of things he's said so often to so many people. They are like the stories I tell when I first meet someone, that canon of basic information and reliable jokes I know so well.

Then he shows us the leather thong on the reigns, tied there so we can whip the animals to urge them faster. Askaa mounts his horse, brings his elbow up over his shoulder and down, hand following up and down, thong following like a wave, leather slapping hide with a crisp thwack! and his horse starting, startled, quickly reined in and turned back around towards us. The pain sparked something wild in his ancient eyes, quickly reined in by the cold steel bit in his mouth. This is how they ride horses in Mongolia. But I will not hit De'art.

We'll trot the whole way if we have to. I'll nudge him, and if that doesn't work, we'll try something else…

But riding around the dusty courtyard in front of Askaa's house, I feel that I won't have to—De'art is young, strong, and mindful that I'm a smaller, weaker animal in his care. Shifting my weight and gently pulling the reigns makes him turn, and he speeds up and slows down with the tone of my voice. He doesn't understand English, but wrapping my legs around him, leaning down over his neck, I feel a sort of sublingual connection. My challenge with this rented horse is to create a meaningful relationship with just enough control that I can lead him, gently, so that he wants to follow. Things break when you force them—I learned that in martial arts and it holds as true on the mat as on a horse and in relationships of every kind.

Christina wears hiking clothes and an orange backpack, screws up her face in a comic grin and bounces up and down on her stationary horse, a city girl having entirely too much fun in the country. Click. Another photo for my scrapbook. Now Juliana can't figure out how to steer her horse as it turns in slow circles while she scolds it in German. I'm not sure which one, horse or girl, to feel sorrier for.

Josh's horse has a long white streak tapering between his eyes, pointing down towards his nose like an exclamation mark. He hasn't ridden a horse before—not for real, like this—but in his brown trench coat and mirrored sunglasses, with his jeans and boots and lean face, he looks the part. He exudes the part, that of the modern tourist cowboy: one part Cool Hand Luke, one part Clint Eastwood, set astride a beautiful animal in a dusty town somewhere far off the map.

Our motley crew follows Askaa across the street, through some empty lots, down a hill and out onto the steppe. We're riding across pastureland to the Buddhist Manzushir Khiid (in Mongol, Khiid means "Monastery") a few kilometers away—it's our lunch spot, and affords a nice view of the long valley leading up towards the temple.

* * * * *

De'art and I have worked out a system—I press my heels into his ribs, lightly, and lean forward when I want to go fast. He's a hot blood, a born runner, and he makes great time over the pool-table-smooth steppe. The land rolls gently toward hills in the distance as we ride through a large valley, past a flock of dirty white sheep grazing on scrub grass. A Mongol teenager in light wool clothes stares at us while an old military truck rolls slowly along a distant road. The wind is clean, clear, filled in here and there with De'art's smell and the sound of sheep bleating. This is what I paid for, what I've needed since Seoul. We're ahead of the pack, not leading so much as continuing the straight line Askaa seems intent to follow up the wide valley.

I lean forwards, press my heels into his ribs, come on, boy! a firm tone praying for speed. I'm not wearing underwear! I say in the same tone, Your mother smelt of elderberries! the messages increasingly bizarre, each delivery the same with the tone spurring him faster. He might not speak English, but he understands my inflection, and that's so much more important—to at least

131

be understood. We have different languages, but every creature understands friendship and abuse. I have not whipped Da'ert. We run fast and free across the steppe, two wild souls sharing the journey and having a helluva time.

I understand this horse more than I understand Josh.

Authentic meals included...

We'll get some real Mongol food now, here in this ger—that's the Mongol word for yurt. There are two gers and a pavilion here by the monastery, where our horses stand tethered by their reins. A thousand and one boulders poke up from—or sink into—the scrub grass. It's cloudy now, and a little chilly, being summer in Mongolia. It doesn't get too hot on the steppe, just warm, and the wind washes away your odor.

This is a public ger, akin to a pavilion in a park—a refuge from whatever you leave outside, a place for visitors to sit on benches around a table. Askaa lays out our lunch, taking it from a backpack and narrating in that memorized English that makes me wonder if he knows what he's saying, or just knows the patter. "Meat," he says, opening a Tupperware container with brown hamburger. "Goat."

Then he introduces "carrot"—long, thin carrot slices carved on a cheese grater and fermented in vinegar and oil. Then "cheese," from goat milk, and white rice, tomato slices, and white bread in a plastic sleeve like the loaves you buy at the store. He'd bought it at a store.

"Authentic Meals Included," the flier said.

The goat is greasy, slimy-white; the fat melts in my mouth and makes the meat taste wonderful—especially with some fermented carrot and a slice of tomato all mixed in. We eat from plastic bowls with plastic spoons, comfortable in our tradition while Askaa digs in with his fingertips.

Warts on Easter Island...

An old monastery sat here on the side of the valley. A new

one sits just down the hill, but it's smaller; tiny, actually, and painted bright red and blue in their custom. The ruins are out back, and down the hill is a small reception building with a taxidermy-animal display. Marmots. Wolves. Birds and rodents and beasts, if living anywhere on the steppe, are represented here by some unfortunate cousin caught and stuffed and posed. They sell postcards, but I decline.

We climb the hill towards brown, sandy ruins, past the small red monastery—it doesn't interest me too much, and besides, right here is a steep, rocky hill to climb. I love climbing. Maybe in another life I was caught and stuffed and put on display and that's why I run and climb things now, since I'm able.

Josh follows, taking his time, breeze ruffling his trench coat like he's in a movie. Nonchalant. Horse tied up and grazing in the background, he is a cigarette or beer shy of a magazine ad.

The ruins I scamper across were once the rest of this khiid, a much larger compound than the new one just downhill. The old monastery was destroyed by politicians—or picks and dynamite, if you want to get technical. Communist leaders like absolute control—no dissenters, no detractors, no higher authority and no greater good than the one they prescribe...so they hate religion. Think of the Fulaun Gong in China; Buddhists in Cambodia. Monks in Mongolia fared no better in the early 1900s.

Caught up in atheist zeal, the communist government purged their land of religion everywhere they found it. Monks were driven out or killed, temples sacked and desecrated. In Ulan Bator a few monasteries were allowed to remain, for reasons that may be no better than whims or fancies; temples and sects farther away, though, disappeared into the landscape. Ghengis Khan would not approve.

This monastery had six or eight buildings, each of brick and wood, each hand-built and then hand-destroyed, the thick, winter-strong walls collapsed and jagged, weathered now on all sides by snow and rain and wind. I climb one and perch at the top like an awkward bird with black pants and a floppy hat, trying to imagine what these old walls enclosed.

We walk up the hill, towards a sacred spot marked with a

rock pile anchoring a stick wrapped in a blue prayer shawl. It might be a grave, though the tradition is to leave them unmarked; it might be a meditation spot, one of those places where energy transits earth to heaven through a seated man praying.

Back home we call that lightning.

The slope is strewn with small boulders like warts on Easter Island. They don't move as we scramble up, to a rock pile and then to a ledge where Josh sits in a boulder hollow-topped and worn smooth like a seat overlooking the valley. A tiny dirt road far in the distance trails off around a tiny forest of anorexic trees, around the bend and out of sight towards some town far away.

That's where we came from—some town, far away—and where we're going. Today, yesterday, tomorrow—another week, another town. Ever onwards.

Roughin' it...

Josh slips his daypack into the trunk of a white four door car on the green, velvety steppe. We're at a cluster of gers just a few miles outside of Zuunmod. This is the homestay part of the trip, but he's heading back into town, to clean bathrooms and warm sheets while we have an "authentic Mongol experience." These are real nomads, we're told—Askaa's mother and her neighbors, his cousins. Inside her round, leather ger is an iron stove; how is that portable? There are fur-lined wool blankets on a single-wide bed to one side, a chest and a sleeping mat on the floor on the other, and between them a knee-high dinner table. There is a linoleum floor, but you can feel the dirt and rocks through its veneer. Cows meander around and around and around the gers in search of something better to sniff or chew.

We're home for the night.

Askaa's mother embodies my image of a Mongol grandma: skin like oiled leather, glistening brown eyes that seem to search through heaven and time and space, her hair a rainbow of silver, one shade for each of her two or three hundred years moving around the steppe. She walks with purpose, but not speed, in her striped grey woolen shirt and paisley skirt. Her hair back in a headband, her ears wiggle from silver balls swinging on short chains, the sort of earrings you sell by the ounce when times are bad.

A straw hat hangs from a thin rafter inside her ger, a ladle from another rafter, and some clothes hang drying. Our bedroom is floor space opposite the stove, so we put our bags there and walk back into the late afternoon.

The neighbors are members of Askaa's extended family. They tend the half-dozen listless cows. Black plastic bags, slit open to make tarps held down with bricks, cover piles of dry dung patties they can burn for cooking or heating fuel. It's a renewable resource, and burns cleanly—no off-tastes, minimal soot. There are no trees anywhere near, and no bushes taller than the scrub grass that grows in tufts and clusters spread far and wide; the only fuel comes from propane tanks and dung, and now, in the summer months, there is enough surplus to save dung patties for the winter.

I watch two young boys at their evening chores: dragging two calves towards a tie-down stake so they don't wander too far from the gers. The children are barely taller than the calves, the scene like two grown men manhandling cows, but shrunk down to one-fifth scale—one even has a foam baseball cap like his daddy. Faces stern, squeaky voices admonishing the calves, their struggle is hilarious. Our horses are tied up, too. Horses are runners, not fighters, being keenly adapted to sleep standing up (or lying down) and make haste at tremendous speed across the steppe. Should one get spooked in the night, it could run for miles.

Dogs roam the camp, sniffing the girls and me, sniffing the horses, lifting their legs in the doorway where our scent is strong. The grandmother scolds them, chasing them with a swatting hand. They protect the calves and horses from wolves, and their barking warns the cluster when something interesting approaches. Thus is the utility of wild dogs—not pets so much as sentries.

The latrine is over by the road—a slit trench not terribly deep, marked with a few sticks jammed into the dirt. It has a fantastic view of the highway, being twenty wide-open meters from the pavement; you can wave at traffic while you wipe.

A motorcycle leans against the grandmother's ger. She bustles over to the ger next door, walking past a huge satellite dish and a solar panel on a wooden pole. With the economic disparity, our dirt-cheap night on the steppe is more than a month's average wages, so with just a few nights' inconvenience, Askaa's mom can live the high life. I get the sense that she lives in the ger with the satellite dish, entertains tourists in this other one, and hasn't moved in a very long time. We stay in the traditional-looking accommodation, sleeping on the floor, while a game show blares away next door.

No satellite TV for us.

Nectar of the gods...

I open the Chinggis Wodka and pass it around to Askaa, the grandmother, the grandfather (who showed up just in time for dinner), Askaa's cousin (or friend, or...who knows), the German girls...there are a lot of us dining together on the fermented carrots and rice porridge in goat milk, on mystery hamburger, sliced cucumbers, and goat cheese. It's a spirited reprise of lunch, reflecting the slim pickings way out here. I don't think they eat much better when it's just them, though they might.

They certainly have the Mongol Thirst—my bottle comes back nearly empty, and I haven't had a taste yet. Swig. Terrible. For being a former Soviet territory, for bearing their hero's name and image, their name-brand vodka is horrible.

Absolutely horrible.

Take the cheapest swill you ever drank, set a glass of it downwind of an outhouse, refill whatever evaporates with rubbing alcohol, bottle it and charge three bucks. I've seen this label holding broken glass together on the sidewalks; bottles turned upside down in tribute to sacred images painted on boulders; for sale in a dozen shops...this is the people's vodka. This is what real Mongols drink. The men (and grandma) knock it back with laughs and smiles like it's the very nectar of the gods. I pass it around again; Askaa and his cousin finish the liter and set it capless on its side.

I've never been so glad to be sober.

* * * * *

I wake up fully clothed and teeth-chattering, legs-shaking –freezing. The grandmother and grandfather sleep on opposite sides of the ger, opposite sides of the door, twin snoring sentries. I pull my blanket tight and contemplate snuggling up against Christina—I gave her my "extra" blanket earlier. The ground sucks the heat out of you, so I'm wrapped up on three sides in the too-narrow blanket like a grey woolen taco gone cold on the floor. The stars shine brightly—I can see a halo of them in the wide open space between the stove's smokestack and where the leather is cut away around it.

Grandma is intuitive—she rustles, turns, looks at me with sleep-sagged eyes. She clucks her tongue, head swaying side to side, and throws me one of her blankets. For a moment I feel bad taking an old woman's blanket, but then I sleep well for the rest of the night.

Left to our own devices...

I'm not on De'art today. We woke, ate hot rice porridge with fried eggs, white bread, cucumber slices with a ketchup-like sauce, and waited for Askaa to finish breakfast. He's in a grumpy mood, and avoids eye contact with everyone as we wait for him to saddle the horses, wait for him to do a few chores, wait...for about two hours before he forces us up on different animals than before. I can't pronounce this horse's name, and we struggle to form a connection; he's a dark brown horse, almost black, with a sturdy body on almost comically short legs...but he doesn't have De'art's spunk. That vigor. That close-cut Mohawk mane. I try to make him go fast, but his only speed is a gentle plod, plod, plod, following Askaa's horse, the whole group moving as fast as a hungover man on a—that's it.

Askaa's hungover. My speedy De'art, the horse I rode cackling across the steppe yesterday is tied up back at the gers.

We're on unfamiliar horses so that...we don't go too fast for Askaa's throbbing headache.

Nor do we go too far—past the slit-trench latrine, across the road and over a hill, pointed generally back towards Zuunmod. The last hour of our ride, which is barely two hours long, follows telephone lines parallel to the road straight back to town. We arrive well before the day's first mini bus back to the capital, so we have lunch with Askaa's wife and daughters in their kitchen.

She serves soup with several kinds of meat, some carrot slices, some cucumbers...their universal ingredients. I'm sore and tired from a cold night of poor sleep on a bumpy floor, and ask for more soup; there is none. The kitchen is comfortable and homey, but in a sparse way—no hand-stitched samplers on the wall, no "Yurt Sweet Yurt," no superfluous comforts in this hand-built house with the plywood floors curling up at the edges. At least my soup was good, and the family was all smiles. On my way outside I pass the glass display case in their living room, where the youngest daughter—maybe ten—calls in broken English "buy wodka? Cigarette?"

"That was unexciting," I say to Christina.

"I'm still hungry," she says. "Wanna find a store?"

"I just want a drink." The dirty streets, dust-caked façades, the second day of riding over before noon...with my gnawing hunger and the old illness rattling in my lungs, I really need a drink to burn away the outside world and leave me in that peaceful void where you breathe slowly through your nose and try not to cough.

We look around the main street, but can't find a bar; Askaa rode off with our horses, gone to return them to the steppe for a few days until the next batch of tourists. No one told us when to expect the minibus; his wife just smiled and said "come back later," and then, "buy wodka?"

Left to our own devices, Juliana stays behind with her palm-sized video camera, showing the youngest child some footage of countries she would probably never see. "I'll find you if the bus comes," she says in careful English with her surprisingly deep voice.

"How'll you find us?" I ask, and then look around at the tiny, desolate town. "Nevermind."

We try the first bar-like place I see. The door is open just a crack, so we push it wide and step inside, surprising a table full of scowling Mongol men playing cards. It's a motorcycle parts store, with tires on the back wall, belts and chains and drums of oil, four men at a table with a bottle of vodka and a Russian semi-automatic pistol on the table, pointing at the door. They stare at us. We stare at them.

I don't need a drink this badly.

* * * * *

Askaa finds us on his steps, staring at the dirt, and with an urgent call leads us down an alley between close-built apartment buildings. Scrap metal and twisted wood make long, freak-show fences and I'm not sure if they're supposed to keep terrible things out, or in. The minibuses leave when they're full, so after Askaa has a lively conversation with the driver, we wait half an hour until enough people trickle out of the alleys to fill our bus.

Crammed in the back with the windows shut tight, we retrace the route we rode this morning. I see the grandma tending a calf beside her satellite dish. Life goes on in Mongolia.

Josh is on the computer back at Idre's. "How was it?"

"Not worth the time or money today," I say. He frowns.

"Yesterday was pretty cool," he says. I agree; it was a great experience that should have ended there. After he left, we felt as if in the family's way as they made modest concessions to our presence. Then Askaa, hungover from draining my vodka, suffered us just long enough to pack us onto the first bus back where we came from. I tell Josh as much, and he dismisses me as if to say man, you just don't have any fun.

"Should have come back with you," Christina says, sitting down by Josh to check her email. He smiles at her, empathy pulling at the corners of his mouth—as if our same ordeal engenders pity for her and disdain for me.

That's when I notice his new earring. "What'd you do to your ear?"

"Tell you over lunch."

To destroy something beautiful… The Glorious People's Crumbling Department Store… The only Mongolian BBQ in Mongolia… Ironic statuary and the man who doomed his country… London to Ulan Bator: the road trip from hell… Joe Cool didn't smoke the filter…

We're at a Turkish restaurant, eating kebab sandwiches with hummus and sour cream sauce, cucumber slices, and tough meat in amazing spices. They cost a buck each—expensive, but I'm tired of authentic Mongol food and ready for something comfortable. Kebap, a close culinary cousin to kebab sandwiches, is my favorite food; I haven't had it in years—we don't have much authentic Turkish fare in St. Louis.

Josh woke up in a funk, and his callous mood back at the hostel probably came from that. "Damn near got run over this morning," he says. "I was looking at how the buildings are just smeared down the street, you know; it was terrible. Then out of nowhere, wham. Damn near got run over. I'm ready to move on." Agreed.

"So, you…" I say, pointing my fork at his ear.

"…found a Korean barber shop that does piercings and paid them ten bucks to jab a piece of metal into my face."

"It looks a little…" I want to say gay, the way kids fling the word like an insult, but we're not kids anymore, and that's the wrong way to explain that it isn't the look I imagine for him—that it doesn't fit the image I have of Josh. But maybe the image I have of Josh doesn't fit anymore, either. Though in fairness, it does make him look a bit light in his loafers. "…silly."

"I just wanted to destroy something," he says. "This choking apathy, this…I don't know. I just wanted to hurt myself a little." This place resonates a self-destructive vibe. The street is a grand drama of apathy and despair—broken glass and rust, drunks and glares. Wanting to hurt yourself a little makes sense, if only right now, in this place, at this time. I feel it too, but turn the energy outwards in vitriol and hard words. Josh got pierced. To each their own.

"Gone in two days, man," I say.

"Not soon enough."

The Glorious People's Crumbling Department Store...

There is one shopping center in Ulan Bator, a hulking grey concrete building chocked full of washing machines and clothing, jewelry and televisions, computers, folk art, and food stalls. It's falling down, like every building the Soviets left. I swear the Cyrillic sign reads "Glorious People's Crumbling Department Store."

Aside from groceries, you can get everything you really need here, at what is properly called the "State Department Store." Nothing comparable grows in its formidable shadow. There was no free market competition under communism—just the same products, in the same packaging, for the same prices. I saw that in Havana, Cuba, and can easily imagine it here.

Weird.

When the Soviet Union collapsed, shrapnel from the imploding empire tore down their smaller experiments around the world. Now Ulan Bator is the capital of Mongolia the nation, Mongolia the culture, and Mongolia the capitalist economy... such as they have one. It's home to their government and the Mongol Stock Exchange, the least-capitalized exchange in the world—which fits, as Ulan Bator's population (just a bit over a million people) is comparable to Louisville, Kentucky; if every Mongol voted, they'd cast fewer ballots than the St. Louis metro area could.

And they invest their money in vodka—not the Mongol Stock Exchange.

There are fifteen large shopping centers in Louisville. Seventeen shopping malls in St. Louis. And one State Department Store in Ulan Bator.

So I think back on Havana and their sign-less shops, sans-advertising because everyone knows where they are, and it doesn't matter much to anyone where a certain identical product is bought, because the proceeds all go to the government anyway.

There might as well be one large distribution center—one "State Department Store."

Underwear? Outer wear? Home furnishings? All right in one spot.

Efficient. Easy. Done.

That was a long time ago, but things haven't changed much. The "free market economy" is their new economic paradigm, but…the locals still shop at the department store, and while capitalism hasn't radically altered the shopping experience, it has widened the selection. I'm told that never before have there been so many different things in the department store; so many electronics and other pure luxuries. Most striking is the top floor, given over entirely to art.

I'm wandering the aisles now, stacks of oil paintings—originals, signed by the artists—in plastic archival bags twenty, thirty, forty paintings deep. Larger, framed pieces hang on the wall. I'm surrounded by art of all different sizes, priced by the square inch.

I have a friend in America who sells her drawings for twenty thousand dollars each; they're huge, and beautiful, and celebrate the intersections of art and literature, creation and reflection. The sixteen inch by twenty inch paintings here are twenty thousand, also—twenty thousand tugrik. For one of her drawings, I could buy every oil painting stacked on these shelves, and a few of the framed ones on the wall.

That collection would thoroughly celebrate life in Mongolia. This one here has a ger with two horses somewhere on the steppe, the sky and ground meeting in that nebulous way it looked from the train, like the ocean meeting the sky, an indistinct and utterly meaningless line because you could ride for days and never get there—never climb over that line and fall onto the other side. So it's meaningless, just a vague abstraction of where two infinite things rub against each other, and I'm looking at the horses anyway.

Mongolia is a vast and magnificent country.

Most of the paintings celebrate this folk Mongolia, these romantic images of gers and horses, sheep and steppe, old

Mongols holding their breaths forever. These artists don't go so much for the abstract, the avant-garde.

Sixty percent of Mongolia lives outside of Ulan Bator, many of them in gers, and of those, many still pack up and move with the weather and their herds. They may use old jeeps to haul hand-fashioned trailers, but they're still at it—still in the old ways, with clothes that will last them most of their lives and tools from their grandparents. They embody that grand notion that the world is an ancient place and we are merely stewards of the environment and customs that existed before and will outlive us all.

* * * * *

The children on these stacked canvases will grow into the men and women in these other pictures, who mature into the old women and old men on the hanging paintings; the same ones who will die and be buried traditionally in shallow, unmarked graves on the steppe like Genghis Khan himself.

He's buried somewhere in the Onon Valley, where legend has it the river was diverted to flow over his grave so it may never be found. Another legend says his army planted a forest over the grave, another, that the burial detail killed everyone they came across on their way to and from the site. The point being that man is made from the earth, lives close to the earth, and returns to it again, a cycle seen in every religion practiced on the steppe. So it is the tribes' tradition to bury their dead in the earth and forget the place, holding the ground sacred instead of the body. This sense comes through in the paintings, which could as easily be of imagined ancestors or current neighbors; of years ago, or years from now.

I poke around, and come back to the horses with the ger; I look at stacks of oil and water color paintings, and come back to these horses. That ger. The sky and the steppe. They remind me of De'art, and the ageless day we shared. In the negative space on the canvas I feel the dust blowing in from the desert, hear the silence that is older than everything else.

That's the thing about negative space—about silence—about the vast expanse of the Mongol steppe. We scream and laugh and cry, sounds welling up from the silence, stark against it, faltering, fading like they grew. From nothing, a gust of wind blows away into nothing. The steppe was silent before us; it's silent in the background now while we're alive and screaming. It is patient. It is waiting to welcome us back.

* * * * *

Here on the top floor they also sell dolls and little figurines wearing the "traditional" Mongol garb—gold thread and bright colors, like they're ready to sing a musical about the wind whipping o'er the steppe. Some have highly detailed, painted faces with basic furs and leather straps. A few have hard eyes and flattened expressions painted on plain wooden heads with exquisite fur hats and clothing that impresses without wowing, authentic but without kitsch; I buy two of these, a man and a woman, for my mother. There's something about the home-spun stereotype in their clothing, that hard winter, animal skin image you think about when you hear "nomads" and "Mongolia" in the same sentence; then you have their faces, those plain brown wooden faces with the stern eyes and flat expressions that feel, to me, so quintessentially Ulan Bator, that in these two dolls I find the perfect marriage of kitsch and by-God authenticity that earns precious space in my framepack.

Everything we buy—for ourselves, for others—we will carry with us for the rest of the journey; at the earliest, we might mail things home in Poland, where the mail is reasonably reliable and somewhat affordable. For all the tempting artwork and black-market goods, there is only so much space in our packs—only so much weight we feel like lugging around.

But these dolls must come with me for my mother's collection; the painting of the gers and horses comes with me for mine.

The only Mongolian BBQ in Mongolia...

"Shu Shu's Mongolian Barbecue" was my favorite restaurant

years ago. Birthdays, dates, anniversaries… I'd use any excuse to go there. "I love Mongol food," I told my friends, and they oohhed and ahhed appropriately. What's it like? "You take a little bit of everything, you know, chicken, lamb, bean sprouts, cucumbers …" the sorts of things Sysco delivered every Tuesday "…and they cook it up on a giant Mongol wok" made by Lexmark somewhere in Kentucky.

Shu Shu's was at the cutting edge of our obesity epidemic, an all-you-can-eat place right in the plaque-clogged right ventricle of our Heartland. Prices rose as the locals wiped out their buffet with increasing gusto, until they priced themselves right out of my teenage budget. Eighteen bucks a person? In the nineties, in a strip mall in a cornfield? Forget about it.

But I always wondered…

Now I wonder no more.

A few days ago I wandered into a mom and pop restaurant where I was, judging by the all-Cyrillic menu and the shock on my waitress's face, probably the only white guy to ever lighten their door. I pointed to a random item on the menu, and ate what came: a soup of carrots and potatoes, celery and meat chunks that could have come from just about any type of animal wandering around the hutongs.

It tasted fantastic.

There were tall, skinny red bottles with Cyrillic labels at each table. Their mouths were wide and designed for fast pouring, so I flagged my waitress and tried to order a bottle to see what it was—a juice drink? Some kind of booze? Mongol soda? I made the "I want to drink" motion, then pointed with my thumb to the bottles.

She knew what I wanted, but had absolutely no idea how to respond.

I gestured again, so she borrowed a bottle from a few puzzled locals and brought it to me. They watched as she turned the label to face me, and read it—in Mongol. I still had no idea until I unscrewed the cap and took a whiff.

Hot sauce.

An outdoor café near the State Department Store served

another fantastic meal. A few thousand tugrik bought a mystery meat shish kebab served with cucumbers and fried rice that, bless them, had onion chunks. It was fantastic; especially so, since vegetables are so hard to come by. The Mongol national foods are meat soups and meat on a stick, with thin-sliced cucumbers and that fermented carrot stuff. Throw in the fried rice, and you can combine the same things in enough ways to make it through a week without repeating yourself too much. But it's a hard place for a foodie to spend much time.

When we need something different, there are Korean restaurants and our Turkish place with their great kebab sandwiches. No one saves their pennies for a food tour of Mongolia, but the offerings are good for carnivores; vegetarians might want to stay on the train.

But nowhere have I found the authentic version of my elusive former favorite, that staple of my cultural enlightenment on the prairie—no Mongolian Barbecue.

Except at DB's Mongolian BBQ near the embassies, which has a big, well-lighted sign and an outdoor deck that's painfully reminiscent of beach-themed "Margaritaville" restaurants in landlocked places like Des Moines. DB's is an American chain, no less. If Mongolian Barbecue exists in Mongolia, I'll find it without taking the cheese in a tourist trap.

But near as I can tell, it doesn't.

So when Josh said he's going to DB's for dinner with the Ohio graduates from the train, I had to come along.

The ingredient bar looks familiar, and they have a small sign explaining how they proudly "locally source" their meat and vegetables—a nod to the present American craze over buying local and eating organic. DB's, after all, caters to Americans... even here.

After loading my bowl with the usual ingredients, I report to the giant grill in the back to watch a Mongol guy cook my dinner with three foot long chopsticks in a near-perfect reproduction of Shu Shu's back home.

It smells, looks and tastes the same—a well-seasoned dichotomy of comfort food and disillusion. Even the price is authentic, destroying two days' budget in one sitting.

DB's Mongolian Barbecue—authentic Midwest strip mall food in the heart of Ulan Bator.

Ironic statuary and the man who doomed his country...

"See Genghis Khan's army ride again!" the advert said, so we bought two non-refundable tickets for the show on this, our last morning in town. According to the flyers and a meager website, re-enactors dress in furs and leather armor and ride horses past a grandstand, whooping and hollering and shooting arrows. The worst reviews were still pretty good, and the best were glowing, so we parted with an insane amount of money—twenty bucks each, nearly a week's housing budget here—to see history come to life.

Except my chest cold is back and Josh didn't sleep well last night, neither of which should stop us, but add the fact that it's raining and the storm drains are backing up into murky, deadly lakes and suddenly our motivation is gone. We splash down the sidewalks towards the bus to the show, talking each other out of going while walking onwards nonetheless. That last-day-in-town feeling has a strong hold. We need to see something—one last anything. Maybe not a muddy horse riding show in a downpour, but something.

At last we write off the show—twenty bucks each, gone—and between the rain and my fever, I almost don't care.

The puddles are coffee-black, with discernible currents. You can't tell how deep they are, so any puddle might be paper-thin or bottomless. The floating detritus looks like a fraternity's dumpster overturned upstream, with empty beer and liquor bottles, trash bags, chip bags, a condom undulating like a squid...

We risk our lives crossing the street, thankful for waterproof boots, and head towards Sükhbaatar Square. The Square has another of the ubiquitous Genghis Khan statues, honoring the man who united these ancient lands and spread the Mongol Empire across three continents. Near Genghis is a statue of Sükhbaatar, who tried to build his own Mongol Empire and doomed the region entirely.

Sükhbaatar led the Red Army against Baron Ungern von Sternberg, and died before the campaign ended. With the help of his partisans, the Red Army killed Sternberg, drove out the Chinese, and set Mongolia up for the communism that economically and socially pillaged their country, leaving them an empty shell of a nation with rampant poverty and alcoholism. The statues of Sükhbaatar and Genghis are nearly the same size, and each has the sort of stern, forward-looking eyes that radiate nobility.

Except the square is named for the man who doomed their country.

London to Ulan Bator: the road trip from hell…

We take refuge across the square at an outdoor bar attached to a hotel. My feet are the only dry part of my body as the rain soaks down my legs.

"You want to go to the Natural History Museum?" Josh asks. He went there alone yesterday, standing in awe of the dinosaur skeletons dug from the steppe and Gobi. "Pretty cool stuff in there."

"Not really," I say. It's barely nine in the morning, but the bar is open already and we share its refuge with a crowd of scraggly, red-eyed Brits already long into their drinks.

There are rows of battered, beaten, and mangled cars parked out front—a VW Bug with a roof rack and roll bars welded on, a Jeep that looks like it drove through the wrong hundred miles of Iraq, a strange vehicle that must have started as an SUV before mutating into a brutish monster…it's the automotive equivalent of the Tatooine dive bar in "Star Wars."

"She's a beaut, ain't she mate?" asks an unshaven, wild-eyed man. "Begged, borrowed and stole to get her here, I did. And we made it, by crikey!" He's ecstatic in a worn-out way, a child at the long end of the greatest birthday party ever, loath to go to bed even though he's clearly pushed through his limits.

"Where'd you drive in from?" Josh asks.

"London!"

"Good Lord, man," I blurt, his eyes sparkling and face lighting from my surprise. My astonishment fuels him, feeds him; he perks up like a flower after rain.

"Just got off the ol' Mongol Rally, we did. London to Ulan Bator, three weeks, two days. And nine hours!"

"Buy you a drink?" Josh says, ordering three breakfast Carlsbergs.

That battered old VW Bug was his—was, until he parked it there out front of the bar. The rally starts in London with about 400 people in 200 cars, which they spend considerable time decorating and outfitting for the harrowing journey ahead: from London to Ulan Bator at whatever speed they can manage, covering 10,000 miles on interstates, country roads, back roads, and off road. Some go through Russia, cursing broken axles in Siberia; others go through Kazakhstan, or south through Turkey and the Middle East on their race towards the rising sun.

The vehicles are limited to those with engines under 1,200cc (ideally, under 1,000cc), specifically not designed for off road use, and they cannot be modified in any manner that precludes their normal use by the receiving charity in Mongolia. Style points are awarded to those vehicles most comically adorned, or comically ill-suited to the task ahead. It's a grueling endurance rally for vehicles that are not in any way designed for endurance rallies... which is all part of their fun.

And it's also all for charity. Leftover funds from the entry fees, along with mandatory £1,000 minimum donations from each team, go to charities like "Send a Cow" and "Save the Children."

Each car has a team, generally with two drivers. One drives, the other sleeps, and occasionally they pull over to sleep in fields, rest stops or motels—wherever it's safe or possible. He didn't sleep much through Kazakhstan. "Had to bribe a few gits on the way," he says. "Pack a smokes usually does the trick. They pull you over, demand your transit papers, your ownership papers, and you can't really do much, 'cause they've got the gun, right? Then they want to know what cargo you've got, and you tell 'em 'oh, spare parts, this is where we're going, no room for anything else,' but you can always find a pack a smokes to hand 'em. That's all it takes, and you get your papers back and drive on a few hours and do it all again."

"So you spend four weeks stuck in the car?"

"Right. You get to know a bloke real well that way," he says. Suddenly our train cars don't seem too bad. "You make some friends along the way, sometimes find out you really don't like a guy. Never know. Never know what's gonna happen, you're alone just the two of you so long. All that matters is you get here, there's no course. Lot of guys don't make it, their cars break down, they can't slice it, whatever, they ditch the car and fly home. Don't get to keep the car anyway, so you've got nothing to lose."

"Don't keep the car?" Josh asks.

"Naw, you leave it here and fly home, and the government gives it away. That's how we get transit papers to drive here, promise we'll leave the car, so it's like a trade. It's the experience, is what it is, something you just gotta do." In my own pathetically inadequate way, I can relate. I must do this; I must do the Mongol Rally.

"You get prizes?" Josh asks.

"Naw mate. But you ever meet anybody who's done it? Driven from London to Ulan Bator like a bat outta hell?"

"Nope."

"There you go," he says. "Everywhere I go now, I'm that guy—that guy who's done it. Had the adventure. Got the stories. Can't take that away from me, mate, and can't just buy it neither."

Joe Cool didn't smoke the filter...

Josh spends his last night in Ulan Bator getting hammered in a bar by the embassies. They serve a mixed crowd of diplomats and expats, with a number of Mongols who like rubbing elbows with ambassadors. The bar has peanuts and pretzels, pictures of actors, Budweiser adverts, NASCAR paraphernalia, and decidedly Western prices. I joined him the other night for a Manhattan, only because it's named for my final destination. It was terrible, and in my lodging-metric, cost two nights at Idre's.

While he's closing this week with his own ceremony, the German girls and I hop a cab across town. We visit the giant statue of Genghis that looks over Ulan Bator from a hillside across the river. From up here the city lights look like a schizophrenic's Lite-Brite, in crazy colors scattered hither and yon; even the streetlights don't follow straight lines or patterns. The dark spots on the periphery are hutongs with gers, and I see fires flickering around the very edges of the capital.

This is the only capital I've ever visited where half the population lives in tents; where I've found animal bones (chickens, a cat skull) pressed into dirt streets. The downtown, of course, is all broken concrete and shimmering glass shards, but out where the other half lives—out past the monastery, up on the surrounding hills—that's where life goes on unaffected by time and the alien notion of an "outside world."

Click. My camera is set up on a tripod, slowly burning the city lights into images that I'll print and put in a scrap book to reassure myself I was actually here. Genghis rides his mighty stead above us, somewhere between human and god and lit with spotlights that dress the heavens in his shadow. Josh could see the monument from outside the bar. Click. But from up here, the view is scattered lights and darkness.

"Cigarette?" a twelve year old boy asks, staring at me. I have an iron grip on my camera strap, and immediately look behind and around him—looking for someone sidling towards my camera during the distraction.

But it's just him, and me, and the German girls.

"No cigarette," I say. "No smoke," using that English as a Second Language dialect I adopt on the road. I mimic the English phraseology wherever I go, chopping suffixes, inverting adjective/noun orders, generally abusing my mother tongue to mimic the locals' grammar. It follows that if someone I'm speaking to doesn't use plural forms or verb tenses, they might not recognize the important words when I conjugate them...so "no cigarette, no smoke" is my direct way of saying "Sorry bub, you're shit outta luck."

Besides, he's twelve; who gives a twelve year old a cigarette?

Juliana.

You don't just bum a cigarette and wander off—now we're stuck with him. He idly smokes while scowling at me and hitting on Christina.

"I man," he says in pre-pubescent alto, pointing at his chest. "Want see home? I show."

"Oh, you're a big man," Christina coos as if to a puppy, "I'm sure you have plenty of girls."

"No want," he says. "Want Europe girl. Very beautiful. Show house, come!"

Click. I blind him with the flash, trying to catch the way the cigarette dangles inexpertly from his lips, bouncing desperately while he talks; he tries to smoke like an Italian lover in an eighties movie—foreign, dark-skinned, experienced and debonair, too good for this silly German girl but for his sense of charity... It's a desperate comedy. I want to dropkick him over the balcony.

"And you have a car, I think," Christina prompts.

"Brother has car. Get anytime, big car!" The car, that grand indicator of maturity and status in every nation... You haven't come of age in America until you have a car, and American ways—seen in those old movies piled high on the television back at Idre's—set the standard. Is this our greatest legacy in the third world?

His cigarette burns through the filter as he smokes the tiny stub, inhaling God knows what nasty chemicals. I'm embarrassed for him, this desperate, inexperienced show the very opposite of cool. He coughs and flicks it into the darkness, calling over his shoulder—Joe Cool—to Juliana for another one without even turning to look at her.

"Nein," she barks. "No more!" Now he's trapped—there were more in her pack, everyone saw that. Now she's telling him no, ending his invitation to badger us; but he hasn't won his girl just yet. What would Chuck Norris do? Flex his muscles, maybe raise his voice? Somehow get his way to impress the girl? Of course.

Except he doesn't remember how that part of the movie goes, and thankfully, he doesn't adlib. He makes a few more passes Christina shoots down with sudden, icy tones that chase him into the night.

"New rule," I say. "Nobody gives cigarettes to twelve year olds."

They laugh. Click.

Good riddance.

Top: **Most Russian trains—local and long distance—are electric**

Bottom: **Commercial vessels at dock on Lake Baikal**

Lake Baikal Region
24 August, 2007

confiscate it and hit the playback button, there's a completely legal and totally silly picture of me, and another one, and then one of Josh scowling.

They make me smile. We've been on this train for awhile, cooped up prisoners of each other's idiosyncrasies, and I'm still sick. Little things are irksome, and it's mutual.

The guard leaning into our car is the first blonde local I've seen on this trip; there have been blonde tourists, especially the German girls, but she's the first natural blonde local…and the first Russian I see in Russia. Her English is clipped and courteous and makes her sound like a ne'er-do-well from a James Bond movie. She wears a large semi-automatic pistol on her belt, a badge, a ribbed black sweater, a radio that chirps in Russian, and an electronic passport scanner with an antenna.

She is the very antithesis of the Mongol cop at Idre's; the antithesis of Mongol everything. It's fashionable to say that people are people and the differences between countries are more political than personal, but that's wrong—we're in Russia now, where there are rules, they are enforced, and things are quite a bit different than the Wild West back in Ulan Bator.

How? We've only heard stories, but she sets the stage just perfectly.

Another guard walks by with a club in his hand, banging on the heating ducts, pulling up the edges of the carpet in the hallway (I didn't know they even came up), banging on the ceiling, looking for hidden compartments or things stuffed in places that should ring hollow. There are more bangs and clangs from below, and I glance outside at a platoon of Customs officials with little mirrors on long poles and short clubs gnawed and gnarled from years of clanking around on steel train carriages. Their eyes are set and mouths unsmiling, like they won't be happy until they find a Chinese refugee strapped to the bogeys or a half-ton of cocaine shoved into a fake heating duct. Maybe then they would smile.

It doesn't occur to me that, in their peculiar way, they are smiling.

* * * * *

The German girls behind at Idre's with our other single-serving friends, Mongolia and China receding from the train and short term memory, we're bound for Irkutsk. My previous experience of Irkutsk was watching my little red star-shaped armies wither under my father's merciless dice-rolling in the board game Risk. Other than that, I don't know much about it at all, but later—well after the fact—I'll understand the many reasons our guidebooks call it the Paris of Siberia…

…which really got going thanks to Nicholas I, who had a certain flare for breaking up a party. Following Alexander I's death and his brother Constantine's abdication of command—he was next in succession but didn't want to be Tsar, and probably for good reason—Nicholas asserted his royal blood and claimed control over Russia. That didn't sit too well with a number of people, for reasons I still don't understand, but can well imagine—people are resistant to change. Remember "New Coke"?

Nicholas I was the New Coke of Russian Tsars, and about three thousand people gathered with rifles and knives and big sticks with ugly knots in them to protest in the square in front of the St. Petersburg parliament buildings. Nicholas sent a general to speak to them; he was promptly shot. Then Nicholas dispatched a cavalry unit to disrupt the mob, but it being a Russian winter and the cobblestones being covered in ice, that didn't work out too well.

So screw it all, he thought—blast 'em with the cannons, which he did, killing many. The rebels scattered, and regrouped on a frozen river not far away, which was also blasted. Those who weren't killed outright fell into the suddenly-not-so-solid-anymore ice water and drowned in a giant slushy of disgusting Russian river water, blood and cannonballs.

On the upside, some of them survived—mostly the aristocrats who incited the movement and got out of the way before the shelling started. They were rounded up, a few were executed, and the remaining rebels were banished to Siberia, which was even colder and even icier than the capital and considered to be a giant, frozen prison. Cutting socialites off from social life and high society and making them, you know, work to survive, somewhere out in the hinterland with the serfs and savages, was considered a humiliating fate nearly on par with death but just so much more exciting for the victors back in Moscow.

Harrumph, said the scores of banished intellectuals, artists, aristocrats, and other muckrakers; we'll be just fine. And they were, mostly, because Nicholas—being a good sport about the banishment—let them import their servants and most of their wealth. Many of them settled in Irkutsk, either coming in from the surrounding land or dumped there by official means. The largest internal city in the far-flung eastern end of Siberia (west a good deal from coastal Vladivostok), Irkutsk became a haven for the disabused.

Lake Baikal is about fifty miles away, connected via the Angora River. Known locally as the Irkutskoye, or just Irkut, it gives the city its name: Irkutsk, roughly meaning "River City." But Lake Baikal gives it more than a handy reference point on Google Earth—it affects their weather.

Lake Baikal has the largest water volume of any freshwater lake in the world. Water is much slower to change temperature than air, and having so much of it so close—and surrounded by the Baikal and Taiga Mountains—it has a tempering effect on the harsh Siberian winters. It still gets well below zero Fahrenheit, but the lake's climatic effect keeps the temperatures from going quite so far down as elsewhere in subarctic Siberia.

That made it just a bit more livable; so did the trading routes and roads. The first federal roads were very primitive—they didn't have mile markers and rumble strips when they cleared a path through the woods in the 1700s and called it a road—but they turned Irkutsk into a major trading center. Precious metals and goods came up from China, and the roads connected smaller Siberian communities and independent trappers with fur markets in Moscow and the world via the Vladivostok seaports.

Buildings were of wood, brick, and stone, and the well-to-do hired artists to decorate their homes with scrollwork and carvings. City architects saw broad avenues in the European terms of luxury and elegance—there is no space to spare in Paris, so wide streets have certain cache there. As there was plenty of space in developing Irkutsk, in went the broad avenues with their regal air. Even today, with widespread development and sprawling districts, there are wide-open parks and green space between some highway lanes, and grassy knolls border the river.

The Soviets blighted Irkutsk with imposing concrete tenement blocks and grey-cube government buildings, but they didn't clear the ground of all the low wooden houses; there are still onion-domed churches nestled amid modern Western-style buildings with glass and steel and European architecture. It's like 1990s Havana fell from the sky and landed amid 1800s San Francisco, with the better parts of Chicago growing up through the cracks.

Irkutsk kept collecting banished dissidents and ornate architecture through the Bolshevik Revolution (which saw a fair amount of nasty fighting between Bolsheviks and Tsarists), through the Soviet Era, and is still the eastern retreat for those disenfranchised politically or economically by Moscow. The "Pearl of Siberia" for several hundred years, they developed numerous museums, several universities, trade organizations, infrastructure…the Soviets built a giant dam and hydroelectric power plant, and the Trans Siberian Railroad came through Irkutsk and linked up with the south-bound Trans Mongolian line. There are Irkutsk-connected sidings that go off around Lake Baikal on tracks that cross hundreds of bridges while circling the lake.

Fur pelts still come in from the Siberian countryside, and precious metals still transit these rails; the China trade is still big business, too. Modern Irkutsk is a city built around the railroads, and an important stop on the modern Trans Siberian Highway that, though an official "Federal Highway," often defies what we consider a modern road. But it is a city of higher education, and research; a city connected to the Siberian oil industry, though the rubles mainly flow back to Moscow. It is a city watered and nurtured by Lake Baikal, and that houses the academic institutions and research companies who ply its one mile depth.

These things will mean more when I see them in person.

The Pearl of Siberia awaits.

Dave Norman

The Pearl of Siberia…

We did it once, and we'll do it again—out through the madding hordes at the turquoise-and-white Irkutsk Train Station, push through the touts, stand on the street and make our first decision: left or right.

"Watch out for the tram," as it goes sliding by on rails flush with the road surface, little trenches along the inside edges for the steel wheels. There's an overhead network of sagging cables rubbed silver-smooth on the underside by years of the tram's boom pressing against them, sucking electricity for the whirring motor that glides the car along through streets busy with people and taxis.

"Toksi?" "Takasi?" They almost get the word right, each man with a slightly different intonation. No.

"Left," Josh says, pack on his back, another on his chest. My bags are fastened over a long sleeve shirt and pants, with a light rain jacket I wear against the chill. It's a cool day at the beginning of September, when the foliage is lush and the air brings a crisp prelude to a sudden autumn. I dropped from the Chinese heat ten days ago, and here I'm zipping up the jacket.

We wander through a residential area with green plastic-coated cyclone fencing, wooden panel fences in other places, a mostly-intact sidewalk, single-story wooden houses and the occasional two-story home with the second story windows open to the "summer" air. The signs are all in Cyrillic, of course, and we're having a devil of a time dealing with the ф, and ж, and й in words that otherwise feel maddeningly close to pronounceable.

Josh follows the little black book's instructions, leading us up a small hill that takes an unnatural toll on me. I fall behind, still sick and wishing my bags weren't so heavy, that I hadn't packed so many t-shirts, that…that I could be healthy again. Either the antibiotics aren't helping, or they're the only things keeping me alive. I'm not sure which, but if we don't find the hostel soon, it's this walk that'll kill me. I've said as much; Josh scoffed and walked on, frustrated as much by my sluggishness as his inability to help me. Often, that's the larger frustration, so easily misunderstood.

"It shouldn't be much farther," he says. "Dave?"

"Yeah."

"Oh," and he turns around, noticing how far back I've fallen. "You alright man?"

* * * * *

We didn't find the hostel. That first left—it was supposed to be a right. Something got lost in translation, either theirs, or ours, or fate's, so we abandoned hope after half an hour wandering around that residential area looking for a hostel "in the center of Irkutsk." The trip downhill was easier, back to the train station were we found a cabbie straightaway—we had our pick of the multitude.

He doesn't know where the hostel is, the cabbie says, but will follow the Russian instructions pasted in Josh's book. He chats with us in broken English about his family in Romania. "Much better here for me," he says. "Send money home. Make one day here, month wage in Romania." I thought Eastern Europe was coming up in the world—certainly on par with far-eastern Siberia, at least. "Visit family twice year."

"Do they come here to see you?" Josh asks; no one came to see him in Korea while he worked abroad, but then, he's still a son rather than a father.

"Nyit," he says. "Expensive."

"Are other cab drivers from Romania?"

"Da. Many. Also, I think, Chechnya, Kazakh…" people from bordering areas where a cab driving gig in Russia not only pays better, but is far safer than many local jobs. Russia's presence in Chechnya creates all sorts of tensions and problems and violence; many parts of Kazakhstan are desperately poor, and again, violence is a daily threat among those who have unmet basic needs and nothing to lose. Driving a beat-up Lada bought on credit at terrible rates from the Russian mob to shuttle unshaven tourists from the train station to dive hostels is a dream job for a lot of people. He's a lucky man, and he finds our building without a problem.

"There," he says, pointing at a large, brown, imposing building with a few Cyrillic signs below dark, cavernous windows.

"Is that our hostel?"

"Da." We pay fifty rubles, which is not bad, I think, but I have absolutely no idea…it takes awhile to get used to a new currency, and how much things should cost, and anyway, I'm in something of a fever-fog. Finding the building was easy; locating the hostel within is a different story.

We try the ground level in front, finding a travel office and many locked doors. At the least, we're looking for a speaker box—push the button, convince the voice that you have a reservation, and someone buzzes you in. Hostels are cheap, so they usually operate in dodgy neighborhoods—the kinds of places where you're thankful for an unmarked, heavy steel door between you and the night. This neighborhood doesn't look too bad, but it's an urban environment with far-spaced streetlights and the guidebook warns of knife-wielding muggers after dark. In that way, it's like parts of Chicago. A definite improvement over Ulan Bator's mid-nineties Detroit.

Down an alley, around the back, there's the door with a call box next to it. Buzz. The stairwell inside is hospital-wide, four stories tall, and lit only by the daylight streaming around us through the door. The stairs lead down below street level; they disappear in each direction into pitch blackness, there being no windows. I think of the muggers again, and scenes from "Bonfire of the Vanities" involving dark stairs in Harlem projects—crack smoking, heroin shooting, dice games for money and knives at the ready… What happens in dank Russian stairwells?

Absolutely nothing…at least here.

My flashlight shows only a grimy concrete chute with stairs in it, which we climb to the hostel door and ring another buzzer. We're greeted by a pleasant Russian girl about our age who shows us the cramped little place. This is apparently a theme—hostels are operated by cute college-age girls who speak excellent but self-conscious English and in their accents and trim figures embody the local allure of each place. Golan wasn't terribly tempting, but was a wonderful acquaintance and in her hard-framed brown eyes sparked the nomads' wild spirit. Yan Ying was cute in an alternative-rocker kind of way, and probably saved my life, both of which are kind of cool. The flunky at the desk in Korea notwithstanding, this Russian girl is the latest in an inspiring lineup of cute local emissaries.

Josh hits it off with her immediately, with that flair of his that knows neither shame nor inhibition, conceit nor self consciousness. I tag along through the corridors, our tour clearly for him now, though her short-chopped and softened words drift back to me as well. There is a dorm room to the left, for women only; our dorm to the right, "eight persons mixed"; a tiny little office-come-bedroom for the overnight staff; a long couch with red flowers, DVDs stacked at either end, next to a window; bathroom with one toilet, one shower, one lock, to serve everyone; tiny kitchen with butter and bread and a table where we can find our complimentary breakfast in the morning.

Cozy. At fourteen dollars a night (500 Rubles), it's quite a bit more than Idre's…but there are no broken windows, and it's clean and warm, so I'm going to pass out now on a top bunk that looks out into an alley. Maybe I can sleep off this cold…

A thousand grains of sand…

I slept through the afternoon and all through the night in fully-clothed unconsciousness, merrily oblivious to the world. Josh filled me in later on what I missed—his response to Ulan Bator and spending so much time on the train, eleven hours in customs at the Russian border, and dealing with my funk by proxy. Everything I did, or didn't, got on his nerves, but he had the fairness to see it was the stress of the situation playing us each against the other.

Which is cold comfort, but a starting point.

Mongolia was nothing of what he expected, and very little of what he read about—sweeping vistas, check, but he didn't have any spiritual transformations and wasn't knocked senseless by beauty philosophical or panoramic. It was a grimy place with hard stares, and he spent most of his nights in an expat bar throwing darts and drinking heavily—a response he developed into high art while teaching back in Korea. He misses his friends there, though he doesn't bring it up much; he's at once homesick for the place he left, and the idealized vision of his hometown ahead, each removed now from day to day mundanity and imaginatively painted in the amber glow of ever-distant memory.

Josh is a tough guy, downright existential in balancing past and future, but…no man is quite the fortress he envisions.

He's taken the lead on this trip, and that's fine by me. There only needs to be one of us poring over train schedules and handling reservations; it could be me as easily as him, but I'm thankful for the respite. Less for me to worry about, especially since I've been sick so much…but it's taking a toll on the guy, and by night he renounces responsibility with self-destructive abandon—a well-balanced theater of self-destruction. Perhaps it's not the healthiest way of handling things, but who am I to say?

These things build, though, and you can't wash the stress away with Carlsberg; you can only mask disillusion and annoyance for so long.

A sleepless train ride from Ulan Bator carried the promise of cleaner air and fewer problems, delivering us right to the threshold of our next great challenge: Russian Customs.

The process was long and boring; not the hair-raising type in spy books about the Soviet Union, but agonizing in the subtle, quiet, any-moment-now terror of appeasing a capricious totalitarian regime. Entry paperwork for Russia is complicated and easily fouled up…and expensive to set right again. You must send your passport off for a visa stamp, provide a daily itinerary with correct addresses (in Cyrillic), present a letter of invitation from someone in Russia… Getting it in order, though straightforward, was tedious and irksome—who could possibly care about the level of detail requested? We're tourists, not UN weapons inspectors… Presenting our papers for inspection at the border was utterly nerve-wracking.

The stress and lack of sleep added to our Mongol Funk. Something had to give.

Theater of self-destruction…

I was asleep when Josh made his move. Though a bender is no great departure for him, he learned of a good club and went for it.

"I just wanted to tear myself apart at the seams," he told me, a phrase apropos of his tendency. "I was in the shower, you were asleep, and I just knew I had to wreck myself. You have to, you know, on a trip like this, just to adapt. You've just gotta stop fighting things and open yourself up and let your preconceived notions just get destroyed, then—then—you can realign your perceptions." He talks this way on rants. "The frustrations, disappointment, you've gotta own it, you've gotta take it in and use it to readjust. It's not easy; you think it's some kind of vacation? I thought it's some kind of vacation, but it's not."

"What is it?"

"It's a journey, man. This is a voyage, we're going around the fucking world by train. We're going home, and we're going through Russia. That's some heavy shit."

So he needed a night on the town to unwind, to press control-alt-delete and reboot his attitude—to wash away the Mongol dust and greet Russia refreshed…if hung over. So he met some guys at the hostel, made easy conversation and helped them finish a few liters of Oxhota, a terrible Russian budget-beer in a plastic screw-top bottle that tastes worse than the swill we used as punishment beer in my old fraternity.

Afterwards, they went straight to Akula—"Shark." It was a club, the same as every other club, with a dance floor and stage, dark lighting and loud music. They partied Russian style—vodka with beer chasers, beer with vodka chasers, cheap vodka with high grade vodka chasers, weird-colored martinis in the American style for the ladies…all at prices higher than American bars. There was a time when Russians were broke and starving, no food available and unable to keep up with inflation anyway; in nineteen eighties-era Siberia you could trade foreign currency, jewelry, even pens and pencils, for food and liquor.

Those days are long gone, but a new kind of inflation pillages their wallets—where insane wealth and purchasing power in Moscow skews the cost of things everywhere. The money comes in from Siberian oil fields, organized crime, logging, and construction. Those who have the money set the prices, then everyone races to keep up; but it's not so grim as twenty years ago.

I hear Cold War children complain of high prices over café lunches with plenty of bread and meat and olives on their plates, having a valid point, while their parents horde kopecs out of habit; their children spend wildly from knowing neither work nor breadlines. On the better streets, fashionable young men in suits walk quickly past hunched babushkas in old scarves—a striking tableaux. It seems a country in transition, a fat/lean dichotomy, their pendulum swung far out over the Bering Straits to balance the years of Soviet poverty; I don't know what will bring it back to the middle, but something will give one day.

The bar was one of those polished roads that could go on forever, he said, and probably would if not stopped by the walls. The walls held in the dancers and the drinkers and the merriment, too, though they weren't needed because Irkutsk is not a dancing-in-the-streets kind of town; for the Paris of Siberia, it's awfully buttoned up. So he danced in the dark, emaciated body and lanky limbs flailing in a white boy groove at once hilarious and far, far more dignified than I could ever move. Calories burned by nuclear metabolism, he went back for more Baltika; that's when he noticed the Inner Sanctum, across the dance floor, its door guarded by a brawny Russian in a suit.

"Face Control," locals call it in English, pronouncing it "fice" like a drunk Aussie, or "fece," like a drunk Chinaman, but always "control," always that most Russian of English words: control.

Drunk enough to dance, he was right where he needed to be to challenge the bouncer, so he walked right up with his Baltika Number 3 in hand. He expected a scene right out of the Wizard of Oz, him Dorothy, man-mountain the talking door, nobody gets to see the wizard! But the bouncer stepped aside, gestured him in, proving a thesis he long held—that Josh Vise, English teacher, world traveler, metabolism of the gods, is attractive enough to be admitted to a dark room.

There were girls on stage; not much of their clothing remained. The music was quieter, designed to warm the silence in hushed conversations, to keep the groove light and hopes high and along the wall was another bar doing its part too. He watched the girls in the tinted spotlights, skin grey-blue and nipples black, shadows flowing over their bodies like water. Enticing. Alluring. Russian-blonde, Russian-brunette, utterly Russian in their faces and elegant curves; they wore just enough—a chain, a thong, a sidelong glance—to hide a final mystery that burned and pulled more than the secrets they revealed. He drained his beer in a single gulp.

He ordered another, turning back to the dancers, watching the prettiest of the pretty people, the cutest of the cute, talk and flirt in this sanctuary where everyone is pretty and young and flush—this concentration of the best Irkutsk has to offer. A girl walked past—no, a vixen with a woman's eyes and appetite in a teenager's body—and he wanted to reach out, to connect with someone, to…to penetrate that wall between foreigner and local. The American, speaking no Russian; the Russian, knowing nothing of real America. It's a boundary you know when you're wasted in a foreign country trying to find a kindred soul, a friend in the darkness. He was the foreigner; this was her club, with her kind, in her country…he knew nothing of the scene around him—a drop of oil on water, surrounded but not part of his surroundings.

That's what it's like to be the stranger in a strange place; to be pulled by familiar desires towards familiar routines in a place you don't belong, and not being able to get past step one. He had no opening move, this man with the unfailing charm and smile and disarming voice like a younger brother, this man with so many stories and jokes and such insight; he watched them slink past, hips swaying like a heart-shaped carrot on a stick he knew better than to follow.

* * * * *

His friends wanted to stay, but Josh had enough; all worked up with nowhere to go, and nearly skint of the rubles he bought at the border, he hit the street for home. Don't go out after dark, every guidebook warns.

He gets this wild look in his eyes as he tells me the story, and I know it's the look he wore on the street—his navy blue knit cap with the khaki stripe pulled down, accentuating the width of his face, eyes focused to cut through the alcohol and see only one of the doubles of everything. Focused, feral, knit cap battling his furrowed brow, my friend looks outright insane.

Not man in a Bullwinkle costume waving a rifle insane, but guy on the Greyhound bus who'll decapitate you with a can opener insane. I'm not sure if he cultivates that look, or if it comes naturally at that hour, but the smiling and peppy optimist Jekyll I know by day puts on the Hyde mask when he needs to. If I was a cop, I'd shoot him on sight, and he knows it.

There is only one kind of knife-wielding Russian mugger who would mess with Joshua Hyde—the kind of sick vermin God Himself would have a devil of a time stopping; luckily for Josh, that sort of stone-crazy killer was asleep already, because the Hyde mask is all latex and makeup and I'm not sure he could throw two punches without losing his balance. Smoke and mirrors blow away in the wind.

It was a twenty minute walk to the bar, which he could have taken in a four minute cab ride. An hour and a half after leaving on foot, though, near four thirty on our first real morning in Russia, he was still lurching through the streetlamp shadows looking for the right concrete building with the correct alley and specific buzzer-box to welcome him home. Nothing doing. He hailed the only cab he saw, dove in headfirst, and reached an apocryphal hand over the seatback with his little black book and his last two hundred rubles. Two blocks later he was home—broke, exhausted, and victorious.

Ten thousand rubles should feel more satisfying...

How do you get money abroad? Years ago, you took a lot of it with you and then changed it as needed. That posed many problems, all of which revolve around theft and being left penniless with no recourse but sneaking out of your hotel in the dead of night and seeking asylum at the embassy.

Then came traveler's checks, which could be replaced if lost or stolen, and could be cashed directly into the local currency at more or less the going rate. There were fees involved, but it was safer than carrying cash.

During my pre-trip research, I read "Adventures of a Continental Drifter" by Elliott Hester, found his email address, and dropped him a line. After requisite cooing over his book—which is legitimately excellent—I asked a simple question: "how do you get cash in odd places?"

ATMs, he said. Same as high school kids in suburban malls.

Many credit cards charge a "foreign currency conversion fee" as part of their grand scheme to rip you off, so you really don't want to use them a lot abroad... Enter the modern miracle of ATM and debit cards. There are fees, yes, but generally not so bad as with credit cards.

The ATM craze, like the cell phone craze, swept the planet and left our cities dotted with blinking steel mini-banks with disease-ridden touch pads that connect us to our life savings a little too easily for my comfort. I've made a grudging peace with them, but still don't like anything about sticking a card in a machine and having complete access to my bank accounts from somewhere in Siberia.

It's just unsettling.

Nevertheless, a menacing little machined just dumped ten thousand rubles into my hands, which I divide between my neck pouch and another around my leg. I'll try to live off this through Perm, our next stop after Irkutsk. If I can live for two weeks on two hundred seventy five dollars, I'll be doing well in Russia. The dastardly little machine told me how much is left in the account, like looking at a clock counting down my adventure. I'm doing alright so far; I can make Portugal, and charge naked and screaming into the Atlantic to close things out properly.

But Russia is one of the most expensive countries in the world...and we just got here.

Yes dad, I'm still alive…no, call off the Marines…

"Haven't you seen the movie 'Hostel'" my friend asked in an email. "You're going to wake up in a bathtub full of ice, or hunted for sport in some rich guy's sick game." Apparently there's a horror movie about people staying in hostels and getting killed terribly; what I've seen could not be farther from that, but Hollywood has a firm grasp on popular opinion, fear, and mis-education.

Use general ignorance and a bit of stereotype, and you can sell just about anything to the uninformed. So take the idea that cheap places have to be dives, and crime happens in dives, and when you're a naïve American in some far-flung country with no one to hear you scream, well…there you go. Sounds about like the plot to "Hostel," though I could be wrong; I'm boycotting it on moral grounds.

My parents are good Midwestern folk who've travelled a little, but always cautiously, and back when the world was safer. They stayed in decent hotels or with friends, and now they watch too much TV…so naturally, they're astounded we have not yet been robbed, kidnapped, beaten, stabbed, and set on fire (in that order). Relieved, I'm sure, but also rather astounded…especially since I'm following Josh, who they remember as a goofy high school kid from too many years ago.

But petty theft is a grand annoyance, no matter how you slice it. Most hostel theft is the crime-of-opportunity type—pass out drunk on your bed with your pants on the floor, and your wallet might get pilfered; leave your camera unattended, and it might disappear. Put your valuables in their little lockers, though, with a lock, and you're usually safe.

Tourists don't normally disappear into the Chinese prison system or get dragged off into the jungle by lemurs. In reality, we have a few harsh words with some guards, maybe spend a week waiting for the embassy to get us new paperwork, have some good food in the process and maybe a spot of adventure, and we're home with unexpected expenses and a fantastic excuse for missing work. It's as stressful as you let it be; as romantic as you paint it…and hard to realize until you've faced the tiger and found it to be a kitten.

That said, I sleep with my passport and ATM card in a pouch looped around my neck and tucked into my underwear. If someone is good enough to sneak in there undetected, they've earned it.

Basic precautions—that's all you need.

I don't apunya your mayo...

Morning, and I'm off to Lake Baikal. Josh is passed out in last night's clothes, stretched lengthwise across the couch, the TV flickering the home screen for some action DVD.

I follow my Lonely Planet guidebook to a bus station, where it says, in effect, ask around. The ticketing window makes it a bit more formal than a Mongol bus stop, but even with my ticket I'm not much closer to Lake Baikal—now I have to find the right one of the dozen idling microbuses. Trial and error time: I hand it to the nearest driver.

"Nyit!" he barks abruptly, but not painfully. He asks me something in full-speed Russian.

"Nyit punyamiatsun, pa'Rooskie," I say in one of two phrases I know.

He points vaguely at the other buses and waves me away.

My fiancée gave me the Pimsleur Russian Language CD kit a few months ago. I didn't tell Josh about that; I just planned to wow him by chatting someone up in their native language in front of him—an ignoble goal, but motivating. More honorably, I thought I could unlock a little bit of the culture by learning the language of their renowned novelists and intellectuals, artists and scientists. With work, maybe I could read a page of Tolstoy in his native language and country.

Or at least, order a beer without turning too many heads.

I kept the CDs in my pickup truck. There I was, speeding through rainstorms on I-70, passing tractor-trailers at eighty miles an hour, stumbling through "vi punyamiatsun, pa'Rooskie? Nyit. Ja apunyamayo..." I never got past the first CD; I never told Josh I tried; I can't chat up the Russians, and even in translation

Tolstoy is often a mystery to me.

So much for that grand experiment; but I'm getting pretty good at working around the barrier with sign language and oh-golly-farm-boy grins; humility is my secret to getting by. The third bus driver looks at the ticket, turns it right side up, and points me towards the back.

"Thanks," I say.

"Da," he grumbles, not unkindly.

Well-ventilated fish...

They call it the Blue Eye of Siberia, and unlike the Great Wall, you actually can see Lake Baikal from space (or so I hear). In the vast Siberian wilderness of pine trees and mountains is a continental rift, where two plates are slowly pulling apart from each other, leaving an enormous rift on the fault line. More than three hundred streams and rivers flow into that tear, filling it half a mile deep on average, more than a mile deep in other places, with a silt layer that contains who knows how many skeletons and sunken ships and scuttled military research projects—you can hide a lot of things in the world's deepest lake.

It doesn't take up as much surface area as the combined Great Lakes, nor even Lake Victoria in Africa, but by virtue of its depth and thirst it holds far more cubic miles of water than any other freshwater body on the planet—nearly one fifth of all surface freshwater, actually.

It spreads before me, the far shore just barely visible at this narrow point to the south, the village of Listvyanka behind me, with hills rising fast towards the clouds. The homes are bright yellow and red and blue, bright green and sometimes all of these colors on trim and shutters and doors, each like a wildflower in bloom by the roadside. The sun is marvelous and warm, warming me just enough to roll up my sleeves and take off my hat to feel the Baikal breezes. There are red, white and blue fishing boats flying little striped Russian flags; they sit quietly, great hulls resisting the tiny waves wind-whipped towards the shore. An old woman fishes from the road, her long pole casting tiny fish on hooks into a river below, where the water carries the bait into the lake and, she hopes, towards the omul.

Omul are one of the main fish the locals hunt, with nets and hooks and no end of patience. They are silver-sided, long and slender, like salmon; powerful fish, they're fun to catch. They sell easily at the market.

People eat them smoked, their bellies cut open and their guts pulled out, the body run through on a spit and held open with toothpicks. Their lifeless eyes harden like glass as they're smoke-roasted, skin and bones and all. The smoked fish are set out in long rows for the choosing. Old Russian women with hard stares and meaty arms tend stands with the fish stacked high; they are women with the kinds of bodies that withstood the Soviets and the Siberian winters and alcoholic husbands, these women who work more in a month than I have in my life. They do all this and sell their fish for a few rubles each.

This market is a Russian adaptation of the Chinese affair, with rows of stalls facing outwards so that the hawkers can stand or sit or wander back and forth behind their tables with their other wares, their change, sometimes their sleeping rolls. Teenage girls, daughters and granddaughters, sell jewelry and ceramic statues of birds and frogs and seals. There are young fishmongers, too, learning from their aunts and grandmothers how to gut and roast and haggle, their fortune in these stalls. Their mentors portend the future.

This is how so much of the world gets their food: open air stalls, no plastic gloves, no sinks or refrigerators, the food cooked and left sitting out for you, with such turnover that it's not usually a problem. I'm sure they wash their hands and clean their equipment now and again—the charcoal fireboxes self-sterilize, at least.

But I'm not used to the sight of smoked fish held open with toothpicks, lying on a table, bones and eyes, and flies buzzing around. Omul are a delicacy I'll pass up. Other tourists wander around eating them like corn on the cob, picking their teeth, nervous about what to do with the tiny bones—just throw them on the ground? Is there a trashcan around? Of course not—who would empty it, and where?

So the bones fall surreptitiously onto the sidewalk, and everyone seems to enjoy the fish.

* * * * *

The lake is too cold for swimming, but just right for sunbathing. Teenagers cover the narrow, sandy beach (imported from a quarry, no doubt) with blankets and pale bodies. I wish it was a topless beach—these are the first Caucasian women I've seen in a number of weeks—but there are also many families and wrinkled grandparents, so modesty here is for the best. I join them in my own way, sitting on some boulders with a bottle of water and some chicken satay. The forests breathe the clean country air I crave, and the temperature is perfect; the water is wide and sparkling-blue. The bathers chasing each other and laughing are the perfect background to an afternoon recharging my spirit. Josh had last night; I need today. I close my eyes, smiling and reaching my face to the sun like a flower.

Now, I can get well.

But can you eat the nerpa?

Seals don't live in lakes, except here where they're called "nerpa." Technically called the "Lake Baikal Seal," I see "Nerpa Tours" advertised on bilingual signs, the "Nerpa Sculpture" made of white rocks with a blowhole-style fountain squirting from its head (who knows why), and "nerpa" statues for sale in the market.

Nerpa, nerpa, nerpa. It's a fun word to say for awhile, but I haven't seen any yet; they're probably as hungry as I am.

Apparently they dive a hundred meters down to the realm of the "Baikal Oil Fish," another critter unique to this lake. Translucent and slippery little devils, they get their name from the curious way they dissolve into a bony puddle of oily goo when exposed to sunlight. Nature is truly strange.

Thankfully I don't have to go swimming for lunch—just for a hike along the waterfront, following twenty meters behind a

Russian woman who looks suspiciously like an old girlfriend. Catching her in profile, I call out "Hey, Hea—" and then, catching myself, "—ello!" She smiles dismissively and walks on, in the same direction as lunch. A minute later she looks nervously over her shoulder, and seeing me, hurries on faster.

The flower-like bright-painted houses pass on my right. There are occasional brick houses with stucco walls, too, together forming a mishmash of designs plopped down in Siberia. The oddest, and saddest, building has a large taxidermied bear out front. I'm a hunter, so taxidermy animals don't generally bother me, but a small English sign under a large Russian banner just pissed me off: "See our ferocious Siberian bears! 300 Rubles!"

Bears abound in the wilderness around us, and if you're not going to eat it, I believe you really ought to leave wild things alone. There are ways as easy as they are inhumane to get bears for a tourist show, and all sorts of cruel ways to make them seem ferocious; even under ideal circumstances, at those rates for the occasional tourist heartless enough to get off on that kind of attraction, there's no way the bear can be properly fed, cared for, or housed. Things like that make my blood run cold, so I cross the street just to avoid the place and avert my eyes in second-hand shame.

Past the bus stop is a small market with trinkets instead of smoked fish. An old man grills a dozen shish kebabs on a rectangular charcoal grill. In a large aluminum pan over a propane heater, he makes fried rice by the gallon.

I have no idea what meat this is—nerpa?—but it doesn't matter. A good Siberian lunch is pretty close to a good Mongol one: large chunks of stringy meat, roast tomatoes with black-cracked and shriveled skin, and pungent onions served over fried rice. At a hundred fifty rubles it's pretty expensive, but just exactly what I need. On the way back to the village, back near the bus stop, I sit for an hour on the sunny side of a steep hill overlooking the lake and the village below. This is the cleanest air I've breathed since camping in New Hampshire; this village is so quaint I just want to shrink it down and put it on my mantle.

I thank God for days like this.

If it's stupid but it works, you're still getting laughed at...

Flowers don't get sunburned. I need to remember that the next time I think I'm a sunflower basking in the rays—I'm a pale German-American who tans under fluorescent lights. I don't think my ancestors ever left the beer hall.

So of course I'm sunburned, and now I wander Irkutsk in search of the remedy. This is a long and tree-lined street with houses at one end, businesses down at the other, and a blonde German in a brown tank top punching keys in frustration on a stubborn ATM.

"Christina?"

"Dave!"

Of all the ATMs on all the streets...

"Are you following me?"

"No," she says, "why would I do that?"

"So I'm not interesting enough to follow, is that it?"

"I would follow someone more important, perhaps."

"So you admit it, you're a spy with low standards!" We laugh at the post Cold War subterfuge, the catty glances and playful tones, and she tries to hug me hello but I pull away. "Sunburn."

"I see!" she remarks, stepping towards me and very slowly, very carefully poking me in the forehead to watch the color drain. "Doesn't that hurt?"

"Only when you poke it. Have you been to Lake Baikal?"

"No, going tomorrow, I think."

"Can I tell you about it over dinner?"

So we're off, but first things must come first: I need some aloe cream for the burn. We duck into a pharmacy, where I try asking the girl at the counter for sunburn cream.

"Nyit." No, she doesn't have any, or, no, she doesn't understand? Surely they must have some; sunburns are universal, even if language is not. I point to the burn and she laughs at me, nodding vaguely down an aisle full of the same medical contraptions and boxes as every pharmacy in the civilized world.

Does every pharmacy the world over get issued the same

boxes of Band-Aids and cough syrups and non-slip shower mats…

Ah. Here it is. I can't read a thing in Cyrillic, but the label has an aloe plant. It's on a squeeze bottle with a clear gel inside, that tempting little aloe plant assuring me that I'll get the relief I need. Christina agrees with a snicker that it's worth a shot, and hey, what have I got to lose?

Out on the street, she holds my pack while I squirt a palm-full and rub it all over my face and neck, massaging it behind my ears and down the bridge of my stinging nose, shaking it with my eyes closed and squirting on more, more, more, the cool gel soothing the burn and calming the tingles. Christina starts laughing, and can't stop.

I open my eyes as a group of Russian women hurry past, mouths agape, avoiding eye contact. Other people walk wide around me, eyes averted. They wear the first real smiles I've seen in Irkutsk.

Then I see the only English on the label: "Gynecologically tested."

What the hell, it works.

Leaping off the straight and narrow…

She's staying at some other place in town, a real dive, she says. Our hostel is full; we checked on our way to dinner, and they have no room. Such are the risks you take when traveling by your wits with no reservations. It surprises us that we ran into each other again, but really it shouldn't—we are traveling the same direction on the same railroad, taking the major stops along the way. I wonder how many other little cliques form and disperse and reform again, fate and luck and probability reuniting casual friends in this mobile community of young travelers.

Christina planned the major components of her trip and left the details to fill themselves in. Then she arranged to have her neat little life shipped in boxes back to Germany, bought train tickets all the way to Berlin, strapped on her backpack, and left the real world behind.

That's something you don't realize at first—the paradigm shift between life as you know it, and serious time on the road. The real world keeps going, unsurprisingly enough, while a new sense of time evolves…one that started when you left and will end when you're back, neatly and precisely starting and stopping like almost nothing else ever does.

With her boyfriend and possessions gone for the moment, no apartment behind and no job ahead, she says that she immediately took on a new, somewhat blank identity—something she didn't expect. Something Josh and I can relate to, but not with such freedom as the truly solo wanderer. We talk about this over an appetizer, and she says I enjoy this kind of travel.

What was she like, I ask, before her boyfriend—seven years ago or longer, the girl who turned into the woman sharing a bowl of olives with me in this small café.

Well, I was younger, she jokes, having to start somewhere, and probably having not thought of the question much before. She had a good German plan for her life, but he wouldn't commit and now his job is gone along with the friends and the lives they had in China. Now she has no plans beyond the train schedule; no reservations. She trusts herself, and herself completely to…

"Fate, is it?" I ask.

"Yes, that is a word for it," she says.

"God?"

"Nein." She is not religious, a trend in Germans my age that I don't entirely understand. Though Israel is the cradle of Christianity, Europe was its greatest home for centuries. European Catholics crusaded back and forth across the continent and the Middle East, spreading their religion, spawning offshoots of all sorts and flavors. Italy is heavily Catholic, Vatican City is in Europe, Martin Luther was German, the English, Dutch, and Spanish brought their faith to the world (usually on the tip of a sword)… I inherited my Christianity from German ancestors who carried their faith to America. We are a God-fearing people, and we learned it from the Europeans.

But this European, of my generation, brushes religion aside like waving a hand through tea-steam and says, eh, fate…

She explains that religion, among her friends anyway, is lumped in with the "old ways," and not something of interest. There are the practitioners, and certainly the fanatics, but the congregations are aging without much replacement. What affects her life more than a supernatural being, she says, is simple luck—the having, or the not having, as decided by fate.

"And fate," she says, "is a roll of the dice."

So she rolls through her trip, Shanghai to Berlin, tumbling along come-what-may and really wishes she could stay with us, but—oh well. Would I like to see Lake Baikal with her? No, I've seen it once. Alright, then.

A month ago she'd spend her weekday in an office, on the phone and deluged with email; now she decides to take a bus or a walk based on whims and weather, letting fate entertain her until her next train departs. She could live a lifetime here in a week, and maybe wake up in Moscow as a different person—as whoever she chooses to be. This is the space between one life and another. I have religion; Josh has a little black book; she has fate. We each make it up as we go.

The real world seems so far away.

Trans Siberian interlude... Trans Siberian Railroad, Highway, Orchestra... Cold food and frozen stares... The only quiet place on the train...

There it went; that was it; Irkutsk gone behind us, my dinner with Christina like a one night stand without the sex or intrigue. Lake Baikal: bagged, tagged, stuffed into .jpgs on a memory card in my camera and gone, baby, gone. The Trans Siberian Railroad rocks us like a great steel cradle, the wind rushing past our window, silently because we can't open it—the frame is screwed shut.

The toilets open onto the tracks, just like on the Trans Mongolian line, and the bathroom doors are locked a mile out from each station. The attendant has a special key that slips over a triangular post in the lock-hole; if I had one of those keys, I'd be a lucky man. The train stops every hour or two, making the real bathrooms a constant gamble—when will they be locked, or open, or locked and forgotten? When the doors are locked I stand in the bobbing antechamber between the cars, accordion-plastic pulled between them, steel plates sliding around underfoot, and aim for the flickering railroad ties down through the bouncing triangular space between accordion and plates. These spaces in between the cars are smokers' lounges and bathrooms, and bottlenecks on the great foot highway fore-to-aft.

This train is full of Chinese engaged in varying forms of commerce; many of them, right there at the stations. We keep our door shut and locked against the constant stream of bodies through our car, transiting our hall to get back and forth from the Chinese-originating cars mixed into our line at Irkutsk. They don't get off at the big stops, or even the little ones, so I wonder if the Chinese and their plastic-wrapped bales of brand-name imposter clothes are going all the way to Moscow. Maybe St. Petersburg.

Every stop is a market for them, every platform a sidewalk sale. When the train slows they rush with extra haste, unpacking fake designer jeans and sequined shirts on hangers that they dangle out whatever windows they can open, every doorway they can crowd. Since no one gets on or off their cars, they take over those antechambers, affixing hangers to the doors and windows and each other until the side of the train is covered in denim and cotton.

The haggling is furious, Russians on the platform having just a few minutes to shop and get into their cars, the Chinese having that same narrow window to make deals and get the products back inside before the train lumbers off. Old women lean out of windows (their windows still open) with fists full of yuan and rubles, taking money, throwing bras and jeans and fake Nike shoes into the crowd. It's a frenzy of travelers and bags, shouting in Russian and Chinese and English, brand names Diesel, Hugo Boss, Adidas, mispronounced in many tongues.

Then the wheels turn and the train stretches, each car loath to follow its coupling west—west, to the next tiny town visited only by train, the next village huddled in the pine trees and forgotten. The land looks like a flat New Hampshire. I know there are mountains and hills but I can't see where. Two sets of tracks run parallel through this solid corridor of trees, each tree the same height, the same width, the same type—planted by log barons who made money clear cutting around the tracks two generations ago, then planted new trees to harvest later. It's later now. The trees are still here, nature's air filter, like a brown picket fence flickering past.

It's a comfort to be in motion; it's a blessed curse to be drawn ever onwards, to feel that pull somewhere—west, for us. To Portugal, to the Atlantic, to homes in New York and St. Louis. I feel that pull now, missing my fiancée, feeling drawn west and onwards by schedules and fate—as if I am just a car in a train pulled inexorably onwards through life.

Then there's that lust to see what's coming, to charge full-bore into the next great adventure. My strength is back, the sickness finally gone, and Irkutsk…was boring. Seoul, Beijing, Ulan Bator…a cold war, a Great Wall, constant danger on the night-darkened streets… It built as a wave out at sea, rushing inland, rising, lifting me and now we're carried on by our own inertia—a country a week! Adventure!

It's a comfort just to be in motion again. In Irkutsk we were stationary, in a way, yet the feelings persisted—feelings of being pulled onwards while stuck in one town. The only thing to do was hop this train and get going at top speed across Siberia. It's a luxury that becomes a need, this freedom to pick up and go, to have the means to get somewhere else. I wonder if I can ever again be comfortable without it.

There is a broken window hanging open in the hallway of our otherwise stifling car. It reminds me I'm moving again and it's refreshing, like water to thirsty lungs; I'm loath to exhale, my head thrust out, eyes closed, face basking in the afternoon. This is why dogs hang their heads from cars. It's a dream, a moment's peace to have my head in the slipstream and my smile in the sun.

This, too, shall pass.

Trans Siberian Railroad, Highway, Orchestra…

The Trans Siberian Railroad was Tsar Alexander II's bright idea. He looked east from St. Petersburg, staring dreamily at buildings and trees front-lit from the afternoon sun and said why, I think we ought to build a railroad out that way, straight out to the ocean. He knew the Pacific Ocean was way out there somewhere and held direct shipping access to Asian countries, and he knew that a reliable rail system transiting his empire could open up the Siberian east to settlement. It would bring goods to the eastern shipping ports and food from Europe to his vast interior. Supplies could come north from Korea and China across the permafrost to feed his people as they expanded his empire into the wilderness.

His son inherited the project, and appointed Finance Minister Sergei Witte to facilitate the project with public funding and the empire's full engineering, construction, and military might. Soldiers worked with hired laborers and convicts to clear the land, grade it, fell the timber for the ties and force the rails east from Moscow (already connected by line to St. Petersburg) towards Vladivostok. As with the Trans Continental Railroad in America, another crew started at the same time in Vladivostok, pushing their line west along a route it took ten years just to chart.

They began in 1891 and met in the middle twenty five years later, opening the line to coal-fired trains pulling passenger cars and freight. The line skirted around existing cities, rather than smashing through them and creating land disputes and bad blood; many of these burgs, then, redeveloped around the rail station, shifting the town's center by adding hotels and warehouses along the tracks. It changed the towns forever.

The difference between a settlement and a forgotten campsite was whether trains would stop. People gathered where the trains pulled in—where access to food shipments and timber markets nurtured communities and businesses. That scheme remains today, even in the age of airplanes and helicopters, where a glance at a map of Siberia shows most settlements tied in some direct way to the Trans Siberian Railroad.

Primary construction finished just before the Bolshevik Revolution. The White Army moved troops and supplies west along the rails, where they encountered eastbound Red Army forces. The Reds won their civil war, of course, and established the Soviet Union.

The Soviets added an ambitious spur to the already impressive route—a 2,000 mile Baikal Amur Mainline that branches off the Trans Siberian four hundred miles west of Irkutsk. It took them three times as long (seventy five years) to construct a line one third the length of the Trans Siberian Railroad, owing to the digging, bridge building, and tunnel blasting required.

The Trans Siberian Railroad is more than just a straight shot from Moscow to the east coast. It connects to the Trans Mongolian, which runs all the way south to Beijing—how we got here. Western lines connect Moscow to St. Petersburg and Warsaw, Poland, where riders can jump on the European train system all the way to Lisbon, Portugal—my plan. The truly hardcore can board in Vladivostok and not stop for more than a few hours all the way to Lisbon, for around a thousand dollars and about ten days of travel.

The Trans Siberian Railroad is part of the three longest continuous-service rail lines in the world. The record line stretches from Moscow to Pyongyang, North Korea, along most of the

Trans Siberian. The second longest line starts in Kiev and goes to Vladivostok, and the third longest is the Moscow-Vladivostok service that claims the proper title "Trans Siberian Railroad."

The first locomotives plying these rails were wood-fired tankers that used steam to power their wheels. They followed slowly behind the workers as they built the lines rail by rail. The next generation used coal, until replaced by diesel locomotives. Now they run on electricity, like streetcars in the wilderness.

The electrification project was completed in 2004, and brings power to the line itself and to many smaller villages otherwise unconnected to major electricity grids. Modern Trans Siberian locomotives have a spring-loaded boom that rises to meet overhead power lines, completing a circuit that powers large motors that can pull trains twice as heavy as many of the old coal burners; liberated of the need to carry fuel for combustion-driven power plants, more of their hauling capacity is available to passengers and goods than ever before.

The romantic image of the boiler tank locomotive breathing thick black smoke into an azure sky is a thing of the past…at least on the Trans Siberian. Coal-fired locomotives still ply the rails on some Mongol spurs.

Our tickets each cost $172 to get from Beijing to Irkutsk, and this leg is $291 for the two day trip to Perm; add another $93 each to get to Moscow, $114 to get to Warsaw, and the hundred dollar Belarus Transit Visa, and we've invested $770 each and twelve days purely in railcar transit to accomplish the same thing as a half-day flight…but no one ever had a coming-of-age odyssey on a fourteen hour plane ride.

The cheapest long-range Trans Siberian tickets are for nonstop trips—nonstop in that the train stops at each station, but we're still on it when it pulls away a few minutes later. Well connected deal-seekers score "kupé" (second class, four-bunk sleeper berths like ours) tickets to get from Moscow to Vladivostok for just under a hundred bucks. If you want to stop for awhile enroute, the price goes way, way up.

So for the thru-traveler, it's a pretty good deal to go one-way nonstop from Moscow to the coast…the route plied by a number of Russia's new age entrepreneurs. They ride all the way to the seaport to buy American, Japanese, and Korean-made luxury cars fresh from the container ships, then drive them all the way to Moscow. Of all the goods shipped across Siberia, these cars, perhaps, have the strangest story.

After they purchase a car from the sprawling lots in Vladivostok, drivers negotiate with mob figures who rather brazenly advertise "protection" like brand representatives at a convention. Carjacking and murder are rampant on many sections of the "Trans Siberian Federal Highway," a series of mostly lawless roads that form the defacto route. Most—though not all—highway bandits are employed in organized crime rings, so buying protection from the right people in the right combination improves their odds of getting a Lexus to market in Moscow or St. Petersburg across 6,800 miles of rural anarchy.

Car bought, mob paid off, the drivers swathe their vehicles in cardboard and tape, even covering the windows—leaving holes just large enough to see through—to minimize scratches and body damage from poor quality roads and hazards along the way. Then they set off for a two week—at best—drive to Moscow, or Yekaterinburg, or St. Petersburg, to sell the vehicles to the nuevo riche oil-money-crowd for just enough profit to pay their family's rent and grocery bills, and to buy another ticket east to Vladivostok...

We have a much better ride in the train than they do on the highway; they have better stories, but I'm happy where I am. The drivers take the eastbound trains—ours is westbound—so I won't be able to sit down over a bottle of vodka with one of them and hear tales of holdups and hijinks and micro-capitalism crossing former Soviet Siberia...oh well.

The rest of the merchandise westbound from Vladivostok gets loaded onto the freight trains, these mile-long affairs packed full of wheat, raw sugar, and imported hardware and machinery. The Trans Siberian Railroad is eastern Russia's lifeline, and crossing it is a rite of passage for backpackers like us. We're seeing parts of the world our friends will never see; riding a legendary line they've only read about. It's pretty cool.

I went to a Trans Siberian Orchestra concert when I was a teen—they're a new-age group that covers Christmas carols with funky synthesizers and guitars. I listened and watched and tried to fathom a connection between a bunch of people playing electronic instruments and the Trans Siberian Railroad, or the Trans Siberian Federal Highway, or anything Trans Siberian at all, but couldn't. I'm sure they explain their name in the liner notes, but I still can't figure it out. The band is as strange and distant on the railroad today as the railroad was at their concert. I wonder how many fans of each have tried the other.

Trans Siberian, indeed.

Cold food and frozen stares

The dining car is gross and overpriced. It's a smoking car, too, which doesn't help. Imagine the Diamond Truckstop Cafeteria on the side of I-44 in the fetid bowels of Missouri, at 3am when it's mainly alcoholics and desperate lunatics who are ordering dinner. Now put the tables in a row and fumigate them with unfiltered Russian cigarettes that burn like cannon fuse, and remember that no one sulking at those tables has had a shower since Vladivostok, or Irkutsk at best. Their hard stares read like warning signs of foul tempers and disdain.

Everywhere you eat, food reflects the cook's mood, if just a little bit. It shows when they take pride in their work, when they're in a good mood and generous and do everything right because each dish reflects back on them. That holds true for all moods; I've had marvelous street food from proud hawkers and absolutely terrible food at fancy restaurants. Take this clientele here in the nicotine-stained dining car, and face them every day for years and see what happens to your mood; see what happens to your food. Forget the decorations or the signs, the menus or their English, I judge a restaurant's appeal first on their staff— I've never gotten food poisoning from a happy cook, and they generally work among a happy staff.

A man in a tired uniform hands me a menu, scowling for no reason, and snatches it back immediately. He looks at it, turns it back towards me and points nyit nyit nyit at dish after dish on each side. Always nyit. No—no, they don't have that, or no, the cook won't make it for reasons entirely his own. The result is the same.

Everything in me says don't eat here. I look at the menu anyway—borscht for as much as a steak dinner back home. Dishes with impossible Cyrillic names and improbable English translations, for a few hundred rubles each. Someone scratched out the original prices and hand-written new ones—higher, no doubt, as if the surly cook with the sweat-stained shirt is trying to price us right out of bothering him.

The staff used to sell the food to hard-up folks on the platforms in these little towns, charging insane prices for bulk ingredients the villagers couldn't get any other way. Enough rubles went into the till to keep the accountants happy back at the office, and the balance was a tidy sum towards their own black-market needs— an interchangeable surplus that no one really owns, just passing it fluidly across Russia. What is money if not a placeholder for wealth, between the thing you sold and the thing you need?

The tradition of "no" lives on: nyit, spat like profanity at a dog. No, they don't have most of the things on the menu. No, they won't accommodate your fancies. No, this won't change. Get used to it.

The guidebooks prepared us for this. Josh turns to his sodium-bomb soup-in-a-cup meals with hot water from the samovar. I have some fruit and a bag of muesli. My paltry supplies last one day, and then I'm hungry and have nothing to eat, and no desire to brave the dining car.

The attendants in each car are like books, in that they're full of information but just sit there doing absolutely nothing until you put in some effort to engage them. Our attendant speaks passable English, I say in contrast to my two Russian phrases ("Do you speak English?" and the obvious lie, "Yes, I speak Russian"). When I get hungry I ask him how long the next stop will be. I don't chance the ten minute stops, but right around meal times the train stops for thirty minutes—as if understanding the dining car's shortcomings.

Josh dumps another load of boiling water into his instant soup cup; I hit the platform in search of a meal.

There are tiny shop windows, many covered over with cardboard, some open, with teenagers and men leaning against the glass on the inside. Their bodies are framed with soda cans and beer bottles, Pringles, foil bags of junk food... No Turks selling döner kebap? No tiny little sausage or hamburger stand, no shish kebab grills? The schedules are posted, the trains are mostly on time, and they're always packed with hungry passengers...with just a little foresight, a guy with a modest grill could make a killing selling lunch around here.

But alas, my options are junk food or beer. Poking around, I find an old woman selling bread, but without cheese, butter, or meat, what's the point? There's a small shop with a door instead of a window, where I find a tray of cold chicken halves and white cheese that looks like Swiss but with a different smell. The prices look cheap, but are based on 100 gram units—just shy of two ounces. I order a small meal and balk at the price.

I stand at the far end of that romantic idea of glamour and adventure in crossing Russia on the Trans Siberian Railroad... holding a cold chicken carcass and some funky cheese, romanticizing lunches back home.

The only quiet place on the train...

I've been in this great steel anaconda for two sweaty days, snaking my way through Siberia. The walls are wood veneer in our second class carriage, and I'm about ready to open our screwed-shut window the dramatic way with a stainless steel thermos. Yesterday, the broken window across the narrow hall hung open, which made the hallway pleasant and cut down on the funk from four people jammed into each tiny room. But sure enough, a team of workers hoisted, shimmed, and screwed the window shut. Apparently, the second class peasantry is not allowed an open window on a beautiful summer evening; of the many broken things on the train, the first fixed are the happy accidents that actually improve our quality of life.

Certainly the air conditioning would improve things if it did, in fact, work at all, which it doesn't, and our compartment would have just enough room for two, if it didn't house four of us. Our compartment mates are an obese Russian who drinks like Stalin is coming back with a sickle, and his equitably portly wife, whose obsession with low-cut tops is obscene. If in my sleep I roll out of bed, there's a chance I'll bounce off the fold-up table, onto her bunk, and suffocate in her cleavage.

I might never even be found.

They don't speak English, which is fine, but they spend each waking moment scowling like little girls practicing their pouty faces in a mirror; even as they sleep they scowl, as if their dreams are as unpleasant as they must find everything in the waking world.

Across the language and attitude barriers—we're American, we smile; they're Russian, they scowl—there is a sort of compulsory silence. I feel the social pressure not to talk to Josh, not to break that silence, and he obliges. They say nothing; we say nothing. I used up the battery in my iPod; the last song churned up on shuffle was recorded by a friend of mine. Out of the blue, there in a surreal moment of awkward silence in a clacking train car crossing Siberia, my friend Suraj's voice crooned through the headphones with a song he wrote for a cartoon. The battery died, lodging the cloying refrain in my mind for hours. The only other sound is of the wheels lurching over bumps and across slight gaps in the track, and my lingering coughs. With the windows screwed shut on four sweaty people our compartment feels like an armpit.

There is no fresh air in the dining car. There are twenty Russians chain smoking and scowling, each trying to out-smoke and out-scowl the others in a contest of hideous aesthetic. No air moves through the place, it just swirls accusatorily around you and drives the smoke deep into your clothes. You can tell that no one wants to be here, and that further, they are here because anywhere else on the train would be worse. The butter costs a dollar US, the cheapest soup is six bucks, and the "meals" start at twelve…if you can stand the atmosphere, which I can't.

But on the way back to my car is a hidden gem—a side door

propped open at the end of the "kitchen." It lets in a flood of fresh air. Without grimy glass in the way, I feel the beautiful sunshine on a spectacular late-summer afternoon. We're passing through a patch of white ash trees, the wind on my face and their trunks flickering black and white like riding past a white picket fence on a motorcycle. The air is simply magnificent, and reminds me of summers in New Hampshire. The tracks are so smooth here, the joints so flush there is no clacking, barely any swaying, the wheels rolling with a steady swooshing and none of the jerks and lurches we normally feel.

I have firm hold here of a little slice of heaven, and quit noticing the steady flow of Chinese—they truly are everywhere—in and out through the doors to my right. Drowning in air, basking in light, I drift deeper towards the happy center of this cathartic moment.

Then great rushing wind hits me, the sound and the fury terrifying me in a cold moment of instant panic and noise and darkness. The sun disappears. The wind rips at my shirt as air pours off a train bound in the other direction. There are blue cars whipping past as flashes of color and shadow, at one hundred and fifty miles an hour—we were each doing probably seventy five in our own direction—with red cars screaming past with great shrieking and clattering. The tremendous noise and wind feel like they want to rip me apart.

But the windows don't shatter, the trains don't collide, and anyway, I'm back just a step from the open door, so…I know I'm safe. I am the master of this moment, and in a moment, that train is gone. All is trees and sun again, and all is peaceful with the gentler wind peeled off the slipstream. I breathe out, realizing I held my breath for the entire show. In with the fresh air, the sunlight, the peace—out with the stress of life on the road. I'm completely relaxed.

Wham wham wham on the wall above my head as I leap across the passageway as if struck by lightning, twisting sideways towards the noise from the hateful smashing of a Russian woman, her forearm bashing wham into the wall where I just stood. The cook in the galley behind me, she beats that wall with unbridled hate and spews Russian epithets like a furious machinegun. She's smaller than me and stronger, wider, terrifyingly ugly, and her face is all screwed up in rage. The gist of her tantrum is "get out of here, you're fouling my air," though far more savage and spiteful as she berates me for—what, exactly?

She's blocking my exit, her fist coming now at my face, the open train car door to the forest behind me and now I'm far from that sacred place, far from Zen, my back towards an inglorious death in the weeds by the tracks. I block her punch, sizing her up for a quick twisting shove, one that would send her out the door in my place to become a long grease stain for the bears. She's brought me down to her level, hatred and violence from nowhere, nowhere at all, the most terrifying kind. If it's her or me by God she's going to eat gravel and die broken in the wilderness.

How dare I stand here? How dare she come out of nowhere to attack me with noise and violence and drive me backwards towards the door. No, lunch lady, you do not want a piece of this.

Never have I incurred such immediate and surging hate, and certainly not from standing quietly by myself. And so I begin, with hard words in hateful English screamed straight in her face, my hands up and ready to strike—to grab, twist, shove—to make my escape through the end-of-car door.

There is no fear in her eyes. She's been threatened by worse than a pale American tourist. Maybe she'd welcome getting thrown off the train; maybe she'd bounce along like an iron cannonball, snapping trees as she goes. No wonder her mother's generation repelled the Third Reich with old guns and farm tools.

I slip past her, escape being the best solution, and hear her slam that open door closed behind me, sealing off the beautiful evening and sealing in the cigarette smoke and sweat—locking herself in a tin coffin with filthy plates and twenty hard-scowling men. The life she chooses.

I sprint back to our berth.

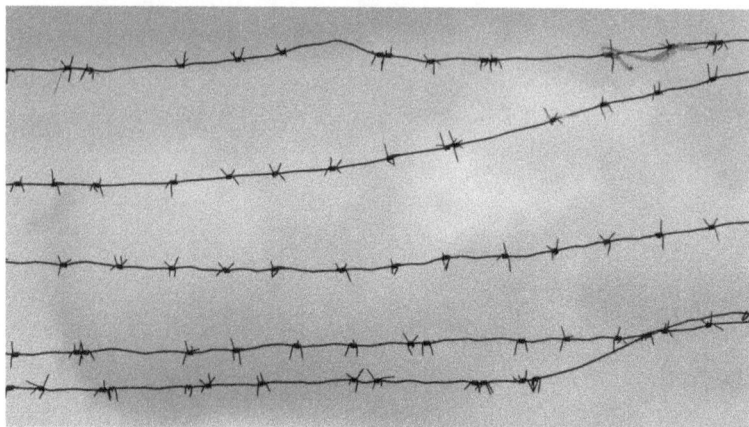

Top: **Barbed wire between the gulag's yard and the sky**

Bottom: **Bunks in the Perm 36 Gulag**

Perm 36 Gulag
28 August, 2007

Perm, Russia

A foreign country is not designed to make you comfortable. It is designed to make its own people comfortable.

—Clifton Fadiman

Russia's Detroit... Dick Tracy on the radio... From Chernobyl to your table... In search of Number 1... Gulaged... Degradation World Tour... Big fish stories... One-day friends bearing gifts... The great absinthe bender... Perm and my existential crisis... Not coming this way again... Right where I need to be...

Perm is Russia's military-industrial equivalent of Detroit. The city has ammunition and explosive manufacturing plants, factories for field artillery and an open air cannon museum; take a walk along the riverfront near the end of Komsomol'skiy Prospekt and you can watch MiG aircraft flying low over the Kama River. A hundred fifty years ago they built steamboats here, and there were paper mills along the rivers. Some companies produced industrial chemicals. Those industries expanded, and soon came ship building yards and massive production, with delivery possible via the rivers. During the Bolshevik Revolution, this success was highly unfortunate—the city was valuable to both the Whites and the Reds, bringing extensive combat to its streets.

The victorious Soviets rebuilt and expanded Perm, making it a center for military goods manufacturing as well as the old civilian commerce. Their lingering influence glowers down from large concrete buildings: tenement block apartments, government offices, and even hotels in matching shades of Communist Grey. Many of the streets are straight and parallel, with a wide avenue every few blocks that could support military traffic, parades, and revues. There are long established bus and tram lines to move the masses. More than three quarters of the town's population still work in manufacturing.

The Bolshevik Revolution was violent; so were the two world wars that kept the weapon plants open around the clock. Even the ensuing peace after World War II was overshadowed by constant fear...of the US, of Western European powers intervening in the Soviets' Eastern European land grab, etc. The Cold War was status quo for a country born of violence and simmered for seventy five years in various states of conflict. The city wears that legacy like its grey façade—heavy, cold, omnipresent.

Perm was off limits to most Russians and just about any foreigner for most of the twentieth century—it was too sensitive to have non-essential people and potential spies and saboteurs wandering around. As such, it developed little tourist infrastructure—few hotels, shopping limited to what was necessary to support the workforce…restaurants enough to feed their own people. Under Soviet Communism, the people had clothing and food and basic medical attention, but very little beyond their needs…with almost no infrastructure to meet the people's wants, and little commerce vying for the discretionary cash they didn't have.

There are two basic kinds of infrastructure: primary infrastructure that keeps people alive and makes things work, and secondary infrastructure that transcends the basics of mere survival and makes those lives enjoyable and rich. These secondary businesses are new to Perm in the last twenty years, and doing an interesting job of carving their niches in old Soviet buildings and shiny new post-modern construction. The old industries survived, but the old paradigm is gone.

They have a fantastic ballet company at the Tchaikovsky Theater; there's Perm State University, and the multi-building Museum of Arts overlooking the river. During the summer, a landing along the Kama comes alive with tents and music, Baltika and Oxhota flowing long into the night. It's not a party town by any means, but there are things to do and an emerging leisure scene—even a few shopping malls in new buildings with glass facades in place of the old concrete.

So it's not a college town; it's not a tourist hotspot. Perm is open to foreigners now, and still trying to figure out what to do with us.

Dick Tracy on the radio

The railroad station is right next to Perm State University. Kids just barely younger than us wander around with backpacks and bush-league scowls—genetic relics more than their parents' Soviet-hardened countenances. They barely remember the Soviet days. A few choice facts, perhaps, maybe the day the regime change became real to them, but they weren't raised with the promises and exhortations and the growing, gnawing disillusions that weighed down their parents' frowns. They have the Russian Scowl, but little credibility to back it up.

We hop a cab, watch the world go by and now we're on Lenina Street, a wide affair that bends around a pedestrian median as we pass a paved-over village green and large fountain. The old buildings are concrete, the old old buildings are wooden, but few and far between—many were destroyed in the revolution or erased by time and several flavors of progress. The new buildings look like any city in the American Midwest that just makes it up as it goes.

Our hotel is different—straight back to 1975, a poster for all that's wrong with Soviet architecture. The Hotel Ural is probably the ugliest building I have or will ever try to fall asleep inside. Behind three-foot-thick concrete walls, part of the main floor is blocked off for noisy, dusty renovations. The rest is cold stone and hollow space, with chunky black buttons for the elevators and a long row of closed positions at an understaffed welcome desk—like they're waiting for a crush of people who aren't scheduled to arrive yet, and probably won't. Ever.

The woman at the counter speaks perfect English and her blend of American-British-Russian accent is downright intoxicating. She inspects our passports, and stamps our papers for the same fee as the hostel back in Irkutsk—100 rubles each. The government requires our paperwork to be stamped every three days, by the companies we told the Russian Embassy in New York that we would be lodging with; a stamp on a piece of paper tucked into a pouch in my pants doesn't help them track my current whereabouts one wit. The ink doesn't cost 100 Rubles, nor does the moment it takes to stamp it. But the infrastructure is there, and the infrastructure is hungry.

The police can give us a hard time if we can't present our paperwork on demand; if it's not filled out perfectly, and in Russian;

if there are not enough stamps to make the three-day average, or more than a three day gap in the sequence; if the stamps are for places not on our government-approved itineraries… Yes indeed, life can get downright ugly if the constabulary wants it to, and even manic attention to niggling details is slim protection. Bribes work better, but for a conservative cheapskate from a Midwest corn town, that's cold comfort.

This has me wrapped around the axle not because of perpetual fear of harassment—I've never been asked for papers outside a border checkpoint in my life—but because it's expensive and silly…Security Theater. It's an old system that is so easily circumvented or manipulated that I can figure out cheats and shortcuts…and it's designed to inhibit spying? To keep track of potential enemies of the state, who will, of course, be professionals and prepared for the stamp-and-paper game?

Really, now…come on. Surely they can do better than outmoded Soviet paperwork policies that serve mainly to annoy backpackers. If the Russian government is so hard up it can't live without the hundred dollar visa fees, if their tourist infrastructure is truly contingent upon four dollar tourist stamps, there are much bigger problems than worrying about where a half-crazed writer and his emaciated friend pass out at night.

Oh well. The space between theory and reality is a chasm full of absurdity and sticky red tape, and we're chest-deep in it. She hands the passports back and gives us a key to the cheapest two-bed private the hotel offers.

I believe in historic inertia—that sometimes it takes a traumatic event to undo the plodding regularity of the same old routine. So when I feel the elevator shake and shudder I look for signs of obvious and recent trauma; finding none, I conclude that no matter how dodgy it feels, no matter this we're-all-going-to-die spike in adrenaline, if it hasn't plummeted earthwards off its chains yet it probably won't on this ride. It's probably safe until something changes, as everything changes for a reason. In the absence of reason, carry on.

Our room is on the right, at the end of a long hall which itself is at the end of a long hall; the carpet changed from worn-out-functional to downright threadbare and the walls way down here are a sickly, sticky yellow like beeswax. Our key opens a door into a narrow room with enough space between the beds to stow our bags upright against the windowsill, and a plastic radio straight out of a Dick Tracy comic. It has four buttons; I press one, making it sing a big-band song. Two other buttons don't work, but the last switches it to talk radio—all in Russian, of course, which sounds menacing and conspiratorial coming out of such a box in a cut-rate dive room at the back of a Soviet hotel.

"We're home," Josh says.

From Chernobyl to your table…

It's dinner time and we haven't had a proper meal since Irkutsk. We head for the shopping mall on the next block, but the food court is closed already and the shops are drawing their security gates across their doors. We find a trendy café, but the prices are high and the atmosphere isn't right; the crowd is a bit too stylish for the likes of us. Back outside, we cross a parking lot to a restaurant with a menu all in Cyrillic.

How many languages do you expect to find on a menu deep in the American heartland? That's Perm—just awakening to the tourist concept, deep in their own country and serving their own people, Perm is one of those cities that doesn't feel any need for translations. It's not xenophobia—there just aren't enough helpless foreigners here to justify multi-lingual subtitles.

My instincts tell me this isn't my scene, either—with the motor scooters parked outside, the 50 ruble specials on the sign… I want vegetables after so much cheese and cold chicken. I want hot, quality food after scrounging around the railway platforms for days. My blood sugar is completely out of whack, and I'm just beginning to realize and understand the effect that has on my personality.

"I'm going in," Josh says. "Looks fine, price is right. Comin'?"

"Enjoy," I say. "See you back at the hotel." He walks up the steps as I round the shopping center, back towards Lenina Street.

This restaurant is open—it looks like a chain "family

restaurant," somewhere between an Applebee's and an all-day diner, with Russian kitsch on the walls. The food is served cafeteria style in a back room—grab a tray, wander around the hot bars and cool bars and grab little plates of chicken or pâté or pizza or…all sorts of things. I grab a grey square of something, a chicken breast in red sauce, some mixed greens, mixed vegetables, and a bottle of water. Twenty bucks US, and I consider it all an appetizer.

The grey square is inedible, the chicken isn't particularly good, the mixed vegetables are raw (which would be fine, had I expected it), and the mixed greens taste like they haven't been washed since being harvested near Chernobyl. Back at her work station, my waitress scowls-giggles-scowls with her coworker in a way that completely baffles me.

What a strange place.

In search of Number 1…

By luck and gestures I find a grocery store near the hotel. I have bottled water and bananas, some apples and an orange in my basket, and am always looking for that perfect something more. More than ethnographic windows into local culture, grocery stores are becoming a source of torment for me. There are large cuts of lamb, pork, and beef, some goat in plastic wrapping, a bit of chicken…a fair amount of sausage, instant coffee in disposable tubes and—God provides—real coffee by the half-kilo.

There are vegetables and other fruits, chicken breasts and spices, deli meats and a few really nice looking steaks…all of this and more.

But I have no kitchen. I can't cook anything that needs more than a candle, and our room doesn't have a refrigerator. A month on the road and I really miss cooking; this far in, I'm tired of the raw fruits and vegetables I eat to offset the two meals I eat out every day. There are people who eat out for every single meal, day in and year out, but I can't live like that; I've used the hidden Velcro tabs to expand my pants several times already. I crave hot vegetables and plain, wholesome chicken. I'm surrounded here by the healthy food I crave, even the tools I need to cook it, but

I have no way to make it happen. I'm back to the twenty dollar dinners and sodium-as-a-food-group fast food.

Ew.

But forget the produce. Forget the fresh stuff entirely. I'm on a mission here, to find Baltika Number 1. Baltika is the unofficial Russian national beer—the brand you find in specialty stores back home if you know where to look. I have a history with Baltika, and that elusive Number 1. There are nine different types of Baltika, some worse than others, from ales and lagers to non-alcoholic brews and the "9 Extra Lager." We tried eight of them one summer's evening back home—eight, because we couldn't find Number 1.

So we are sworn to that purpose: finding it here. Perhaps it is too rank even to dump on the Siberian market; perhaps too good for the brewmasters to relinquish. Perhaps it bestows immortality, or maybe the Germans stole the only recipe back in the long cruel winter of '44.

Who knows. It's not here, though, just two through nine. Back to the hotel...

* * * * *

I pass Josh on the way to our room; his dinner was alright, he said, and really cheap—its main virtue. He sits, smoking—since when?—with some locals in the hotel bar. I glanced at his drink menu, then the empty bottles on his table, and see where his savings went. "Want some chocolate?" he offers, handing me half a bar in a green foil wrapper. "It's got absinthe in it."

"Is that absinthe too?" I ask, nodding at his glass.

"Yeah," and he offers me a taste of the strange green liquor. I taste the drink, then the chocolate; yup. Absinthe-y.

I head up to the room; I don't drink at hotel prices. He turns back to his newfound friends and picks up wherever he left off.

Gulaged...

There isn't much reason to visit Perm, except the ballet, and they're out of town this week. There are no hostels. The locals wonder why we're here.

We came to see the Perm 36 Gulag. We took a minibus to Chusavoy, the next town over, then a taxi out into some country that would be pretty if not for the wooden prison we came to visit.

Josh put it best a minute ago, slowly ambling around the lane inside the gates: isolation. The word has a cold echo in the isolation rooms—concrete cells with wooden doors so heavy they block out sound, tiny windows too high up to see out from. Isolation—in a square, stone room with a drain hole in the corner for a toilet, a heavy wooden cot chained to the wall, and no hope of escape. The Soviets learned from the Nazis, and built their gulags like smaller, wooden Dachaus.

There is a high wooden fence around the gulag to keep prisoners isolated—from what, who knows. A sparring amount of barbed wire tops the fence, because of the rows and layers of wire inside, out of sight from the world beyond. Just an inch-thickness of Siberian timber, and a few strands of wire, made a cage in which so many died.

A few buildings stand near the gulag, old wooden things that have been there for a long time, but not forever; they remember the days when political prisoners were dumped here to be forgotten and die quietly, but theirs are not the kind of walls that talk. There's a new-ish school, but that's the only recent construction; no demolition or abandoned buildings, either. This tiny village, half an hour from Chusavoy, doesn't seem to have been affected when the gulag closed down in the '80s—like its walls worked both ways.

If a prisoner escaped the barbed wire and searchlights, dodged the guards' bullets from the watchtowers, they would merely escape into a vacuum—nothing but western-Siberian trees and cool summer, frozen winter weather as far as the strongest man can run. The villagers knew better than to aid escaped prisoners, lest they suffer far worse than mere incarceration.

I could be perfectly happy in this wilderness for quite awhile with my framepack full of clothes and a tent, a little food, some matches and a hatchet. But after being fed only a thousand calories a day in the gulag, and carrying no food and dressed in thin cotton clothes, no prisoner would last long out under the stars. Chusavoy is several days away on foot; anywhere else is even farther. Perhaps that deterred escape more than barbed wire.

Isolation—no contact with the outside world, and nowhere even to escape to.

Facing the collapse of their empire, the Soviets ordered the KGB to destroy the gulags—in case any of their leaders would be hunted and tried in Nuremberg for the unsavory things they'd done in the name of Mother Russia. So the evidence burned down, fell over, and was bulldozed into the swamp…except Perm 36, and I have no idea why. Sometimes these things just happen.

A historical society maintains this gulag as a monument to Soviet political oppression and brutality. Even as the Nazi concentration camps were being liberated in central Europe, the Russians were building similar things throughout Siberia. They didn't gas millions, and wholesale executions were exceptions to crueler norms—millions were incarcerated during the Soviet Era and then systematically worked to death.

But the principle was roughly the same: undesirables, inconvenient people, political opposition, intellectuals who got in the way of doctrine or defied orders, artists and other miscreants who wouldn't work or follow the rules and norms…they were loaded onto the Trans Siberian Railroad and shipped off to the gulags.

Punishments had little to do with crimes. Speaking against the government in public, or being turned in on rumor of doing so in private, garnered a nasty fine for those who paid the right bribe as well. Everyone else was sent to Perm 36, or another gulag, for thirty years of hard labor beside murderers and spies and poets. Concentrated in these camps, dissidents and common criminals were removed from the Soviet machine and put to work felling trees, hewing lumber, digging train tunnels and laying tracks… rendering materials and creating infrastructure for the good of Soviet Russia—paying their "debt" to the cause.

Ukrainian poet and political dissident Vasyl Stus was named a candidate for the Nobel Prize in Literature the year he was beaten to death by guards in that building over there.

* * * * *

There are three people working here today: a man in the guard tower by the front gate, a woman in an office, and the portly baboushka showing us around the buildings and providing an absolutely riveting historical narrative. She points out rooms and buildings, lanes and trenches, explaining the significance of each in minutia and broad historic context—I think. She doesn't speak English, but that doesn't slow her down at all. We get the drift readily enough from displays and the general sense about this place, despite English being rare on signs. This museum is intended for Russian students to see the horrors of man's inhumanity to man, as enabled by corrupt ideology…except that most people our age don't care a whit about that. Indeed, we're the only ones visiting today, and the nearest date in the visitor's log was three weeks ago.

I imagine that any Russian old enough to remember the gulag's threat probably has sufficient psychic scars to stay away from here forever. Chusavoy is pretty far away from the Trans Siberian stop in Perm, which itself isn't terribly popular. Perm 36, even after the fall of Communism and now in the internet and mass-transit age, is still isolated and obscure. This is a shame.

I read about gulags in history books; but I read about concentration camps first. After a chapter on Auschwitz, a few paragraphs on gulags didn't sound so bad—thirty year sentences, after which you're done? No institutionalized slaughter, just three decades cutting wood in the fresh air? Terrible, yeah, but not too bad in context—the Diet Coke of evil.

Then I came here. Whole. Different. Story.

Degradation World Tour…

Back in high school we joked about taking a spirit quest, one of those trips into the great unknown where you expect to be tossed and pummeled by fate and have your old world view smashed at your feet and replaced with true understanding. The kind of thing you hope to learn from, because the process isn't much of a reward in itself. It's an old Native American tradition, the spirit quest in the wilderness…but now we have planes and trains and insurance, so it's tempting to arrange something a bit more comfortable, a bit more exotic, than just wandering into the woods with a hatchet and plenty of time to kill. The modern equivalent, for people our age, is to backpack around Europe, or volunteer in Africa…even trek across the Sonora Desert with a tin cup and a pocketknife in a "wilderness survival" school.

We're on such a trip now, but years ago Josh and I joked about a very different plan: the "Degradation World Tour." We wanted to turn the fluffy-self-discovery notion on its ear. Leave the pampered luxury of St. Louis suburbia for its polar opposites. Start in Auschwitz, we said, then "diplomatically observe" our way through one of the regular flare-ups in Gaza, thumb our way south through Darfur, hop a flight to Cambodia and finish off at the Khmer Rouge's killing fields. Then we might have some perspective; some insight; some understanding of human nature just as real, and just as opposite, as whatever you get out of playing drums in a village in the Peace Corps.

It was the sort of unromantic anti-adventure that boys joke about, and then grow into men and forget all about it before realizing how absurd and offensive the childish fantasy sounds.

We haven't forgotten about the "Degradation World Tour," though the irreverence of our adolescent joke has a strange new sourness. We sought out Perm 36, going out of our way to seek this gritty, unpleasant side of history—possibly to bear witness, possibly to record the grim side of human nature lest we all go merrily blind on pop-culture Kool-Aid; maybe we're just sick after all. But the purpose of preserving places like Perm 36 is to remind the future of the lessons learned by spilled blood and past terror—to avoid more of the suffering endured already.

Maybe under childish bravado we knew that long ago—that we must preserve lessons from the worst, along with celebrations of the best. Not for balance, per se, but to avoid repeats of history's darker chapters.

Now the trendy travelers rave about Moscow and its fashion scene, about the music in Berlin and the clubs coming up in Tel

Aviv, but these places have unpleasant lessons and warnings in the shadows behind the neon. Buy into the new wave without knowing where it came from, and the ruined lives invested in warning you are wasted. All the pretty flowers grow from dirt— the mulch of dead things.

* * * * *

Josh wants to leave. I can't stop taking pictures, framing the courtyard through the guard tower windows, capturing a hopeful sky framed in rusted barbed wire. This is an evocative place and I could pack emotions into pixels all day with morbid content. He can't handle the vibe much longer, and I can see it.

He wandered around the buildings and the brick kiln, and sat for awhile in eerie silence in an isolation cell, where he ate an ironic candy bar. "This is so wrong," he said, "but it tastes so good to eat a Twix in a gulag." Despite his gallows humor, and perhaps in light of it, I can see on his face the psychic toll the place takes on him. Coming out of the "punishment cells," he wore the exact same I don't want to deal with this, and might not even acknowledge its reality scowl I know from hard-faced Russian strangers.

It's the scowl of a person who saw too much and will never be able to forget it. Josh has been to the killing fields in Cambodia, handled the disarmed mines and talked to one-legged volunteers about the families they watched get murdered; I wonder if this is familiar territory for him, however traumatic the familiarity. Russia is a pretty big downer so far. I hope Perm 36 is the nadir— nowhere to go but up, if so.

"Come on man," he says testily, "let's go."

Be careful what you wished for as a kid.

Big fish stories…

I wasn't hungry at Perm 36, but now back at Chusavoy it's long after a lunch that never happened and I could eat anything— even borscht, of which I have an unnatural beet-based fear. We wander the bazaar near the minibus stop in search of food. There are clothing stalls and people selling shoes from tables under tarps, in the Chinese Bazaar style, and a number of permanent shops in long buildings. The only restaurant has a picture out front of shish kebabs and fish. Few people speak English around here, so I take a picture of the sign and walk inside.

When I raise my camera, the woman at the counter freaks out and starts screaming and waving a baseball cap at me like a sword. Chill Mellow Yellow… I turn the camera around, lens facing me, hitting the "play" button. A picture of her picture of shish kebab appears on the screen. Mmmm, I say, pointing at the screen, then my belly.

Oh.

Nyit! she spits in the native fashion.

"I think they're out," Josh says in that slow, teacherly way he doesn't realize is condescending. "We'll get you food somewhere else." Perhaps it's from being a teacher, or maybe the roles we play now, but the grammatical subtleties poke at my irritable mood. We'll get food means we're in it together; but when he says we'll get you food, in that tone especially, there's an uncomfortable distance between us that stands me apart as a weak link.

Weakness—my greatest embarrassment…

Or maybe I'm just irritable; it snuck up on me. I shouldn't be this quick to anger, yet I am.

Wandering on, we find an outdoor supply shop that sells fishing supplies, pellet guns, small outboard motors, scooter parts, and knives. Not good knives, but good looking knives in cheap generic boxes. The man at the counter speaks passable English and revels in the chance to show it off, cracking jokes (I think) and asking where we're from. San Luis! he says. Good!

"I fish," I say, pointing to the board on the wall where anglers staple yellowing Polaroid pictures of themselves holding stringers heavy with fish. "Bass," I continue, puffing up my chest and lowering my voice, "this big." I hold my hands two inches apart. He cracks up and points to a picture of himself with a shiny silver fish bigger than anything I've seen short of the display wall at Bass Pro Shops. We ooh and aah appropriately, and return to staring at the knives. He hands Josh a comically oversized lock blade; I point approvingly at a butterfly knife, the kind where the blade hides down in the handles that swing apart three hundred and fifty some degrees. I play with it, doing a few tricks I learned when I should have been studying in college.

"You like?" he asks. The fighting knife in my waistband beats this low-grade Chinese junk in every way, except it's pretty, so I say very good, thank you and hand it back. "No, no," he says. "Send photo from America," pointing at his wall. "Send photo for me." Josh gets to keep his knife, too, and the sheet of paper on which the man writes his name and address in Cyrillic. We make a promise we fully intend to keep, and walk out smiling—our day has completely turned around. All it took was free weapons.

One-day friends bearing gifts...

Josh plans to skip dinner, as well as lunch; I'm ready to sign away my future children for a good fajita with extra peppers. This restaurant is way fancier and more expensive than it looked outside, but that's alright—by which I mean we're the only customers, our waitress is gorgeous, and she's very eager to practice her English. Each meal she describes sounds better than the last, and I ignore the hand-written translation she wrote and slipped into the menus, closing my eyes and letting her guide my lunch fantasies.

The lamb with roasted potatoes in an herb crust sounds amazing; so does the asparagus side and the bread, the potato soup with the cream and chives... Russian food so far has been unimpressive, but if the cook can deliver on her promises I may never leave.

I fall for the lamb, if not her accent also, and Josh says make that two. I talk him out of it so we can try a wider range. He thinks that's a good idea—I shouldn't feel this flattered—and orders the next thing she mentions, a beef dish with tomato soup. She keeps my coffee cup full with real coffee, our table stocked with bottled water, and has one of the kindest dispositions I've ever met in a waitress.

Our dinner showcases Russian culinary potential; as a one-off dinner mid-Trans Siberian Odyssey, it's like a peek at Heaven on your walk through Newark. For dessert, she brings an oversized book of prints by a famous Russian photographer who invested a hundred full-color pages documenting the changing seasons and light in the Ural Mountains. They are among the best color landscapes I've ever seen, and bound in a fantastic hardcover. "You like?" she says, and my heart clings to the edge of a precipitous drop—we're the only ones in here. The only way she can make up for this slow afternoon is to warm up two tourists and then rip them off on a souvenir. My hackles are suddenly on high alert, blood quickly boiling. She reads my fear and anger and says "if you like, it is my gift."

"Gift?"

"Yes. You are photographer, so I think you like this to remember Ural region. Really, a gift if you like it."

"I can't pay for it."

"Oh," she says, flirting, "silly American. Do you ever pay for gift?" Sure enough, both our hearts just melt. I have her sign her name and a short inscription on the title page, and we head off to the bus stop with two free knives, two full bellies, an amazing book, and one-day friends we will never forget.

The great absinthe bender…

On the minibus back to Perm, I watch the Nicholas Cage movie "Lord of War" dubbed in Russian. I don't understand a single word, but I watch it for the gorgeous cinematography, and to try to piece the story together…and because the highway looks like any country road back home. I still feel a little guilt when I turn away from the unique place around me, to some electronic or other distraction—like I'm turning my back on an opportunity. Like I'm electing to miss part of the trip.

But it's getting easier, a sign that I've fallen into the groove of being rootless.

I'd like to see this movie in English; without words, going just by camera angles and body language, facial expressions and cinematography, it looks like a scathing indictment of war in general and arms-based profiteering in particular. It's rather heavy-hitting, and with Perm 36 behind us and one of Russia's premier military-industrial cities ahead, it's prescient...and irksome.

Back at the hotel we change into our last clean clothes, having not done laundry since Ulan Bator. I can get two days out of one pair of boxers, four days from a pair of socks, and I've worn the same pants every day for a month. That's how we pack light, and we're used to it...but tonight we dress to the nines—we're going clubbing.

Yesterday I bought a half-size bottle of absinthe, the kind with thujone extracted from wormwood—the "real stuff," like what made Picasso go mad and drove a generation of writers into the sort of insanity I admire. They drank in Parisian cafés, while we're on the edge of Siberia, but that's fine—we are men of the occasion, wherever the occasion finds us. Tonight, it finds us sitting on the floor between our beds, trying to light an absinthe-soaked sugar cube on fire.

One incorrect way to drink absinthe, I've heard, is to put the sugar cube on a slotted spoon, over the mouth of a glass, and slowly pour the liquor over it until the sugar completely dissolves. This method requires enough room-temperature absinthe to kill a rhinoceros. The proper way is to do that for one shot, then again for three to five shots of water, recirculating the beverage until the sugar is gone. Naturally, the idea of diluting the absinthe appalls us.

Or, we could set the cube on fire, which we figure will at least be more entertaining; with 140 proof booze, that shouldn't be hard.

It's not.

The sugar turns black and drops from the blade of my butterfly knife into his metal travel thermos, setting the inside on fire. We smother it with the lid. Mom would be proud.

And so begins the Great Absinthe Bender.

* * * * *

Josh walked past this club yesterday, and leads us right back like a dog coming home. We smile at face control, who bars the way. Nyit! None shall pass!

Josh gives up without trying, in a way that suggests he has a plan; for the moment, that plan involves the Korean-style karaoke bar next door. I stay outside the club, chatting up some college girls who look like they should speak English. They don't. Awkward…

Abraham Lincoln was the "Great Negotiator." With him at that end of the spectrum, you can find me just about as far on the other side of cool. But every now and again, fate lets me slip one past the goalie. "You speak English?" I ask the bouncer, in English.

"Da." Yes.

"V'punyamiatsun pangleski?" I ask—do you speak English?— in Russian.

"Yes." Da.

We've described a circle. Time for the kill. "So can my buddy and I please go inside? It's cold out here."

"Nyit!"

"What if I come back in five minutes?"

"Da." Really? "Bring friend." Cool.

Five minutes into the bar, Josh is already friends with a drunken Asian man, and is "re-imagining" the Bangles' song "Walk like an Egyptian." The absinthe has clearly taken hold, and the locals are eating up his performance like candy coated valium. He could be at this all night. The song finishes and I give him the good news. "Dude, we're in." He isn't interested.

"This is Roger," he introduces, using the man's English name, "and this is…"

"Petrov," blurts a surly looking Russian on Josh's other side.

"They bought me this round," Josh says, obliged to stay. "They're good guys. You should drink with us." Already deep into drink-swapping with the locals…and he's been here five minutes?

And fired out a Bangles song with a head full of absinthe?

My friend is a drunkard savant.

"Dudeman, we're in, we've gotta go before the bouncer changes his mind." It takes Josh another song, Berlin's "Take my

Breath Away" of all horrors, some more cajoling and a parting round for Petrov—who physically grabs Josh and says you don't leave, we have good time—before we're out one door and in through another.

After today's emotional rollercoaster, I could use a distraction. Not being a club guy is the best reason to hit a Russian club—to really challenge my comfort levels. Absinthe seems necessary for this, and who are we to argue?

The bartender pours a splash of the potion in each of two goblets, spreads two napkins on the bar, swirls the booze and sets it on fire. Then he turns the flaming goblets mouth-down on the napkins while pouring us shots of straight green fairy. He bends two straws, lifts the goblets just a little and urges us to stick them underneath and suck out the scorching fumes. They taste like burning turpentine and don't smell much better as I exhale through my nose. After that, the straight shots aren't half bad—a little heavy on the fennel, really heavy on the aftertaste.

The club has four rooms, divided into two levels, with a wall separating the bar from the dance floor. Upstairs on the far side is a lounge area overlooking the thronging mob and the t-shaped stage cutting out into the masses—I'm up here where it's a little quieter, and I can see everything pulsing and gyrating below. There are cages on each side, open at the backs, with go-go girls doing painfully slow stripteases. Granted there's tease in striptease, but we're of the internet generation—scroll down real quick, hit fast forward, skip to the good stuff and move on, an entire body ogled and forgotten just that fast. Not so in real life, and not so in the cages, the tease so slow that empires can rise before their micro-skirts fall.

There are plush couches with liquor stains you can't see in the darkness, bodies writhing on the dance floor like tubeworms in a current, gyrations timed to the techno songs that change seamlessly, the beat carried on by the house DJ in a booth in the corner. We're the least-fashionably dressed; I'm the least-shaven, and in general, have no idea why the bouncer even let me in. Because I'm American, and that's a novelty? Perhaps; I'll take it. Whatever it was, I'm happy to be loopy in a sea of Perm's prettiest twenty-somethings while fairies dance in cages. Wherever Josh is in that seething madness, I hope he finds a more interesting place to sleep tonight than alone in the bed beside mine.

Perm and my existential crisis...

The blues—a hockey team in St. Louis, a music style, and a metaphor for despair. How many songs start with a gravelly voice singing I've got the blues so bad, uh-huh... But the songs don't make you feel so bad—they make you feel so good, those tales of ire and woe with the hopeful voices and the dirty, beautiful music reminding us that life goes on despite the troubles. It's good music, about bad things—an exorcism of the demons, such that you know the guy feels better for getting that off his chest; better out than in, right? Giving voice to the blues is salvation set to music.

I can't sing; for a harmonica, I have a pen. Life doesn't unfold like a path drawn on tourist maps; it's an adventure, best enjoyed when you're open to spontaneity and wandering around interesting places others might not go. Want to get out of the grooves? Get off the sidewalk.

But even amidst adventure I can't shake this funk that's been dogging me since Beijing, so I grab my camera and do a little Zen Navigation—an idea I stole from the Douglas Adams novel I read on the train. In Zen Navigation, I clear my mind of all hopes and desires and wants and needs, trying to ignore any hunger or curiosity or concept of how the city is laid out, and then—devoid of internal stimulus as much as possible—I slowly open my mind to ethereal suggestion.

It's very, very foofy, but I do it in combat boots, which balances things.

Something amazing happens when I Zen Navigate—I actually feel compelled to walk in some direction, and invariably, something interesting happens. In a busy city with shops and restaurants and parks and trams clanging through the streets, something is bound to happen wherever I go, but...the payoff is more special than chance alone could deliver.

At the least, it's an exercise in leaving the fugue behind—a little urban meditation. Sometimes from that clear mind-state I think of something and let that idea turn itself over and around until I feel compelled to walk somewhere, and—no, really—every single time I find what I'm looking for.

It's kind of creepy.

Today I just want something to photograph, something that teaches me about Perm…and in the process, rediscover that lust I have for traveling. Off to the river I go, along Komsomol'skiy Prospekt all the way to the concrete stairs leading down a knoll. I follow my impulse, ignoring the Museum of Arts and the teenagers binge drinking on benches (it's barely after lunch). A trail branches off from the sidewalk—it's just a narrow swath of bare ground where the grass has been trampled into submission, leading to a stand of trees. Here I find a fire pit and a giant mound of plastic Oxhota beer and vodka bottles, broken glass bottles…a hobo camp? The nocturnal hangout for those teens drinking above? It's an eyesore, and not very well hidden…further suggestion where none is needed that there is little entertainment for the locals beyond the Bolshoi and alcoholic oblivion.

I cross some railroad tracks and follow a trail through more trees, then wander through a park and along a sidewalk down by the water. A family sits, young father, young mother, baby, on steps at the water's edge—not playing, just sitting quietly together staring out at the far shore. They're all scowling, of course. Even the baby scowls, but I'm learning to sense the moods underneath—they're wistful. Maybe longing for something lost—childhood? Innocence? A job?—or maybe for something on the way, like another child…who knows what really fills another man's heart?

On down the sidewalk, to a restaurant—too expensive for me—and through their parking lot, down a gravel road, to a hardware store that sells concrete lawn fountains and landscaping material. I go inside, a white guy in a white guy's country attracting a strange amount of attention for reasons I don't understand—I'm unshaven, yes, but even at that I don't look different in any truly outstanding way. They must know I'm different somehow, perhaps with that intuition a duck has for finding his flock on a crowded lake.

I grew up rehabbing old houses with my father, fixing and building things in our workshop, and playing with power tools. Hardware stores for me are like creeks for salmon—an old way home—so it's strange to see the Russian electrical plugs on familiar tools, the prices in rubles thirty five times higher than in dollars back home, and familiar brand names rendered in Cyrillic. It doesn't feel like every other hardware store I've ever been in, the way stores feel back home, and I'm not sure what's so remarkably different. Maybe the expectation, or the possibility—between my workshop and the hardware stores back home I can build anything. Here, on the road, there is nothing I need to build, and nothing to build with—things here are just parts and pieces on display, rather than components in something I have the means to bring to life.

The shop next door has a buxom silhouette on a sign adorned with hearts and arrows; I stick my head inside and, sure enough, just what I expect: walls covered in dildos and shrink-wrapped lube, dirty DVDs stacked high. Some things you find everywhere—booze, hardware stores, and sex shops. With the ammo factories and jet flyovers, the military history displays and museums too, Perm is a strip club shy of a testosterone meltdown.

But Perm doesn't do much for me. Today's meandering tour brought me in touch with familiar things in foreign contexts, and gave me some perspective I didn't know I wanted…but there's still a void in my heart and I'm not sure what it needs to feel full again. Maybe to be in motion; maybe adventure. I snap a few pictures of a crumbling train station long out of service, catch a bridge lit up in late afternoon splendor, and wander back to the hotel; maybe Josh wants to get dinner. I don't want to be social, but I'm not really in the mood to eat alone.

* * * * *

In no rush to get back, I Zen Navigate through a park with a glorious fountain glowing at the trailing edge of the "photographer's golden hour," that time just before the sunset where the sun's long rays coat everything in a warm amber veneer. I work the angles, freezing the water in mid air with fast shutter speeds, stretching it into frothy honey-milk with long exposures, catching the light from every angle as it cascades over bronze sculptures. This is how I enjoy photography, using it to deconstruct both space and time—a few degrees per image; a little piece of history. If a photograph is a moment saved forever, a long exposure is a minute, a full memory with motion and change that looks different the way a day is different than an hour. I see things with photography that I can't with my eyes alone; it becomes a focused meditation and the world outside the frame just goes away.

So I'm startled when two girls speak to me in Russian. Ny'punya…

"Oh," one says. "You are English?"

"American," I say. They titter.

"You like to make photos?" Yes. "Make photo of us?" Sure.

Their backs are to the sunset, so I turn them around and pose them to get the golden glow on their blonde hair, on the one girl's blue eyes to make them sparkle like the water dancing in the fountain behind her; I carefully search the ground I'll have my back towards while distracted, in case this is a setup. Click.

"Tourist?" she asks.

"Journalist." They titter again, and I take another picture, then show it to them on the LCD screen. While they're distracted, I look around again for anyone approaching; no pickpockets, no one in my blind spots. Maybe they're just friendly after all.

"What magazine?" National Geographic, I lie; someday, if I'm lucky, maybe… "Oh really!" their eyes are all hope and awe. "You like Perm?" Yes, I lie again, the women are very beautiful. That part is true.

They giggle and walk away, their English expended and my mood lifted for the moment. It's nice talking to cute girls, to see twinkling eyes and smiles burst from scowls like April flowers, and to have an actual exchange with a stranger that isn't a come-on or setup. Everybody wants something, but sometimes a cute girl being curious is just a cute girl being curious.

I give a wide berth to a group of teenage soccer hooligans

singing wild drunken songs in a pack; not wide enough, though. One of them comes towards me, making eye contact; I sling my camera across my body, tucked under an arm where it can't be grabbed, right hand empty for fist, or knife, or to shake hands with the stranger. I shake hands. He speaks to me in Russian, then in English.

"Football fan?" No. "Perm has great football team!" Really, that's nice. I walk away but the rest of the mob surrounds me, laughing and singing; it's cool to be in the center of a drunken, screaming football mob, if for the novelty alone. I can feel the fraternity around me, the safety in numbers, except—it's theirs. I'm the outsider, and now I'm surrounded. I dodge out of the pack, dogged by its leader.

"Drink with us, friend!"

"Yes!" scream two more, "drink!" Then they launch off into a song, the mob behind and around me like a horseshoe. They can't get the camera, they can't get my wallet in its hidden pocket, but…I'm in no mood to deal with whatever else they have in mind. "That shop!" the leader says, "we must drink together! Buy first round, we drink with you, friend! Buy a lot! That shop, right there…" I begin the standard evasion—I have no money, but I'll drink with you, lads, you get the first round and I'll wait here. Teach me a song, I say, but get me a drink first, yes, I'll be right outside. They've hustled me across the street now, in front of the corner shop, heavy traffic on two sides.

Then a car balks, considering a left turn or a lane change, creating a small gap in the traffic and I dart across at top speed. The gap closes behind me, cars honking, but I'm gone and safe on this side of vehicular pandemonium. I lock eyes across the busy street with the thwarted pack leader, and see the sort of malice I feared.

They amble down the sidewalk and back towards the fountain while I laugh with long and jeering relief.

* * * * *

"Any ideas?" Josh says, staring at the intersection of Lenina and Komsomol'skiy.

"Adventure food," I say. "A little Zen Navigation." We walk back towards the club, then take a right down a narrow side street where someone sculpted a one-third scale ship bursting out through a ground floor wall. There are cannonballs imbedded in the brick and a crow on the mast, but no sign or explanation. In Perm, it makes as much sense as anything.

"What'd you see today?" I ask.

"Just wandered around, you know. Saw some art, the cannon park..."

"Any good?"

"Lotta cannons." Then, "You?"

I tell him about the girls and the soccer hooligans, but he's unimpressed. "They just wanted to drink with you, man." Right... How can two people see the same thing so differently?

Or maybe he doesn't; maybe he's offering me a revisionist perspective couched as correction, a dubious goal—if we lie our way into painting a happy past, what blindness lies ahead?

Maybe the look on the pack leader's face was Russian for rejection; maybe he was pouting.

Nah. I like my history authentic.

There are restaurants clustered in this part of town: a fancy Italian place, a sushi place (this far from the ocean? No thanks), several cafeterias with buffet-style self-service... "Anything?" he asks.

"Nope." We cross a street, and then—I see it. I have no idea what the sign says, but it's down a staircase along a gorgeous brick wall, box planters hanging on the wrought iron fence around the stairwell, there's a Greek theme to the Cyrillic sign... "Athena's Café," maybe. "That," I say with conviction, "is where we're going."

"Cool."

The waitresses all wear togas—classy, classic-style togas with golden cords around their waists and olive wreaths in their hair. White and green sheets hang from the domed brick ceiling in this centuries-old basement; vines grow up the exposed brick walls, quiet Mediterranean music seeps from hidden speakers, the tablecloths are fine, white and expensive, and everything is clean and ethereal. It's heaven in a restaurant. I'm still grouchy and depressed, but much less so now.

Our waitress is a siren, a Russian blonde in a Roman toga with a leather-wrapped menu in one hand and a bottle of wine in the other, the angel I need right now. No wine, though; Josh talks me into a beer, a Belgian bottle served cold in a goblet that helps it breathe. We stumble through terrible mispronunciations of the menu, lauding this and damning that like two old critics on the town. It's great sport making fun of words you can't pronounce, and it's nearly fun, but then it wears off and I'm no better for it.

"What do you need, man?" he asks.

"Lamb and a lot of veggies."

"No, like really—what's going on with you?"

"I've got some stuff to work out," I say; I kind of want to punch him in the face for his impertinence, but the anger and impulse are gone as quick as they came. He cares, after all, and that's a comfort. "I'm doing it, working it out and such. Slowly, but it's coming." Josh had his meltdown in Irkutsk, when he threw his hands up in surrender to fate and embraced self-destruction at the club. Now it's my turn to wonder wide-eyed about the future and recoil from the harsh country around us, but it's hard to stay depressed in this restaurant. I try, I really do, but everything is perfect, and a few sips into the Belgian double-bock I'm able to check my baggage at the door.

"This isn't what I was expecting," I say. "I thought it would be a vacation."

"The Trans Siberian sucks," he says. "Not what I expected either, but hey—it beats working." We toast that truth and for a glorious moment feel just how lucky we are.

It's three in the morning and I can't sleep.

Now it's eleven, with noon coming up fast, and I haven't slept—not really—just closed my eyes to the passage of time. Nothing refreshing, nothing reinvigorating. I don't like Russia, and can't recommend it for tourism, though Lake Baikal's luxury hotels and expensive tourist traps are superb for those with more dollars than sense. I lose another night on this crazy junket with every twenty dollar meal, but can't live on cup-o-soup and raw vegetables. Moreover, that golden promise of a new beginning just over the horizon feels less like a viable plan and more like a gilt fairytale—alluring, but unrealistic. It's closer than before, but feels farther than ever from being obtainable.

I was doing better until the incident with the lunch lady, that random act of violence and hate right in my most vulnerable moment, and now I'm pickling in a morose state that surprises Josh. He can't deal with it, or else, doesn't want to; I can't blame him—why let someone else bring you down in the midst of adventure?—but at the same time, I'd appreciate a bit of compassion.

That, and strangling the Joshua Teacher right out of my old friend's voice. You don't mind the little things until they become daily irritations in cramped quarters.

I'm lashing out now, cruelly, because it feels nice to a sick soul. This lack of energy baffles me; my apathy, this depression. It feels a bit like homesickness, which I don't normally get on the road (too many things to see, do, eat, try…). My appetite has changed from gluttony to fasting and back again, stuffing myself some days and, others, barely eating; today I didn't even feel like getting out of bed, though each day is a precious gift that holds adventure if only I would roll off the mattress and crawl out into the sunlight. In my futile attempts to email home, I expend great time and prose without saying much of anything—eloquence without substance. Noise in a vacuum.

The dignified course, as I'm learning, is to say nothing—at least until which point as I have something otherwise useful, or at least entertaining, for others to read. It's well after noon now, and I scribble these notes half-heartedly, alternately staring at a novel I don't like. I'm not really reading it—there is no movie in my mind, no characters moving through the scenes as their destinies unfold…just words I forget as quickly as I read them. They keep other thoughts at bay, and their hollow sound pushes back against my doubts and fears about the future.

How will I make my living in New York? How will I provide for my fiancée, and lay the groundwork for building the family we want? I love my freedom as a bachelor—here I am in Russia on a glorified lark—and the freedom of freelance sports writing, with its abundant travel and ability to chase which assignments I want and work anywhere in the world…but the bottom is beginning to fall out of that market, and even in good times it can't support two people. Status quo is no longer good enough. Other jobs don't interest me, and their concomitant lack of freedom is appalling.

Growing up sucks.

I thought I was all grown up in college—drinking, carousing, sleeping around. I got some writing work to support an enormous apartment and all my bills, doing all these things adults do, and loved it. I thought I was there, that I had arrived.

Nope.

Then in grad school, more of the same. I'm not an undergrad, I said. I have a more expensive apartment, more writing jobs, school, older friends…now I'm an adult, and it's pretty cool.

Wrong again.

The nineteen year old corporal, married with a kid back home in Georgia while he dodges mortar fire in Kabul, has done a lot more growing up than me despite my extra years. I'm still play acting…and why can't I stretch it a little farther? Why can't I venture into the real world, snatch my girl, and carry her back into my weird post-college stasis? Why can't we have it all?

Last night I prayed for help finding answers to my questions, and for serenity while I searched. The prayer was answered immediately: this is the very business I set out to work on—the heart of the trip, the center of the story, an existential crisis between two paradigms…just as I had advertised.

I billed this trip to friends, family, and editors as a personal journey from youth into adulthood. While Josh was carousing around downstairs again last night, running through his money at the hotel bar, I was having just the sort of growing pains I asked for.

I'm past the mid-point of this quest—there isn't enough odyssey ahead to keep the real world at bay. I see a great, dark cloud ahead, with my fiancée glowing warm and radiant in the middle. There will be time enough to figure things out, to carpe the hell out of some diems, but for now that world is terrifying and I swear I can see the Manhattan skyline looming just ahead of us...

Not coming this way again...

Goodbye, Perm. We're at the station catching the Trans Siberian to Moscow. Each arrival is like a chicken waking, memory-erased, to a brand new day. Each farewell is an opportunity to let go and have the pieces fall where they may behind us. We're leaving Perm with a kick in the ass and no hard feelings.

Maybe that's cheating—using a change of venue to cinch one time and start the next one clean and fresh, but we do it. Every New Year's Eve we welcome a virgin year chubby and ripe with possibility and hope. We even make resolutions that the next year will be different; we'll be different; for the sake of Auld Lang Syne.

Sometimes it works.

Right where I need to be...

I wake up screaming, face to face with a Russian man sleep-scowling. Josh is asleep below me here in Car 16. Perhaps I was only screaming in my dream; I was definitely screaming there.

My father told me as a child, "There are two things no one ever really wants to hear about—movies you've seen, and dreams you've had." That was one of his hard and fast rules of human nature made up on the spot, applied to a single instance, and not intended to live on in my brain.

But maybe he was right. I'll take that risk...

While tucked precariously into a train bunk as wide as a knife's edge, my mind drifted back to my grandmother's home. My parents sat down with me to our regular Sunday dinner. "We're so glad you flew home for this," grandma said. I was shocked to be there, with Josh continuing our adventure alone. Why had I come home for dinner? It made sense in that way things work out in dreams, but I was horrified.

Over the first bites of comfort food, I felt my stomach and my spirits racing each other down a bottomless hole. Everything I talked about and hoped for on the trip, its implications and meanings—coming of age—had been seriously and irrevocably undermined.

Josh was poking around Perm 36 while I was eating roast beef with grandma. The sense of loss felt like abandoning a brother in the thick of things...and selling myself short in the process. I needed to work through the road-weariness and dissatisfaction, to master them and grow stronger...not bug out when it got tough.

It felt like pure cowardice. Moments before the strawberries and angelfood cake, I started screaming...

...which woke me up face to face with that Russian man snoring like he swallowed a chainsaw.

I've never been more relieved to be so far from home.

Top: **St. Basil's Cathedral in Red Square, by night**

Bottom: **Paintball tank at a secret facility**

Moscow, Russia
4 September, 2007

Moscow, Russia

Moscow remains the most free-wheeling city in
Russia; for the cynics there are no surprises, and for
the ambitious and connected there are no limits.

—Lonely Planet

Don't step in that man's last meal... Home, sweet hostel... My hero is a Dutch Tyler Durdan... The millionaire's lunch... Infiltrating the red parade... My kind of albino black-sheep... Brothers in Moscow...

Of the nine train stations in Moscow, we arrive in the Yaroslavsky Station, the Trans-Siberian hub. From here it's a quick hop to the subway, following Josh through the madding crowds of transients and travelers, morning-drunks and bleary-eyed backpackers, down a long escalator through a throbbing subway station, and then by subway through the tunnels with a crowd-muted swoosh.

We're right in time for Moscow's 860th birthday, which is counted from the date of its first mention in history: the record of a fabulous party thrown by Yury Dolgoruky in 1147. It was born as a hard-drinking party town on the eastern end of the Vodka Belt, suffered a lot of rough times[1], and gives every indication of honoring their roots—the event posters all over the place and the red eyes and bleary stares in the subway suggest a thriving midweek party scene.

We lurch into the Kurskaya Station, a stop on the blue subway line, with glorious marble architecture and high arched doorways. The colored tiles and stained glass, heavy blocks of fine marble under bright fluorescent lights, shame just about every subway terminal I've seen before. We take the escalator to the street, to a line of taxis we don't need. Not thirty feet away, I see a man passed out in a puddle of bloody vomit, red and orange goo dripping from his nose while his body convulses. His eyes are closed, his twitches the last acts of a man dying on the street in his own filth. A policeman stands a few feet away, staring off into space.

Home, sweet hostel...

Our hostel is near a small church, just off an avenue that leads straight to Red Square. A mile from the city center, we're

1   For my take on Russian History, see Appendix A

in a quiet neighborhood that has a shocking amount of traffic on the one-way streets hemming us in. Most of the people over forty have "the stare," the one that seemed noble on propaganda posters in the fifties; in real life, it looks hollow and defeated. Those under forty, the Cold War Children, wear either a hardened version of urban apathy or a blank look without expression at all. The people our age, young professionals, are well dressed by comparison to Perm—think New York's Upper East Side vs. the Soulard working class neighborhood in St. Louis.

I identify more with Soulard.

Someone painted a cartoon train beside the buzzer, the only indication that the Trans Siberian Hostel is in this building. The hallway has a hand-painted map leading upstairs, following a black line past red dots—Moscow by the door, to Perm and Irkutsk and Vladivostok upstairs. "Check it out man," Josh says, pointing out a few of the names, "We've been there."

"How cool is that?" You see some amazing things in retrospect—perspective we get in trade for being acutely aware of the diminishing time ahead.

My rule holds true—another hostel, another cute college-age girl working the desk, taking our passports, charging us to stamp our papers, showing us the kitchen and the dorm room with twelve beds and a large Russian man passed out face down on a mattress in the middle of the floor. Home, sweet hostel.

My hero is a Dutch Tyler Durdan...

The eastbound Trans Siberian line is more popular this week than the westbound line—half the people here have tickets to Vladivostok or China. The other half are just here "on holiday," as non-Americans refer to vacations. Two Dutch Brothers, as they refer to themselves, are retracing our route to Beijing. We sit in the kitchen, watching some television program on Russian fighter pilots, talking about the trip and giving them advice for the road ahead. Once you get tired of talking about home—about three weeks in—you start giving advice to anyone who'll listen.

Which is really annoying on the receiving end, but fun when

you're the offender.

The Dutch Brothers tell stories about their lives and hometown as a tag team, alternating quips and finishing each others' sentences. This would be mortifying for many of my friends with siblings, but par for the course with the Dutch Brothers; I don't suppose they'll have many problems getting along with each other in cramped quarters. They figured out a long time ago, they explain, how to get along together under one roof; as an only child, that's a whole skill set I've never learned.

Apparently having a brother comes in handy on the road—they've travelled together through seven countries this year alone.

"It's what people our age do," says Pim, the older brother, who has a rounder, more innocent face; the younger brother, Sander, has the lean face of a daredevil, and they both dress in black and white with dyed hair like heavy metal rock stars on tour. Incongruous to their appearance—that's just my bias—they are among the kindest people I've met. "On time off from school, we just travel," Sander chimes. "There's a law, where even if you work, you have to get a month off every year without being fired, and you can take, I think it is, six months or a year off once in your life and you can't be fired for it. Just tell 'em you're going, and go, and your job has to be there when you get back."

"Do you still get paid?"

"Oh no, not usually, but if you save up you can come back with nothing and it's okay 'cause you still have your job. Then it's life as usual. Everyone does it." He even draws money from the government, like a cross between welfare and a scholarship. So long as he's a student, he gets government assistance, much of which funds his adventures. "That's why there're so many students in Holland. There's no reason ever to quit!"

It must be nice.

Sander has a girl back home, and they're serious; she doesn't travel much, but that doesn't stop him from going abroad. It's part of life, and each lives, he says, as they see best. Since that's good enough for them, it's great for the relationship. Few worries; everyone does it. Poland for the weekend? No problem. Hop a flight to Helsinki? Sure, it's cheap from Amsterdam. Stay in hostels and you've got beer money on even a modest budget.

It's amazing—here's a lifestyle I've never encountered back home. Many of my friends have never left America, and some have never left the Midwest. Flights to the coasts are expensive, and then there are hotel bills and food, and what is there to do, really, when your friends are back home working? For the young traveler on a tight budget relying on public transportation, there aren't many places in America to go.

But we can hit Europe on thirty bucks a day once we get there; we can hop a four hour train and be in another country, or fall asleep in the train car and wake up on the other side of the continent...all without any planning whatsoever. For Europeans, it's just a few hours' ride back and they're home in time for work or classes on Monday. We just can't do that from St. Louis, unless you like taking the Greyhound to Effingham Illinois...

...but having Warsaw, Frankfurt, even Moscow, right there for a weekend getaway? That's a whole different world, with a totally different culture surrounding the freedom.

I know folks who work sixty hour weeks and make fun of the French for only working through Thursday. They can't imagine taking multiple weeks off in the summer, though that's normal in Europe. "No wonder it takes so long to get things done," they say, or, "look what we've accomplished in America in two hundred years—bettered Europe, and they've had centuries." Great. Thousands of Chinese worked themselves to death on the Great Wall to leave the world an enduring monument to...to... certainly not to the workers' quality of life.

I've got my head so wrapped around the idea of making money and supporting a family and building a name and...here's a guy my age and his kid brother who live on the dole and are kicking around Moscow for the hell of it—perpetual students with the easiest smiles and most genuine laughs I've found on the road. What, them, worry? I'm sure they do, about something, but... They're not locked into the American college-work-retire-regret-die formula.

Of which I no longer want any part. Maybe the cost of this "enlightenment" is ruin, but death is a certainty anyway and if I die smiling, what have I lost?

Christina is somewhere along the line, searching for brötchen and sausage, leaving tomorrow safely where it is while she enjoys today. Josh stepped quietly around the dying man this morning, and while I never want to be so callous as he appeared, I could stand to be more carefree—less affected by the world, perhaps, or at least the parts that drag me down.

I've learned how to haggle, how to escape drunk soccer mobs, how to ride like Genghis Khan...but I haven't learned yet how to sit back and let go—let the chips fall where they may, and let what doesn't matter truly slide.

Chuck Palahniuk wrote that about Tyler Durdan in "Fight Club." There's a character to look up to...but it worked for him. The book's protagonist was so caught up in his tiny little life, in making money and being the perfect adult, that he completely lost track of what really matters. Then he invented Tyler Durdan, the carefree alter ego that set him free...in a way.

Maybe I need an alter ego that is everything I want to be but can't—a James Dawson for everyday life. Or maybe I just need a good brushfire to clear the tangles from my mind. Then I can grow up on my own terms, embrace the adventure for what it is, and enjoy each day to the fullest like some lame aphorism come beautifully to life.

The Dutch Brothers do that every time they leave Holland— they leave behind whatever they have to do, and get on the road towards what they want to do...and that's alright. It's just a different way of living.

And it's incredibly refreshing.

The millionaire's lunch...

Tripping on youth and freedom, and that giddy sense of getting away with something that comes from freely wandering the streets on a work day, I Zen Navigate for lunch. Across town from the hostel, I find a place that has it all: roast chicken, braised pork, lamb, fish, salads, jiggling Jell-O desserts, macaroni, Baltika on tap, coffee and tea and ice cream...it's a high-class cafeteria just over a bridge from the Kremlin, and it caters to a well-dressed jet set on their lunch break. I go for the chicken and salad, some steamed veggies, avoid the borscht, and score a bit of fish in red sauce.

A cute brunette version of the cafeteria gremlins back home rings up my order, waggling her finger at each tiny dish. 1,000 rubles? More than thirty bucks US for a modest lunch? It's insane.

Welcome to the most expensive city on earth, or so say the groups that keep track of such things. It's a balanced lunch, yeah, but…that's excessive. I look around at the well-dressed diners with elegant shoes and briefcases, feeling acutely impoverished amid businessmen and women who dress the part of Moscow's new wave of executives and politicos—millionaires, not least of all because their rubbles are worth around thirty to the dollar.

The food is arranged on the ground floor beside a trendy dining space. An elegant stone-and-iron stairway leads up to the second floor bar with mezzanine seating. The place is packed on both levels, and I'm lucky to score a two-seater table with a view out the front windows, down over the two-way street thronging with shiny black sedans and people in suits and dresses bustling every which way. There's a McDonald's across the street, a Pizza Hut down the way, and a few local Russian restaurants…I thought this would be better than fast food, but cheaper than a table-service place. It's a cafeteria, after all.

Turns out that I'm eating authentic to the new Russian economy, well above my lowly station…and the food is amazing, even though it costs more than a night at our hostel. Another day on the trail, gone; the Baltika here is five bucks a pint, which is on par with bars in Manhattan. I certainly can't afford a night on the town here.

But the sun is warm and wonderful through the window, and this ranks among the best meals I've had on the road. If this is how Moscow eats, I'm in for a treat…and destitution.

Infiltrating the red parade…

I have no idea where I am, but I know how to get back—this

is how I like to explore. Even if I'm wrong, I have some rubles and the little black book. It's no problem to hail a cab and let him find the way; the better cabbies have GPS and in-dash navigation. Only the Koreans love high-tech gadgets more than Moscovites.

The sun pokes at the western horizon, looking for a soft place to bed down for the night. I hear brass instruments and percussion on the next street over. Then comes cheering, and between the buildings I see people walking through the streets carrying banners. They look happy. All the guidebooks say to stay away from demonstrations and rallies and large public gatherings... advice I'm incapable of taking.

They're all about my age, these girls with soft and hopeful faces and guys with angular brows and tight skin. They're dressed a little better than my fraternity t-shirt and black hiking pants, but ignoring that, they look just like me. My kind of people.

College kids.

They're marching through the closed-off streets behind banners that identify their departments, or maybe where they come from, in some kind of high-spirited collegiate parade; there are thousands of them, and the avenue is lined with people waving and cheering—not Thanksgiving Day Parade crowds, but about what you expect from a farm town at homecoming, spread thin along the route. There are waves and cheers and the band plays on.

So of course I slip in among them, quick-walking ahead to join a group that didn't see me cutting in from the sidewalk. We march and wave and smile to the people and cameras along the way. Where are we going? Who cares! What's the end of the line going to bring? I have no idea. Is it fun?

You know it.

My kind of albino black-sheep...

There was a Russian writer named Aleksey Maximovich Pyeshkov. As Samuel Clemens adopted Mark Twain, beloved Russian author Aleksey went by Maxim Gorky—"Gorky" being Russian for bitter. He was a favourite author of the Stalinists, and is considered the father of "Social Realism"—consider it the anti-fairytale style where real life is depicted in real ways...which sounds impossibly obvious, but even the most obvious things had to start sometime.

In 1892 he saw one of the first moving pictures ever presented in Russia, a video showing innocuous street scenes and people going about their daily lives in Paris. He commented, in Russian of course, to the effect that "moving pictures" were neat and all, but soon the dark side of human nature would drag the medium into portraying violence and indecency. He hit that one right out of the park—seventy nine years before Dirty Harry and the Spice Channel.

So I've got a lot of respect for him, and at the moment, this crazy parade I'm in is heading right for the park that bears his name. It's a low-standard amusement park with a large pond and small rides, some trees and food stalls, beer stalls and a giant stage. But I don't know that yet—I'm still in the crowd, making a right turn, looking at the thronging students behind me and the horde massed up front. Everyone has a little plastic card on a flimsy elastic string around their neck, and I'm sure the card is important. They have little flyers—schedules, maybe, or propaganda to save the albino black-sheep or who knows what—and buttons. I watch the street, picking up a barely-trampled button, a new-looking flyer, and when my herd yells and cheers and waves their signs, I yell and cheer and wave my flyer. I thrust my arm in the air so my button rattles and my voice joins their chorus.

Save the albino black-sheep! Love the outcasts who fit in!

In any crowd you'll have a couple people who lose all the things they're supposed to bring—forget their wallet, their papers, or, like some poor schmuck, lose his id card in the madness. It's around my neck now as our herd stampedes the park gates. A long line of guards give the once-over, checking cards, keeping out the interlopers, scrutinizing me, waving me through, and suddenly I'm inside the iron gate with my kind of people.

* * * * *

I'm scribbling on the back of that flyer, standing among three thousand, four thousand, five thousand college students, swaying rhythmically amidst the throng at an open-air pop concert in this park as the last of the parade stampedes through the gates. They're on the other side of the diploma from me, a threshold you can't cross backwards. I'm one of a very few "adults" here, if only because I call myself one, and certainly the only American. Russian pop doesn't sound that different from American pop, if you stand in front of the speakers and shake to the rhythm of drum machines and manufactured beats. Russian college kids look no different from those in America. I could be back at Westminster College, or Mizzou, or Dartmouth; but I'm in Gorky Park, in Moscow.

The giant stage glows pastel to match the singer's sequins and the outfits on her entourage—they dance and jiggle in all the MTV ways, and half the crowd eats it up. The other half is making out, texting, or laughing in cliques. I feel right at home. A cute brunette looks my way, catches my eye, and we smile at each other. She's standing in a group of girls, huddled for protection from boys, no rings on their hands; single. I'm engaged. You can't go home again. She turns back to the stage, and I turn back to writing.

* * * * *

I thought it would be high school graduation, but no, it was the first week of college that put the kibosh on my childhood—which sure beats taking mortar fire in Afghanistan, as some old friends of mine did when their lives switched over.

This trip is supposed to end-cap my college days, and start me on the red-necktie-road to adulthood. But on my first day in Moscow, I'm back in student mode, crashing a concert. Perm is a working man's town; Gorky Park tonight is college in all its glory, and I haven't felt this good in a long time. I'm dancing with kids I swear I know from somewhere, identifying with this mob I don't belong to anymore. But I suppose you never have to leave, not in your heart—how sad would it be, if everywhere we went, we had to leave completely?

I guess you have to move on; but you never have to forget.

Brothers in Moscow...

Josh is gone, off drinking with the Dutch Brothers; no email this evening from home, and my ears still ring from the concert. It's a perfect night for a run, to take this energy in my blood and fly through the streets without touching the pavement—never mind my boots clomp clomp clomping like hooves.

Ulitsa Maroseyka Street is quiet, with a few restaurant lounges open and fashionable women sipping neon drinks in the windows, and a snack shop carved just six feet deep into a building— little more than a display counter and a cash register and enough room to turn around. There's an all-night coffee shop on the corner with a logo ripped off from Starbucks...and similar prices on the menu posted in their window. I jog past at a dead sprint, filling my lungs with night air and enjoying the freedom in motion. It's after midnight, well after midnight, and the couples I dodge on the pavement are drunk and don't notice me until I dart past; I pass so close to them my flapping shirt sleeves brush shoulders, daring to see how close I can get unnoticed. I could run down the middle of this quiet street, but this is much more fun.

Red Square is beautiful at night—wide open and clean. St. Basil's Cathedral glows at the southern end, bright-colored and spotlighted onion domes alive and glossy. The Kremlin's red walls dominate the western horizon—long, clean lines leading to the Moscow River and Lenin's Tomb. In their stoic, soft-glowing smoothness I understand what it is to be a wall. I have no idea what is on the other side, and beyond Google Earth, I will never know; and that's alright. I can jog through the city's streets and I can run alongside that wall and never see, never know what it looks like on the other side, and still I'll have a helluva good time.

There are police on foot patrol who watch me run past, nothing in my hands, no women screaming about their purses; there are no other joggers and few pedestrians at this unholy hour, and nothing else to watch but me—some strange man in olive drab shorts and combat boots sprinting manically around the Kremlin at two-thirty. Tut, tut...aren't tourists strange?

Perhaps we are, but this fills my heart with joy. The city lights reflect on the river's edge as I sprint near the water, imagining myself a bird skimming low over the ripples. Lovers and conspirators whisper in the shadows in the parks around the Kremlin walls; they understand the night. Gorky Park is probably still full of students, the ones who feel in their bones that these are moments to savour until the sun comes up and forces tomorrow on us all. The policemen walk their beats, quiet shifts in the resounding silence after the workday chaos, enjoying the open spaces on the desolate boulevards and the true width of the day-thronged sidewalks. We appreciate the night. Sweaty, drunk, conspiring, vigilant, revelling, running...we are brothers in Moscow.

Paintball Cold War...Moscow's para-paintball underground... Cold War toys...

It's inevitable; business creeps into every pleasure trip, but that's alright when it brings more adventure. Josh is up for it—we're meeting a man named Nick who runs paintball scenario games around Moscow; whatever else he does for employment, he doesn't say. We don't ask. There are more billionaires in Moscow than anywhere else in the world, and they employ armies of interesting people to do interesting things on and off the record.

Nick has a short grey-stubble beard and eyes that could comfort or kill at any moment. He is very cordial in emails and warmly invited me—a stranger whose work he is vaguely familiar with from paintball magazines—for a tour of the Moscow paintball scene. I get a mob-vibe from the guy, so my heart skips when he pulls up in a blue sedan and says in heavily Russianized English, "Quickly, get in."

We creep through the one-way streets to a thoroughfare aimed away from the heart of the city, out from inside that central loop around the Kremlin. That's the high-rent district behind us, where Russian corporations share the skyline with government buildings and luxury apartments. Paintball takes a fair amount of land, and doesn't bring in that much revenue, so fields spring up on the periphery rather than in the urban centers, though in such a huge place as Moscow, it's difficult to get away from the zoning ordinances and traffic.

Now we're reverse-commuting out of town, so the traffic is snarled and stuck on the other side of the divider but flowing fast and free around us. We shoot through the open spaces between traffic pockets, Nick weaving deftly to show off his talent and the car's agility. Nick and Russian cab drivers live for this sort of thing. It's the same in New York, Seoul, Beijing...and despite my white knuckles, I love it. We are all alike, though far from being all the same.

We pull into the field with tires smoking. Just off a highway circling Moscow, it's a prime location, he says, because Moscovites can get to it easily once they get on the beltway. Then it's a hammer-

239

down run around the capital on six open lanes in each direction, towards the large plastic banner on telephone poles at the edge of the property. "Paintball," it says in Cyrillic, struggling against the wind. I can see apartment complexes not too far away—we're still within the city, though forty five minutes worth of traffic away from our hostel.

"There is a subway station not far," he says, "and plans to put a bus stop right near the parking lot. Now, it is a subway ride and a short walk." I'm used to driving many miles through cornfields and forests to find paintball venues; arriving by subway is mind boggling.

So are the special effects they installed at this field. At first glance it looks like any course back home: wooden pallets, khaki sandbags, empty metal drums, like a junkyard with the corners rounded off. There's a cannon in the corner, made from plastic pipe and plywood, with a spent artillery shell on the ground near it. Start one team with the cannon, another with the cartridge, and whoever brings these two elements together first wins. The field has basic, well maintained props. I don't notice the wires in the treetops.

"This is what makes the field special," Nick says with the pride of an inventor showing off his laboratory. He leans nonchalantly against a giant switchboard built into a plywood-backed map of the field. "Flick these switches," he says with a chuckle, indicating the silver tabs that correspond to a dozen bunkers around the field, "and boom—all dead."

"All dead?" I ask, balking at the term we avoid on the US paintball scene—to distance our sport from war-play, ironically, even as we run around in camo shooting at each other.

"All dead," he declares bluntly. "We have a system of pyrotechnics rigged in the trees and on posts over the bunkers. When the referees get bored, or in a game with artillery strikes, they set them off one, two, three… Anyone within five meters is eliminated from the game. It gets their attention when things start exploding."

The Russians clearly have no compunction about playing at war, and none of the political correctness we use in our publications. Part of that is pure entertainment; part of it has to do with the clientele. A lot of it is pure Russian chutzpah.

* * * * *

They use a lot of fireworks in paintball, he says, walking me around the field; multi-colored rain-swollen balls lie slowly deflating on the dirt.

Back home, we fill surgical tubing with paint until they swell like elongated eggs, then cap them loosely so on impact a ball bearing dislodges and they spin around, squirting paint. We call them "paint grenades."

The Enola Gay pyrotechnics company makes "grenades" for the Russian scene: grey plastic reproductions of a German "potato-masher" hand grenade from World War II. He hands me one. "Enjoy." I pull the pin and chuck it across the field. It bounces once, twice, nose-heavy at the end of the handle with its warhead full of goopy paint.

Boom.

Pink paint splatters on everything in a forty foot circle, the plastic peeled back like jagged flower petals. A moment later the kachoo echoes off the apartment buildings across the highway.

It's all part of the experience—it's what the customers want, and the customers are king in Russia.

Paintball isn't cheap in America, but you can play all day for fifty bucks. Here, you'll barely get on the field with rental gear for a hundred dollars—due to the cost of transporting gear from America, paintballs from England, and paying the utilities, taxes, and bribes it takes to stay open…especially the bribes, which are the difference between keeping to a construction schedule and abandoning hope in the fourth circle of Paperwork Hell.

So rather than marketing paintball to teenagers, like we do, they go after the thirty to fifty year olds; teenagers can't afford to play in Moscow—at least not enough to make them a viable demographic. But the world's most expensive city has more billionaires than any other metropolitan area on earth right now, and they employ well-paid staff members by the hundreds of thousands. These are the men (hardly any women play paintball in Russia) who eat hundred dollar lunches of caviar and vodka; who work long and tedious hours in suits and offices far removed from the natural world; who compete with their minds while their bodies atrophy; who spend hundreds of dollars on golf.

These are the people who can afford paintball, and they get interested when you show them videos of men in camouflage dodging incoming fire and explosions. You don't get shot at on the golf course, but here's a way to shoot and get shot at without risking injury; here's a place where things blow up, where that pure animal adrenaline flows in buckets, where the air is acrid with gunpowder the way Russians for hundreds of years have smelled it, but they can be back in the office unscathed on Monday… and for lunch, this paintball field has a gourmet restaurant with a thick glass window so you can watch the action as you slurp your borscht.

There are heated floors and personal lockers in the shower room, and a pro shop where you can buy all the supplies to come back with your own gear next time—everything just like a golf course tailored for the elite, but plunked down adjacent a paint-splattered playground for men with soldier fantasies.

"I think there is nothing in the world like paintball," Nick says. "Nothing except maybe the real thing," without a trace of humor, whist or sarcasm—Nick is inscrutable, and I'm not sure just how much he fancies the notion of firing a real weapon in anger. Maybe a lot.

I really want to play paintball against him, one on one. You really get to know a man when you're hunting each other, mind vs. mind at the other end of a projectile-launching device. You really get to know yourself under fire, even if it can't actually hurt you. Regional flavors exist, but everyone I've ever played against approaches the game differently—each according to their own personality. Some come at you hard and fast, quick on the trigger, ignoring risk to themselves in a blind headlong charge; others move defensively, eager to see what you throw at them, reactionary and cautious. There are as many combinations of aggression and defense as there are players in this world. Everyone is different— an opponent to respect, and a challenge to savor.

I think Nick would feel me out with a series of defensive moves, shooting at bunkers I could advance to, encouraging me not to go to them, so as to guide my movement without me even knowing; and then I imagine he would move in for a kill in a burst of speed I don't expect from him—not from his stocky build and how he started so conservatively. He would be relentless, practiced and calculating, not stopping until I was hit or he ran out of paintballs and then, if that happened, he would charge shooting harmless bursts of air from the muzzle with such a war cry as hasn't been heard in Moscow since 1941.

I want to hear that. I want to fight The Bear, just to see what it's like. And then have vodka with him.

* * * * *

We have lunch instead of combat, sitting down in the restaurant to watch the shadows change slowly on the paintball field. He orders for me, a Baltika and some borscht with extra sour cream—the sour cream is critical, he says, and so very Russian—and a meat dish: pork something, breaded and fried and smothered in gravy. Three rounds, he says, one for each of us. I face down my borscht-fear out of dignity and respect—Nick is staring at me hopefully—and because Josh is lapping it up with terrifying earnest.

It's fantastic, and the sour cream makes it even better once I stir it around. Nick smiles, a treat as rare in Russia as fine dining at paintball fields everywhere else. He tells me more stories.

Some players build armored vehicles, he boasts, and then—between bites of breaded pork—asks if I would like to see the paintball equivalent of the Red Oktober Factory. "The time they brought me, they blindfolded me, put me in their car and drove me in circles before taking me to a large garage with no windows. It is a very secret facility. The other groups know nothing of it. I have no idea where I was, but it is very interesting to see. I can arrange a tour..."

It's the Cold War all over again, but this time with paintballs— how could I say no?

Moscow's para-paintball underground...

From an empty and intimidating alley, we turn through a metal fence topped with curled razor wire and park by what looks like an auto shop. Automobile-shaped lumps under tarps are parked along the fence. White splats blanch in the sun, powder now with their gelatin shells in tatters and all the water evaporated into the clear blue sky—I know these faded marks from fields around the world, left behind like bullet holes in cities under siege. To the untrained eye they look like any random splatter, background detail in an urban environment; to me, it's an unmistakable sign there are folks nearby who play my game—who share that connection and the sporting community around it. Old dried paintball splats, to me, are like graffiti marking friendly territory.

This courtyard doubles as a firing range for exotic paintball markers mounted to armored vehicles. There are a lot of splats clustered tightly together on the side of an adjacent building, either shot by a marker with tremendous accuracy or a cannon with a tight bore and good sabot.

Josh stayed behind to explore the city while I take my guided tour of the paintball underground. I watch Dmitry, the man in charge of this madness, tug back a corner of a tarp covering something big next to the fence. Nick rushes to help with a speed I've not seen before—he shows Dmitry great respect. Neither of us was blindfolded on our way here, a theatrical inconvenience Nick thanked him for sparring us today. There's a fine line between men play-acting their scenario roles, and scenario players taking the game too far. With Nick's tarp-peeling duty, I can see their respect is genuine and surprisingly formal.

They uncover a scaled reproduction of a Russian T-34 tank, complete with an air cannon jutting out of the turret. Dmitry helps me climb aboard, pointing out where the façade won't hold my weight—the tank is a plywood body fitted over an old truck chassis with a diesel engine. It will only go five miles an hour—a nod vaguely in the direction of safety—so they retooled the engine to idle at that speed without the pent-up horsepower destroying its gearbox.

The driver looks out through a slit in the body, forward of the turret, just like in the real T-34...and the turret gunner can swing his cannon around three hundred sixty degrees to shoot foam rockets at other tanks, or clusters of paintballs like grapeshot for anti-personnel use. On the sides are real entrenchment tools and gas cans in their authentic positions, painted to match the tank... and quickly detachable in case the crew needs to clear an obstacle from its path or refuel under fire.

Dmitry and Nick are beaming. I've never seen this sort of glee in adults...and here they are, two hard-scowling Russian men with grey-stubble beards grinning like kids with Willy Wonka's golden tickets.

Dmitry made another tank from an old Volkswagon, which they used because of its reliable engine and smaller chassis. It's less impressive—an earlier attempt, it's crude by comparison and intended to look generally like a tank, rather than to replicate a particular model.

He has field artillery as well, which Nick apologetically tells me is broken at the moment but soon to be fixed—as if I might be sad that we can't fire it within Moscow's city limits.

I am kind of sad. Oh well.

A half-dozen middle aged men are hard at work in the garage, turning an old van into a new, historically accurate tank of some sort; in another bay is a mostly-finished armored personnel carrier that, eyeballing it, could probably hold about six fully outfitted paintball players. Today is Wednesday, just barely after lunch, and these men grind and saw like it's their job; perhaps it is. Dmitry owns a scenario team and the event production company—so that's why Nick is so respectful—so maybe these guys are on the clock. He introduces me to each by name, a flurry of Vlads and Pytors and Mikhails I can't hope to remember, and then takes me upstairs. Nick dodges into a side room, out of sight.

"You have such things in America, yes?" he says, standing with me at a window overlooking the shop floor.

"The tanks, yes," I say. "But nothing like this facility."

"Ah yes, good. It is special. Even in Russia, there is nothing like it." Then, "Nick has told you about the fireworks?" Indeed. Specially trained players carry pyrotechnic mortars into the games, making the air explode and rain popping firecrackers on the players. His face changes minutely towards a frown. "Have you seen them?" No. "Ah!"

There's that elusive Russian smile again.

"Come, I show you," and he sits me at a giant computer screen filled with icons for promotional videos he made by mixing Russian military music with game footage. For the next five minutes I listen to absolutely terrifying Red Army Choir hymns punctuated by explosions and illustrated with close-in shots of paramilitary-types firing automatic paintball markers. Half of me wants to run screaming for Switzerland, but the other half is ready to grab a marker and dive right in. That's when Nick bursts through the door firing a Luger—a German 9mm handgun from WWII.

Dmitry grabs his own shoulder, twisting to the right; grabs his belly, doubling over. Nick cackles, brass cartridges spinning on the floor as he blows smoke from the muzzle like an old west outlaw. Dmitry straightens up and laughs, clasping a hand on my shoulder. "Blanks," I hear through ringing ears. "Watch this." He leads me to a window as Nick leaps out onto the metal stairs, pointing the pistol out over the work floor. Blam! Blam blam blam!

Workers scatter like roaches when the lights come on—all but one, who spins in a practiced movement towards a rag on top of a tool chest and pulls from it a model 1911 handgun, the US answer to Nick's Luger. Blam blam blam!

The men exchange blank fire until their magazines run out, and I wonder for a moment how many other loaded handguns they stashed around the building. "It's real," Dmitry says. "I have license. I collect them from that period."

"Sometimes during games," he adds, handing me the Luger—real alright—"we like to shoot blanks too. It scares the players just enough. Come. We drink vodka with my crew."[2]

---

2   Read about vodka's peculiar history in Appendix B

Cold War toys...

Nick takes me to an early dinner, one of those courtesy things that offers a chance to extend the conversation. There are trendy coffee shops, but when he said ...or a bite to eat, I jumped at the opportunity for food. Here we are at another of those high-class cafeterias, a personal favorite of his that has a great selection. There are cabbage dumplings, borscht—not as good as at the paintball field—and strudels, bread, lamb, fish, fruits...it goes on and on as if to make up for the decades of breadlines in this same neighborhood. I grab a coffee and load up on dinner. It's four o'clock, but I'm in financial-crisis-mode and figure a big, free dinner could last me all through the night.

He laughs at my over-burdened plastic tray. I explain it's my way of really getting to know a place—by eating the local food. All of it. In this case, an entire culture in one sitting. He pays thirty bucks US, buys a coffee for himself, and I feel bad—really bad...embarrassed-bad—but chalk it up to saving enough for another day on the road. The accounts are looking grim now on the flickering ATM screens and we're stuck for a few more days in the most expensive city on earth.

We talk about the paintball scene, but it quickly turns to more interesting subjects—after his tours, there isn't much ground left uncovered. What did you do before paintball?

"I sold equipment to certain agencies," he says, completely casual and noncommittal.

"Like the KGB?"

"They paid in cash. I liked that."

"Ever play with the stuff yourself?" I imagine what I would do with access to Q's spy-toys—how great would that be? No good would come of it, though—wreaking havoc is much more fun.

"Nyit. I was in the business of selling such things; not using." Then, "I collect firearms like Dmitry. Do you shoot?" Yes. "Perhaps next time you come, we go shooting. You would like my collection."

We talk about the social liability of collecting firearms, and how in the US you can make friends fast in collecting circles or, more frequently, alienate and terrify people when you openly talk about enjoying guns. It's one of those things you either get, or you don't, and the national trend is away from hunting and sport shooting. On airplanes I hide my Guns & Ammo inside a National Geographic. He laughs and says it's similar in Russia.

"Those my age all served in the military," he continues. "There was a time when it was great, and we were young. Russians have a long military tradition. Today the trend is away from that, so young people are not so interested in these parts of our history." But he is.

"Yes," he says with a devilish smile. "I am not so quick to forget."

Burrito "Frogger"... Burn bright, burn out... Goldilock and the peroxide toothbrush... Those left behind... iPhone perversions and the way Josh wasn't hit by a tram...

We're living on snacks—Josh stays faithful to his Cup-O-Soup while I fetch burritos from a liquor store across six lanes of heavy traffic. There's a subway stop a few blocks away, and I could cross under the street there, through a corridor lined with tiny stalls selling shampoo and cologne, cheap pocketknives and belts. Someone must have gone through Grand Central Station and decided to replicate that station-stop capitalism here on the Red Line.

But the tunnel is too far out of my way. As a kid we had one of those early home computers with the green and black display, and a game called "Frogger." Your character had to hop across a busy road without getting splattered by traffic—that's me going for dinner.

Stoplights somewhere far away stagger the traffic so I have to sprint here and stop there, let some cars pass, identify a gap and move again; there's a reason they let us cross for free underground, but I like to live on the edge—one of those stupid guy things where the more you risk the more you feel alive, even if in the end you have nothing to show for it but a greasy burrito.

The shop has half a dozen brands of vodka, Baltikas two through nine, and an ancient cylinder of meat slowly spinning in front of a heat lamp. They shave that into a round flour shell, load it up with lettuce and onions and sauce from a bottle with no label, and two dollars later I've got dinner soaking through a paper bag as the cars whiz honking past.

Such is life on the cheap. I went to a grocery store, a maze of foil bags and cellophane where ground floor apartments used to be. I grabbed some soft cheese in foil triangles, crackers, smoked fish, and fruit, avoiding the caviar—which I'm sure is good, but it's expensive and not really my thing. I like my eggs scrambled, with bacon and toast—not squirted from a fish's nether regions into a can that smells like a shrimp boat.

That light snack cost eighteen dollars. These burritos will get me through.

Going back to the hostel, I pass a man on the street who is passed out drunk against a wrought iron fence; this is not newsworthy here, not these days when the rich pass out on high thread count sheets while the peasants sleep where they fall. What's newsworthy is the association it brings, this man on the sidewalk, with the first drunk we saw passed out cold on the street—this one is also covered in vomit and shaking, but not bleeding out. He'll get better; he might even wake up before dark.

It's just two in the afternoon.

Burn bright, burn out...

"I can't keep this up," Josh says, sitting down with his rehydrated soup. He looks tired, and I wonder how late he was out with the Dutch Brothers last night.

"All the salt?"

"No, the cost. I'm not too hopeful. We've got tickets to Warsaw, but I don't know how much farther I can go."

"Where do you want to go?"

He gets this blank look; not the conquering hero's ponderous gaze, not the survivor's hollow stare, but something exactly halfway between them—two parts whist, two parts despair...and one part boredom. His fingers bounce on the table like he's full of energy with nowhere to go. "Take a run," I say. "Burn some energy, clear your head."

"No one runs here, you crazy?" It's true; there were old people pumping away on public exercise machines in Beijing, but here, not so much as a jogger out in the open.

If you can call city air fresh, he's had plenty of it. He's toured the nighttime social scene with friends made fast in this hostel. He goes out with the Dutch Brothers, with some French students, with anyone who has plans and a warm smile. They buy each other drinks, round after round, as if paying rent for their tables. It takes a toll on the mind and body, and especially on the wallet. He's been burning bright; I'm surprised he hasn't burned out.

Then he says "I want to see Ireland. I want to get away from here. I've been in Russia too long."

Goldilock and the peroxide toothbrush...

Josh went orange. I'm staring down at him passed out in his bunk with the sheets pulled up to his ears. An enormous Russian bouncer lies face-down on his mattress in the middle of the floor, the other beds are either full of sleeping people or peeled back like banana peels...everything looks normal except for Josh. There's no denying it—his hair is bright orange in that off-blonde way you can only get from a bad dye job, like a hangover for your appearance.

Last night I drank Baltika with the Dutch Brothers under the tree outside our hostel, and called it an early night; last time I saw him, Josh was emailing home and had unremarkable brown hair.

He tells his story over breakfast.

"It was the right thing to do," he says. "I had to try something different, like totally destroying my appearance."

"It kinda matches the earring."

"Yeah, my mom's gonna freak out." He shifts his weight and stares past me, mulling over a thought. Then he adds, "You know, I can get an earring. I can quit my job. I can dance with whoever I want to, or get trashed and stay out all night, or turn my hair orange. I don't know if it's self-destruction. Maybe it's just an extreme form of exerting my will on my surroundings. Maybe it's just exercising freedom."

It happened last night in those witching hours known to insomniacs and people like Josh. I know that hour, too—the dead of night when the energy comes and the world is quiet and I'm the last man on earth, leaving a record, brutal and honest, for no one. While I write, or jog through Red Square, he comes into his own somewhere else, seeking kinship with others who gather in the night for come-what-may. They're his people, while I walk alone.

The curly haired girl at the hostel is one of us; one of them, rather—Josh's people. They sat up talking and laughing as he unwound six weeks of stress, sharing his life and listening to hers, the last two people awake in the hostel—the last two people on earth. He was taken by her accent, he said, by her voice at first and then he found he really liked the girl. Maybe they would never hang out in St. Louis, but late at night on the road he was a different Josh than his mother would recognize; perhaps she, that curly haired Russian, was a different girl as well. Off the clock; not working, really—but living. Just two crazy people up late, laughing the world away.

So he took off his shirt as she dissolved some powder in a bowl, making a foul blue concoction to mark the occasion with. She worked the cream through his hair with a toothbrush—he left his comb in Mongolia.

"Don't brush your teeth with that," he said, the blue chemical goo burning his scalp and staining the bristles. "Don't want your teeth to go blonde." They laughed at the absurdity of blonde teeth, and of dying your hair at three in the morning with a toothbrush. His hair became the dumping ground, he explains, for weeks of stress; like the earring in Ulan Bator, like the bender in Irkutsk, a bonfire for his vanities so that in the morning he may rise from the ashes—free. It's how he does things, and for him, it works.

She washed her hands in the kitchen, swaying back and forth and washing each finger carefully. It was strangely erotic, he says. Her voice, accent heavy with sex, made him want to abandon everything he knew and leave the world behind. We've come too far, he says, too fast, so it all seems now a barrage of color and emotion—Korea, neon, Beijing, smog-yellow, Mongolia, brown, Irkutsk, blue, Perm, grey, Moscow…Moscow red, like blood pumping through a healthy young body that needs to forget the rest of the world for a night.

If he wakes up in a new city with new clothes, a hole in his ear and orange hair, could he wake up as a different person? Palahniuk's thoughts again…

Josh keeps changing the outside, but it's the inside that's on fire.

"It burns," he said.

"Oh, you're a tough man," she teased, drying her hands on her shirt. "It's not my fault if your hair falls out tomorrow."

"I'd hold the toothbrush responsible," he said, and then, "You should dye yours too."

"No way," she scoffed, scowling and sparkling, in a way he notes as distinctly Russian. "Maybe," she said on second thought. "But just a streak."

"Alright; take off your shirt…"

"Joshua, you're crazy!"

"Had to try…"

And there it is—she walks through the kitchen and I see it: amid the curly brown, a shock of orange that matches Josh. They didn't sleep together, no, that's not his style, but what they shared was just as meaningful; maybe more. She ambles groggily past our table with her breakfast in hand and a conspirator's smile just for him.

Those left behind…

Vladimir Putin dismissed the Russian government today. Only the parts he didn't like, apparently, but doom-and-gloom headlines like "Putin Dissolves Government" are all over the US news websites. The Russian Prime Minister won't be around too much longer—his term is coming up—and there is opposition to Dmitry Medvedev, the man Putin intends to appoint as his successor.

So Putin fired everyone who opposed him, which is better than locking them in cages with starved hunting dogs like his long ago predecessor, Ivan the Terrible, did. Modern politics are just so…boring.

It's an exciting time to be in Moscow, though, and a great evening to drink room temperature Baltika Number 3—unless you've been pounding round after round all day, like some of the men stumbling through the streets. I remember the guy passed out against the fence, there one hour and gone the next—maybe to the outskirts of town in the back of a van with no windows and an unpadded metal interior, easy to hose out at the end of the day.

The streets are clean, for the most part, and the trash has to go somewhere the good comrades won't miss it—the taiga forests are thick and keep their secrets.

Then there was that man unconscious before nine in the morning in a bloody pool of his own vomit, dying just a few meters from an unconcerned cop in a city exploding with money and power—no justice if you can't afford it. Every seventy two hours we pay someone to take down our passport numbers and stamp our paperwork so the Russian Federation can track us while our embassy remains oblivious that we're even here. What if we couldn't afford the stamp?

The food is rich and the spirits divine, and you can't sneeze without spraying someone important. So who cares about two broke guys living out of backpacks? We could slump down with our Baltika and close our eyes and disappear like millions before us, hauled out into the forest and left to the bears like writers before glastnotz; like the ousted officials feel right now; like what might have happened to those bums.

Perhaps this is the modern Russia: streets full of people going up, up, up in the most expensive city in the world, walking wide around a pile of bloody vomit seeping out of a crumpled failure. Did he have a home or a claim or a friend in the world? Does anyone here, or is it a race against even their friends? What about those who don't run so fast, who can't keep up with the pace or the rent and fall by the wayside; what happens to them?

Russia has never had a race like this before, no culture where anyone can run after hopes and goals and business. The old serfs, the old communist rank and file, followed orders and worked to survive. But now there's opportunity, and today the power structure was fired inside those old red walls a mile from our hostel.

Now what?

Those who can't keep the pace drink Baltika on benches around the war monuments. They fell out of the race and hard on the sidewalk, broken, beaten, damned. The juxtaposition is too much, so we're off to a concert to forget it all for awhile and spin our wheels while time slides by. Poland is coming fast, but we're not done here just yet.

The Bloodhound Gang is playing Moscow tonight.

iPhone perversions and the way
Josh wasn't hit by a tram...

The opening band was fantastic: Montreal, a German punk band with bleach-blonde hair and Aryan eyes crashing around the stage like they were the main act. Their confidence infused the music with angst and emotion—never mind that it was all in German. Then raunch-rockers Bloodhound Gang took the stage for some pure magic. Pure drunken Russian magic, with seven dollar beers from the two bars in this cavernous place filled with slam-dancing Russians and horrible, terrible, wonderful lyrics. This isn't the kind of music you play for your family.

I discovered the Bloodhound Gang back in high school, drinking stolen beer with my friends in my parents' basement with our ears pressed against the speakers while my parents slept upstairs. This band was the first real not in my house music I listened to, and still probably the best—if you're into stalker love ballads to porn stars.

But why do we still listen to raunchy music when we're old enough to know better? Because it reminds me of when I wasn't. Because this band is legendary for their live shows and here, in Moscow, where anything goes for the right price in dark rooms packed with foul-minded young people, we're likely to see some crazy stuff...

...like one of the singers chugging a pint of Baltika, vomiting it back into the glass, and chugging it again, to our amusement. These are not the things you talk about in polite company—nor are they the sort of things you can ever un-see.

I'm thoroughly entertained in a way I'm not proud of.

Apple released their iPhone three months ago, and they're the coolest tech-toy in the US right now. They're not for sale in Russia, but of course the band has them, and they're eager to show off. They have one running a slideshow on a screen behind the band, showing twenty-foot-tall videos and pictures dredged from the internet's festering nether regions. It's all part of the show, to see how far they can take perversion as a public art form, to push the envelope so far past tact that we have one of those "novel experiences" we'll never forget. It seems like shock and filth is the new cultural frontier, which appalls me, but it fits with our theme tonight: to see just how far we can go. To run screaming out of our comfort zones and see if we fall apart, and if not, go farther, faster, until we do. It has something to do with being young; so here we are at a bawdy concert in Moscow, and there's a naked man onstage dragging an amplifier by a chain attached to his penis.

We down our beers and scream into with the madness, singing along with "You're Pretty When I'm Drunk" in a room full of writhing Russian beauties. This is exactly what we paid for.

Videos from tonight are going to wind up on YouTube— find one. Look in the corners of the screen for some drunken Americans throwing shockers—that'll be us. We're on the Jumbotron, we're on the sauce, we're hooked on the Moscow nightlife. The writhing, moshing horde screams along in Bond-villain-accents, throwing beer on each other and the band. Evil Jared tries to crowd surf to the bar, but gets detained by security— they're protecting us from the band.

The concert lets out far too early, and we flee into the streets ahead of the drunken stampede. Kids are punching and shoving each other, not a scene we want to be part of, and the sidewalks are full of coked-up hookers with knives. They flash come-hither eyes above stone-set scowls, shirts so tight they might as well be painted on; they have more courage than pride. One reaches out for Josh, but he smiles and dodges away.

We cross the dark street towards a subway stop under a grassy knoll, keeping our eyes on the packs of teenage guys arm-linked and swaying through the streets. For the moment they're peaceful. A gaggle of hoodlums sit on the concrete steps towards the subway stop, drinking Baltika and smashing the bottles at their feet. It's the only possible thing to do at this hour. They're high on good times and booze-bold like us. The whole world is young tonight, young and reckless and dodging electric trams and trying not to get stabbed—euphoria in dangerous places, as delicate as balloons in the dark.

Now I'm ready for the adventure to begin. Ready for Poland, ready for Europe, ready for whatever comes next and eager to start now. The adrenaline courses with the night wide open and the future ahead, like a fever breaking and leaving the baggage behind with my flu.

Let's not waste another minute.

"Dude, let's find a bar!" I cheer. I haven't said that all trip, but the mood is on and I'm up for diving headlong into this madness, seizing opportunity and running with it all the way to Portugal.

"No, man," Josh says. "I'm broke."

Top: **Leaving Russia behind. Photo by Josh Vise**

Bottom: **Brest Railway Station**

Brest, Belarus
8 September, 2007

Belarus

Like all great travelers, I have seen more than I
remember, and remember more than I have seen.

—Benjamin Disraeli

Let it begin... The new Berlin Wall... When bribes don't work... Spoon-fed to the bear... Ian Fleming, where are you now?... The taxi full of porn... The bitter taste of cowardice... My $363 lunch in Brest... Parting shots...

"I'm getting off in Poland," he says like it's the weather report...scattered clouds and sunny, with a hundred percent chance that this is it...

"We're both getting off in Poland..." but I see where he's going.

"No man, I'm getting off in Poland. I'm broke. We've done it man, we've done the Trans Siberian. I'm going home."

He turns his face out the train car window, his gaze ignoring the Belarusian farmland as it searches for a home five thousand miles to the west.

Somehow, I expected more—maybe getting robbed at gunpoint and him screaming I've had it! or staying out too late and waking up on a hospital flight home, or...I kind of feel cheated. I kind of feel...like I won. Outlasted him. But a victory that leaves a friend behind is nothing to celebrate.

A little riff goes through my mind, a piece of a song they over-played long ago—every new beginning comes from some other beginning's end...

He arranged his ticket while I was touring with Nick. The won-flush millionaire is broke—his parents paid for it so he wouldn't have to wash dishes in Warsaw. Now he's in the hole a couple hundred bucks to his old man, but their food is free and his room in their basement is just the way he left it—Soundgarden poster on the wall, amp in the corner, with a tricked out computer he built as state-of-the-art in 2003.

It's unsettling to see the end of his adventure looming—he knows the very minute he leaves. He has an itinerary. On most trips you know when you'll be back before you even leave, imbuing each successive moment with a mounting sense of urgency. That urgency just burst out of nowhere, and just as quickly passes me by—it's not my fate, after all.

Something clicked for me at the Bloodhound Gang concert, as if assailing my eyes and virtue with vile rot and absinthe awakened that same part of my mind that used to enjoy pushing loose teeth out with my tongue. That same overdrive which kicks in when things get too weird, or frightening, and suddenly I'm in control—the conductor on the runaway train. Just as doomed, perhaps, but empowered by the struggle.

It's his time, I guess; time to get back to the reality he left years ago.

"I've emailed this guy at a public television channel," he says. "I'm gonna try to get a job there. Might go back to Mr. Chiu's," the Chinese place where he washed dishes in high school, "just for a little while. Gotta pay off the credit cards. I'll figure it out…"

Belarus looks like Kansas: gently rolling wheat fields in unbroken gold slipping by like time in life's best years. Some people work this land knowing nothing different; Russian, Belarussian, communist, capitalist…those are just details in lives lived close to the earth. They work the land, pay their taxes, raise their kids to work these fields when their fingers are brittle and their skin forgets its color. I hope he does something with his Master's degree. I hope he saves a lot of money. I hope he travels again; he's been everywhere, man, but there's still so much beyond these fields.

The new Berlin Wall…

Most Americans go through Latvia and Lithuania to get to the easternmost ramparts of Fortress Europe, because you need a transit visa to go through Belarus…which lies on the most direct route from Moscow to Poland like a giant tollbooth. An old Soviet territory, Belarus is that Kansas-sized chunk of land west of Russia that was downwind of the Chernobyl disaster. They're not doing too well, but can't blame it all on second-hand Ukrainian radioactivity.

When the Soviet Union crumbled, Belarussian fortunes were looking up and their manufacturing was strong with plenty of laborers and functional infrastructure. They sold heavy machinery and grain to Russia, and did pretty well if you compare their fledgling capitalist success against their old expectations… but without the old totalitarian ways, without the strict market controls and micromanaging, it all fell apart.

Now most of Belarus is unemployed. They're landlocked, so they rely on regional trade and transit taxes to move goods through their territory. Poland used to be their gateway to Europe, but then the European Union essentially dissolved their internal borders, meaning that you can drive from Lisbon to Warsaw with no more hassle than driving through a handful of US states. This freedom is afforded largely by the strength of their borders with the rest of the world—like a bug with its innards protected by a hard exoskeleton.

Drug interdiction and immigration, passport and visa control, import and export tariffs…it all happens at the shipping ports and land borders with non-EU countries. Belarus is so close…but so far, being on the wrong side of the fortress walls.

Hopeful of brighter days in different environs, scores of Belarussians fled to Poland in the nineties and early two-thousands. They got jobs and sent money back to Minsk… and then Poland joined the EU in 2004, and the border rules changed substantially. This trapped a number of Belarussians in Poland where they had work and support networks, but lacked the requisite paperwork to conform to the new rules. Visas and transit papers are hard to come by for Belarussians now. Rather than make border runs back home—through the gauntlet of paperwork and guards—the Belarussian diaspora stays where they are and lies low. For them, the border is now something like the Berlin Wall, with bureaucracy instead of machineguns.

So Belarus doesn't have much going for it, except as a toll station for gas lines and rail traffic…and transiting tourists. The visa is expensive, and some fees are arbitrarily levied by the person issuing the permit at the Belarussian consulate—Soviet-era corruption is rampant at home and abroad. The visas never cost less than a hundred bucks, which is what I paid in person, in cash, at their embassy in a high rise office building in Manhattan. My visa is stamped September 8—no stops before Warsaw, just a night on the train as we pass through Minsk.

Josh's transit visa is stamped September 7-9. The devil, they say, is in the details.

When bribes don't work...

I'm sitting in my underwear eating breakfast and minding my own business. Josh lounges on a bunk, staring out at another standard-issue Soviet train station here in a border town named Brest. There's a knock at the door, and I'm annoyed—I'm eating, leave me alone, go away.

Knock knock knock! and something barked in Russian.

I locked it against people and problems and the mind-numbing boredom of a train trip across the eastern European steppe; it's locked against the irritation of this immigration officer and the day-wrecking catastrophe he portends. He looks at me disapprovingly—my unshaven face, mussed hair, lack of pants.

He grumbles the Russian equivalent of "come with me," hands Josh his passport, and stomps into the hallway, blocking one direction so I must walk the corridor before him. Great. We have a protocol for this: whoever gets singled out takes enough cash and the appropriate clothing to endure an unexpected overnight, abandons his bags as if they all belong to the other man, and the lucky guy left behind carries on to the next stop without complaint. We've heard of hassles on the train, the malice and caprice of corrupt or hostile or just plain mean guards, and figure that one person detained with no luggage is infinitely better than two people detained with all our worldly belongings subject to confiscation. I don my pants, grab my camera, and walk into the hallway.

"Bags!" he barks, pointing back in the room.

"Leave?" I ask, pointing to my camera bag.

"Nyit! All bags!"

I point to the camera bag again, "All bags," and shrug my best awe shucks, I got robbed the other day and this is it, look.

I'm forced off the train, whereupon another guard explains, pointing to the passport I'm not allowed to touch, that my transit visa is expired. My watch says "September 8." My visa says "September 8." He laughs and says nyit, nyit, buy new visa.

I protest; I offer small bribes, but it doesn't work. I don't want to offer large bribes, as there are multiple authority figures around me on the platform—meaning that it either wouldn't work, or would get very expensive—and I feel that I'm in the right anyway. I'm poor and indignant. My papers are in order, the greedy bastards...

So much for a hundred bucks and a day spent at the embassy in Manhattan. We got through all of Russia without a hitch or glitch or problem, and here at the last stop before the European playground, my luck runs out.

Good luck can't last forever.

Spoon-fed to the bear...

The officer walks me across the platform to a cab stand and introduces me to a fat man who smells of rancid sour cream and onions; they have a few words, and the cabbie fixes me with a look of equal pity and hunger—fresh meat. I'm a clueless American, and we're all rich, of course; we're piggy banks stuffed full of hundred dollar bills, waiting to be broken. Naturally. That's what's in his look when he smiles like a jailer and says in a terrible British accent "Come, I take you to police chief."

I need an embassy—a Belarussian one to straighten this out, or an American one with Marine Corps guards to protect me. Of course the embassy is closed today, he says; it is Saturday, everything is closed. The embassy would probably be closed on Monday, too, or Wednesday or any other day for that matter, but—and I'm in luck, apparently—he is friends with the police chief who can get me a transit visa for only $250 US. Cash.

I don't have that, I lie; I have five hundred dollars between thigh and neck pouches the officer never saw me strap on, and the wallet hidden inside my pants he doesn't know is there. I left the train with my camera and my passport, that's all; I was robbed, I say, I have no more money. Throw me in jail, what would it do? My visa's valid, the piggy bank is empty... They converse in

Russian, laughing at me.

"You have bank card?" the cabbie asks. "I take you to ATM, no problem!"

Right…

"Hurry, train leaves soon," he exhorts.

I've been spoon-fed to the bear so the officer walks away, leaving me with the cabbie, my passport, and my mantra, "I have no money, my visa is valid…" I watch the officer mount the train car's steps as it pulls away from the platform, Josh, bags, and hope rolling slowly away from me.

Hello, Belarus.

Ian Fleming, where are you now?

I thank the cabbie, swipe my passport from his hand, and trot off down the platform with cold panic in my blood. I find the first educated-looking person and ask when the next train will be along, in a few hours maybe. Then they add but that one will be back in a few minutes, pointing down the tracks at the one I just left. They are swapping the bogeys.

Of course! Europe has a different railroad gauge—this is like the crossing into Mongolia, and my train will be held up while I figure this out. I have to consult Josh, and maybe the guards are done with the car entirely…maybe I can sneak back on. I sprint down a siding, listening for the rack of a pistol slide or click of the safeties on the guards' assault rifles, but the milling Belarussians just watch me with curiosity as I sprint boots-flailing across the rail yard.

The car is up on lifts, the people still inside, faces at the windows watching the workers in their grease-splattered grey uniforms below. They stop, stare at me, and scowl—I reach up for the bottom stair, to pull myself into the car, and a worker tries to block my way. Nyit! he blurts; I brush him aside. There's another worker, on the stairs, holding out his hand to help me, and when our eyes meet he makes the come on motion with his hand that says money, money.

"Nyit!" I bark, scared and insulted and threatened, pulling

myself up into the car like it's a jungle gym. Back in our compartment, Josh says "what was that all about?"

"They say my visa expired."

"Get a new one."

"Where, a damned vending machine?" He reclines on the bunk, thankful this isn't his problem.

"I got a three day transit visa," he says. "I'm set."

"They give three day visas?"

"Duh."

The train will circle around the station on a set of narrower tracks. Then the guards will board, hand the passports back to the passengers and send it on its way to Poland. I would fit in the storage bin under the bottom bunk in someone else's berth (they'd look for me in mine), and I could pay them not to say anything to the guards—I'd rather pay a stranger double what the system charges, out of spite and resistance.

"That's completely stupid," Josh says. "Just pay them off."

I could... I could...

A hundred James Bond scenarios run through my mind, but each ends the same: the scraggly tourist gets caught by guards who revel in worsening my plight; I get beaten up, thrown in jail for the night, robbed, and dumped on the next train out of the country in the morning—if I don't get bayoneted or shot or suffer some worse fate in this corrupt place where I have no status.

I jump out of the elevated railcar, roll through a summersault to break my fall, spring to my feet and bound off down the tracks—the first time in my life that trick comes in handy. The workers shake their heads dismissively, rather like Josh. I'm just another crazy tourist bound for trouble.

The taxi full of porn...

No one wins against the system. An officer intercepts me on the platform, sweating against the autumn chill, confiscates my passport and marches me into a back room. Here I meet my interrogator, who wears a similar uniform but with a few more ribbons and a shinier pistol. He sits me down on a hard plastic seat in an empty, antiseptic marble room with a giant map on the opposite wall. He knows hardly a word of English. We go through several languages, none of which we have in common, before settling on German: we speak it equally terribly. He knows the textbook phrases like how are you today? and I know profane pickup lines, but it's a start. His Russian voice interrogating me in German is one of the most surreal experiences I've ever had.

"Are you a tourist?" Yes. "Are you American?" Yes. "Are you a spy?" No. "Are you a soldier?" No. Then he points to my combat boots, my black hiking pants, and my general demeanor under pressure; maybe someone radioed to him about my adventure in the mechanic's shed... "Na man," I say, copping terrible street slang, "Ich bin tourista, es alles. Ein artiste." I can fake some words with people who speak a different portion of the language.

"Ah, ah," he says, pantomiming understanding. "So you are... soldier, eh?" I'm sure he interrogates better in Russian...

This is a farce; here I am, being held for self-ransom with a valid visa they won't accept for reasons of greed and maybe a slim chance I'm actually in error...but the principle of the matter percolates up through my diminishing fear. I got the transit visa. I paid my money. I'm not smuggling anything, or immigrating illegally; for probably the first time in my life, I'm not trying to get away with anything—I'm just trying to get to Poland, and I've done everything in good faith to play by their rules.

So this is how they treat me? We've been on the road so long, maybe today is the 9th, or possibly the 7th; maybe I did screw something up...their earnest and my road-weariness have me questioning my fundamental beliefs, like what day it is. But even so, what's a different number worth on a piece of paper—certainly not $250. A good day's wage in Belarus is 10,000Belarusian rubles; the cash they want from me is equivalent to 710,000 rubles, seventy one days' wages...paid to the police chief friend of the cabby who the smirking guard introduced me to.

Yeah, this seems legit.

With the train still in the station, their guns still in their holsters, my wrists unshackled, that initial fear gives completely over to indignation...which will get me nowhere, so I swallow the bile and try to bribe the interrogator.

He'll have none of it; that matter is between the commander and me, who returns as if on cue and urges me out of the station with him, back to the same cab driver. Now it's like getting stuck in a riptide out at sea—best to go with the flow and save your energy for when you can actually do something on the other side of whatever ride you're being taken for.

The cabbie hands me his cell phone; the voice on the other end says, in practiced English and a menacing accent, "Go with this man. Give him two hundred fifty American dollars for emergency visa, fine, papers, and his services." The line goes dead.

This is how they pump up their economy...seventy one day's wages at a time. But I'm still acting broke and once-robbed already, playing for any shred of human decency that might help me.

"You come from Russia, no?" asks the cabbie.

"I'm American."

"But you come from Russia, no?"

"Yes."

"You like Belarus?"

"Not yet."

"I am from Michalkow, you know where is?" No; I don't care, either. "Was part of Russia, then Germany, then Soviet Union, now Poland. Same place, it is border town just across river. My family is there, but I met girl across river, on this side. That was during Soviet time. We married, but she could not move west, so I move east. Then things changed, and now I'm Belarusian citizen, and I can't go back to Poland."

He actually has my interest now, though I admit it's with a tinge of glee that the man scamming me has a central pain in his life—pure schadenfreude.

"So hard to get into EU now," he says, "and visa so expensive. I apply and get turned down, and apply again, and get turned down, and give up. We had nice life here, but now—no work for most people. The factories close, the farms need no one more. Our 'president,' he is not what you would call 'president.' He is dictator!"

Now his blood boils like mine, each of us hot for different reasons, and in our angst we share something; we are indignant against corruption, him against the government, me against him. "Lukashenko, he has made it so he cannot be removed until he quits. No term limits! Even Russia has such things, but not here, no more. You know how many leaders we have since Soviet times?"

That was thirteen years ago, so I guess "two?"

"Lukashenko only! And he make it criminal to criticize government, two years in jail, just like Soviet times. We had jobs under Russia, at least, but not now—now the jobs go to other countries and our ruble is worthless. Lukashenko did this."

I have only the most tremulous grasp of eastern European economics, so I have nothing to add. Thankfully or not—I'm unsure—he keeps the silence full between us while driving me through another standard-issue post-Communist city of bright painted concrete and aging Ladas parked in the shade.

"You organize political party but government does not grant recognition?" he asks, rhetorically. "Then you get investigated by secret police. Andrei Suzdaltsev, he spoke out, he organized to oppose the government. Suzdaltsev was arrested and poisoned! We have democracy, Lukashenko says, but is this democracy? We have worst of both, and our votes? Worthless, like our rubles. I cannot even buy way back to Poland with my wife, so I drive taxi. Taxi is best business now, only way to make money."

He's right, of course—about being able to turn a fast buck as a taxi driver at least. Post-communist countries have thriving black-markets and easy money for the corrupt and those who ferry suckers into their schemes...

But there's something terribly inconvenient about this very human side of the man—he's just a guy trying to get by, cut off by politics from his family, stuck in a place he doesn't like. I can relate—that was Perm, but at least for me, Perm was both voluntary and temporary. He carries on, Lukashenko this! and Lukashenko that! until we arrive at a shopping plaza with a bank on the corner.

He needs to make copies of my documents for the

"paperwork," he says, and apparently the police station doesn't have a copier; right... Against better judgment but without another option I watch him disappear with my passport. While he's gone I pull exactly two hundred and fifty dollars from the pouches strapped to my body.

With your cash hidden away, you can show someone your wallet with only cab fare in it and nothing more; that's all you're worth. Take it, just don't hurt me. Later you can un-strap the pouches and check into the Ritz Carlton. It works.

The cab is a beaten-up Lada with nearly comical rust, slashes through the itchy fabric seats, and gouges on the vinyl dashboard, like an animal tried clawing its way out. The door pockets are full of porno DVDs—explicit pictures and Russian titles with English below, Anal Debutants, Teenage Amateurs, Daddy's Home. There is no way those girls are eighteen.

I hate this man, and I hate his country; I'm hungry and about to lose ten days' budget, but all I can do is sit here rifling his car. This is how a scam feels from the inside—loathing, frustration, and boredom, trapped inside a taxi full of porn.

The bitter taste of cowardice...

The police station is unimpressive; just another concrete building on another side street, an emblem over the doorway but nothing special. A man meets us at our cab and leads us inside, up some stairs, through a dim corridor past closets and a locker room, to a large office. He's wearing a polo shirt and jeans, hardly the uniform of a police chief; he looks completely out of place in this office, but knows exactly where to find the roll of stick-on visas that look like low-quality reproductions of the one I got from the embassy. There's another man with us, a hulking, body-builder type who stares at me without blinking. No doubt about his role in this little game...

The chief looks at my passport, writes some information on the sticker, and with it, obliterates another entire page of the little blue book—two more border entries and exits gone from its potential. He hands me a form to sign, all in Russian, and my paranoia shouts out loud.

This is how they really get you. What am I swearing to in Russian—that I'm a criminal, a spy, an enemy of the state begging for mercy, that I imported drugs or sabotaged a railway or... That's what some regimes do with prisoners: give them a smile and a document in a language they don't speak and then show the world their "confession" and signature while the poor dupe gets bludgeoned in a prison cell. It happened weekly during Vietnam, and happens even now in the Middle East. This is just another Podunk country too impoverished to be at war with anyone, but the memories of those horror stories well up a little too easily. My "confession" might go all the way to my President, who'll say "well he's our boy, but Jesus, we don't what that kind of sick freak back," with the diplomats agreeing that it's a matter best resolved quietly in the shadows as per local custom.

And then I may as well have tried to run screaming towards the Polish border and hoped for mercy from the machineguns.

So I politely say no, I won't sign, and with anger equal to my politeness he forces the issue. The bodyguard stands up, smirking, my pen the only thing that can keep him back.

So okay. I did it. I admit it. I smuggled that car full of whatever, I burned down the orphanage, I'm the Lindbergh baby...just...lemme go.

"How much do I pay?"

"Nyit," he says. Reprieve? Once I have that passport back, what I'll pay will go down, down, down...and they know this, so he hands it to the cabbie and says "pay him" without pinning down a number. We're hurried out, the station locked behind us; back to the station in the porn-mobile, while the cabbie prattles something off into his cellphone—probably to the guard at the station.

The visa in the passport, my money in my pocket, I could park this car around the corner from the train station and they wouldn't find his body before I'm safe in Fortress Europe. It's tempting... but just another daydream for the doomed, of retribution for the slighted; an image of power for the powerless.

I'm just another schmuck in a cab. Another meal for the

system.

The cabbie demands my money before driving the rest of the way back; I reach past my knife and go for the cash, the cold blade still feeling like a good idea while the money burns with humiliation. Every man has that hero fantasy, that tough-guy-under-fire dream he hopes is true, but that dream mocks me today as I'm faced with my Moment of Truth. I've been had, and when I tried to get out of it, I chose sniveling and lies. Now with the chance to kill him—a seriously disproportionate sin—I roll over and pay, permanently souring any delusions I ever had of being a tough guy.

My righteous rage isn't so immaculate. I make a thousand excuses for myself, like a thousand men before me, buried in a pile of shattered ego. I give him my money and we drive the rest of the way in silence.

My $363 lunch in Brest...

Nadir below me, my day gets better. With a few hours to kill until the next westbound train, I wander around town and spend about three dollars on lunch at a grocery store. The main course is smoked fish with cheese on poppy seed bread, with a banana and a liter of fruit juice. I'm leery of the vegetables and grain—they grow from ground irradiated back in 1986—but I'm hungry and one meal of glowing produce won't kill me.

Take the hundred bucks I spent on the first visa, the two fifty I spent on the second visa, the ten bucks I spent to change my now-useless ticket to one for the next train out of Belarus, and three bucks for this food, and I've got a $363 lunch in a town whose name that sounds like "breasts." For that I should be drinking champagne with Donald Trump, but here I sit on a bench in a sunny spot trying to keep the pigeons from stealing my bread. Such is the life of a paintball journalist on the fringe.

This park is my reprieve from the train station, from the cabbie manning his leaning spot against the side of his car, ready to feed another sucker to the beast that's never satisfied. The sky is an electric-blue like it can only be on autumn days like this, and a fierce wind whips leaves across the paths in the park. Parents walk by with one shoulder high in the air, holding their children's hands and hurrying between buildings. They know I'm different; they're not sure how. I catch their sideways glances, women darting their eyes away and forward again, or down towards their children. Do they know my shame, or do they just not see that many tourists?

For the troubles I've had here, Brest is rather attractive—like a nicer version of Perm. There are yellow buildings and shopping centers, color everywhere, and the little kiosks on the street sell coffee and newspapers and Russian porn. The people are dressed in their weekend best, and the apartment buildings—here at least—look more European, less concrete-box-Soviet. Not a bad place, economy aside.

I smile at the flock of pigeons stalking my bread, bobbing their heads as they walk, impatiently stamping three-toed feet, and wonder if they are conscious of any difference between themselves, Russian, and Polish pigeons—they are all just pigeons, after all. I read that scientists found some tonal differences between dogs of the same breed that were reared in different countries—dog accents. They could tell an English poodle from a French poodle by more than the ribbons in its hair. But do the dogs notice?

And do they care anywhere near as much as we do?

We invented "nationality." It's unnatural. It envelops our traditions and gives them definition through boundaries—some way to discern "us" from "them." We need something easy that avoids the unhelpful realization that people are just...people. Families and herds are the largest social group most animals recognize. Pigeons don't seem to care at all.

But people do. And because my blonde hair and blue eyes are different from the blonde over blue on the other side of a border, I spent $363 to have an unscheduled lunch in Belarus.

We're funny creatures.

Parting shots...

The passport control officer has a huge steel and rubber stamp in one hand, my passport in the other, and stamps my original visa. Then he flips idly through the pages, finds the one I bought today, and fixes me with a look of tired pity that says it all. He cancels that one, too, and hands my passport back.

It's dark now, the platform lighted with electric lamps high on rusting poles. The same officer who stopped me this morning is still on duty, and smiles at me like a used car salesman with my money in his pocket and another lemon moved off his lot.

I'll never see Josh again if I kick him in the balls…

* * * * *

My emergency ticket leaves me status-less, and a special guest of sorts—but special in that bottom-of-the-list sense. The guards plunk me down in a half-sized compartment where the attendant rides, knees bouncing against the yellowed outside wall of this car's bathroom. Through the thin sheet metal wall may come all sorts of agonized sounds. Great.

I unpack a plastic-wrapped blanket and pull it over myself, using my camera bag as a pillow. The attendant comes back from his rounds and is surprised to find me in his compartment. I expect another hassle.

But by his grace and the pity on his face—man, is everyone in on the joke?—he leaves me alone, shutting the door that does not open again for some time. Then it slides back, the light waking me up and silhouetting a Polish woman's face, her sweater tight across an attractive chest, pistol in a shiny leather holster, bar scanner in hand.

I surrender my passport, mentally preparing for the worst because that's the theme today, and she hands it back with a Poland entrance stamp. "Welcome to European Union," she says with an honest smile.

Even bad luck can't last forever.

Top: **"Stalin's Gift," the Palace of Culture and Science**

Bottom: **The Author, gone native. Photos by Josh Vise**

Warsaw, Poland
9 September, 2007

Warsaw, Poland

Two great talkers will not travel far together.

—Spanish Proverb

Laughter in Warsaw… What is an "Art Hostel"?… A bucolic playground of destruction… Divesting the clutter… Going native… Turkish street food snobbery… Anxious in Purgatory… When the time comes, you'll know it… One free lie… Leaving Josh…

I step off the train after midnight, half-awake and surprised by the modern station. There are glowing advertisements everywhere, which I didn't realize were missing from the former-Soviet stations; long glowing fluorescent tubes, too, and gleaming tile walls. Many sets of tracks run parallel through this station, and trains arrive on several other levels too—local trains run underground, international lines pull in right here. It's a modern train station for modern times. Urgency in motion. Europe proper.

* * * * *

The night is full of people my age, bundled against the chill that whips through my thin jacket and makes my skin clammy where the camera bag presses against my shoulders. Knots of twenty-somethings sway down the sidewalk, talking at drunk-volume; it's their laughter that gets me. Their gaiety in these wee hours is refreshing because it was missing from the street scenes in Russia. What are darkened weekend streets without young voices laughing? They were mean and lawless in Ulan Bator, and millions of people schooled like honking, hawking salmon through Beijing; there was such noise and neon back in Seoul…

But here the people laugh.

They're out tonight in Warsaw and all over the western world, their laughter the same in Poland and Paris, New York and St. Louis; if I squint hard enough I could be almost anywhere at all—even home. Then I shake my head and read a sign and I'm back in Poland, back in the first steps of a new adventure through another country, fresh off the trail, catching up to Josh…right where I need to be.

Dave Norman

What is an "art hostel"?

Who needs a cab on a night like this? It's cool and breezy, yes, but so alive, with such different energy from the Russian streets that were empty and felt so much colder. My little black book is open to the OkiDoki Hostel page, which leads me through a nighttime profoundly different on this western side of the EU border. There is a sense of freedom in the air tonight. Where the ambiance of Perm was a hard scowl, here I almost giggle, and the instructions to my home for the night feel intuitive in that way a duck just knows when it's flying south. This is the right path, yes, through the right place and on foot is the right way to get there.

It's hard to navigate a new town's streets without a map, in the dark, alone at one in the morning, but the instructions and the instincts hold up—I can keep the Palace of Culture's clock tower on my right hand side, and there are tram tracks on Marszałkowska Street as advertised. I get distracted by a little park and wander around its bushes and benches and trees, watching a couple stroll down the street and out of sight.

The hostel's door is poorly marked but the instructions take me right to the buzzer, where someone watches me through a night vision security camera. I must look sufficiently "youth hostel patron" —like because the lock buzzes open for me. I walk past the side entrance to a bank and up some smooth stone steps towards a buxom mermaid with a shield and a helmet that she wears at a rakish angle, the words "Hostel Oki Doki" and an arrow painted on the wall beside her.

There's a party in the hostel pub where people my age drink cheap beer long into the night. An exhausted-looking girl works the front desk. She hands me a key and points farther up the grand stairwell, towards the dorms on the floor above.

The girl explains that this is an "art hostel," a term I'm convinced she made up; but it's the best way to describe the place. The walls are painted shocking colors, like orange-tinted pink, bold red, yellow…paintings and drawings hang everywhere, some done right on the wall. An artist could probably trade a good sketch or quick painting for a night here, and seems like many have done just that. The rooms, she says, each have different themes—travel themes and art themes, special colors and decorations and unique art on the walls…the kind of place that makes you glad for words like "eclectic" and "funky," relatively useless words but without which there would be no way to describe it at all.

The bathrooms remind me in look, size, and smell of my freshman year in college. Our dorm is at the end of the hall. The theme inside is "office, sweet office," as the space was recently and unimaginatively converted from a drab, standard-issue corporate office. Apparently the artistic flourishes haven't reached this far, and that's fine. I'm so tired, I just want to find an empty bed and pass out—there's something about a warm, dark room full of lightly snoring people that takes all the energy right out of me. The only empty bed is a top bunk—my favorite—and has my framepack in it…

Though I knew it was in good hands with Josh, the sight of it makes me beam in the dark—my clothes, Urals photo book, Mongol art…my toothbrush…all there, reserving me a clean, warm, stationary bed.

Statues don't sleep so peacefully.

A bucolic playground of destruction…

Warsaw is a Post World War II city with the wonderfully ironic motto "Semper Invicta"—Always Victorious. Countless times it has been sacked, looted, and burned, in the time-honored German tradition of exercise and adventure at Poland's expense. The landlocked city's coat of arms features a mermaid with a sword and shield, which is reproduced in the hostel's stairwell—with a few bonus cup sizes. The city retains a tiny number of authentic buildings dating back to the eighteen and seventeen hundreds, which is unusual for Europe, where even the tiniest hamlets have buildings from the seventeenth, or even sixteenth centuries. Much of the reason Warsaw doesn't, is attributable to their history as Eastern Europe's whipping-boy.

Warsaw began as a military settlement for the native Polish, with their first fortress named Bródno. It was replaced two hundred years later with Jazdów, which was promptly sacked. The survivors rebuilt Jazdów on the site of a nearby fishing village, where it remained for two hundred years before Prince Bolesław II renamed the settlement Warszowa, from whence derived the name "Warsaw."

Filled with arable land and on the way to Western European kingdoms, Poland was a popular thoroughfare for armies and bandits heading across the Central European Steppe. They were a welcome mat for armies heading east, and even hosted skirmishes with Genghis Khan's Golden Horde. It was sacked in World War I by the Germans and company, and then sacked again in World War II. Try as they might to cling to peace, their location made Poland a historic playground of destruction.

The Nazis had a tremendous military presence in Warsaw during the early 1940s, driving locals out by the thousands and drawing the full fury of the Red Army and Allied bombing raids. Ahead of their retreat, the Nazis bulldozed and blasted any buildings and supply caches they thought would aid the advancing Allied armies, or that might protect those locals caught in the middle.

Between the carpet bombing, shelling, and demolitions, Warsaw was reduced to a smoldering pile of rubble. Then the rubble was blasted into even tinier bits, in an orgy of violence that would make General Sherman proud.

In the final days of the conflict, Russia quietly claimed Poland for their Soviet Empire. The people came back, and brought with them heavy machinery and the resilient Polish pride that has rebuilt their country time and time again. Their economy didn't fare too well as an Eastern Bloc country, but their pride in being Polish never dulled—forged in adversity, tempered in the flames of their homeland, there are few bonds so strong as their national identity.

More European than farther-east countries, with ocean ports and borders with Western countries, Poland fared much better coming out of the Soviet era than Lithuania, Ukraine, and Belarus. In 2004, they joined the European Union, and haven't been invaded in awhile.

They seem pretty happy about that.

Divesting the clutter...

Today is September 10th, I'm vaguely aware that it could be a Monday, and I'm cold. Not freezing to death in the White Mountains cold, which feels very different, but I'd rather be warmer cold, which is so much easier to rectify. At the moment we're in the Polish Post Office, but in a few minutes we'll be on the street again and looking for the next warm place—this is early autumn in a northern climate, but I packed for Beijing heat. Siberia was cool, but not cold, much of the difference being that we were there in late August and anything less than scorching Chinese heat felt downright refreshing. Autumn comes fast in Warsaw, with September highs in the mid sixties and lows in the forties as they sink towards October—jacket weather as the first leaves start turning.

This looks like any big city Post Office in the Midwest, with blue-uniformed workers behind desks handing out boxes, poring over forms, weighing and measuring and busily guarding the gates to an international network of cheerful men in small trucks and windowless white airplanes with Post painted on the cabins. There is no bulletproof glass, no armed guard, no man in a green uniform with a red star on his hat standing at the door as in our last few countries; just dogged smiles upturned with joy at helping me figure out the customs forms to mail a box of artwork and t-shirts home.

Value of contents? A few old fraternity t-shirts that smell like a Russian railcar, a gorgeous photo book with a priceless inscription from a friend, irreplaceable Mongol dolls for my mother...useless, valueless clutter in the grand scheme of things. I write a big number anyway.

The Post Office brings backpackers face to face with the reality that so many of the things which mean so much to us are of so little objective value. I mail home only the things I think are worth saving—words I choose carefully, knowing they are not otherwise worth the expense. I could donate my shirts to a local charity, or to trade the hostel's lost and found for something I need. But I have unhealthy sentimental attachment to these things I know aren't actually worth $78 to mail home…

Moving out of my apartment before this trip, I sat surrounded by boxes and disassembled furniture and realized that I'm completely comfortable living with only the few things I left accessible. Sealed away from the extra clothes, the old spices and spatulas, the drawer-clutter dumped in boxes that will, in turn, be dumped back in drawers somewhere else, I didn't feel any comfort in ownership—no attachment to the things that fill and define my space.

Just freedom from the possessions that came to own me. The boxes could disappear from my life and I'd still be happy…except if I thought about what was in them.

So I look down at this box of t-shirts and souvenir clutter I don't need, and the price of three more days on the trail just to ship it back to myself, and think…just let it go.

"I'm not worrying about it," Josh says. He has a few things in his daypack to mail, but not at these prices. "I can wait," he says.

But I can't; I need to stay light and mobile—able to dump everything in that pack and hump it over the next hill on foot, just in case. I need the room for some cool-weather clothes and… more clutter, I'm sure. There go two and a half days on the trail, the future traded to preserve these parts of my past that only I value.

Which is good enough for me.

Just let it go, the voice says again…

Going Native…

I like getting good and lost on purpose—leaving the worn out tourist trails and bushwhacking my way through the real country. I look in windows and pull on doors and find all sorts of neat places…and trust in Zen Navigation.

I need some warm clothes, I think, clearing everything else from my mind. I'm drawn towards Josef Stalin's "Palace of Culture and Science." There's a glass-sided department store on the way, but it doesn't interest me so much as a warehouse that looks like a run-down Kroger grocery store without the broken carts in the parking lot.

Inside, it's laid out as if a train carrying a Macy's collided with one carrying a Thai night market and the debris was arranged by Chinese merchants. There are tightly packed aisles lined on both sides with tiny stalls fashioned from shiny steel grates and solid paneling, every vertical surface covered with layers of shirts, pants, belts, underwear...

One booth specializes in bridal gowns, with bolts of fabric stacked high behind displays. Two "Army Surplus" booths sell military patches and camouflage-pattern street clothes. Several booths specialize in American-style hip-hop fashion, with comically oversized jeans, t-shirts with shimmering gold lettering and pop-art designs, baseball caps just waiting to be worn backwards...

There are all-pants booths, all-shirts booths, kids' clothing booths, even an old woman selling fried foods and soda at a snack counter in the corner. There are no prices posted on anything. This is exactly halfway between the Western European department stores and the dense warrens of independent merchants that comprise Far Eastern bazaars.

Fighting the sensory overload, I pick out a thick brown sweater with a quarter-length zipper, a style I've seen on the street already, and ask for the woman's best price. She doesn't speak English, but gets the drift, and uses a calculator to show me 150PLN—about forty bucks.

"Thank you," I say, bowing instinctively in the Asian custom that doesn't apply here but is, nonetheless, recognized as being polite. I bowed in Korea and China—just little lowerings of the head, my shoulders moving a few inches, nothing major—and I bowed in Mongolia, and always it was returned. I bowed in Russia and, coming up, often found the same hard scowls unmoved and unchanged despite my civility, such that I embraced the bow that was foreign to us both out of spite instead of respect—I'll show you common courtesy, the thought went, whether you like it or not.

Bowing has apparently become a habit. Whoops.

I punch 50 into her calculator and she sucks a long breath,

making a staccato sound with her tongue. 125, she counters; the hostel costs 40PLN a night. Three nights' stay for one sweater seems kind of high; I peg currencies to strange indexes.

It's cold outside, and in my hand is the solution…but there are nine more aisles to hunt. A few minutes later I find the same sweater for sale at the same price, and ultimately, the same bargain. I thank her and move on, but there are no more sweaters in the building, so I go back to the first woman with the cash in my hand.

I'm loyal in strange ways.

Back on the street, I need something warmer than my black baseball cap. I wander east past cafés and bakeries, a curious soup shop, and find a farmer's market along Nowy Swiat street. An old man unloads quarts of fresh-picked grapes and apples. I buy a half-kilo of raspberries for three bucks and munch my way down the sidewalk, fingers turning red with sweet juices.

I lick the seeds from my teeth, wipe my fingers on my pants, and walk into a haberdashery. The little bell on the door rings behind me. The owner emerges from a room in back, where through a drawn curtain I see a Styrofoam head with chalk lines and felt strips. She greets me in Polish.

"Howdy," I say. I remember half of the Polish word for hello, but don't want to mangle it. At least saying howdy implicates my nationality, and thus, which flavor of foreigner I am.

The walls are hung with black Polish fedoras, hand-knit women's caps in blue, white, and beige, straw hats with colorful bands, felt hats with maroon or green ribbons tied in flat-pressed bows opposite small red feathers… These are the hats old men wear the world over. I've found where they're made!

I have in mind a fleece hiking cap, the kind that will keep me warm in a Polish autumn and wherever I go next, the temperature dropping as the leaves turn gold. She doesn't have that sort of thing, but I need something, so I try on the hats she made and each one makes me look older and closer to the grave until I find the perfect style: a sloped-dome cap of pressed rabbit hair, jet-black with enough space for an insulating layer of air. It has the old-world aesthetic I've seen time and again in pictures of immigrants fresh off the boats at Ellis Island…and several times on the street already.

Yes, in the full-length mirror, with this brown quarter-zip sweater and black cap, scruffy beard and scuffed-up boots, I'm the very image of an old world immigrant; more importantly, I fit in on the streets in a way I haven't anywhere yet. With my old wardrobe on its way back home, I'm slowly going native.

Turkish street food snobbery…

I'm addicted to döner kebap. Like a smoker who quit years ago, the shakes are gone but I know I'll always be addicted—the smell, the taste, the comfort of pita bread filling my hand with hot shaved mystery meat and garlic sauce… I fell in love so naively, so innocently, sneaking kebap into my host family's home on an exchange trip to Germany. I was a kebap-a-day addict, eating against time, knowing that in a few weeks I would fly back to the kebap-devoid Midwest. There are gyro shops in the malls, yes, and they have sour cream sauce and shaved lamb, but it's not the same—not the same at all, like a hamburger patty when you crave filet mignon.

But that analogy is backwards—kebap is more like the hamburger, a cheap, greasy thing slapped together for a few zloty in tiny shops that wouldn't pass American health inspections… which makes them that much better. That much more authentic. They do terrible things to your bowels, and that's part of it too— the Full Kebap Experience. My friends don't understand, which sets me apart in those comforting ways that make it easy to fancy myself a World Traveler, a Man of Experience, the kind of guy who drinks vodka with Mongols and pines for things he can't spell without an umlaut. Yes, all these delusions and the belly-filling warmth of meat in a bread pocket come wrapped in foil at the döner kebap stand.

I hand the woman twelve zloty—a green and white bill and a two-color coin with a faux gold band around a silver center. She hands me a kebap with extra meat and chili pepper flakes, strands of shredded lettuce poking out of the garlic sauce like the arms of drowning men. There's quite a line behind me, of guys in hardhats sipping coffee next to students and women with leather briefcases—kebap, the people's food.

This is my homecoming in Europe; it wasn't real until now, this taste I associate with my first real trip abroad—this misplaced anchor to Germany, country of my heritage, misplaced because it's Turkish and I passed authentic German restaurants to get it… but I ate it in German parks and now, alone in a crowd on a Polish street, this kebap is a direct pipeline back to that freedom and heady excitement. This is an adventure we're on, and Josh is off somewhere trying to feel the sort of emotion I just bought with a three dollar lunch.

The meat is as wonderful as I remember, but the shell is different—a soft white pita instead of crispy wheat bread. No goat cheese or red onions either, so it's not perfect…but it'll do.

And do quite nicely.

This is the alpha moment of a new adventure. Now that I'm back in the land of kebap, I'll eat all the different types and pit them one against another like gladiators. Where's the best meat-stuffed pita pocket in Europe? How far can I push this adventure, now that I'm back on top?

I'm going to find out.

Anxious in Purgatory…

"How can you eat that?" Josh asks. We're back at the hostel, in a lounge that overlooks a park, where I've been waxing philosophically about kebap; but how can you explain the nature of love? Of memories and hope and salvation wrapped in a bread pocket?

"Whatever makes you happy…" he says. He's got the furtive look of a man about to charge down the stairs and out of sight, suddenly gone forever. I usually find him chatting with someone, holding court over drinks or food or maps, but now he sits strangely alone. Forlorn, almost. I wonder if he needs more now than that old Josh magic; more than flirting with intimacy with interesting strangers; more than he's had all this while, which seems now not to be quite enough after all.

He says, "I leave in two days," dropping the words like bombs—carefully, dangerously, intending their dramatic effect. The air goes tense immediately. "I moved some things around. I've got an overnight layover in Dublin. I'm done."

"That should be...fun." It feels like I'm being left behind; dumped cold, though that's not the case—feelings are only tenuously tied to reality.

He looks out the window, his words echoing off the cold glass. "I can't afford a hostel. I've got just enough for a few buses and to see some things, then if I stay out all night I can just show up at the airport and sleep on the way home."

"You stopping in New York?"

"Just to clear Customs, then I'm going home. I can feel it already, that pull... When I get on that plane, I'm just gonna want to get there, you know? No delays, just get it over with." That edge in his voice, those pensive eyes...

So much has changed. Now he's the one keyed up, stressed out, road-weary and eager to just get on with things...and get them over with—the way I felt in Mongolia. Just enjoy the ride, man, I want to say, flinging his words back at him. But his angst goes deeper than illness, deeper than the stresses of one place or a few hard days.

He's been abroad for over a year, in the sort of isolation he needed but didn't seem to know what to do with; he missed being part of all the family happenings and holidays back home, where it increasingly seemed he needed to be. To show for all his stories and misery and excitement and work, he has the clothes on his back, a new line on his resume, and is in debt. What was it all for, he seems to wonder in that place deep within his stare.

Maybe he was only after a good time; he had that. Maybe he suspects the answers—to questions of identity and his place in the world—lie in wait in St. Louis, making the time between now and his arrival seem like eternity.

Or could he see that golden hope as, itself, another false prophecy—just a carrot on a stick, first dangled over Korea, then Moscow, and now yet another place with only more questions and doubt? You make your place in the world, after all; you don't just find it. There is no magical solution. All this time he's been looking for it as a location, as a fact, as a sacred jolt from some strange new stimulation. But if it worked like that—if happiness came merely from relocation or adventure itself or interchangeable stimulations—then he should have his answer.

Rather, his place in the world lies inside him, as a state of mind and perspective hidden within; the same is true for me, and now I see it. Happiness is something you make with the tools you have and the inspiration you find. But it's not a destination, not a place; perhaps our desperate, failed attempts at finding happiness rather than making peace are what caused the friction between us.

Seeing my friend now, sitting before the window on a gray-sky day, face contorted as he twists around towards me again, I realize that this path we've been on is a scenic lark. The changes I expected of myself, from the graduate student to the man ready for marriage and responsibility, don't necessarily happen riding horses across Mongolia or during Russian absinthe benders. They happen on far more frightening journeys—journeys within oneself.

That's a shocking realization; one that comes at the far end of a heavy trip for the mind and the heart, an around-the-world-in-a-train-car voyage open to anyone who dares to truly question their place in the world. You don't even have to leave home to take it; yet so many do—as we did—without knowing that the process is an inward journey.

Now Warsaw seems at best a diversion, at worst a confrontation with the fact that he's been—that we've been—misleading ourselves even as he led me across Eurasia. Now the end can't come fast enough for Josh. He's ready to get on with things, on with life back where he left it, on with the search he must take alone. These last two days will unfold for his body in Warsaw, a place his mind has already left; a place he doesn't truly want to be any longer.

His Purgatory.

Two days more… Too much time to sit idly by this window and simply wait. The nervous energy coils inside him, this tension that makes him seem ready to bolt at any moment.

It reflects how I must have felt all along, without knowing it. I need the time, the space from those who know me or knew me, to take that trip my spirit needs—a Trans Siberian Railroad for the soul.

On the train away from Perm I realized that I am, after all, right where I need to be. Strangers don't know us; we can be anyone when we're alone somewhere truly foreign. More boldly, we can be ourselves…and see who that is.

Changing your surroundings really helps…but it is a tool, not an answer.

Looking at my future without Josh and his plans, his guidance and example and companionship, I see the terrifying freedom I require to become the man I need to be. Alone and acutely aware of my cowardice and courage, I'll have no one else to rely upon or blame; no one to check myself against, to distract me from the voices and the thoughts that come when left completely to myself.

Few things can be more terrifying; few things can be more freeing.

The paralyzing reality of such complete freedom, of course, is that among its infinity of options there are no rules, no structure save for that which you allow to limit your freedom. I will answer to my harshest critic, the only man who can set me free to become who I am destined to be: me.

With those simple words, I'm getting off in Poland…I leave in two days, he gave me my freedom, and took his own.

This is that moment where the rollercoaster mounts the hill and pauses, that flash of calmness where the pull of the chain beneath the car is done and you float light as a breath before gravity takes over. Poised between two adventures, the one behind and the one ahead, I find peace to hold onto.

I'm ready to be done with the pre-booked tickets, with the reservations, with plans that supplant my need to control my own fate. I'm ready to go where I please; to test my courage and wits and spirit as I guide myself across the sea of endless possibilities.

These are the final hours of his yearlong sojourn to Asia, a journey to discover himself and figure out what he needs from the future. He's ready to come home; I wonder if he's ready, now, to start finding some answers.

My journey continues where it must: on the road.

When the time comes, you'll know it...

So we go to dinner to talk things out, like there needs to be a sort of formal peace between us. My head swirls with these ideas of looking without and within, of my carrying on and his going home—of knowing when the time is right to come out of the woods after a spirit quest.

My black book is open on the table between us, the white pages glowing yellow in the lamplight. "I prepaid nine bucks to the Goodbye Lenin in Krakow," he says. "That's the last reservation I made. We don't have train tickets, but the schedule is right there." He points to the pages. "You'll be alright alone?"

I want to tell him of course. I want to explain to him that now I know why people go to Europe to find themselves; that I've seen the clever mechanics behind the veil of that cliché. Of course I'll be fine—I'll finally be alone to take stock of things, a process neither of us can do while traveling with the other. I want to speak of the wonderful and terrifying opportunities that come with solitude.

He strikes preemptively, as if to avoid such treacherous ground, firing a single question like a marksman.

"Is Jake still coming in?"

Jake... Did I invite calamity?

Jake answered that email I sent from Mongolia. He lands in three days. So self-absorbed was I, in existential crises and my own affairs, that I forgot all about—Jake.

We are to meet him—I am to meet him—in Krakow, the last city in my little black book, where I figured that either Josh and I would be soul-brothers or not speaking at all. Either way, I figured the end of our little black itineraries would be the end of our story, and a good time for a great friend to arrive.

I also figured that there was no way he would be able, on such short notice, to take time off for an expensive, no-plans junket across Europe. I was wrong. It wasn't an empty invitation…I just didn't expect it to work. But now Josh and Jake will pass in the air over the North Atlantic, and I'll trade one old friend for another on this journey I lately realize must be taken alone.

Jake is five years my junior, an inch taller, and a good deal smarter. An accomplished engineer at only twenty, he has the boyish charm of a kid brother with the caprice and intellect of a mad scientist—he has a long way to go on whatever spiritual journey life has in mind for him. I wonder if I'll become his Josh.

Is this luck or insanity?

"Yeah," I say at last. "Yeah, he's meeting me in Krakow or something."

"Use my reservation for him," Josh says. "Don't worry about the deposit."

"Then let me buy your dinner."

"Sure," and he smiles, leaning back. "Thanks." He bought our first meal together, back in Seoul; it fits that I should buy our last.

"I'm gonna miss you, man," I say. Though I mean it, I can't get the edge out of my voice—the I've been practicing this edge. I will miss him, but I need to be to take off on my own now. To quit following Josh, and…start leading Jake? I don't know about that… But I'm tired of stale city air and concrete buildings, of shimmering glass where trees belong, of Joshua Teacher where I want Joshua Friend. It's been great, but when the time comes you just know it.

So I'm losing Josh after five weeks, six countries, two continents and a lot of good times; in a few days I'll gain Jake—another person who knew me back when, and who only knows how to interact with the guy I was in grad school. That was me recently, yes, but how things—and people—can change…

I look out the window and see the faintest reflection of myself—black cap, brown sweater, scraggly beard—as a different person than I was in Seoul; a very different person than I was back there, where Jake knows me from. I don't write home much anymore, and when I do, I write trivial news and platitudes. I've run out of things to say that wouldn't cause serious confusion, and

I can imagine eyes back home glazing over as I tell my stories, old friends and family unable to relate; I imagine being a stranger at my own party. Besides, I need to think new thoughts and mull them over with strangers; writing home lures me right back into being the person I was before.

Inviting Jake seems like a terrible idea.

But Josh smuggled my bags into Europe for me. He lent me money in a pinch, and beyond his utility, he's my friend. Damn it all, I enjoyed having him along, and I realize in a broad, fast stroke how thankful I am to have such a companion.

Looking at his now-familiar orange hair and pierced ear, his features sallow in the lamplight, I fancy I know the man across the table. Perhaps not the Josh he was in Korea, nor the man he'll be back home, but the person he is right now—right now with the hummus clinging to his cheek.

Maybe Jake will see my clothes and beard and realize in an instant that I'm a different person, like I didn't realize about Josh in Seoul. Probably not; and maybe there aren't that many changes. It's hard to be objective about yourself.

"Has he been out of the country before?" Josh asks.

"Yeah, Nicaragua." A college trip, where the behavior of the other students shocked him—it was not in fitting with who they were back at school…but they weren't at school anymore, so of course there would be differences. We are all dynamic.

"How's he going to handle Poland?"

"He'll manage. I'll drag him along to Prague, maybe," I'm just making this up on the spot. "Then Germany. Or Hungary. Who knows. He has ten days on the continent, plenty of time to make a man of him." We share conspirators' smiles. "Hell, it'll be good for the kid."

I have the plans; I'll email him cab-friendly directions from the airport to the hostel, so he can just print them out and hand them to the driver. I'll figure out our schedules and keep things organized so the poor guy isn't overwhelmed, and so he can have an adventure…following me.

"So you're gonna show him the world, huh?"

"I guess I am."

One free lie...

Every trip has The Story—the anecdote you tell to people when they ask "so what all did you do?" No one wants to know what all you did, they just want to hear that you went exotic places, had fun, and now you're back and all is normal again. Rare is the saint with the interest and attention span to hear the whole story. We need a sound bite for the masses, and something more—fun?—for longer conversations.

"We each need a big one," Josh says. "Something that if I tell, you're right there to back up, or if someone brings it up later, you can be like 'yeah, and then...' and tell the same thing so they believe it."

There's been so much that stretches credulity already; so many insights and truths I don't want to undermine. Why this?

"Just for the hell of it," he says, and then I realize that no one will believe much of the truth anyway. "That night in Perm, remember the bar?"

"Yeah."

"And the blonde Russian bartender chic?"

It was a dude with brown hair and a scowl... "Right, and she kept pouring you free absinthe?"

"Trying to get me trashed, but I had her drink with me..."

"And you went back to her place, right?"

"Yeah, but the thing was—it's her brother's bar, that beefy guy up in the VIP."

"He was so pissed when he came home..."

"...and found me drunk with his sister, so I had to bolt out the window..."

"...nearly broke your leg!"

"...naked with just a sheet I pulled off the bed on my way out."

"Should have been arrested, you crazy nutter..."

"...and if you go to that club now, hanging up over the bar, are my boxers—like a captured flag."

"Saw it with my own eyes, I did."

"What's yours?" he asks.

I need to think, because big lies—at least about my exploits and adventures—just don't sit well with me. But not sharing in this covenant feels like leaving a buddy in the cold, so…

"You got hit by a tram."

"I what?"

"Jakeman expects to see Eastern Europe with us. But you're going home. You didn't run out of money, bro…you got hit by a tram."

"Had to get flown home."

"And you're going to be fine—not Jake and me fine, but you know, fine in your own special way…"

"Hurt like a son of a bitch when I woke up…"

"Surrounded by police…"

"The Eastern European nurses were gorgeous…"

"Kind of jealous myself…"

"It was a bar night…"

"And we were wasted on absinthe."

"Right on."

"That's it. You were tripping absinthe and got hit by a tram and in your memory…"

"Hey, I'm not dead…"

"…in your honor, then, I'm going to take him out on an absinthe bender and scare the willies out of the kid."

"You're a sick man."

"It was your idea."

Leaving Josh…

It's eleven o'clock on a Tuesday, about which I care only because I have to be on time for the Krakow train. We walk past a bread stall on the street and I point to a circular pretzel, about six inches across, and say "Hey, it's Ethiopian belt-bread!"

"There's something cruel about you," he says, and perhaps he's right; I get punchy when I'm stressed, and this is the point when everything changes.

Josh is in super-teacher-mode, leading me like a puppy on a leash. "We take this street," he says without needing to—it's the same street we each took from the same station three nights ago. At the station, he reads the departure board aloud for me though I can read just as well—the l's have lines, the o's have accent marks, but if you mispronounce them the same way each time the echoing words make a sort of sense...

My ire rises with every obvious point he makes, every word he reads for me, and I'm ready for that promise to split off with no hard feelings. I thought it would be harder than this, and while there is no malice in my heart, the annoyance makes it easier.

* * * * *

I wondered how it would go; would I wake up somewhere and he'd be gone, a note for me at the hostel desk...or if I'd do that to him. If I'd want to see Budapest, he'd want to see Paris, and we'd shake hands and take trains bound in opposite directions... or if there'd be a fight. Something climactic, something anti-climactic, but not a crowd of people milling around as he drags me from window to window to find a ticket I can get for myself, like he's trying to bundle me off. But that's not it...this is just how he deals with stress—a cultivated response.

Joshua Teacher, under fire, is a man of action. I respect that, even when his action is to treat me like a wayward student, a silly kid who can't be trusted with his own welfare. Belt-bread indeed; eat a sandwich, you skinny bastard, which I mean with all due love. I think about those old married couples who fight within an inch of divorce because they know this isn't really it, but the heat of the moment makes it easier to vent what's bugging them. It's not healthy, but it happens.

So goodbye, Joshua Teacher. We'll be different people in a month, different again when we see each other next. I'll write you from the road, tell you of my adventures, the places I go and the things I see, and your eyes will glaze over because try as we might, we can't relate to places we've never been, or who our friends become when they're away. We'll always have this trip together, but you can't come with me where I need to go, and I don't want to go back in time with you. I'm vitriolic now because that's easier than saying goodbye to the best friend I've ever left in Warsaw.

I watch him through the train window. He's wearing the jazz hat, waving goodbye.

Leading

Jake

Coming in 2012
from
f/64 Publishing

The adventure continues in **Leading Jake**, where Dave meets his best friend in Krakow — a medieval city with an ancient soul and a youthful lust for life. Their coming-of-age story is set against rich historic and cultural backdrops as they explore Krakow and Prague. Then alone at last in Germany, land of his ancestors, Dave must make peace with former loves and other trauma before embracing a new life.

From absinthe bars to Auschwitz, a fire-breathing dragon's lair to Oktoberfest — and that space between extended adolescence and adulthood — **Leading Jake** is the provocative, laugh-out-loud sequel to **Following Josh** that will inspire you to fall in love with life...and laugh with every breath.

www.f64publishing.com

Appendix A

A tale of two Ivans...

The Trans Mongolian Railroad dragged us across the legacy of two Ivans: the Great, and the Terrible. Ivan the Great is the man who coalesced Russia as a country, incorporating Novgorod and Tver into his territory and driving the Great Khan's forces out of Russia with politics and violence. He set in motion the eastward migration into Siberia, accomplishing this all before his sixty fifth birthday. Rather than retire in a country without golf, he promptly died.

His kingdom is the heart of modern Russia, and the spirit of his easterly quest lives on in the Trans Siberian trains bound east for Vladivostok.

But it was Ivan the Terrible, grandson of Ivan the Great, whose reign in the 1500s nearly caused the end of the world in 1962...

* * * * *

Ivan didn't stand a chance at becoming a nice guy. His father fell through history's cracks and died of an infected pimple on his leg, leaving a wife and three year old Ivan. No one lets a toddler run their country, so the high-muckities clamored for power within the ranks of Russian nobility. They killed his mother, and spent the next decade keeping the child at heel so he wouldn't get any ideas about taking power away from them; supposedly he developed a temper and began abusing animals, like a rumored episode of throwing puppies from a parapet.

When he turned fifteen, Ivan assembled the ranking nobles—the Boyar Council—and called them to account, singling out one man in particular: Prince Andrew Shuisky. The door burst open and in charged tough men whose acquaintance Ivan had made in secret. They seized the prince and dragged him to a courtyard where they locked him in a cage full of starved hunting dogs that tore him limb from limb in a gruesome public display.

The world met Ivan the Terrible.

"The Terrible" is an English approximation of the word "grozny," which could also be translated as "strict" or "powerful," or even "awesome"—but not in awesome's modern sense of fantastic and wonderful. It was a name he certainly earned by antics, but also through his legacy as Russia's first Tsar.

Ivan led his army and a contingent of Don Cossack mercenaries down the Volga River against the two khanates his grandfather missed, neutralizing them and swinging east to root out more. Their charge added new energy to that great eastward migration that went all the way to the shores of the Pacific. This is how Russia built a country full of white people that stretches across the entire width of Asia.

Ivan overhauled his country's judicial system, leaving cracks just wide enough for bribes to slip through. In territories beyond Moscow, he sold judgeships and political positions and got away with it—an example followed by scads of other politicians throughout history. Ivan married several times and was doing pretty well for himself…except for losing power over his own neuroses.

Ivan was militarily awesome, but increasingly paranoid—he feared he would lose power, and the Boyar Council would overthrow him.

So he purged the Boyars from his court, ordering them to serve in the cavalry, which demoted them to the working class and allowed him to seize control of their estates…just like the Communists would do a few hundred years later to the entire country.

Breeding Communism...

Here's where the story starts to sound a lot like that of Soviet Russia; indeed, Soviet Russia could not have existed without Ivan the Terrible.

He redistributed property, setting another precedent, and held the new land owners responsible for the yield of their estates. It was the first time they were held accountable to standards beyond their own needs and market forces. If their yield wasn't up to the Tsar's expectation, the guy who threw puppies from towers might do who-knows-what to them... So they came down hard on their workers, turning serfdom into outright slavery.

This created an aesthetic of hard work that paid off in terms of personal survival and national success. That became a vital part of the Russian psyche, which you can see in the old Communist posters that came well after the serfs. So the working class leaned hard on their vodka and built a society that grimly accepted their fate and carried on for lack of any other choice. The nobles gallivanted; the serfs worked; the aesthetic deepened.

Which worsened the schism between the rulers and the ruled. Those who fought in the broad-ranging armies returned to work until their dying days, serving the greater good by fighting for their own survival, then working themselves to death—Red Army veterans of WWII could relate. For the rest of Ivan's reign and onwards through history, this idea of a dignified working class as nobler in spirit than their rulers spread and strengthened and grew into Communist ideology and values.

At the heart of their dream is a system where everyone works as hard as everyone else, where no one is supported without contributing their skills and labor, and everyone gets what they need and desires nothing more. That's the best a serf could hope for, she of becoming one of the lords they hated.

It was Ivan's property redistribution and quotas that got the ball rolling—contributing largely, though not single-handedly, to Russia's legacy of formal Communism.

Following victory with quagmire...

The Moscow we find is filled with tall buildings and large glass facades, bright colors and new construction...but these stand out from a vast background of dull square buildings, drab concrete structures left over from the Soviet era. The Seven Sisters Buildings, alike in their towers and Soviet-Gothic style—where concrete was formed into quasi-Gothic Architecture—are visible from just about everywhere in town.

Babushkas shuffle down the busy sidewalks among men in fine tailored suits and girls in tight skirts. It's a place that's trying hard to embrace the future, without necessarily trying to forget the past.

So we can't help remarking on the old buildings in the background, with their fire escapes dangling from cheap concrete walls. Ivan himself walked through Saint Basil's Cathedral, and he may as well have built those drab apartment blocks in the distance—they are as much his legacy as anyone's.

And so was the fall of Soviet Russia, in repetition of Ivan's own troubles.

Ivan's Russia spanned the divide of two continents, and included fertile land that was highly desirable...meaning, of course, constant struggle with their neighbors. In response to regional aggression, he started the Livonian War—the Cold War of his age, in that it was disastrously costly and all-consuming.

It dragged on for twenty five years, bleeding his country of men and resources and pride. His country saw little return for the men they sent to die, and after their success against the khanates, the Livonian quagmire was embarrassing...equivalent to following the Red Army's route of the Nazis with their 1979-89 debacle in Afghanistan.

At one point Ivan fled the capital in shame, only to return and exile those who criticized him. He further shook up his court by banishing perceived enemies and creating something of the Boyar Council v2.0—called the Zemschina. They were sent to Novgorod and put in charge of the rest of the country, while he and his closest advisors focused on political housekeeping in

Moscow and directing his far off wars.

Ivan's best mercenaries were exploring Siberia, having a smashing good time while the rest of his military was getting beaten up by the Livonians. Paranoid land owners were working their serfs to death—and towards certain revolution—and trade was disrupted by all the fighting. Things were pretty grim, which of course Ivan blamed on the Zemschina, those poor souls he sent to govern the interior from Novgorod. They pointed the blame back at him.

So he set off from Moscow for Novgorod with what forces he could muster, and sacked his own city.

Most civil wars are about…something. Economics, identity, religion… This miniature civil war was about Ivan not weathering an insult.

Terrible…

Cuban missiles for Ivan…

While he was gone, the Crimeans sacked Moscow without breaking a sweat. They took what they wanted and ambled off. Russia's other foes were growing stronger while Ivan the Terribly Paranoid reshuffled his government. Again.

In the 1900s, the Soviet Union was under attack not physically by Livonians, but ideologically by capitalism. Democracy and capitalism spread fast after the failure of the Japanese Empire and the Nazi dictatorship. The Soviets dug in for an ideological fight, spurring their industry to out-produce, and thus shame, our capitalist system. With the space race, we fought over pride in scientific development and conspicuous accomplishment. Our militaries raced to amass the larger stockpile of nuclear weapons, well beyond what it would take to destroy the world…and neither country backed down. Ivan would have understood. Too much pride was on the line, and cold wars are fought by image more than bullets…though I'm not sure he would have understood that part.

But the Soviet system was sick with spies and snitches, from block captains up to the Kremlin. Ivan didn't trust his own government, either, who didn't trust each other or him, in the same way that was rampant at all levels of the Soviet Union. The same flavor of paranoia vexed the tsar and wracked the Soviets.

On top of the arms race, the space race, and everything else, the Soviets spent more money on protecting the communist system from their own people than on developing infrastructure to sustain their society—like Ivan worrying about Novgorod while his capital burned. That business with Novgorod was his Cuban Missile Crisis, except he caused it within his own government and territory whereas the Soviets picked their fight with us. Had Ivan the Terrible been in the Kremlin during Khrushchev's Cuban Missile Crisis, I would bet my soon-to-be-vaporized life that he would push the button. Twice, at the very least.

Ivan only lived to be fifty one, dying of natural causes during a game of chess. His government was in shambles, but without an invader taking over or any move for a new form of governance, his son Fyodor was confirmed and carried on the tsardom.

The Soviet Union barely lived longer than Ivan, collapsing under its own tangled weight in 1991, at age sixty nine. The Soviet Union melted into history, and many of their former territories— even Russia itself—more or less democratized. The Soviets came to be along Ivan's dubious course...though they might have avoided their downfall if they had learned from the rest of his example.

The capital city they had in common saw the coming of the Khan, the clash of the Red and White Armies, dictatorships and communism, and finally a capitalist democracy emerging from the ruins of communism...they've been through a lot. All the while, the Russian workers just keep at it, raising grain from the land, turning much of it to vodka, and enduring those things which regular folks have no power over anyway.

Appendix B

Honey for the bears...

Vodka is to Russia like beer is to summer, or rain is to storm clouds. It originated somewhere in European Russia, possibly in the Pontic-Caspian Steppe with its historic abundance of grain. Though it can be distilled from any biological matter with high sugar or starch content, traditional Russian vodka is made from fermented wheat or rye. Poland, Ukraine, and Russia each fervently claim vodka as their national drink; the informal "Vodka Belt" stretches from Finland to Vladivostok, across the Balkan countries and south to the Black Sea.

I drank a lot of vodka in college because it mixes easily into punch and cocktails, and we could buy it cheap in plastic bottles. We believed that vodka, being a clear spirit, had fewer impurities and caused less severe hangovers—a theory too precious to criticize despite contrary headaches.

But we were kind of onto something there...

The vodka stillmaster (like a brewmaster, but for hooch) distills and filters the wort three, four, or more times, until the alcohol content is up near ninety percent—180 proof. That's not pure ethanol-alcohol, but it's very nearly there and water accounts for the rest. Distillation removes the particles, and charcoal filtering removes other chemicals. When they're satisfied with the wort, they use water to dilute it down to around forty proof.

So when we slammed a shot of vodka, screwed up our under-aged faces and pretended we liked the burn, we tasted straight alcohol diluted in plain water and very little else. The ethanol still dehydrates you and aggravates your insides, but unlike with other spirits, we weren't imbibing ethyl lactate, ethyl acetate, methal alcohol (a rather nasty impurity), or fusil oils. So the ethyl alcohol puts the marching band in your head the next morning, but it's all the other stuff that turns up their volume. We were onto something in college after all—lotta good it did us though.

And the Russian aristocracy, so closely tied to political power, was on to something when it came to making vodka. Around the time of Ivan the Terrible, the government seized control of liquor production. Nowadays our government just taxes the hell out of liquor based on alcohol content, but in the fifteen hundreds the Russian government was the only entity allowed to even make or sell it.

They established the first bars in Russia as the exclusive distribution points for standard Russian vodka. As demand grew in the cities and countryside, and takeaway service (by the thirteen-liter-bucketful) got going, they needed more distilleries in more places to keep up with demand. They experimented with selling licenses to the aristocracy to produce the alcohol, and private business boomed. Many aristocrats licensed their licenses, entrenching themselves in the revenue stream without further investment.

A combination of greed and class fear set in, what with all the lesser citizens starting small distilleries and seeing quick success; every ruble given to a businessman was a ruble not given to the nobility…and a measure of power given to the underclass. Clearly the traditional ways of elevating yourself into nobility—not being able to, basically—were under the same threat as the nobility's former monopolistic liquor enterprises.

So the government banned the competition and rather energetically closed down all distilleries not tied to the established nobility.

Later, even that wasn't good enough—the government needed more rubles for their military and urban development. Again they seized exclusive control of production, and the money it generated. This went back and forth for hundreds of years…

...as the landowners defiantly made their own supplies onsite. From there arose a rich tradition of flavored specialty vodkas that survives to this day in Poland, Finland, Ukraine, and the gas station down the street from my old fraternity house. It's patriotic for modern Russians to consider any flavored vodka as anathema—imposters not fit to swill on the darkest night. But in the eighteen hundreds, their land barons made small batch, flavored vodka into an art form.

They flavored their vodka with everything from sweet fruits to bitter herbs, to pepper and even grass, adding the flavors late in the distillation process. It produced brown and red vodkas, green and yellow vodkas, and all sorts of shades with all sorts of flavors that varied from estate to estate. Having custom vodka made only on your estate was a matter of regal pride.

Russia experimented with their own alcohol prohibition in the early 1900s, and like ours in the Roaring '20s, it failed spectacularly. The always-thriving black-market flooded with a tsunami of homemade hooch. Food distribution was badly disrupted, as sugar and grain disappeared by the trainload to fuel the underground distilleries; they backed off in the mid '20s, and things got better for tipplers, bakers, and especially the tippling bakers. The communists brought back the booze and kept production the exclusive right of a special government branch.

Enter Mikhail Gorbachev in the 1980s, a leader saddled with the sagging and desperate communist empire embroiled in the Cold War. They had tremendous expenses, inefficient bureaucracy, and their seventy year old totalitarian system wasn't doing so well...a terrible time for a third of his population to be raging alcoholics. That number is highly disputed, but a pretty good low-ball figure. Gorbachev discouraged his countrymen from drinking, and tried to stem production.

The people were furious, and their outrage contributed to his resignation. So much for that.

Russian history is pretty violent; their days under communism were pretty grim, as viewed by those of us who've known only democracy's freedom. Most of their chapters open with a massive military action and such casualties as I can't fathom, or close with victorious comrades expelling the last invaders from their utterly destroyed city. There are plagues and blights, serfdom and revolution, and always a tendency for the upper echelons to keep the other ninety nine percent in as abject poverty as possible.

Russian life right up until the turn of our new millennium seems incredibly rough. The scowls make sense in context, especially after touring the gulag and reading a lot of Dostoevsky on the train. No wonder they embraced the vodka so readily, for so long; no wonder they fought prohibition so vehemently. Vodka was reliable, comforting, and stable through a history that was anything but.

They tried a US-style free market approach to vodka production in the nineties, where the government could back off and make money for nothing by taxing the businesses that took over the distilleries. With deregulation came another vodka-tsunami from the black-market, as bathtub hooch, "fake" vodka, industrial chemicals mixed with water, and all sorts of other concoctions came to market claiming to be the genuine article. Selling vodka in Russia is about as hard as shilling ice cream in hell, so every man with a few friends and a wild notion started producing hooch.

A lot of people went blind. Many more died. The reputation for Russian vodka on the world market tanked from fear of getting a well-disguised fake full of drain cleaner.

So the government got back in the distillery business and ran damage control on subpar companies—after all, their national image was at stake. Now it's safe to drink Russian Standard; Stolichnaya is good to go. Chengis Wodka?

Who knows…but that's all back in Mongolia, and here in Moscow it's smooth drinking all the way.

More Praise for A Tipping Point for Liberty:

"Government is totally out of control. It is the duty of every citizen to learn how and why. Now, thanks to A Tipping Point for Liberty by Adam Dick, there is a valuable guide to what is wrong with government's role in the drug war, the police state, militarism, surveillance, guns and beyond. Buy this book if you need to learn how government fails us. Buy this book if you want to learn how to defend liberty. Dick is a brilliant word-smith for liberty. His prose hits like fireworks on every page. You won't be able to stop turning the pages. I couldn't."

Robert Wenzel, Editor & Publisher of EconomicPolicyJournal.com

"I am thrilled that the Ron Paul Institute for Peace and Prosperity has published A Tipping Point for Liberty, a collection of some of Adam Dick's best writings. One of the joys of working in Dr. Ron Paul's congressional office was hearing Adam's insightful and witty analysis of the government's latest attacks on liberty, peace, and prosperity, and it is wonderful to see him get a wider audience. Everyone who enjoys reading a no-holds-barred defense of liberty will enjoy this book, and anyone who still thinks America is the 'land of the free' needs to read this book."

Norman Kirk Singleton, President of Campaign for Liberty and former Legislative Director for Congressman Ron Paul

Contents

Forward by Ron Paul xiii

Preface xv

Part 1: The Drug War

Part 2: The Police State

Part 3: Militarism

Part 4: Surveillance

Part 5: Guns

Part 6: Government Chicanery

Part 7: Ron Paul and Libertarianism

Part 8: This and That

Forward

I hope you enjoy as much as I have reading this collection of some of the hundreds of articles Adam Dick has written for the Ron Paul Institute for Peace and Prosperity. Chapter after chapter, Adam focuses with keen insight on the issues of the day with an eye toward protecting Americans' liberty.

So many of the topics Adam deals with in A Tipping Point for Liberty — the drug war, gun rights, the Constitution — are topics he helped me with in the House of Representatives. Now, many more people can benefit directly from his perspective and analysis.

A goal in founding the Ron Paul Institute was to amplify my efforts to educate people regarding liberty and foreign policy. Adam and my long-time foreign policy aide Daniel McAdams are accomplishing this goal by bringing important news and education to a large and growing audience at the institute's website every day.

The Ron Paul Institute published my book Swords into Plowshares last year. In Swords into Plowshares, I wrote about the issue of peace. It is fitting that the institute's second book is Adam's volume that examines liberty in America. Together peace and liberty are the Ron Paul Institute's focus.

I want to comment briefly regarding two sections of A Tipping Point for Liberty.

In the "Ron Paul and Libertarianism" section you will see Adam is an able defender of me against the various attacks that mainstream media throw my way. Of course, the real target of these attacks is the liberty movement.

I must also comment briefly on the "Government Chicanery" chapters of the book. I entered politics with low expectations that legislative action alone would turn around a government that had rejected our nation's founding principles of liberty and nonintervention. Before such a major change could happen, there would first need to be an educational revolution. But, even with my low expectations entering politics, I was amazed at the amount of nonsense, deception, and corruption in Washington, DC. Adam understands all of this and communicates it well.

I hope this book does help push liberty over the tipping point. When enough people understand the freedom philosophy and circumstances are right, a peaceful revolution can bring about major changes quickly and out of the blue. As Ludwig von Mises explained, even despotic and seemingly all-powerful governments stay in power only if they have sufficient consent among the people. If consent crumbles away, so does the regime.

Even a small minority, if well informed and very committed, can bring about a revolution.

Now, the freedom philosophy is understood better than ever before.

At the same time, we are racing toward an epic crisis brought about by extraordinary government spending and intervention at home and overseas.

The coming crisis will bring big changes. These changes can be for the better or for the worse. Will liberty and nonintervention win the day, or will even greater despotism win out? The answer depends on how much we can spread the understanding of the freedom philosophy.

A Tipping Point for Liberty expertly applies the freedom philosophy to current events. The book is an important tool for spreading the education needed to ensure we can move onward to a world of liberty, peace, and prosperity.

—Ron Paul

Preface

A Tipping Point for Liberty collects together 105 of my articles from the Ron Paul Institute for Peace and Prosperity's first three years — 2013 thought 2015. The articles are arranged into categories corresponding to some of the major areas on which my work with the institute has focused — the drug war, the police state, militarism, surveillance, guns, government chicanery, and Ron Paul and libertarianism — plus a few articles on odd topics at the end.

In general, the articles included in this collection address issues in a broad manner and with an editorial bent. But, on occasion, a very short or "newsy" article is included, often to fill in gaps and help this book tell a full story.

Before working at the Ron Paul Institute, I had the pleasure of aiding Dr. Ron Paul — the Institute's chairman and founder — for ten years at his United States House of Representatives office. There I was Dr. Paul's primary aide regarding a number of issues and was his assistant for correspondence regarding all issues

In April of 2013, shortly after his retirement from the House, Dr. Paul announced the creation of the Ron Paul Institute, which is tasked with continuing Dr. Paul's public advocacy for a peaceful foreign policy and the protection of liberty at home.

Dr. Paul's institute has had a great educational impact in its first three years. I am glad that he invited me to assist him in the endeavor, and I look forward to seeing the Institute broaden its activities and deepen its impact.

The title for this book is taken from an article you will find in chapter 102. The title expresses an optimism that Dr. Paul and I share regarding the period in time in which we now live. There is much reason to be concerned about the growth of the police state, militarism, and mass surveillance in America. Indeed, the disturbing trend in these areas is discussed in detail in parts 2, 3, and 4 of this book. But, as people say, the darkest hour is just before the dawn. It may be that these dark hours for America are occurring just before the dawn for liberty.

One area in which light is piercing the dark hours is the drug war, which is the subject of the first part of this book. State and local governments are moving away from the draconian war on drugs to follow their own courses, especially in regard to marijuana. The steady advance of this trend is creating great improvements in the lives of people around America. The trend also promises to serve as an example for rolling back other violations of liberty in America.

Ultimately, for liberty and peace to replace oppression and militarism, enough people will need to be educated about the alternative path. It is my hope that this book will help spread some of the ideas needed to ensure that liberty and peace prevail.

Part 1: The Drug War

1

American Hemp Farming Poised for Resurgence Despite US Prohibition

This month Ryan Loflin, along with a group of volunteers, completed on his Colorado farm the first public hemp harvest in the US since Colorado voters approved legalizing the farming and distribution of both marijuana and hemp last November. The Loflin farm harvest is one of several recent developments that suggest American hemp farming that has been suppressed by the US government for decades may soon enjoy a resurgence.

While the Colorado government says legal hemp farming is on hold until regulations are enacted, Loflin jumped the gun, growing his hemp the old fashioned way — without a government permit. As reported in the New York Times in August, Loflin ordered fertile hemp seeds through the mail from suppliers in countries in which the plant is legally grown. He then planted the seeds on his farm.

Despite the fact that hemp is legally included in products from building materials to cloths to food, the US government deems illegal the possession of fertile hemp seeds and the cultivation of hemp. The Times article relates that Loflin, who was upfront about his hemp farming plans and told the neighbors of his farm about his intentions, half-expected US Drug Enforcement Administration (DEA) agents to race down the highway to his farm and burn his crops before harvest.

Loflin's concern about DEA interference is warranted. Hemp is a variation of cannabis sativa L., as is marijuana. Though hemp is distinguished from marijuana by hemp's tetrahydrocannabinol (THC) content being so low that it is impossible to use hemp to alter one's psychological state, the US government views hemp farming as prohibited under the 1970 Controlled Substances Act that defines all cannabis sativa L. as marijuana.

Other individuals who have dared to publicly grow hemp in the US during the national prohibition have faced punishment and the destruction of their plants. Mother Jones writer Leora Broydo relates the overpowering SWAT reaction of multiple federal agencies when some people attempted in the summer of 2000 to farm less than two acres of hemp in a South Dakota reservation in accord with the tribal government's laws:

> Alex White Plume called it his "field of dreams": an acre and a half of plants so tall and strong they seemed to touch the sky; a crop representing hope for a new and self-sufficient life for his family, residents of the desperately impoverished Pine Ridge Indian Reservation in South Dakota.
>
> But on Aug. 24, 2000 at sunrise, just four days before White Plume and his neighbors planned to harvest their bounty, White Plume awoke to the sounds of helicopters. He looked out the window and saw a convoy of vehicles heading for his field.
>
> He raced down to investigate, and was met by a slew of black-clad and heavily armed figures — 36 agents from the Drug Enforcement Administration, the FBI, the Bureau of Indian Affairs, and the US Marshal's office.
>
> When White Plume rolled down the window of his

pick-up to ask what was going on, he says, one US marshal pointed a gun in his face. Meanwhile, the other agents chopped down each plant near the roots and hauled them away.

Twelve years later, David Bronner locked himself and a few hemp plants in a cage in front of the White House in Washington, DC. Bronner then proceeded to harvest the plants as well as process hemp oil from them in an effort to publicize the need to end the US prohibition on hemp farming — until police broke into his cage and took him away in handcuffs.

Bronner's advocacy for American hemp farming is buttressed by his business experience as the CEO of Dr. Bronner's Magic Soaps. Bronner explains in an interview with KPBS television that his company spends yearly over $100,000 importing 20 tons of hemp seed oil from Canada. As Bronner says in a 2012 Reason interview, "We want to give our money to American farmers. And, in a recession, why are we continuing to hand it to Canadians?"

Other American business leaders are likely asking similar questions. Among other considerations, moving hemp farming closer to American production facilities can lower costs by significantly decreasing transportation distances compared to importing hemp from hemp producing countries such as Canada, China, and Hungary. Further, so long as hemp cannot be grown legally in the US, an American business may decide it makes the most economic sense to locate hemp-related production oversees near the legal hemp farms.

The threat of US government reactions including the standard drug war tactics of arrest imprisonment, crop destruction, and property confiscation has held back other individuals who have desired to publicly grow and harvest hemp in the US. For example, North Dakota farmers Wayne Hauge and David Monson jumped through all the hoops and paid all the fees of their state's hemp regulations to obtain licenses in 2007 and 2008 to plant hemp only to have the DEA take no action on their applications for US government approval.

The DEA is incredibly stingy in granting farmers permission to grow hemp. The July 24 Congressional Research Service report Hemp as an Agricultural Commodity notes a now-expired DEA permit for a quarter-acre research plot in Hawaii between 1999 and 2003 but no current hemp growing permits. Looking to the period before the Hawaii permit, the DEA indicates in a March 12, 1998 press release that it had never permitted hemp farming.

Vote Hemp, in a hemp FAQ, lays out bluntly the predicament farmers considering growing hemp without DEA permission face:

> So, what do I risk for planting hemp under state law without a DEA permit?
>
> You are literally betting the farm if you can grow hemp under state law without a DEA permit, which they won't give you one of anyway. Federal civil asset forfeiture is not something to mess with. Your assets are considered to be guilty until the property owner prove them innocent. If all of your liquid assets are subject to forfeiture and that's what you need to prove your property is innocent, well, too bad. You had better get a good pro bono lawyer and pray a lot and you may have a slight chance of getting your property back. But, most likely you're not. Oh, and they don't have to file charges against you or prove that you are guilty of a crime to seize your property. For a little more on the subject please see 18 USC § 981 - Civil forfeiture. Also, there are federal mandatory minimum sentences for the number of marijuana plants grown. [For] 1,000 plants, which at oilseed densities of 10 - 12 plants per square foot is only 4 feet by 25 feet, a person "shall be sentenced to a term of imprisonment which may not be less than 10 years or more than life" according to 21 U.S.C. § 841.

Loflin and other farmers who decide to grow hemp may find some comfort in a US Department of Justice (DOJ) August 29 memorandum. The memorandum, issued in light of the November popular votes in Colorado and Washington for marijuana legalization, provides guidance for US attorneys to exercise some restraint in exercising investigative and prosecutorial discretion in matters involving marijuana. Since growing hemp is considered by the US government to be the same as growing marijuana, the guidance provided in the new memorandum should apply to hemp farming as well. But, hemp farmers beware: similar DOJ memoranda regarding medical marijuana have not ended US government raids on medical marijuana businesses.

Potential hemp farmers may also suspect the US government lacks the capacity to crack down on wide-spread violations of hemp restrictions without the assistance of state and local police and prosecutors. This has been among the greatest protections for people involved in the medical marijuana industry. No matter how much the US government may want to throw them all in prison, it does not allocate sufficient resources to make it happen.

For real security from US government harassment, hemp farmers need a change in US laws. Rep. Thomas Massie's (R-KY) H.R.525 and Sen. Ron Wyden's (D-OR) S.359 are similar bills, both titled the Industrial Hemp Farming Act, that would eliminate the US government prohibition on hemp farming by excluding hemp from the Controlled Substances Act definition of marijuana. Rep. Dana Rohrabacher's (R-CA) H.R.1523, the Respect State Marijuana Laws Act, would restrict US government prohibition on hemp farming in certain states by providing that provisions of the Controlled Substances Act related to marijuana would not apply to people acting in compliance with state laws.

Public opinion and the movement of state governments to adopt more accommodating hemp and marijuana laws are making the legalization of hemp and marijuana farming less taboo subjects in the US Congress. In years past, easing US government marijuana restrictions was debated on the House floor during consideration of the recurring amendment to the Department of Justice appropriations bill that called for respecting state medical marijuana laws. The amendment, though, never received a majority vote. This year a majority of the House did vote for a narrower-focused amendment to limit the marijuana prohibition under the Controlled Substances Act. This hemp provision, which was included in a House-passed farm bill, would end the US government prohibition on colleges and universities growing hemp for research purposes in compliance with state laws. A final version of the farm bill, though, has not been approved by both the House and Senate.

A September Senate Judiciary Committee hearing titled Conflicts between State and Federal Marijuana Laws further illustrates that Congress is taking notice of the shifting nature of marijuana policy in the US. A similar hearing of the Government Operations Subcommittee of the House Oversight and Government Reform Committee titled Examining the Federal Response to Marijuana Legislation that was scheduled for October 2 was postponed along with many other committee hearings during the "government shutdown." Supposing the House subcommittee hearing is rescheduled, it should provide an interesting discussion. Three of the eight subcommittee members are Industrial Hemp Farming Act sponsor Rep. Thomas Massie and cosponsors Reps. Justin Amash (R-MI) and Mark Pocan (D-WI). Amash and Pocan are also cosponsors of the Respect State Marijuana Laws Act.

California is the latest state to adopt legislation favorable to hemp farming, with Governor Jerry Brown approving SB 566 on September 27. The Vote Hemp website provides a good starting place for researching information on the many state hemp bills and laws.

Burgeoning hemp farming promises to return to America a valued crop in US history. Indeed, the promotors of the Virginia Company's Jamestown settlement, encouraged the production of hemp.

In the next century, hemp was a common crop in American farms, including those of Thomas Jefferson and George Washington. Thomas Paine even pointed to the abundance of hemp in the American colonies in his Common Sense exhortation for the colonists to stand up to the British government. Paine wrote, "In almost every article of defence we abound. Hemp flourishes even to rankness so that we need not want cordage."

Over 150 years later, the US government would similarly praises hemp as an important wartime crop, including through the film Hemp for Victory that encouraged "patriotic farmers" to grow more hemp.

Yet, the US government, pointing to the Controlled Substances Act, now tells Americans they cannot grow this crop. Even if it appears inevitable that the US will join the many other nations that allow farmers to grow hemp, as we see in the case of medical marijuana, the US government is capable of inflicting much pain as it is pushed toward an accommodative policy.

As the hemp farming resurgence effort unfolds, look for other farmers to follow Loflin's lead, challenging US drug war policy and exercising their right to farm. In doing so, they will be taking part in an activity as American as apple pie — with some hemp seeds in the crust, of course.

2

November 6, 2013

City Voters Legalize Liquor Stores and Marijuana

Eighty years after the Twenty-First Amendment to the United States Constitution ended the US government's prohibition on alcohol, Jeff Mosier reports in the Dallas Morning News that in elections Tuesday residents of the Dallas-Fort Worth Metroplex cities of Arlington and Lewisville voted to legalize liquor stores in their cities. Mosier explains that the election results in these cities with respective populations of around 365,000 and 100,000 are part of a trend over the last decade of Texans voting to ease local legal restrictions related to alcohol:

From 2004 to 2013, Texans voted in 665 elections

seeking to ease alcohol restrictions, according to the Texas Alcoholic Beverage Commission. Nearly 80 percent passed.

Only two jurisdictions voted during that same time to restrict alcohol sales.

Also in elections Tuesday, Reason writer Ed Krayewski relates that voters in cities in Maine and Michigan, where recreational marijuana use has not been legalized statewide, voted for recreational marijuana legalization.

Since Californians voted to legalize medical marijuana in 1996, referenda and bills passed by legislative bodies have liberalized many local and state government marijuana laws. Laws concerning marijuana in the US have thus increasingly resembled the patchwork quilt of differing, though not outright prohibitionary, state and local laws concerning alcohol.

Without the cooperation of local and state police and prosecutors, the US government will have limited ability to counter state and local marijuana law liberalization. And when the US government does step in to enforce strict US marijuana laws, it may increasingly encounter juries refusing to convict.

Jury nullification will even protect some people charged under state and local laws that lag behind the tide of marijuana law liberalization. Jurors will look to their consciences and neighboring state or local laws for guidance. Even if some cities in Texas take eighty years to legalize marijuana stores, a majority of Texans supporting legalizing marijuana, as do a majority of Americans generally, will give a Texas prosecutor second thoughts about bringing a case against a person caught with a joint or two.

May 18, 2014

Rep. John Fleming's Marijuana and Libertarians Disinformation Campaign

Rep. John Fleming (R-LA) presented his absurd and deceptive campaign against all marijuana use in his opening statement for a hearing regarding marijuana laws held by a subcommittee of the House Oversight and Government Reform Committee on the morning of May 9. In the process, Fleming also made a preposterous mischaracterization of libertarianism.

Fleming's subcommittee statement followed his similarly misleading speech on the House floor in April in opposition to veterans using medical marijuana. And the statement occurred the same day Fleming said he may introduce legislation to block the implementation of a local Washington, DC law that decriminalizes the possession and transfer without payment of an ounce or less of marijuana on private property.

Fleming's subcommittee statement presents a litany of misleading and half-truth assertions regarding marijuana use that needs to be heard to be believed.

We can consider a few of Fleming's assertions at the beginning of his subcommittee presentation to gain an understanding of the abysmal nature of his marijuana disinformation campaign. But, first it is important to consider Fleming's incredible misrepresentation of libertarian ideas also included in the presentation.

Not stopping at spreading disinformation about marijuana use, Fleming also made a flagrantly erroneous assertion regarding libertarians in his subcommittee remarks. Fleming asserted:

> Now there's also a libertarian argument on this, that "Why should government stand in the way of people utilizing a substance if they wish to do so?" And theoretically that makes plenty of sense, but the problem is you never hear libertarians make the claim that "when

I'm unable to get or keep a job and I can no longer support my family that I will also tell the government not to take care of us through our growing entitlement system." So, again, I would always challenge those who argue on a libertarian basis, "You can't have it both ways; if you can do whatever you want with your body, that is, ride a motorcycle without a helmet or whatever, don't expect society and taxpayers to take care of you when you're suffering from those circumstances."

At the subcommittee hearing, Rep. Thomas Massie (R-KY) challenged Fleming on Fleming's ludicrous twisting of libertarianism. The exchange between Massie and Fleming illustrates the nature of deception that also permeates Fleming's comments regarding marijuana use:

Massie: With all due respect, I just want to clarify the libertarian position is not that the government take care of you if bad luck befalls you or you make poor decisions.

Fleming: Would the gentleman yield on that?

Massie: Absolutely.

Fleming: I would agree that should be the libertarian [sic], but I interact with people every day on this subject because of my stance on it, and I can tell you — and I would actually say there is a kind of faux libertarian group out there who make the claim on the basis you say, but they never come with the second part. So, I agree with you — if you were to take a libertarian stance on this, if I were to choose myself, for instance, to ride a motorcycle without a helmet or to use marijuana and tell the government to stay out of my life, then, like you, we should also demand that government not provide us benefits to the charge of taxpayers to take care of us when that happens. So, we agree philosophically. I'm just saying there are many who make a claim under the umbrella of libertarianism, and it's not libertarianism at all as you well state.

Massie: Yea, I agree. Thank you.

Busted for outright misstating libertarian ideas, Fleming rambles about his idiosyncratic interaction with "faux libertarians" before essentially granting the fact that his comment regarding the libertarian position on marijuana use is an absolute fabrication.

Fleming's disinformation campaign regarding libertarian ideas, however, was not deterred by his being corrected during the morning subcommittee hearing. That afternoon Fleming proceeded with a new laughable twisting of libertarianism, telling Roll Call in an interview how libertarians were starting to agree with his plan to have the US House of Representatives require the DC government to continue imposing incarceration and expensive fines on people caught with an ounce or less of marijuana on private property. In the audio of Fleming's Roll Call interview you can amazingly hear Fleming both repeat his earlier mischaracterization of the libertarian view regarding marijuana use and twist Massie's correction of Fleming into saying Massie agrees with Fleming. Here is Fleming in his own words:

> So I think that people who want to relax laws on marijuana are actually people who simply want less law enforcement and are hiding under the umbrella of libertarian movement, but they are not libertarian at all. And, I had a brief conversation with Mr. Massie who, you know, is a libertarian, and he agrees with me on this. He says, "Your right, it makes no sense for us to say allow me to ride a motorcycle without a helmet or to smoke marijuana or use drugs without government interference, but at the same time I should be willing, as a citizen, not to require the taxpayers to take care of me or my family when bad things happen." So, every time I hear the libertarian argument, I always see that they stop short. They demand freedom to do things, but they don't demand that taxpayers be free from the responsibility of taking care of them when bad choices lead to bad results.

Of course, Massie did not express — despite Fleming's claim

to the contrary — agreement with Fleming that people should not be allowed to use marijuana. Massie instead starkly corrected Fleming's misinterpretation of libertarianism by informing Fleming that libertarians believe the government should not take actions to correct problems people may somehow create for themselves by choosing to use marijuana. Further, Fleming, who had just had the libertarian view explained to him that morning by Massie, proceeds to say that "every time" Fleming hears the libertarian argument it claims exactly the opposite — that the government should require people to take care of individuals who are harmed by choosing to use marijuana.

Fleming's assertion regarding libertarianism, like his series of absurd suggestions regarding marijuana — including that marijuana is very addictive and provides no medical benefits not provided by other medicines, is no more than paper-thin propaganda that can be blown over easily.

While the first inclination is to just chuckle at Fleming's comments as quaint Reefer Madness hysteria, it is important to address a few of Fleming's assertions even today when the move toward marijuana legalization throughout the United States almost appears unstoppable.

While absolute nonsense, arguments like Fleming's still present dangers. First, to uncritical listeners, arguments like Fleming's reinforce the status quo of marijuana prohibition, both the nearly complete prohibition on the US government level and the varying degrees of prohibition in the states, territories, and DC. This prohibition leads to arrests, imprisonments, property confiscations, gang violence, police corruption, adulterated drugs, higher drug prices, and other problems inherent to prohibition. Prohibition is also at its core a restraint on a person's exercise of the right to make choices in the nonviolent direction of his own life.

Second, arguments like Fleming's inhibit some medical professionals, especially in states without medical marijuana legal protections, from discussing medical marijuana with patients and inhibit people suffering from medical problems from exploring the benefits marijuana use may provide. A barrage of marijuana use disinformation, especially when coupled with legal prohibition, can be effective in preventing sick individuals from testing the potential benefits of marijuana use on their own or upon the suggestion of friends, family members, or medical aides.

Third, coming from a member of the House of Representatives, Fleming's comments carry additional weight because, with other politicians, Fleming has the power to prolong the war on marijuana and the incredible suffering it creates for so many individuals and families.

Let us consider in turn some of Fleming's initial comments in his subcommittee statement.

In the first two minutes of his statement, Fleming states:

> You know, it was back about 20 years ago, I believe, that there was identified some theoretical value of the use of marijuana medicinally in the case of dying cancer patients, that it gave them some comfort. And of course no one has any problem with attending to the needs of a dying patient, someone with a terminal illness. Somehow this has morphed, though, into claims that marijuana actually cures cancer, that it's necessary to treat nausea, and many other claims that have been completely disputed by the medical community. There is nothing that marijuana treats today that can't be provided by other medications that are much safer.

The distortions in these few sentences alone are astounding. First off, medical benefits of marijuana have been understood and used for centuries — not just identified as having "some theoretical value" for dying cancer patients in the 1990s. In the United States, Irvin Rosenfeld is one of many individuals who demonstrates the very real benefits of medical marijuana dating back over 30 years. Rosenfeld has smoked over 130,000 US government provided marijuana joints that he says provide control of and relief from his congenital bone disorder. Rosenfeld is a participant in a small US government program called the Compassionate Investigational New Drug program.

Maybe Fleming would say that Rosenfeld is a liar or mistaken. But how would Fleming explain the many doctors around the US who have recommended marijuana to their patients and the many people who report they use marijuana for medical purposes. Are they all liars or mistaken as well?

Granted some people have "gamed" medical marijuana systems to obtain marijuana for recreational purposes. If this keeps them out of prison for the crime of trying to get high, more power to them.

But, there are also many people who are using medical marijuana on their own initiative or on the recommendation of a doctor to help deal with medical problems. With people becoming more familiar with medical marijuana and states removing legal barriers to medical marijuana over the last few decades, medical use has expanded and come out of the closet. More and more people know one or more person who benefits medically from the plant.

Many people do not today need to see high-profile medical marijuana user-activists such as Rosenfeld, Montel Williams, Peter McWilliams, or Cheryl Miller to learn the benefits of medical marijuana. They can see the benefits firsthand from their friend undergoing chemotherapy and radiation treatment for cancer, their grandparent with glaucoma, or their nephew with seizures.

An April 2013 Pew poll found that over half of the 12% of American adults who reported using marijuana in the previous year said a medical problem was the whole or partial reason for the use.

Should we just discard as deceptive or delusional several million Americans' claimed medial use of marijuana?

Should we just condemn them to lesser treatment for their medical problems because somewhere out there is a mix of pharmaceuticals and therapies that will help them as much as marijuana if they can just spend the time, money, and effort to discover it — as their medical problems continue to advance?

Should they just be fined and put in prison if caught with marijuana?

Yes, yes, and yes appear to be Fleming's answers.

Switching to grammatical deception, Fleming also asserts in this brief passage that many claims regarding medical benefits of marijuana use have been "completely disputed by the medical community." This assertion by Fleming is both true and very misleading. Many people would hear this comment and assume Fleming is saying that marijuana's medical benefits have been considered in full and rejected by all doctors, nurses, and other medical professionals. But, that is not what Fleming actually said. All he said is that the benefits of medical marijuana have been "completely disputed."

For a dispute to occur there have to be differing opinions. Many doctors, nurses, and other medical professionals believe medical marijuana aids certain patients. Other medical professionals will disagree with some of these assessments. Because Fleming says medical marijuana should never be used and because Fleming is a doctor in addition to being a House member, his opinion alone is even enough to make any and all suggested medical benefits of marijuana use "completely disputed."

Another distortion in these few sentences of Fleming's subcommittee statement is the suggestion that other medications could provide every benefit marijuana can provide not just as well, but also more safely. The US Centers for Disease Control and Prevention (CDC) in its "Prescription Drug Overdose in the United States" fact sheet notes that drug overdose is "the leading cause of injury death in the United States" with 60% of those overdose deaths related to pharmaceuticals. How many of the remaining 40% of overdose deaths were caused by marijuana? None.

Fleming continues with his misleading presentation, stating:

> Now let's talk about the safety of marijuana. Marijuana is an addicting substance. Again, there's a myth out there that it's not. The most common diagnosis for young people admitted to rehab centers today is for marijuana addiction — make no mistake about it.

Supposing we grant Fleming may be right that, technically speaking, marijuana can be addictive for some people, it is important to keep in mind that, even with some of the more addictive drugs like tobacco, some people find it very difficult to stop using a drug while other people can stop using with little effort. Marijuana, however, is not among the more addictive drugs. As Dr. Sunil Kumar Aggarwal explains in the Huffington Post, the often cited estimate from the US government's National Institute on Drug Abuse (NIDA) that one in 11 people who have ever used marijuana become dependent on the plant "is based on bad science and is way over the mark." The percentage of people who could be classified as addicted would necessarily be even much lower. NIDA itself explains there is a big difference between dependence, which is common and expected with even prescription drugs used as directed, and addiction.

Further, Fleming, by pointing to the percentage of people being in rehabilitation for "marijuana addiction," is very deceptively stating something that does not prove what people would suppose it proves. Paul Armentano of the National Organization for the Reform of Marijuana Laws (NORML) explains — in a short, informative article from 2008 exploring the idea of "marijuana addiction" — that marijuana rehab numbers are greatly inflated by courts sentencing people to rehabilitation instead of prison:

> Not familiar with the notion of "marijuana addiction"? You're not alone. In fact, aside from the handful of researchers who have discovered that there are gobs of federal grant money to be had hunting for the government's latest pot boogeyman, there's little consensus that such a syndrome is clinically relevant — if it even exists at all.
>
> But don't try telling that to the mainstream press — which recently published headlines worldwide alleging, "Marijuana withdrawal rivals that of nicotine." The alleged "study" behind the headlines involved all of 12 participants, each of whom were longtime users of pot and tobacco, and assessed the self-reported moods of folks after they were randomly chosen to ab-

stain from both substances. Big surprise: they weren't happy.

And don't try telling Big Pharma — which hopes to cash in on the much-hyped "pot and addiction" craze by touting psychoactive prescription drugs like Lithium to help hardcore smokers kick the marijuana habit.

And certainly don't try telling the drug "treatment" industry, whose spokespeople are quick to warn that marijuana "treatment" admissions have risen dramatically in recent years, but neglect to explain that this increase is due entirely to the advent of drug courts sentencing minor pot offenders to rehab in lieu of jail. According to state and national statistics, up to 70 percent of all individuals in drug treatment for marijuana are placed there by the criminal justice system. Of those in treatment, some 36 percent had not even used marijuana in the 30 days prior to their admission. These are the "addicts"?

Additionally, Fleming's focus on rehabilitation admissions of young people is revealing. Children, as well as young adults still dependent on their parents for support, do not have much choice if their parents tell them it is time to go to rehab for marijuana use. While parents making this choice for their children may do so with the best intentions, these parents' choice does not establish the presence of marijuana addiction, much less serious life-threatening problems related to marijuana use.

Fleming moves forward in the remainder of his presentation with a series of additional misleading and half-truth arguments regarding the use of marijuana. Yet, even if we were to assume that every argument Fleming presents regarding marijuana use — including that marijuana is a "gateway drug" and poses serious health risks for users — were absolutely true, these arguments would not justify Fleming's policy goal of fining and locking up people who choose to use marijuana for medical or recreational reasons.

As any libertarian could tell Fleming, individuals have the right to choose to consume illegal drugs and, should that drug use create problems for an individual who makes this choice, the government does not have the right to require other people to take actions or pay money to fix those problems. Maybe if Fleming hears the message enough times he will stop distorting it. Maybe, he will even think things over, do some research, and change his mind.

4

May 26, 2014

Can Kinky Friedman Bring Legal Marijuana and Hemp to Texas?

Kinky Friedman, who is competing in a runoff election Tuesday for the Democratic Party nomination for Texas Agriculture Commissioner, describes his race as "kind of a referendum on lifting this prohibition on hemp and on pot." Can Friedman, who has gained notoriety among potential Texas voters as a singer/songwriter, mystery book writer, Texas Monthly columnist, and Texas governor candidate, bring legal marijuana and hemp to Texas?

While many people may view Texas as among the least likely states for a candidate promoting marijuana and hemp legalization to win statewide office, polling indicates a majority of Texans support marijuana legalization. Nevertheless, Texas politicians are reluctant to legalize, likely in part because they are concerned about a backlash from the minority of Texans who support the war on marijuana.

Friedman's bold pro-legalization statewide campaign may help subdue this fear among politicians in Texas and around the nation. Indeed, even if Friedman fails to win the runoff, his winning of over 37% of the vote in the first round of the Democratic Party primary (just one percent less than the other candidate making the runoff) is significant. It demonstrates that a bold pro-legalization message does not prevent a candidate from being competitive statewide in the Democratic Party.

Friedman's marijuana stance is indeed bold. His campaign website clearly portrays a vote for Friedman as predominantly a vote for marijuana and hemp legalization. At the top, the home page states in large, red, capital letters "KINKY SAYS LEGALIZE NOW!" and, as if to ensure there is no ambiguity, right next to that statement is the large image of a green marijuana leaf. Further down the page, the Friedman campaign lists six campaign issues, with "End the Prohibition on Marijuana" listed first and "Promote the Cultivation of Hemp" second.

If Friedman wins the Democratic Party runoff, the next test is whether his "legalization referendum" can appeal to enough voters — including Republicans, independents, and people who typically do not vote — to make Friedman the first non-Republican elected to office statewide in Texas since 1994. Achieving that victory would send a powerful message regarding the political viability of marijuana and hemp legalization in Texas and beyond.

5

August 28, 2014

Liberty Across the Board: Ron Paul vs Boston Globe on The Right to Use Heroin

The Boston Globe published this week a guest editorial arguing, as Ron Paul Institute Chairman and Founder Ron Paul memorably did during a 2011 Republican presidential primary debate in South Carolina, that heroin should be legalized. While the Globe editorial presents strong arguments for heroin legalization, it shies away from discussing the right to use heroin. In contrast, when asked in the debate about legalizing heroin, Paul zeroed in on individual rights, saying that protecting the right to use heroin is part of his commitment to protecting liberty "across-the-board."

The Globe editorial by Jack Cole of Law Enforcement Against Prohibition (LEAP) presents valuable arguments for ending heroin prohibition and merits reading. But, the editorial fails to address the important issue of individuals' right to choose what they put into their bodies, including substances that alter their perceptions.

The individual rights argument for legalizing heroin is also in conflict with the Cole editorial's support for government regulation of heroin purity and the establishment of special places where people would consume heroin.

Considering the patchwork quilt of laws governing alcohol in the US, it would be rather Pollyannaish to assume that heroin will be legalized soon in a manner that does not include some government interferences such as "quality control" regulations, restrictions on where the drug may be used, and taxes. Nevertheless, when you make the case for legalization while excluding a discussion of the freedom to use — and especially when you couple that exclusion with an inclusion of recommended government powers — you invite reform efforts that, far from true legalization, involve a lot of tinkering but little overall increased respect for liberty.

Practically speaking, practical arguments alone stacked from here to the moon will be of little persuasive value so long as the rights argument is not widely accepted. Dramatic reductions in government restrictions regarding heroin or another "hard drug" cannot be expected before a large percentage of the American people (for a national law change) or of people living in a state or local government's jurisdiction (for a state or local law change) respect that people have a right to use the drug.

September 6, 2014

Desperate Drug War Beneficiaries Spread Marijuana Legalization Disinformation

While local and state governments continue moving forward with reducing and eliminating restrictions and penalties regarding marijuana, drug war beneficiaries are desperately responding by spreading disinformation. One such effort is the Rocky Mountain High-Intensity Drug Traffic Area August report "The Legalization of Marijuana in Colorado: The Impact."

The report purports to be a balanced analysis of the effects of marijuana legalization in Colorado. In fact, the report is over 150 pages of deceptive pro-drug war propaganda.

One may wonder how much time and money the HIDTA spent on researching, writing, and producing the professional appearing report. Whatever the cost, the HIDTA people must figure it is a good investment of other people's money.

While the Rocky Mountain HIDTA and its private and government allies spent hundreds or thousands of hours creating the agitprop, drug war writer Jacob Sullum had no trouble promptly rebutting a good portion of the report's conclusions and exposing some of the rhetorical trickery that made the report particularly deceptive. Nonetheless, singers of prohibition praise from Cully Stimson of the Heritage Foundation to DARE enthusiastically promoted bite-size packets of the report's disinformation.

As explained by the Office of National Drug Control Policy (ONDCP), 28 HIDTAs, including the Rocky Mountain HIDTA, assist United States, state, local, and tribal law enforcement agencies in fighting the drug war in areas that include 60 percent of the US population pursuant to the Anti-Drug Abuse Act of 1988. While a lot has changed in America since 1988, the US government's drug war keeps going strong.

With more and more state and local governments moving away from prohibition of marijuana and this trend showing no

signs of reversing, the HIDTA people, along with their connected police departments and other allied drug war beneficiaries,
must be having some job security concerns. Drug war arrests,
and marijuana arrests in particular, after all, help keep the police busy. US News and World Report writer Steven Nelson reports some of the Federal Bureau of Investigation (FBI) war on
drugs arrest statistics:

> Data released Monday by the Federal Bureau of In-
> vestigation show there were an estimated 1,552,432 ar-
> rests for drug-related crimes in 2012 – a slight uptick
> from the 1,531,251 drug arrests in 2011. Marijuana
> offenses accounted for 48.3 percent of all drug arrests,
> a slight reduction from 49.5 percent in 2011, which
> itself was the highest rate since before 1995.

> Most marijuana-related arrests were for possession of
> the drug. By mere possession, there was one marijua-
> na arrest every 48 seconds in 2012. Including arrests
> for distribution, there was a pot-related arrest every 42
> seconds, the same interval as in 2011.

HIDTAs (with their $238 million in ONDCP grants) and
US, state, and local police (with their "policing for profit"
through drug war asset seizures) are not the only groups that
benefit from marijuana prohibition. There are many additional
beneficiaries including prosecutors who push defendants who
typically lack comparable legal resources along the guilty plea
conveyor belt, private and public prisons that cage drug war
convicts, treatment centers where people with no addiction
problem whatsoever will opt to take part in court-mandated
treatment as an alternative to being in prison, and arms manu-
facturers who have found new income in police militarization.

While it is important to counter deceptive propaganda with
truth and logic, there is little reason to expect that the Rocky
Mountain HIDTA report and other propaganda efforts will stop
the general American trend toward greater respect for the right
to grow, use, transport, buy, and sell marijuana. On marijuana,
America it seems has turned a corner, with the country mov-

ing toward a patchwork quilt of marijuana laws that overall are much less prohibitionary and punitive than the laws have been over the last few decades of the war on drugs. People are seeing firsthand that very significant loosening of marijuana restrictions in parts of the country did not cause the sky to fall. Indeed, people are seeing that marijuana freedom, despite the prohibitionists' dire warnings and continuing disinformation campaigns, is not dangerous.

With marijuana use coming out of the shadows of illegality, people are more and more recognizing that individuals who use marijuana, on occasion or regularly, are not so different from people who do not. Reality is overtaking hype.

Marijuana freedom is nothing to fear. Instead, as Ron Paul Institute Chairman and Founder Ron Paul says, freedom "brings people together, whether you are liberal or conservative or what, because people like to be in charge of their own life; they like to be in charge of their own money." Despite the efforts of the Rocky Mountain HIDTA and its prohibitionist allies, Americans are rejecting the government and private drug war beneficiaries' propaganda and experiencing the benefits of "live and let live" over "arrest, fine, and incarcerate." Hopefully, this lesson will help create paths to greater respect for other freedoms as well.

7

November 5, 2014

Alaska, DC, and Oregon Voters Legalize Marijuana

State and local governments continued going their own way on marijuana laws in elections Tuesday, with voters in the sates of Alaska and Oregon, along with United States capital city Washington, DC, approving ballot measures legalizing marijuana for recreational use. All three jurisdictions already had laws allowing medical marijuana use, while Alaska also already had legal recreational use but not legal sale of marijuana.

Also in the Tuesday elections, legalization of medical marijuana passed in the US territory of Guam and received a 58% majority vote in the state of Florida. The Florida ballot measure, however, did not pass because state law imposed a 60% supermajority vote requirement for victory.

As with prior marijuana law liberalizations in other states, the changes in law approved Tuesday are unique approaches that will find their place in America's developing patchwork quilt of marijuana laws that is increasingly resembling the diverse, though nowhere absolutely prohibited, legal status of alcohol in America.

While some American politicians and drug war beneficiaries continue to promote disinformation concerning marijuana, more state and local governments continue to join the trend toward greater respect for the right to use marijuana. This trend shows no signs of reversing.

Under pressure from the steady push of state and local governments' marijuana law changes, it appears that the US Congress is starting to backtrack on some of the decades-long US government war on marijuana. Majority votes in the US House of Representatives in May supported requiring the US government to respect state hemp and medical marijuana laws. These votes followed the enactment earlier in the year of a change in US law to allow limited growing of hemp for research purposes where growing hemp is legal under state law.

November 9, 2014

NYPD Union Leader: Reducing Marijuana Arrests is 'Beginning of the Breakdown of a Civilized Society'

Reported efforts to begin following through on New York City Mayor Bill de Blasio's 2013 election promise to reduce marijuana arrests in the city has distressed Sergeants Benevolent Association police union President Ed Mullins. Mullins is quoted Wednesday in the New York Post lamenting that "If the current practice of making arrests for both possession and sale of marijuana is, in fact, abandoned, then this is clearly the beginning of the breakdown of a civilized society."

The city's apparent move to reduce the number of marijuana arrests comes soon after an October joint report of the Drug Policy Alliance and the Marijuana Arrest Research Project publicized that the number of marijuana possession arrests in New York City were on track to remain the same under de Blasio's leadership, or even increase, compared to arrests under Michael Bloomberg, the preceding mayor.

Of course, the truth is that there is nothing civilized about arresting people and throwing them in jail for making the choice to use, buy, or sell marijuana. Such choices have been tolerated or accepted in much of the world for centuries and were legal under United States law for the majority of the nation's history. US legal prohibitions and punishments were imposed in the 20th century, including with the enactment of laws such as the Marihuana Tax Act of 1937 and marijuana's inclusion in schedule one of Controlled Substances Act of 1970, thus applying the most expansive level of prohibition to actions involving the plant. In contrast, looking further back to the origins of the US, we find that Founding Fathers grew hemp on their farms, including George Washington at Mount Vernon and Thomas Jefferson at Monticello.

A time traveler from the American 1800s, when marijuana

and other now-illegal drugs were legally grown, bought, sold, and ingested, would likely find perplexing the comment that it is uncivilized to refrain from arresting and jailing people for such peaceful activities and commerce. Indeed, such a time traveler would probably immediately recognize that it is instead the police-state approach exhibited in Mullins' comment and demonstrated each day in the enforcement of the drug war that is uncivilized.

But, Mullins need not talk with a time traveler; he can witness himself in the states of Colorado and Washington, and soon more American jurisdictions, that even legalizing marijuana is not a step away from civilization.

It is hard to believe that Mullins really believes his dire warning. Instead, as with the response of other drug war beneficiaries to marijuana prohibition rollbacks, Mullins is probably making his Chicken Little pronouncement in a desperate attempt to keep the war on marijuana easy money flowing in spite of the apparently unstoppable move toward nationwide marijuana legalization. Mullins is a police union leader after all.

Mullins also reveals a broader agenda behind his support for continuing the high number of New York City marijuana arrests when he comments in the Post article, "If we're not making marijuana arrests, then we may not pop someone who has a warrant on them or who committed felony crimes." Indeed, the drug war exception to the Fourth Amendment and to similar state restraints on police action has proven a convenient path to abusing people with impunity. And, when you put enough people through the wringer, you will find a person here and there with a warrant or who you can book for a crime.

One of those "crimes" the Post article reports is often uncovered in the city's marijuana policing is illegal gun possession — a victimless crime just like marijuana possession.

As a candidate, de Blasio both criticized Bloomberg for being too severe in the pursuit of marijuana law violators and said, "amen for what [Bloomberg] did on gun control. I think we should go the next step." Might the next step include replacing the marijuana pretext for city police abusing people with a gun pretext? We can hope not. But, the city taking that step may give Mullins some hope for preserving the warped "civilized society" he cherishes — at least in New York City.

9

Ed Mullins Returns with More Marijuana Nonsense Talk

With the recent announcement of the particulars of the New York City Police Department policy change intended to reduce marijuana arrests, Sergeants Benevolent Association police union leader Ed Mullins, who previously lamented that reducing marijuana arrests in the city would be "clearly the beginning of the breakdown of a civilized society," is back with more nonsense talk about marijuana.

Under the new NYPD operations order effective November 19, marijuana arrests are expected to drop dramatically. The new policy directs that police generally should not arrest a person who has 25 grams (about 9/10 of an ounce) or less of marijuana "consistent with personal use" in public view in a public place. Instead, the marijuana may be confiscated and the individual fined up to $100 for a first offense and up to $250 for a later offense. Police are instructed, though, to continue to arrest individuals who are in public with lit marijuana.

Mullins first attempts to disparage the police policy change by labeling it as part of a "far-left agenda." Mullins is quoted in the New York Daily News:

> "Some guys are really blaming de Blasio," Sergeants
> Benevolent Association President Ed Mullins said.
> "The guy just doesn't get it with this whole far-left
> agenda, and he's putting (cops) in a bad spot."

That is not much of an argument. Favoring free speech and peace is often labeled as "left wing" as well; that does not make those views wrong. Mullins' comment does nothing more than reinforce the false left-right dichotomy that diverts people from considering the real battle between freedom and oppression.

We must grant, though, that there is evidence supporting the proposition that nationwide a greater portion of people "on the left" than "on the right" support increasing leniency in marijuana laws. Consider, for example, the United Sates House of Representatives consideration in May of two amendments to tell the US government to respect states' legalization of medical marijuana and hemp. Each of the amendments passed with the support of over 90% of voting Democrat members, while only 22% and 30% of voting Republican members voted "yes" in the respective medical marijuana and hemp votes. This partisan divide is also visible in Americans' views on marijuana legalization as reflected in a Pew Research Center poll in October. The poll results indicate marijuana legalization is about twice as popular among Democrats as among Republicans, with 64% of Democrats favoring legalization, compared to only 31% support among Republicans. Overall, 52% of people polled supported legalization, compared to 45% favoring illegality.

Over at CBS News, Mullins is quoted further regarding the police policy change. He offers two additional arguments for his opposition, both nonsensical:

> "I see this as a very, very lax police atmosphere to which we're sending a message to the public that it's OK to do what you want to do on the street regardless of what the law says," Mullins said.

Mullins said the move is purely de Blasio backing off.

> "I know what his argument is: It targets blacks and Hispanics disproportionately," Mullins said. "But what he's not addressing -- and what no one is addressing -- is that if this is an issue in a black and Hispanic community, ignoring it by not making arrests isn't helpful to the community."

Contrary to Mullins' suggestion, the NYPD's marijuana arrests binge, including nearly 440,000 marijuana possession arrests from 2002 through 2012, was largely composed of arrests in violation of the law or thinly justified through use of the city's corrupt and rights abusing "stop and frisk" policy. As explained in the CBS News article:

> Under a 1977 New York State law, low-level marijuana possession is a non-arrestable offense unless it's in public view or burning. But critics say many of the arrests are the result of New York's "stop and frisk" policy, during which police will make people empty their pockets and then arrest them for having the drug out in public.

Regarding Mullins' bizarre claim that the police are helping communities by arresting people and throwing them in jail for marijuana possession, it would be interesting to see him explain that to the individuals handcuffed in the back of police cars or confined in cells deprived of their ability to direct their own lives. Or he could explain to family members why they should be thankful that their parent, child, spouse, or sibling is manhandled and incarcerated for having some marijuana.

Mullins' worries about protecting civilization, the rule of law, and communities may be about to grow even larger. New York City Council Speaker Melissa Mark-Viverito stated on Thursday that she believes marijuana should be legalized.

10

March 3, 2015

On Marijuana, Young Republicans Say 'Legalize it' but Congressional Republicans Say 'No'

According to Pew Research Center poll results released Friday, 63 percent of Millennial Generation Republicans support marijuana legalization. On this issue these Republicans born between 1981 and 1996 have more in common with Democrats than with Republicans generally. And these young Republicans are definitely at odds with the majority of Republicans in the United States House of Representatives who continue to vote "no" on rollbacks of the US government's war on marijuana.

The further we look back through earlier generations of Republicans, the less support for legalization we see — 47 percent among Generation X (born in 1965 through 1980), 38 percent among the Baby Boom Generation (born in 1946 through 1964), and 17 percent among the Silent Generation (born in 1928 through 1945). In contrast, substantial majorities, ranging from 61 percent to 77 percent, support marijuana legalization in each of these generations of Democrats, except among the oldest polled generation — the Silent Generation — where support registers at 44 percent.

The Pew poll results suggest that the majority of Millennial Republicans and nearly half of Generation X Republicans would be happy with the US House's approval, by a floor vote in May 2014, of telling the US government to respect states' legalization of medical marijuana and hemp. These Republicans also likely would be disappointed by the fact that the vast majority of Republican House members voted against these war on marijuana rollbacks. Only 22 percent of voting Republican legislators voted "yes" on the medical marijuana provision. A bit more — 30 percent — voted "yes" on the hemp provision. Both provisions received the support of over 90 percent of voting Democratic House members.

Americans who identify themselves as Republicans in the Pew poll would likely support both of these war on marijuana rollbacks passed in the House by even higher percentages than their support levels for marijuana legalization in each respective generation. Legalization of medical marijuana or hemp is much less broad an action than full marijuana legalization. Further, many Republicans, of any age, who oppose even these partial rollbacks of marijuana prohibition on the state level also believe that the US government should nonetheless respect a state's decision to follow its own course on these matters.

The trend reflected in the Pew poll results suggests that American politicians will, with each passing year, face electorates increasingly supportive of marijuana legalization — including in Republican primaries. A major shift in marijuana public opinions and policy is ongoing in America. Many politicians will be caught off guard by the major changes yet to come. Expect voters to boot out more drug warrior politicians because of those politicians' increasingly discordant views regarding marijuana. Also watch for politicians to increasingly shift their positions so they publicly support rollbacks in the war on marijuana.

11

March 30, 2015

After HIV Spike, Drug Warrior Governor Grants Limited Temporary Needle Exchange

Indiana Governor Mike Pence on Thursday issued an executive order (EO 15-05) declaring a "public health disaster emergency" in Scott County in southeastern Indiana due to an epidemic of human immunodeficiency virus (HIV) in the county. The extraordinary measures allowed under the executive order include permitting the Scott County Board of Health to seek the state government's permission to design and administer a short-term needle exchange program for the sole purpose of suppressing the HIV epidemic in Scott County.

The Republican governor's executive order further says that all 79 HIV cases the Indiana State Department of Health has confirmed in Scott County since December "directly relate to intravenous drug use." According to the executive order, no more than five confirmed HIV cases, irrespective of how transmitted, are expected yearly in the county.

If you are in one of Indiana's 91 other counties and wish to access new, clean needles to protect yourself from infection, tough. (Less than half of one percent of Indiana residents live in Scott County.) Yet, people outside Scott County will be no less dead or debilitated because of infections they receive from using old, dirty needles.

Pence has a war on drugs to fight, and wars have casualties.

Transferring new, clean needles and injecting drugs into your body are nonviolent acts that, due to politicians like Pence, are declared a legal crime punishable by fines and incarceration. Meanwhile, there are no negative repercussions for the perpetrators, including Pence, of the moral crime of the drug war that is responsible for monumental pain, suffering, and death, including because of the transmission of infections through shared needles.

Eight years ago, as a Republican member of the United States House of Representatives from Indiana, Pence voted for an amendment that sought to prohibit needle exchange in Washington, DC, which has long had a high prevalence of HIV. Indeed, Pence still opposes needle exchanges. Shari Rudavsky reports at the Indianapolis Star that Pence, in announcing his executive order, said he is only making "an exception" to his "long-standing opposition to needle exchange programs."

Pence's drug warrior attitude extends beyond wanting to prevent people from using new, clean needles. He also is doing his best to slow Indiana's participation in the trend of states and local governments decreasing marijuana penalties and even ending marijuana prohibition. For example, Brandon Smith of Indiana Public Radio notes Pence expressed concern in 2013 that state legislation to reduce a list of criminal penalties "was not tough enough on drug crimes" resulting in the bill being altered so marijuana penalty reductions would be less than the penalty reductions for other crimes.

Of course, a needle exchange program run by local, state, or US government bureaucrats is not the optimal means to respect dug users' freedom and protect their health. New, clean needles should be legal for anyone to own; any store to sell; and any individual, business, or charitable organization to give away. And, if you really value people's freedom and health, the drugs injected through the needles should be legal to use, possess, transfer, and sell as well. Just don't hold your breath for a drug warrior like Pence to support such changes.

April 8, 2015

How the War on Drugs Facilitated the Global War on Terrorism

When President George W. Bush announced the Global War on Terrorism in 2001 he did not have to start his war from scratch. Instead, the development of the United States government's war on drugs that President Richard Nixon announced forty years earlier facilitated much of Bush's new war. Two revelations this week provide new examples of the linkage between the two wars.

First, Brad Heath reported Wednesday at USA Today that from 1992 through 2013 the US Drug Enforcement Administration (DEA) collected calling records of "virtually all" phone calls from America to a long list of countries. At the list's peak size, bulk collection was undertaken on calls between the US and over 100 countries. Countries that the article notes were on the list at "one time or another" include most countries in South America, Central America, and the Caribbean, as well as Canada, Mexico, Italy, Afghanistan, Pakistan, Iran, and other countries in Europe, Asia, and Africa.

Heath describes the DEA program as "a model for the massive phone surveillance system the NSA launched to identify terrorists after the Sept. 11 attacks."

Second, Jana Winter reported Monday at The Intercept that the Screening of Passengers by Observation Techniques (SPOT) program of the Transportation Security Administration (TSA) uses as a means for identifying possible terrorists a checklist that is, "in part, modeled after immigration, border and drug interdiction programs." If one of the thousands of TSA Behavioral Detection Officers (BDOs) is watching a person and checks enough boxes on the checklist made up of ordinary human activities and attributes, the BDO can refer the observed individual to "selectee screening" (i.e., "enhanced" frisking and harassment) as well as request the involvement of local police who can interrogate the targeted individual and even bar him from traveling or arrest him.

Like the TSA overall, the SPOT program does not prevent terrorism. It is, though, one means among many the US government agency uses to routinely violate the rights of the people who encounter TSA checkpoints when they dare attempt exercising their right to travel.

These two examples are not the only ways the drug war has facilitated the Global War on Terrorism. Court decisions permitting invasive and abusive police tactics used in the drug war, for example, have created a drug war exception to the Fourth Amendment. This has led to courts being more accepting of the surveillance, entrapment, and other practices outside historic American legal limits that are used regularly in the name of fighting terrorism. Also, the practice of the US military deploying around the world to fight the drug war has made the similar "counterterrorism" deployments more easily undertaken by the government and more palatable to many Americans.

Last month at Foreign Policy, Harvard Professor Stephen M. Walt highlighted another commonality of the two wars — failure. Walt observes in his persuasive article "Just Say No" that the Global War on Terrorism more and more reminds him of the "costly and counterproductive debacle" that is the US government's war on drugs.

13

May 7, 2015

Radical Texas Marijuana Legalization Bill Passes in State House Committee

Texas took a step toward leapfrogging past all the states that have legalized marijuana for medical and recreational use so far. In March, Texas State Rep. David Simpson introduced legislation (HB 2165) that would remove references to marijuana from the state criminal code so the plant would be legal just as are tomatoes. And, you know what, Simpson's bold, no-compromise, forget about "taxing and regulating" move is yielding success in a state many people write off as destined either to never legalize marijuana or to be one of the last states to legalize marijuana. On Wednesday, the Criminal Jurisprudence Committee approved Simpson's bill by a 5 to 2 bipartisan majority — after HB 2165 was moderated in the committee to retain marijuana restrictions for juveniles.

The committee's approval of HB 2165 clears the bill for a debate and vote on the House floor. However, as suggested in the Dallas Morning News, the House may not make time for floor consideration of the bill in the remainder of this session, which is scheduled to end June 1. Still, the strong committee vote for a radical legalization bill in the Texas House committee bodes well for marijuana legalization in the state. It also bodes well for enacting marijuana legalization in America that respects freedom to a much greater degree than does any of the legalization programs adopted in any states thus far.

14

July 13, 2015

Hey, Obama, How About Freeing the Nearly 100,000 Drug War Victims in US Prisons?

With President Barack Obama announcing Monday the commutation of the sentences of 46 US government prisoners, Reuters calculates that the president "has now commuted the sentences of 89 prisoners, the vast majority of whom were nonviolent drug offenders who applied for clemency under an initiative the White House began in April 2014." The freeing of any drug war victims is reason for celebrations. Yet, according to the Federal Bureau of Prisons 95,265 people (48.7% of all federal prison inmates) are in US government prisons for drug convictions. How about freeing them all?

As Obama indicated in his announcement of his newest round of commutations, drug law violations are nonviolent crimes. In addition, they are victimless crimes. With no violence and no victim in drug crimes, it is absurd for the US government to incarcerate a single person for a drug crime for even one more day.

There is no need to wait for clemency requests and laborious study of the facts of each prisoner's case. The proper action is to eliminate the drug crimes portion of all federal prison inmates' sentences. This would result in people convicted only of drug crimes being immediately freed. People convicted of drug and other crimes would be freed as soon as they have served the portions of their sentences arising from nondrug convictions, meaning many of them would be freed immediately as well.

What's the hold up? President Jimmy Carter, on his first full day in office, pardoned thousands of people for the nonviolent and victimless crime of evading the US government's military conscription. Obama could take similarly heroic action by freeing thousands of drug war prisoners from federal prisons.

15

September 3, 2015

Buy the Rights-Abusing Cops Lunch Says Texas Lieutenant Governor Dan Patrick

Texas Lieutenant Governor Dan Patrick issued a statement Wednesday that says that, to counter "America's negative attitude toward our law enforcement officers," people should all-but grovel at the feet of any police they come across. Patrick even suggests that "financially able" individuals (who presumably are already paying cops' salaries via taxes) pay for the lunches of any cops they may see in a restaurant.

Here is Patrick's complete list of groveling suggestions:

Join me in changing this negative attitude toward those that protect us, by practicing the following:

- Start calling our officers sir and ma'am all of the time. It's a show of respect they deserve.

- Every time you see an officer anywhere, let them know you appreciate their service to our community and you stand with them.

- If you are financially able, when you see them in a restaurant on duty pick up their lunch check, send over a dessert, or simply stop by their table briefly and say thank you for their service.

- Put their charities on your giving list.

- If your local law enforcement has volunteer-citizen job opportunities, sign up.

Interestingly, Patrick never mentions in his statement that a major contributor to the negative attitude many people in Texas and across America have toward cops is the many times cops act in manners bereft of respect for the rights, property, health, and lives of the individuals they encounter.

How about the cops who abused Sandra Bland or Angel and Ashley Dobbs in Patrick's home state? "Thank you sir. Thank you ma'am. Please, let me pay for that sandwich!"

While some people would say that these abusive cops are just a few bad apples, reading through articles by Rutherford Institute President John W. Whitehead or journalist William N. Grigg, it becomes clear that the basket contains many bad apples. The fact is that many cops are more intent on harassing, abusing, and dominating people they encounter than on serving and protecting them. Rather than disrespect for cops being, as Patrick seems to believe, some irrational, mystical belief that showed up out of nowhere, the disrespect is a logical response to the horror show of abusive cops that plays out again and again in this age of police militarization.

Though often overlooked, the war on drugs is an underlying cause of the worsening police conduct. Because the growth, manufacture, sale, transfer, and use of drugs are nonviolent and victimless activities, with no complaining victim, police have resorted to all kinds of invasive, deceptive, and destructive tactics in fighting the war. For example, the drug war has been used as an excuse for vast expansion of police practices including covert surveillance, sting operations, pretext traffic stops, asset seizures without any court hearing whatsoever, and SWAT team raids on homes and businesses. All of this is supposedly justified to protect people from themselves.

Of course, the drug war, like alcohol prohibition before it, has also spawned gangs fighting over turf. This violence, in turn, is used as an excuse for the further militarization of the police — in equipment, tactics, and mindset.

But, according to Patrick, we should be thankful for the SWAT team members who raided a home last night, pointing guns at all the suddenly awoken family members, turning the place upside down in an effort to find even a fraction of an ounce of a forbidden drug, and maybe shooting someone or the family's pet dog to boot.

The drug war corrosion runs even deeper. Beyond the SWAT team members, there are also the undercover cops trying to snag individuals in drug sale stings, the traffic cops who make up pretenses to conduct drug searches without consent or pressure drivers to "consent" to searches, and even the deskbound cops who handle the paperwork that allows the drug war machine to relentlessly move forward.

Patrick laments that "America's negative attitude toward our law enforcement officers" may result in less people choosing to become cops. Yet, having less cops around can actually lead to much enhanced safety.

Let's call off the war on drugs, its danger-enhancing police practices, and the related drug war exception to the Fourth Amendment. Let people exercise their right to grow, manufacture, sell, transfer, and use drugs as they see fit. Let the violence prohibition engenders wither. Free the drug war prisoners.

With the end of the drug war, the number of cops can be significantly reduced. Ending the war may also be the single biggest step that may be taken immediately to increase Texans' and Americans' respect for police.

16

End the Marijuana 'Sin Taxes'

Legal marijuana in Colorado has been a boon for freedom, allowing people to make, transfer, and consume marijuana products free from the threat of arrest by state or local police. At the same time, there is an unfortunate side-effect of the liberalization of marijuana laws in the state — the government scooping up great amounts of money via marijuana "sin taxes."

The high marijuana taxes punish people who purchase marijuana by depriving them of money to save, to give away, or to spend on other goods or services. The sin taxes also are a means of controlling people's behavior. Facing high taxes, some people will forgo or reduce their purchases of products containing the plant.

Proponents of the sin taxes claim the taxes are justified because using marijuana is a sin that should be discouraged. But, even if it is granted that there is some truth in that claim, a much greater sin is the use of government force via taxation to control people's nonviolent activities.

There is plenty of marijuana sin tax to roll back in Colorado. Ethan Wolff-Mann calculates in Money magazine that sales and excise taxes increase the price of marijuana by 27.9% in the state.

The gouging of marijuana purchasers is reason enough to oppose the high taxes. In addition, there is the concern that all this tax revenue feeds the government machine that tramples on individual rights, including through enforcing laws against other drugs that are still illegal and even through clamping down on marijuana activities that take place outside the marijuana regulatory system. Recall that New York City cops killed Eric Garner on a Staten Island sidewalk last year in a confrontation predicated on stopping the evasion of one of the highest-in-the-nation cigarette tax rates. Protection of sin tax money streams can be very nasty.

There is indeed much government revenue from marijuana-specific taxes in Colorado. The Marijuana Policy Project places the total for the 12 months ending June 30 at nearly $70 million — 67 percent more than the nearly $42 million in revenue from alcohol-specific taxes during the same period.

How about the government stops taking this money from marijuana purchasers? Let them spend the money on what they choose. Refrain from using the new respect for marijuana freedom as an excuse for imposing oppressive new taxes, manipulating people's behavior, and funding violations of individual rights.

A one day marijuana tax holiday occurred in Colorado on September 16. The interaction of a state government "accounting error" and state tax law provisions resulted in people in Colorado experiencing that day the freedom of purchasing marijuana free from the compulsion to pay much of the taxes on marijuana. But, freedom is for every day, not just for one day a year. Let's make every day a holiday from marijuana sin taxes.

Part 2: The Police State

17

May 31, 2013

Illinois School District Forces Students to Self-Incriminate

What could be less controversial than a US public high school social studies teacher informing his students that they have the right to refuse to answer whether they have done something illegal? In fact, this concept — the right against self-incrimation — is part of the typical high school curriculum. Nonetheless, in Illinois this week the Batavia Public School District 101 school board reprimanded and disciplined Mr. John Dryden, a public high school social studies teacher, for informing some of his students of just this concept.

Dryden, who received a student survey just before his first class of the day, realized his students' names were on their respective survey forms, meaning the survey was not anonymous. He also noticed the survey asked about matters including the students' drug, alcohol, and tobacco use, as well as their emotions. Dryden then informed some of his students they could apply to this survey the right against self-incrimination. The school district found this otherwise routine lesson unacceptable when the lesson stood in the way of school officials reviewing completed surveys.

While the school district argues, as have other school districts, that such surveys will aid the school district in helping students at risk for suicide, students who admit to drug or alcohol use in such surveys have a legitimate concern that this information could be used against them. According to the Federal Bureau of Investigation's (FBI) most recent Crime in the United States report, there were over 155,000 arrests of people under 18 years old for alleged legal violations in the categories "Drug Abuse Violations" and "Liquor Laws" in 2011. Further, students have reason for concern when they consider that some schools invite drug-sniffing dogs to campuses for locker-to-locker and car-to-car drug searches and participate in programs awarding cash for tips leading to school administrative action, arrest, or charging of students for drug or alcohol legal violations.

Many parents and students are also concerned about the widespread use of mental health screening surveys of students that include detailed questions about drug use, sexual activity, and other personal matters and are administered without parents' knowledge and consent. Concerns about mental health screening include the risk of misdiagnosis and the pressure to use pharmaceuticals that may cause worse problems than any mental issues the drugs are supposed to address.

Parents and students also may be concerned that records of drug use or emotional issues could be used against a student who may later desire to own a gun or work in certain kinds of employment

There are many reasons parents and students would refuse to participate in surveys such as the one administered by the Batavia school district. But one reason should be more than sufficient: The information sought in these surveys is private and none of the school district's business.

June 27, 2013

McCain: 'Vote For Berlin Wall!'

Sen. John McCain (R-AZ) is promoting the so-called immigration bill (S.744) in the United States Senate by emphasizing it will create "the most militarized border since the fall of the Berlin Wall." Apparently, McCain believes this argument will convince other senators to vote for the legislation. The "border-industrial complex" we have been warned about is out in the open.

By the way, the militarization for "border security" goes far beyond the immediate border. The American Civil Liberties Union (ACLU) presents a chilling map showing what the ACLU terms "The Constitution-Free Zone of the United States." That zone includes every place in the United States within 100 miles of a border — including international coastlines. Within this area, where the ACLU estimates two-thirds of US residents live, the US Border Patrol, whose funding and employee levels the Senate immigration bill dramatically increases, and other US government entities exercise expanded powers to stop, search, and harass anyone.

Ron Paul Institute Chairman and Founder Rep. Ron Paul warned, in a 2011 presidential debate, about the type of Berlin Wall-style proposals in the Senate's so-called immigration bill. Walls are often built to keep people in rather than keep people out, he said at the time.

August 9, 2013

NH Police Chief: I Need Tanks to Fight the Free State Project!

Mother Jones reports that Concord, NH Police Chief John Duval has backed off his outlandish suggestion that his police department needs a Lenco Bearcat G3 to fend off the terrorism threat posed by the Free State Project and Occupy New Hampshire. Duval had made the claim in his application for a $250,000-plus grant to purchase the armored vehicle that Free State Project President Carla Gericke simply calls a tank.

Of course, Duval still wants his Bearcat nonetheless — even if he does have to amend his application. You see, several other New Hampshire police departments already have the armored vehicle, the Bearcat looks really neat in the advert video with AC/DC's "Thunderstruck" playing, and somebody else is willing to pay for it! Nothing moves the demand curve like "it's free."

We can thank the American Civil Liberties Union (ACLU) for bringing the application into the light. The Mother Jones article explains:

> The application was obtained by the New Hampshire Civil Liberties Union (NHCLU) through a public records request, and is one of more than 250 filed by the American Civil Liberties Union to track what it sees as the increasing militarization of police departments throughout the country.

With the application now public, opposition is mobilizing. Gericke has written to Duval a public letter including demands for a written apology and removal of all references to "Free Staters" in the application. Occupy New Hampshire is meeting tonight regarding the application. The publicity will also allow individuals to attempt to influence the Concord city council members, whose August 12 meeting includes in its agenda a resolution regarding acquisition of the Bearcat.

Maybe Concord, New Hampshire will be the turning point in the decades-long rise of SWAT.

20

September 26, 2013

Is TSA Frisking and Scanning Coming to the Local Mall?

Will American families soon spend Saturday mornings waiting in line for US Transportation Security Administration (TSA) friskings and scannings outside the local shopping center? We can hope not. But, Miranda Green reports in the Daily Beast that the US Department of Homeland Security is "urging shopping malls in the United States to increase security in the aftermath of the carnage wrought by al Qaeda's Somalia affiliate over the weekend in Nairobi."

The US government has over the last few years made extensive preparations for making shopping center checkpoints a reality, including TSA's Visible Intermodal Prevention and Response (VIPR) teams that recreate TSA's airport harassment anywhere and US Customs and Border Protection (CBP) that is pursuing similar Fourth Amendment-free zone activities far from US borders. Meanwhile, the US Department of Homeland Security is moving forward quickly to implement an ambitions facial recognition program in cooperation with state and local police, having conducted Saturday another test of its Biometric Optical Surveillance System (BOSS) at a Kennewick, Washington hockey game.

The US government's acronyms tell us the plan: Show Americans who is the BOSS and sic the VIPRs on them. The recent killings at the Nairobi mall may provide the excuse to take the next step in that plan.

November 13, 2013

FBI v. The First Amendment: The US Government's Investigation of Antiwar.com

Federal Bureau of Investigation (FBI) documents released last week reveal the FBI investigated Antiwar.com, a website regularly publishing content critical of US foreign policy, for at least six years based on the content and audience of the Antiwar.com website, as well as an asinine mistake by the FBI.

According to Julia Harumi Mass of the American Civil Liberties Union of Northern California, which is representing Antiwar.com in a lawsuit against the FBI, the FBI produced in response to a document request in the lawsuit documents confirming "that the FBI targeted and spied on Antiwar.com [and the website's founding editors Eric Garris and Justin Raimondo] based on their First Amendment protected activity and kept records about that activity in violation of federal law." Mass elaborates on the anti-press freedom justifications for the investigation:

> One of the factors that prompted the FBI to investigate the editors of the online magazine was that Justin Raimondo writes under this pseudonym. The content of a writer's published opinions and whether they write under a pseduonym [sic] should never be used to characterize someone as a potential threat to national security, or justify an FBI investigation. The First Amendment protects anonymous speech too. News articles and the comments of the public should not be included in FBI intelligence files unless they're necessary to a real criminal investigation.

> The second flawed factor that prompted the FBI investivgation [sic] is that "many individuals worldwide... including individuals who are currently under investigation" view the website. Presumably people around

the world, "including individuals who are currently under [FBI] investigation" view all kinds of websites and news sources. Being part of a successful media outlet should not make a journalist suspicious and should not be the basis for government surveillance.

In addition, Mass points to a mistake as a third factor prompting the investigation:

The third flawed and incorrect factor was the FBI's mistaken conclusion that Eric Garris had threatened to hack the FBI website. In fact, Garris reported to the FBI that he was the recipient of a hacking threat to Antiwar.com. After reporting this threat, he was instructed to forward the email to the FBI, which he did. The FBI later concluded that Garris had threatened to hack the FBI website and placed him under suspicion.

It is an odd mistake for the FBI to interpret Garris' reporting of a hacking threat against the Antiwar.com website as a threat by Garris against the FBI's website. The flub up could have been rectified and an illegitimate investigation potentially prevented by just double-checking Garris' communication with the FBI. Instead, the asinine mistake remained uncorrected, allowing the investigation to proceed with a justification not rooted in concern about First Amendment-protected expression.

Of course, Garris, in reporting a website hacking threat to the FBI, was doing just what the FBI prominently recommends on its home page:

Reporting Crime

You can report violations of U.S. federal law or submit Information in a criminal or terrorism investigation as follows:

- Submit a tip electronically
- Contact your local FBI office
- Contact your nearest overseas office
- Report online crime or e-mail hoaxes

The FBI investigation of Antiwar.com began in 2002, the same year Attorney General John Ashcroft released new guidelines for domestic investigations that did away with restraints built into prior FBI guidelines adopted after examination of FBI and other government entities' abuses by the 1976 Church Committee investigations. The Electronic Privacy Information Center (EPIC) relates at its website the history of US attorneys general amending the 1976 guidelines periodically over the years, including making significant changes in 1983, to piecemeal strip away liberty protections. In an informative memorandum, ACLU Washington National Office Legislative Counsel Marvin J. Johnson explains how the 2002 guidelines changes allowed the FBI "to spy on domestic groups even when there is no suspicion of wrongdoing" and FBI investigations to "continue longer, with intrusive techniques and with less oversight, even when they produce no evidence of crime."

Of course, also throughout 2002, the George W. Bush Administration, along with advocates in Congress and the media, was working to increase public support for a proposed war in Iraq and maintain public support for an ongoing war in Afghanistan. A website featuring content critical of US foreign policy could hinder these public relations efforts.

Many Americans hoped that the election of a new president and his appointing of a new FBI director would end abuses such as the investigation of Antiwar.com and its founding editors based on shoddy and legally-dubious justifications. However, President Barack Obama has promised more of the same — not change — at the FBI. Obama first extended by two years the term of President George W. Bush-appointed FBI Director Robert Mueler, while praising Mueler for setting "the gold standard" for leading the FBI. Next, Obama nominated for the position James B. Comey, Jr. who, at the nomination announcement, effusively praised Mueller's work as director.

Now that public opposition has prevented a US attack on Syria, will FBI investigations of individuals and groups opposing US foreign interventions increase?

As with US wars, strong public opposition is key for restricting the US government's illegitimate investigation and harassment of people and groups that oppose US government policies and actions.

22

Free Speech Repressing Bureaucrat Threatens Alex Jones and Hundreds at Dallas Gathering

Wednesday night in front of the headquarters of the Federal Reserve Bank of Dallas I witnessed bureaucratic tyranny in action. There a mild-mannered and soft-spoken representative of the Dallas police threatened talk show host Alex Jones and over 200 people with $500 fines if they held signs too close to the road and handed out leaflets.

Irrespective of whether anyone is fined, the threat of fines alone — especially multi-hundred dollar fines — is enough to prevent many people from speaking freely. People may also fear that arrest and jail time may come along with fines.

From around 7:30pm to 9:00pm Wednesday night, over 200 people gathered at the sidewalk by the Federal Reserve building to receive from Jones leaflets and signs related to today's 50 year anniversary of the assassination of President John F. Kennedy and the city government's restrictions on free speech for the time period around the assassination's anniversary. While there, many of those gathered participated in a rally spanning issues from ending the Federal Reserve to questioning the "lone nut" view of the Kennedy assassination to criticizing free speech restrictions.

The time and location seemed well chosen to avoid causing trouble for pedestrians and drivers. I did not notice a single person walking through the area who was not there for the event. With wide sidewalks and a crowd that seemed happy to move out of the way, it seemed like any pedestrians would have had no trouble passing through.

The traffic was also minimal and slow on the ordinary city street and the highway access road next to the gathering. While the police representative commented that people are not allowed to give leaflets to individuals in passing cars, the only drivers I saw given leaflets had requested the leaflets while their cars were stopped at an intersection to turn within three feet of the sidewalk where people had assembled.

It is beyond credulity to believe the Dallas police spokeswoman's threats Wednesday night were anything other than a targeted effort to suppress speech because of the speech's content. Plenty of businesses and organizations have people hand out leaflets on sidewalks regularly.

As far as signs, some people holding signs, along with US, Gadsden, and Puerto Rico flags, seem less distracting to drivers than the common sight in many areas of a person standing for hours at the side of busy intersections holding, twirling, and throwing up in the air a huge arrow-shaped sign advertising a gold purchasing store, apartments for rent, or whatever.

If the Dallas government is really so concerned about accidents caused by distracted drivers, it would be restricting the downtown high-rise buildings that try to one-up each other with flashing, multicolored light shows next to a tangle of intersecting highways. That does not mean the city government should turn off the lights. But, neither should the city government use ludicrous assertions of pedestrian and motorist safety to justify threats to turn off free speech.

23

December 2, 2013

House 'Improves' TSA Instead of Ending It

Following another Thanksgiving travel period with the Transportation Security Administration (TSA) subjecting travelers to infuriating harassment, the House of Representatives leadership has scheduled for House floor consideration Tuesday three bills that will tinker with the TSA while allowing the harassment to continue. The three bills are the TSA Loose Change Act (HR 1095), the Transportation Security Acquisition Reform Act (HR 2719), and the Aviation Security Stakeholder Participation Act (HR 1204).

All three bills are scheduled for consideration under suspension of the rules — a process generally reserved for noncontroversial legislation. Because bills considered under suspension of the rules are not subject to amendments on the House floor, the House Republican and Democrat leadership have ensured there will be no debate or vote on amendments that would end or significantly restrict the TSA harassment.

Up first on the House's suspension schedule is HR 1095. The bill directs the TSA to start transferring money left behind at TSA checkpoints to nonprofit organizations that operate places for military members and their families to rest and recuperate at United States airports.

HR 1095 arguably provides an improvement over the current law that allows the TSA to use the money for its own operations. But, the bill does nothing to reduce the TSA's main source of money — US government allocations. Also, by throwing some "loose change" — about a half million dollars a year according to the House Homeland Security Committee report on the bill — to nonprofit organizations, the legislation risks creating a new special interest supporting maintaining and expanding the TSA harassment. The committee report notes that the bill's requirements have been written such that the United Service Organizations (USO) is the only nonprofit currently qualified to receive the money.

Next up, HR 2719 directs the TSA to take actions including developing and regularly updating a "strategic multiyear technology acquisition plan," making reports to House and Senate committees regarding certain technology acquisition intentions, creating "baseline requirements" for technology acquisitions, and using equipment in the TSA's inventory before acquiring more of the equipment.

HR 2719 does nothing to restrict the TSA's daily agenda of detaining, questioning, and searching people for no cause whatsoever, much less the probable cause required under the Fourth Amendment of the US Constitution. Neither does the bill limit the TSA's regular seizures of people's property. Rather, HR 2719 attempts to ensure the TSA employs technology more efficiently while engaging in these constitutional violations.

Finally, HR 1204 offers a classic legislative solution: it creates a committee. In particular, the bill creates an Aviation Security Advisory Committee and at least four subcommittees that will consult with and deliver periodic reports to the TSA.

If the committee HR 1204 creates were charged with developing plans for reducing the activities of the TSA or increasing respect for individual rights, some good may come from the legislation. Unfortunately, the bill instead directs the committee to develop, at the TSA's request, recommendations for improvements in aviation security. Further, the TSA would appoint every member of the committee. The bill appears to advance the kind of bureaucracy-building exercise you typically see in growing government agencies.

Congress earns its low approval rating through legislative schedules like this. With many Americans having just experienced their Thanksgiving TSA harassment and dreading another round at Christmas, cheers would sound across America if the House passed legislation terminating or, at least, greatly restricting the TSA assaults on our rights. Instead, the House's bipartisan leadership is demonstrating its allegiance to the TSA and the agency's abusive activities.

March 27, 2014

The TSA PreCheck Extortion Racket

Transportation Security Administration (TSA) Administrator John Pistole touted on Tuesday the expansion of TSA's extortion racket-style program known as the PreCheck. Pistole's comments were part of his testimony at the US House of Representatives before the Homeland Security Subcommittee of the Appropriations Committee.

Under PreCheck, travelers in airports who have taken steps including paying $85, giving over their fingerprints, and obtaining TSA approval of their background checks have a chance — but no guarantee — that TSA employees will, over a five year term, harass them a bit less than other travelers.

Pistole recounts in his prepared statement some of the metrics of PreCheck's expansion:

> To accommodate TSA's expansion of program eligibility to a greater number of low-risk passengers, TSA has taken the following actions: expanded the number of airports participating in TSA PreCheck from the initial 40 to 117 airports; increased the number of expedited screening lanes from 46 to 600, with each lane providing the capability for doubling hourly throughput; and increased the number of U.S. airlines participating in TSA PreCheck from six to nine in FY 2013, with plans of continued expansion as airlines are ready. Today, TSA provides expedited screening to over 35% of the traveling public.

PreCheck is just like the old extortion rackets of hooligans selling protection from themselves to store owners and raiders from the countryside demanding that residents of a town pay tribute. Dressed up in the language of law, regulation, and formal application procedures this abusive practice develops a veneer of legitimacy. At its heart, though, the practice is the same whether conducted by a street gang or the TSA: pay us money and do as we say so you may avoid being abused. In the case of the TSA, the offered benefit is limiting the extent of invasive frisking and property searches conducted without even the pretense of the probable cause required under the Fourth Amendment of the US Constitution.

While it may sound extreme to call TSA's regular airport activities criminal, and its PreCheck program thus an extortion racket, the US government recognizes that TSA's regular activities would be criminal but for the special protection TSA has as part of the national police apparatus. When legislation to remove TSA employees' protection from prosecution for their routine on-the-job offensive touches passed the Texas House and appeared about to pass the state Senate in 2011, the US Department of Justice responded with a threat to end all commercial passenger flights through Texas airports given that the legislation would make routine TSA activities illegal.

Fingerprinting, background checks, applications, and $85 are a price many people are willing to pay in the hopes of avoiding some of the enhanced harassment that infuriates travelers in American airports. Yet, once enough people have applied to the PreCheck program, we must wonder if the US government then will make PreCheck participation a requirement for all travelers while eliminating every bit of relief from harassment the program may now provide.

25

June 20, 2014

US House Rejects by 355 to 62 Vote Amendment to Limit Transfer of Military Weapons and Equipment to Local Police

By a vote of 355 "no" votes to 62 "yes" votes the United States House of Representatives voted down Thursday night an amendment offered by Rep. Alan Grayson (D-FL) to the Department of Defense Appropriations Act (HR 4870) that would have curtailed the transfer of US military equipment to local police.

Grayson explained on the House floor that he offered his amendment "to address a growing problem throughout our country, which is the militarization of local law enforcement agencies." In particular Grayson expressed concern about documentation in the New York Times of huge transfers of military weapons and equipment to local police and the overkill use of transferred items in ordinary law enforcement, even in raids to enforce barber and liquor license laws, instead of in response to nonexistent terrorism.

The Times article Grayson mentions documents that the transfers involve a long list of military weapons and equipment including, since 2006 alone, 432 Mine-resistant Ambush Protected armored vehicles (MRAPs), 435 other armored vehicles, 533 planes and helicopters, and 92,763 machine guns. The Times article also lists grenade launchers, silencers, and other items among the transferred military items.

As Grayson explained in the debate, his amendment would have limited effect. The amendment would not reverse any of the transfers that have already taken place, and it would allow transfers of guns and ammunition to continue unimpeded. What the amendment would do according to its language is stop the transfer under a Department of Defense program of the following items: "aircraft (including unmanned aerial vehicles), armored vehicles, grenade launchers, silencers, toxicological agents (including chemical agents, biological agents and associated equipment), launch vehicles, guided missiles, ballistic missiles, rockets, torpedoes, bombs, mines or nuclear weapons."

While the Times article does not list nuclear weapons among military items transferred to local police, Grayson including them to the list makes the point that, as the law stands, there is virtually no limit on what weapons and equipment may be transferred.

In opposition to Grayson in the debate two representatives figuratively put their hands over their respective eyes and ears and said they saw and heard no evil in the actions of local police. They presented this argument despite the decades long rise of SWAT culminating in what Rutherford Institute President John W. Whitehead terms an escalating "epidemic of police violence."

Rep. Rodney Frelinghuysen (R-NJ), who is Chairman of the Defense Appropriations Subcommittee, speaking in opposition to the amendment pronounced the blanket statement that the military items are "not misused" and, instead, are used "to make sure that all of our citizens are protected."

Frelinghuysen then introduced Rep. Rich Nugent (R-FL), whom Frelinghuysen described as a former sheriff. Nugent proceeded to one-up Frelinghuysen's fantasyland representation of police use of this military equipment, stating:

> This is absolutely ludicrous to think that the equipment that is utilized by law enforcement is utilized for any reason except for public safety interests, and it happens across this nation every day in a responsible way.

What happens across the country every day are SWAT raids – tens of thousands of them a year, in fact. And these raids are, as explained by Grayson on the House floor, often employed as a matter of course, even to address suspected petty legal offenses. The result is deaths, injuries, emotional trauma, property destruction, and withering respect for individual rights. Indeed, it is absolutely ludicrous to defend this practice and, even worse, to promote it as advancing public safety.

26

July 6, 2014

House to Vote on 'Expedited and Dignified' TSA Screenings for Some People, Sometimes

The US House of Representatives is scheduled to consider

on Tuesday the Honor Flight Act (HR 4812) that would require the Transportation Security Administration (TSA) to work with a non-profit organization to establish a process for providing "expedited and dignified passenger screening services for veterans" who are traveling with the aid of certain non-profit organizations to visit certain war memorials.

While enactment of this legislation may provide some relief for veterans traveling on these particular trips, the obvious question is why the same basic restraints are not placed on the TSA for its interactions with everyone and for all trips.

Honor Flight Act sponsor Rep. Cedric Richmond's (D-LA) June 9 press release announcing the introduction of the bill encapsulates the very limited benefit the bill would offer:

> Any veteran who desires to travel to our Nation's Capitol to visit the memorials constructed in their honor should be afforded every opportunity to do so in the most dignified manner. It is the least we can do.

"The least Congress can do" is a fitting description of the bill. Are you a veteran who desires to travel for a wedding, funeral, Thanksgiving or Christmas with relatives, class reunion, surgery, job interview, fun, or whatever reason other than visiting a designated war memorial on a US government-approved trip? If you answer "yes," then be prepared to wait in line for your scanning, frisking, and invasive property search. Like so many other people, the TSA will continue to subject you to infuriating mistreatment as a precondition of you exercising your right to travel. Maybe, if you tell the TSA employee you were in the military, he will say "Thank you for your service" as he rubs your crotch.

Also note that the legislation does not exempt veterans from TSA harassment even when they are traveling on a government-approved trip to a war memorial. The Honor Flight Act just says the harassment must be conducted in an "expedited and dignified" fashion.

Though promising veterans minimal benefit, the Honor Flight Act — like the TSA PreCheck extortion racket through which people may pay the TSA in hopes of being harassed a little less — divides travelers into categories for differing levels of harassment by the US government. Such stratification of respect for individual rights is contrary to the equality under the law that is supposed to be a basic standard in American government.

A day cannot pass without multiple members of Congress praising veterans for "fighting for our freedom." If so many Congress members really believe that rhetoric, Congress would eliminate the TSA, restoring respect for a significant portion of freedom denied since the beginning of this century. The Washington, DC political class has determined, however, that it is "too extreme" for Congress members to support eliminating the TSA. Instead of protecting us from the TSA, the House fiddles around the edges of the abusive bureaucracy with the Honor Flights Act and other tinkering bills.

27

August 21, 2014

Send Sunil Dutta Back to the Police Academy... or Not

Sunil Dutta, who has worked 17 years in the Los Angeles Police Department, has some advice for anyone encountering him on the job: do whatever I say and don't complain, or I will hurt or kill you.

Here is Dutta's advice, in his own words, from his Tuesday Washington Post editorial:

> Even though it might sound harsh and impolitic, here is the bottom line: if you don't want to get shot, tased, pepper-sprayed, struck with a baton or thrown to the ground, just do what I tell you. Don't argue with me, don't call me names, don't tell me that I can't stop you, don't say I'm a racist pig, don't threaten that you'll sue me and take away my badge. Don't scream at me that

you pay my salary, and don't even think of aggressively walking towards me. Most field stops are complete in minutes. How difficult is it to cooperate for that long?

Revealingly, every action Dutta says a person he confronts should refrain from taking is a nonviolent action. In contrast, every action Dutta says he, as a cop, may take in response is violent — an assault or a murder.

Dutta's advice amounts to this: Give up on exercising any of your rights — even the right to free speech — and act as an absolute slave when a cop accosts you.

Reading Dutta's outrageous advice, one is tempted to say he should be sent back to the police academy to learn the basics. But, things have changed in America with the rise of SWAT. Dutta pretty much is the police academy. He is an adjunct professor of homeland security and criminal justice at Colorado Technical University in addition to working for the LAPD. Dutta's biography on the university website relates:

> Dr. Dutta's teaching experience goes back two decades and includes teaching police academy instructors as well as high-level police and military professionals at the International Law Enforcement Academy. He has taught at all levels, including high school, community college, and university.

Dutta's disturbing views are commonplace among police due to a dangerous change in attitude that has swept through the police profession over the last few decades. Rutherford Institute President John W. Whitehead explores this change and how it is reinforced in modern police education in his June article "Just Shoot: The Mindset Responsible for Turning Search Warrants into Death Warrants, and SWAT Teams into Death Squads." While it is absolutely worthwhile to read Whitehead's entire revealing article, a couple paragraphs jump out as particularly relevant:

> Yet the tension inherent in most civilian-police encounter these days can't be blamed exclusively on law enforcement's growing reliance on SWAT teams. It

goes far deeper, to a transformation in the way police view themselves and their line of duty. Specifically, what we're dealing with today is a skewed shoot-to-kill mindset in which police, trained to view themselves as warriors or soldiers in a war, whether against drugs, or terror, or crime, must "get" the bad guys—i.e., anyone who is a potential target—before the bad guys get them. The result is a spike in the number of incidents in which police shoot first, and ask questions later.

…

If ever there were a time to de-militarize and de-weaponize police forces, it's now, starting at the local level, with local governments and citizens reining in local police. The same goes for scaling back on the mindset adopted by cops that they are the law and should be revered, feared and obeyed.

Dutta's editorial is one more indication that police brutality in America is not just the result of "a few bad cops." Instead, it is caused in large part by serious institutional problems arising from changes in how cops are taught to perform their jobs and how cops view their interactions with other people.

These institutional problems create danger. They make police brutality more likely, and they drive people to act out of fear — as Dutta recommends — as cops' slaves instead of as free individuals with rights including rights against self-incrimination and warrantless searches.

This danger is compounded by the US government delivering weapons of war to local police throughout America without even the semblance of restraint.

To substantially reduce police brutality, the understanding must be restored among the vast majority of police that the disturbing views Dutta expresses in his editorial are unacceptable in the police profession.

August 28, 2014

Is a Nationwide Local Government Backlash Against Police Militarization Beginning?

KCRA-TV is reporting that the Davis, California City Council voted Tuesday evening, after hearing from concerned people at the city council's meeting, to get rid of the police department's Mine-Resistant Ambush Protected (MRAP) military vehicle. The police department had obtained the MRAP, which is valued at nearly $700,000, for free recently from the US government.

Will Davis, California one day be seen as the beginning of a nationwide local government backlash against police militarization in the US?

With the police crackdown in Ferguson, Missouri, Americans appear to be gaining an enhanced awareness of police militarization and the US government's dumping of military equipment on local police departments. The timing of the Davis City Council vote suggests that this heightened awareness may help reverse the practice of so many local governments accepting the free weapons of war even when, as in Concord, New Hampshire last year, confronted by many vocal opponents.

What to do with the unwanted military vehicle? Maybe, like the cars at the Cadillac Ranch near Amarillo, Texas, the Davis police department's MRAP could be half buried in the ground with its exposed posterior painted in a multitude of colors. As a sculpture, it could serve as a reminder of the wrong turn the local police department had taken and the corrective action that concerned individuals were able to bring about. Maybe similar sculptures would start appearing in other villages, towns, and cities across the nation.

October 9, 2014

The Abominable No Fly List

Last week the US government prohibited poet and journalist Amjad Nasser from speaking at an event to inaugurate the Gallatin Global Writers series at New York University. How did the government do this? By having a policeman at the event inform Nasser that he would be arrested if he took his turn to speak at the event? No, that would be a clear prior restraint on speech in violation of the First Amendment of the United States Constitution — a government action courts routinely rule is prohibited. Instead, the US government simply banned Nasser from flying to the conference.

Nasser recounts the process by which his participation in the event was blocked by a faceless Department of Homeland Security agent on the other end of a phone line at London Heathrow Airport. At the airport terminal, Nasser was handed a phone whereupon the US bureaucrat on the call peppered him with personal questions about Nasser and the event at which Nasser was planning to speak. Nasser relates that, after two hours on the phone, the questioner informed Nasser that Nasser was banned from taking the already booked, and by then already departed, US-bound flight.

While Nasser, a British and Jordanian citizen, had to answer a series of questions regarding his private affairs in hopes that he would just be allowed to board the plane and fulfill his speaking commitment, the US bureaucrat on the other end of the line was not obliged to even provide an explanation for why Nasser was prevented from boarding the plane. Nasser relates how the phone interrogation wound down upon the inquisitor's announcement of Nasser's travel prohibition:

> ... he said: I am sorry. You cannot board this departing plane (It had already taken off) to New York.
>
> - What is the reason?

- I cannot disclose that.

- Do I not have a right to know the reason?

- No.

- Just like that?

- Just like that.

The direct result of Nasser's ban from the flight is that he was prevented from speaking in person at the event in New York City. A second very important result is that anyone who hears the story of Nasser's travel restriction learns the lesson that if you want to travel freely it is best to not speak out about anything that could risk provoking the ire of the US government — or even of any random, faceless US bureaucrat who may hold veto power over your travel plans. This threat hanging over travelers certainly, in the language of US courts, "chills" speech. But, being removed a step from outright speech restrictions, courts would be less likely to find the travel prohibition violates of the First Amendment — especially so long as the government can get away with providing absolutely no reason for imposed travel prohibitions.

While Nasser's ordeal alone is disturbing, what is even more disturbing is that such banning of airplane travel is routinely meted out by US bureaucrats upon travelers both foreign and American. And, as in the case of Nasser, these other blacklisted travelers are regularly provided absolutely no reason for the deprivation of their ability to exercise their right to travel.

The treatment of Nasser and other people subjected to the US government travel blacklist is properly describable as Kafkaesque, reminiscent of the arrest of Josef K. at the beginning of Franz Kafka's novel The Trial:

> "I want to see Mrs. Grubach ...," said K., making a movement as if tearing himself away from the two men - even though they were standing well away from him - and wanted to go. "No," said the man at the window, who threw his book down on a coffee table and stood up. "You can't go away when you're

under arrest." "That's how it seems," said K. "And why am I under arrest?" he then asked. "That's something we're not allowed to tell you. Go into your room and wait there. Proceedings are underway and you'll learn about everything all in good time. It's not really part of my job to be friendly towards you like this, but I hope no-one, apart from Franz, will hear about it, and he's been more friendly towards you than he should have been, under the rules, himself. If you carry on having as much good luck as you have been with your arresting officers then you can reckon on things going well with you."

The US government's No Fly List operates in opaqueness, like the arrest of K. An individual on the No Fly List is administratively denied the ability to exercise the right to travel, as well as to exercise rights that travel facilitates — from free speech to participating in commerce to visiting family and friends, all without any of the due process the US Constitution guarantees. By an entirely secret process your name ends up on the No Fly List. You find out about your travel prohibition by showing up for a flight and being told you cannot fly on your booked flight, and that's that. It is you at the airport with Transportation Security Administration (TSA) bureaucrats offering at best a mix of platitudes, warnings, and "helpful advice" about how if you jump through all the right hoops you just might be able to convince the government to again respect — until it may decide arbitrarily not to again — your right to travel. They may well even tell you that they are sticking their necks out for you by talking with you for a few minutes.

Want to know for sure if you are on the No Fly List and, if so, why? Here is what you do: Make a federal case of it; sue the US government in federal court. That is what several people did with the help of the American Civil Liberties Union (ACLU) over four years ago. On Friday the federal district court judge hearing the case ordered the US government to disclose by January 16 whether the 14 plaintiffs, who have been barred from air travel, are in fact on the No Fly List and, if they are, why.

Justice would be better served if the US government just followed the US Constitution. The Fifth Amendment prohibits the US government from depriving any person of "life, liberty, or property, without due process of law." Due process would involve the government being required to prove in a US district court all the elements of a statute permitting the denial of travel rights. And that statute would have to have become law through the constitutionally prescribed method, be clear in its meaning, be consistent with constitutional limitations of government power, and be publicly reviewable. Employing due process would also involve the person the government seeks to deny the ability to travel having all his rights respected as should be the case for other defendants in court actions brought by the US government — rights such as the right be represented by an attorney, the right against self-incrimination, the right to confront witnesses, the right to a jury trial, and the right to appeal an adverse district court decision to a US appellate court.

The current Star Chamber system has none of these liberty-protecting attributes. For a window into the depraved manner in which the No Fly List, along with the related Selectee List and Terrorist Watchlist, operates, read Jeremy Scahill and Ryan Deveraux's July 23 exposé that begins with the following account:

> The Obama administration has quietly approved a substantial expansion of the terrorist watchlist system, authorizing a secret process that requires neither "concrete facts" nor "irrefutable evidence" to designate an American or foreigner as a terrorist, according to a key government document obtained by The Intercept.

> The "March 2013 Watchlisting Guidance," a 166-page document issued last year by the National Counterterrorism Center, spells out the government's secret rules for putting individuals on its main terrorist database, as well as the no fly list and the selectee list, which triggers enhanced screening at airports and border crossings. The new guidelines allow individuals to be designated as representatives of terror organizations

69

without any evidence they are actually connected to such organizations, and it gives a single White House official the unilateral authority to place entire "categories" of people the government is tracking onto the no fly and selectee lists. It broadens the authority of government officials to "nominate" people to the watchlists based on what is vaguely described as "fragmentary information." It also allows for dead people to be watchlisted.

Even beyond these lists and their employment in rights violations, President Barack Obama claims the authority, and has acted upon this claimed authority many times, to order the "targeted killing" via drone missile or otherwise of anyone in the world. The related list he approves in secret is the Kill List, and the creation and use of this list also provides for absolutely no due process protection.

In January, Rahinah Ibrahim became the first person ever reported to successfully gain removal from the No Fly List. Her victory occurred after a five-day federal district court trial that was held largely in secret, at the US government's insistence to protect "state secrets." Bringing to mind the typographical error that puts in motion the story in the movie Brazil, it turns out Ibrahim had been added to the list in 2004 because a Federal Bureau of Investigation agent checked the wrong box on a form.

While the US government chose to force Ibrahim to proceed all the way through a long, costly, and burdensome court battle to correct the error that placed her on the No Fly List, the government has long known the list is a mess. The multi-agency FBI-administered Terrorist Screening Center (TSC) that maintains the list in January 2007 determined that tens of thousands of individuals included in the No Fly List did not belong there. The TSC recommended the people instead belonged on the lower-level Selectee List that calls for greater airport harassment, but not a for sure travel prohibition, or belonged on neither list. Here is the rundown from a redacted September 2007 US Department of Justice, Office of Inspector General report:

In July 2006, the Homeland Security Council Deputies

Committee issued guidance on how to correctly apply its criteria for including individuals on the No Fly list. Subsequently, the TSC submitted all TSDB [(the TSC's consolidated terrorist screening database)] records associated with individuals who were on the No Fly list to a comprehensive quality assurance review using this guidance. When the TSC began its review in July 2006, the No Fly list contained 71,872 records. The TSC completed its special review of the No Fly list on January 31, 2007, determining that the No Fly list should be reduced to 34,230 records.[15] The TSC recommended 22,412 records for removal from the No Fly list and placement on the TSA's Selectee list.[16] For another 5,086 records, the TSC determined that the individual did not require inclusion on either the No Fly or Selectee list.

The current size of the No Fly List is not publicly available. According to an Associated Press article from February 2012, the names on the No Fly List more than doubled from 10,000 a year earlier to 21,000, including 500 Americans, around the time of the article's publication.

Whatever the number of names now on the No Fly List and the airport "enhanced" harassment guaranteeing Selectee List, the lack of anything approaching due process in the determination of who is on the lists and in how the lists are used to deprive respect for individual rights guarantees that many people in addition to Ibrahim are being harassed and denied the ability to exercise their rights for no good reason. Given the US government's entirely shoddy and unjust No Fly and Selectee Lists system, the presumption should be that everyone, such as poet and journalist Nasser, who is singled out for special harassment at an airport or is barred from a flight is a victim of rights violations by a government bureaucracy operating in absolute violation of individual rights and constitutional constraints.

October 15, 2014

Committing Highway Robbery to Fund Police Militarization

The militarization of local police in the United States is not being fueled just by the federal government providing military equipment, including machine guns, grenade launchers, and armored vehicles, to local police departments. The police are also funding the rise of SWAT with billions of dollars obtained through asset seizures that amount to highway robbery under the guise of law enforcement.

In an October 11 Washington Post article, Robert O'Harrow Jr. and Steven Rich offer some revealing details concerning how state and local police have raised billions of dollars since 2008 via asset seizures associated with the US Department of Justice Equitable Sharing Program that allows state and local police departments to take 80 percent of the proceeds of seizures conducted in cooperation with US government agencies. In addition, much more police revenue has been gained through asset seizures outside the program and without direct US government involvement.

What do the state and local police do with the money obtained through asset forfeitures? As the Post article explains, much of it is pumped into expanding surveillance and police militarization:

> The police purchases comprise a rich mix of the practical and the high-tech, including an array of gear that has helped some departments militarize their operations: Humvees, automatic weapons, gas grenades, night-vision scopes and sniper gear. Many departments acquired electronic surveillance equipment, including automated license-plate readers and systems that track cellphones.

Police departments even use the Equitable Sharing money

to pay incidental costs related to military weapons and equipment obtained from the US government's 1033 program:

> Ten agencies have used the asset forfeiture funds to pay their fees for the Defense Department's excess property initiative, better known as the 1033 program, which enables local and state police to buy surplus military-grade equipment at cut rates. The equipment includes automatic weapons, night-vision gear and clothing.
>
> Police in Sahuarita, Ariz., paid $4,300 to outfit a Humvee obtained through the 1033 program. The New Bedford, Mass., Police Department in 2012 paid $2,119 for shipping costs for M-16s from the military.

In addition to the harmful uses to which the Equitable Sharing money is employed, O'Harrow and Rich point out the absolute injustice of the asset seizures that feed money into the US government program:

> Of the nearly $2.5 billion in spending reported in the forms, 81 percent came from cash and property seizures in which no indictment was filed, according to an analysis by The Post. Owners must prove that their money or property was acquired legally in order to get it back.

You read that right. The way the asset seizures work is the police just take your money or other property even without the slightest basis for proving you committed a crime, much less that there is any relationship between an alleged illegal activity and the property taken. Then, turning on its head the fundamental American legal principle of "innocent until proven guilty," victims of asset seizure must prove they had acquired without ties to illegal activity whatever was taken before they can have it back.

Revealingly, only in 19 percent of the asset forfeitures were indictments even filed. This is despite the ease with which grand juries that only receive the information prosecutors put before them issue indictments — thus the quip that a competent prosecutor can convince a grand jury to indict a ham sandwich.

In so many asset seizures seizing the property is the goal, and an accusation of legal violations is nothing more than a rote step in reaching that goal.

Michael Sallah, O'Harrow, and Rich explored in a September 6 Washington Post article the outrageous schemes used by police around the country to seize assets. Here is how the process often begins:

> The Post's review of 400 court cases, which encompassed seizures in 17 states, provided insights into stops and seizures.
>
> In case after case, highway interdictors appeared to follow a similar script. Police set up what amounted to rolling checkpoints on busy highways and pulled over motorists for minor violations, such as following too closely or improper signaling. They quickly issued warnings or tickets. They studied drivers for signs of nervousness, including pulsing carotid arteries, clenched jaws and perspiration. They also looked for supposed "indicators" of criminal activity, which can include such things as trash on the floor of a vehicle, abundant energy drinks or air fresheners hanging from rearview mirrors.

In short, anyone can be a suspect.

From there the police can pressure people into "consenting" to a search, or they can attempt to use a drug-sniffing dog's signal or other additional excuse to allow a search. Once property such as a few thousand dollars in cash — something absolutely legal for any person to carry on his person or in a car — is found, the police then seize the property. To make their claim to the seized property even stronger, the police may then move on to threatening their victim with prosecution for drug or other crimes unless the victim signs a form disclaiming ownership of the property.

You may be tempted to call Equitable Sharing Program asset seizures "highway robbery." In many instances that description is spot-on. The October 11 Washington Post article relates:

> There have been 61,998 cash seizures on highways
> and elsewhere since 9/11 without search warrants
> or indictments and processed through the Equitable
> Sharing Program, according to an analysis of Justice
> data obtained by The Post.

The asset seizures are, however, in some ways even worse than the highway robberies of private criminals. When confronted by a private robber, you may legally flee or exercise your right to defend yourself and your property with force and, depending on the circumstances, even deadly force. But, try to escape from or just nudge your elbow into the arm of a policeman who is in the process of seizing your property and you can be charged with a catalogue of crimes and misdemeanors. Plus, unlike private criminals who may cease robbing people or even be caught by the police after a while, the police, with courts' help, have institutionalized their property seizure practices.

Where is America's Robin Hood?

31

Fed Asset Seizures Rollback Less Than Advertised

While headlines in Yahoo News and Raw Story blare, respectively, "U.S. attorney general bans asset seizure by local police" and "No more asset seizure: Eric Holder bans controversial 'war on drugs' tactic," the truth is that United States Attorney General Eric Holder on Friday changed US Department of Justice policy in a manner that will result in at most a small rollback of asset seizures.

It is true that there appears to be a rollback in the police state for a change. The catch is that the rollback is nowhere near the monumental change that some people in the media are trumpeting. The many and broad exceptions in Holder's order all but swallow the announced headline-garnering rollback. Depending on how the order is interpreted and implemented, it may provide almost no asset seizure relief.

Holder's order terminated immediately on Friday a portion of the US government's Equitable Sharing Program. The program has funneled billions of dollars to local police departments via seizures of people's cash and property without any demonstration required of a relation between the person deprived of the assets, or the assets themselves, and criminal activity. In particular, the order ends some uses of "federal adoption" — a process defined narrowly in the order as when seizures by only state or local police and based only on state law are categorized as being US government seizures. The bulk of the proceeds so "adopted" may then be routed back to the involved state or local police departments.

Otherwise, the order leaves US asset seizure policy unchanged.

The Department of Justice announcement of the policy change further notes that the US Department of Treasury is issuing consistent changes for the Treasury asset seizure policy.

The limited scope of the rollback is admitted in the Justice Department announcement. The announcement states:

> Indeed, adoptions currently constitute a very small slice of the federal asset forfeiture program. Over the last six years, adoptions accounted for roughly three percent of the value of forfeitures in the Department of Justice Asset Forfeiture Program.

Several limitations spelled out in the order illustrate the small impact of the order and the potential for the order's rollback to be easily circumvented. The order states:

> This order does not apply to (1) seizures by states and local authorities working together with federal authorities in a joint task force; (2) seizures by state and local authorities that are the result of joint federal-state investigations or that are coordinated with federal

authorities as part of ongoing federal investigations; or (3) seizures pursuant to federal seizure warrants, obtained from federal courts to take custody of assets originally seized under state law.

With the growth of the national police, as well as national criminal law, and the increased integration of state and local police departments with the national police, these limitations very much diminish the scope of the order.

The limitations may also create new problems. A very worrisome potential consequence of Holder's order arises from state and local police now having an incentive to incorporate the US government as a partner in even more police activity in an effort to obtain adoption benefits. Thus the order may advance the ongoing process of militarizing police.

Notably, Holder's order also says adoption can continue without change in regard to "property that directly relates to public safety concerns, including firearms, ammunition, explosives, and property associated with child pornography."

Do not be fooled into believing the listed types of seized assets compose the entire exception. The order outright states that adoption may continue to be used for any property under the "public safety exception" so long as the Assistant Attorney General for the Criminal Division gives approval.

Further indicating the limited protection the new order affords, the Justice Department explains in the announcement that, given states' enactment of their own oppressive seizure laws over the last few decades, the US workaround is no longer needed to ensure police can continue violating individual rights with impunity:

> The Justice Department's policy permitting federal agencies to adopt seizures dates from the inception of the Asset Forfeiture Program in the 1980s. The Treasury Department's adoption policy has been part of its Asset Forfeiture Program since its inception in 1993. At the time that these policies were implemented, few states had forfeiture statutes analogous to the federal asset forfeiture laws. Consequently, when state and lo-

cal law enforcement agencies seized criminal proceeds and property used to commit crimes, they often lacked the legal authority to forfeit the seized items. Turning seized assets over to federal law enforcement agencies for adoption was a way to keep those assets from being returned to criminals. Today, however, every state has either criminal or civil forfeiture laws, making the federal adoption process less necessary.

While the rollback contained in Holder's order is far from the grand achievement suggested in some news headlines, even a small rollback can lead to relief for some individuals. It can also serve as a starting point for further rollbacks.

To the extent state laws provide greater protection of rights in the limited cases in which adoption will no longer be available, the rollback may help protect rights. Also, to the extent the rollback will result in state and local police departments' asset seizure proceeds being directed to general revenue or elsewhere instead of back into police departments' own budgets, the incentive for asset seizures may be reduced. Further, with the US government workaround limited, some state and local governments may find more reason to impose greater limitations on their own asset seizure policies.

Yet, if the US government does not follow Holder's order with action to significantly back off from asset seizures and demonstrate much more respect for privacy, due process, and property rights, it is unlikely that people demanding an end to rights violations associated with asset seizures will feel much satisfaction. For these advocates, the progression toward medical and recreational marijuana legalization in America may show the path to success: Big rollbacks in cash and other property seizures in America will likely only come as a result of increased public opposition to the seizures coupled with state and local governments reversing course and directly opposing the seizures.

January 30, 2015

To Stop Tracking of Car Movements, States Can End License Plate Requirement

Despite Chairman Chuck Grassley (R-IA) and Ranking Member Patrick Leahy (D-VT) of the Senate Judiciary Committee expressing concern about the US government using a license plate tracking system to monitor vehicle movements in America, we should not expect the US Congress to pass any significant rollback of the mass spying program. As we have seen with the US government's telecommunications mass spying program administered largely by the National Security Agency (NSA), a large-scale effort to defeat any significant rights-protecting legislative response should be expected. Further, only insignificant to counterproductive "reform" legislation — portrayed deceptively as a major rollback — will likely be pushed through the legislative process.

If Congress will not act to protect the people's rights, who then can limit the license plate tracking program? State governments can. Without license plates, there can be no US government license plate tracking program. A state government can protect individuals from the US government's snooping by ending the state's requirement that license plates be displayed on automobiles. In taking this action, a state would also protect people from spying and tracking by private individuals and entities, as well as by state and local government police, bureaucrats, and contractors.

As Judge Andrew Napolitano, a Ron Paul Institute Advisory Board member, has explained, the US government's mass tracking of automobiles via license plate readers is a violation of the Fourth Amendment of the US Constitution and reminiscent of East Germany domestic spying practices.

April 14, 2015

Ending Vaccination Mandate Exemptions in Australia and the US

Under a new government policy announced by Australia Prime Minister Tony Abbott, many Australian families are respectively facing the denial of thousands of dollars in welfare and tax benefits over a year's time because their children have not received all the vaccinations listed on a government schedule. Meanwhile, in America, recently developed pro-mandate momentum threatens to end the most commonly used exemptions families claim to exempt children from mandatory vaccinations.

The new Australian policy cuts welfare and tax benefits if parents rely on a conscientious objection — often referred to as a philosophical objection in America — to deviate from the government's vaccination schedule. While the conscientious objection option has been available to parents generally, the religious and medical exemptions that may still be asserted under the new policy are only available to a subset of families. Indeed, CBC News quotes the Australia social services minister predicting that very few families will be able to obtain an exemption under the new policy:

> Social Services Minister Scott Morrison said he only expected a very small number of families to be exempted from the new policy.
>
> Morrison said parents seeking a religious exception would need to be registered with their church or similar organization.
>
> "That's the only basis upon which you can have a religious exception, and there are no mainstream religions that have such objections registered so this would apply to a very, very small proportion of people," he said.

"It'd be lucky to be in the thousands, if that."

The new Australia policy is an example of the danger of "do-good" government programs, such as welfare, morphing into a means for punishing and prohibiting the exercise of individual rights. John Odermatt passionately addresses this concern about the new Australia policy at the Lions of Liberty, stating:

> The law blatantly targets the poorest in society and gives the rich a pass. I don't see how any rational person could see this as anything else than an attack on the poor. The law is immoral because it uses coercion to influence behavior. Lawmakers and the people who support this travesty believe that individuals do not own their bodies. To endorse this law is to endorse outright tyranny.

Once the new policy has been implemented for a while to limit some families' welfare and tax benefits, the concerns Odermatt expresses about the disparity of the program's impact will likely be used by mandate advocates to argue that mandatory vaccinations be made the policy for everyone.

In America that would be termed "closing a loophole" or "expanding a successful pilot program."

A requirement to comply with a government vaccination schedule for families to receive welfare and tax benefits is not the policy in America. But, state governments do impose vaccination requirements on children attending institutions such as public and private schools, and even day care centers and camps, with available exemptions varying state to state. Some sates even impose vaccination mandates on homeschooled children. Considering the combined effect of mandates with states' compulsory school attendance laws, vaccine mandates reach the vast majority of American children.

The New York Times reported in February how extremely restricting vaccination mandate exemptions causes a significant increase in vaccination rates, pointing to Mississippi as an example. Mississippi has among the strictest vaccination requirements in America — barring philosophical and religious exemptions and allowing only a medical exemption for students in both public and private schools. In the 2013-14 school year the Times reports that only 17 out of 45,179 kindergarten students in the state were exempt from the state's vaccination mandate.

Residents of California, which is home to over ten percent of American residents, may soon be subject to vaccination mandates like those imposed in Mississippi. Last week, the California Senate Health Committee passed SB 277 that would, if it makes its way through the entire legislative process, eliminate the state's personal beliefs exemption for vaccinations, leaving Californians with only the usually unavailable medical exemption option. In California, the vaccination mandate is imposed on children in any public or private elementary or secondary schools, as well as, child care centers, day nurseries, nursery schools, family day care homes, and development centers.

Whether in Australia or America, expanding vaccination mandates is part of a march toward tyranny.

34

June 13, 2015

The Prosecution of Dennis Hastert and the Government's War on Cash

Back on March 31, the US Department of Justice (DOJ) announced what many media reports heralded as a big rollback in the use of structuring allegations to justify seizing assets from individuals. Yet, here we are less than three months later with the DOJ prosecuting former US House of Representatives Speaker Dennis Hastert (R-IL) for two crimes — structuring and lying to the Federal Bureau of Investigation (FBI) about why he employed structuring.

Despite the DOJ's March 31 talking points used to allay people's worries about the US government punishing people for the nonviolent action of moving cash in or out of their own accounts in a manner the US government disapproves, the Hastert prosecution shows that business as usual continues at the DOJ. In fact, the willingness of the DOJ to undertake this very high-profile prosecution where there is no alleged crime beyond structuring and lying about structuring may well indicate an escalation in the US government's structuring crackdown.

According to the DOJ, Hastert faces punishment of up to 10 years in prison and a $500,000 fine if he is convicted. It is thus hard to argue that Hastert is in a better position than the many people whose money has been seized because of structuring allegations but who can choose to just walk away with a significant monetary loss. Hastert's legal bills are mounting to defend himself against the DOJ that can spend without restraint in pursuit of a conviction. Even if Hastert can beat the charges or make a deal so he can walk free, his financial loss will be very high.

Though allegations are flying that Hastert has committed "sexual misconduct" (criminal or not), none of that is used as a basis for his prosecution. Instead, as Conor Friedersdorf notes in The Atlantic, "The alarming aspect of this case is the fact that an American is ultimately being prosecuted for the crime of evading federal government surveillance." "That has implications for all of us," continues Friedersdorf.

Indeed, Ludwig von Mises Institute President Jeff Deist categorizes Hastert's prosecution as part of the US government's larger war on cash that puts Americans' privacy and liberty in peril.

One of the great benefits of using cash for transactions is the anonymity it can provide, allowing, for example, buyers and sellers to keep their identities secret from one another and from the snooping eyes of third parties, including governments. But, this benefit from using cash is under attack in America. One of the primary means of attack is the US government's practice of seizing cash from individuals who at one time move $10,000 or more in cash, or who engage in multiple actions that together move $10,000 or more in cash.

Carl Menger Center for the Study of Money and Banking President Paul-Martin Foss lays out in his article "The Kafkaesque World of Financial Reporting and Asset Forfeiture" the process by which American financial institutions — from banks to money wiring services — have been ratting to the US government on their customers' cash activities. Foss explains how the US government has in turn used that information to seize large sums of money from people without the presentation of any proof that the individuals committed any crimes — other than moving their own cash. As Foss details, financial institutions are required to report all cash transactions of $10,000 or more via a "currency transaction report" as well as, via a "suspicious activity report," all transactions of less than that amount that may be seen as "structuring" to avoid the $10,000 reporting threshold. Foss points to the enactment of a law nearly thirty years ago as putting this process into high gear by relieving financial institutions of all liability for their betrayals of customers' privacy:

> Because the Money Laundering Control Act of 1986 released banks from liability for reporting "suspicious" transactions to law enforcement, there is no reason for banks not to report your transactions to the government. They cannot be held liable for reporting too much of your information, but they could be prosecuted by the government for reporting too little information, if the government decides that suspicious activity was taking place and was not being reported. So to cover their own derrieres and keep from going to jail, banks report as much information on you as they can.

The result is the government seizing people's cash though there is no proof whatsoever that the individuals did anything illegal aside from moving their own cash. The burden is then on the seizure victims to go through a difficult and often unsuccessful effort to regain their funds. The process to regain seized money can be very costly with high lawyer fees that may be impossible to pay because of the deprivation of the seized funds that started all the legal mess. As Foss notes, this is Kafkaesque.

Ron Paul Institute Advisory Board Member Andrew Napolitano relates in an April Fox News interview some of the absurd travails of dairy farmer Randy Sowers from whom the US government — through the Internal Revenue Service (IRS) — is keeping nearly $30,000 dollars it seized from him based merely on the fact that Sowers deposited large amounts of cash from his farm's sales in his own bank account. Going to the root of the problem, Napolitano explains that "the true culprit is the Congress that intentionally wrote these laws very loose so that the IRS does not even have to have any evidence that the structuring is unlawful; it could just be coincidental."

Rachel Wiener describes more of Sowers' predicament in the Washington Post. Initially, she relates, the US government had seized $295,220 from Sowers. That seized money was used against Sowers as leverage to pressure him to agree to allow the government to keep 10 percent. Wiener concludes that, three years after the seizure, Sowers has not gotten back any of that 10 percent "and almost certainly never will." This puts Sowers in the same boat with many other victims of the US government's seizures program. Wiener explains:

> Based on Freedom of Information Act requests, the libertarian Institute for Justice has reported that the Internal Revenue Service has seized almost a quarter-billion dollars in such cases from 2005 to 2012, about half of which was never returned. A third of those cases, like the Sowers case, did not involve allegations of criminal activity beyond the structured deposits themselves.

Some hope for restraint in the US government's pursuit of such cash seizures may seem to be offered by the issuing on March 31 of a new DOJ policy directive. The press release announcing the policy directive does have a promising title: "Attorney General Restricts Use of Asset Forfeiture in Structuring Offenses." But, from past experience with DOJ policy changes supposedly restricting prosecutions of people complying with state medical marijuana laws and "equitable sharing" of property seizures with state and local police, we are well advised to be very skeptical of any DOJ announcements of limitations on policing or prosecuting powers.

While the DOJ received some media coverage heralding its March 31 announcement, a close look at the supposed rollback shows that it is illusory, amounting to little more than an appeal by the US government for us to just trust it to behave better.

Looking at what the policy directive says, its restrictions on asset forfeiture are underwhelming. A listing of a few of the significant problems with the supposed rollback follows.

First, to the extent the memorandum defining the DOJ policy directive includes restraints on asset seizures, those restraints only apply to seizures based on the allegation of structuring. The memorandum does not address, and thus leaves unrestrained, seizures arising from reports of deposits or withdrawals of $10,000 or more. It should go without saying that moving $10,000 or more in cash at one time is no more wrong and deserving of punishment than are several actions that over time add up to moving $10,000 or more in cash. Nevertheless, if you dare to move $10,000 or more in cash all at once, the memorandum does not offer you any hope whatsoever.

Second, the DOJ memorandum confesses no DOJ wrongdoing concerning any asset forfeitures it has ever undertaken or defended. Indeed, no concern whatsoever is expressed in the memorandum for victims of the asset seizures. The two introductory paragraphs of the memorandum make clear that the DOJ is in no way admitting even one instance, much less many, where its seizures based on structuring allegations were unjust. Instead, the policy announced in the memorandum is described as arising from the DOJ's "ongoing review of the federal asset forfeiture program." Consistent with this "housekeeping" explanation for the origin of the policy change, the memorandum declares that "The guidance set forth in this memorandum, which is the result of that review, is intended to ensure that our investigative resources are appropriately and effectively allocated to address the most serious structuring offenses, consistent with Departmental priorities."

There you have it: The purpose of the policy change is entirely to promote DOJ efficiency in accomplishing its priorities. Those DOJ priorities are in no way changed by the policy directive. Liberty violations caused by asset seizures are not taken into account, and the priorities of asset seizure victims are not considered relevant.

Third, the DOJ memorandum continues to allow asset seizures based on nothing more than multiple cash transactions adding up to over $10,000. In the first paragraph of section one of the memorandum the Justice Department seems to be saying it is prohibiting seizing funds for structuring except when a criminal charge has been filed or "unless there is probable cause that the structured funds were generated by unlawful activity or that the structured funds were intended for use in, or to conceal or promote, ongoing or anticipated unlawful activity." Even this language alone would leave incredible leeway for seizures as it allows the DOJ, based on its own assertion of probable cause, to seize funds without even having a court hearing at which the person whose funds are seized can argue his case. Further, the memorandum goes on to weaken even the internal affirmation that must be made in an asset forfeiture by stating that "For these purposes 'unlawful activity' includes instances in which the investigation revealed no known legitimate source for the funds being structured." There you have it. The person whose cash is seized is assumed guilty until proven innocent.

Fourth, while the DOJ memorandum includes a promising general rule that cash seized based on structuring must be returned after 150 days if a prosecutor has not filed "a criminal indictment or a civil complaint against the asset," that rule offers little real protection. Initially, this rule still allows keeping the cash with no court process even initiated for five months. The power to, on a whim, retain a person's confiscated money for nearly half a year also gives the DOJ plenty of leverage to pressure an asset seizure victim to enter a deal allowing the US government to keep a chunk of the seized money, just like dairy farmer Randy Sowers did.

Further, the "protection" that kicks in after a victim has been deprived of his money for nearly half a year allows for the bypassing of the criminal system that can hold the government to higher burdens of proof. It also maintains the government-aiding fiction that the structuring of the cash itself is some sort of crime by terming the cash as the "defendant" in a legal action.

Even this rather weak protection can be entirely bypassed via an exception you can drive a truck through. Here is the exception: The cash can be kept forever if approval is obtained from the right higher up in the DOJ — a US Attorney or the Chief of the Asset Forfeiture and Money Laundering Section (AFMLS) of the DOJ, depending on the circumstances. So, the DOJ has to go to a court after several months unless a DOJ manager says not to bother with that.

Fifth, the DOJ memorandum "graciously" mandates that settlements that might provide for the return of a portion of cash seized for structuring must comply with requirements found in two DOJ policy manuals. If you maintain high hopes that these manuals will protect the rights of cash seizures victims, you haven't been paying close attention. The system is stacked in the government's favor. This provision, like other provisions in the policy directive, mandates little to no improvement in how victims will be treated.

Sixth, the concluding paragraph of the memorandum makes clear that the DOJ is not bound by anything in the memorandum, noting that the memorandum "is intended solely as a guide to the exercise of investigative and prosecutorial discretion, and does not alter in any way the Department's authority to enforce federal law." And to put suspenders on the belt, the paragraph continues with a sweeping renunciation of the idea that the memorandum amounts to any change that any victim may rely upon, stating, "This memorandum is not intended to, does not, and may not be relied upon to create any rights, substantive or procedural, enforceable at law by any party in any matter civil or criminal."

The Hastert prosecution, however, is probably the clearest indication that the March 31 "rollback" is nothing more than public relations cover for the US government continuing its anti-structuring prosecutions, its asset seizures, and its larger war on cash. Initiating such a high-profile prosecution in direct conflict with the public relations message of the March 31 DOJ policy directive announcement is a pretty definitive way of saying "we really didn't mean any of that rollback stuff."

A real rollback, or even the total abandonment, of privacy and liberty violating policies comprising the war on cash can only be hoped for if public pressure for such a change increases instead of being mollified by government PR efforts.

The many Americans who despise Hastert for his activities in politics or alleged sexual misconduct should remember that in his legal battle against the DOJ Hastert is just another victim, like dairy farmer Randy Sowers and so many others, targeted for destruction by the US government. The government can persecute and steal from these individuals because it refuses to tolerate privacy from its prying eyes. If we want to end the US government's war on cash, war on privacy, and war on liberty, how can we turn our backs on Dennis Hastert?

35

July 23, 2015

Sandra Bland is Everyman

Waller County District Attorney Elton Mathis is characterizing Sandra Bland — who died last week in a jail in the Texas county — as being "very combative" and "not a model person" during the traffic stop that led to her arrest and incarceration. His disparaging assessment appears to be far from the truth.

Recently released dashboard camera video of Bland's arrest shows that throughout her ordeal on a Texas roadway Bland behaved appropriately and much as would many other ordinary people in a similar situation. Bland's response may even have been more muted than average considering the infuriating nonsense she had to deal with — an out-of-control cop pulling her over for changing lanes without using a turn signal and then proceeding, for no good reason, to force her out of her car, throw her to the ground, handcuff her, and send her off to jail.

Bland's response to the police harassment and brutality is commendable. Unless you accept the police-state mindset that Mathis' comments suggest, you can't help but admire Bland boldly standing up to a cop who literally had the power of life and death in his hands on that Texas roadway.

In the video we see and hear Bland being brutally attacked and arrested for expressing her opinion (after the arresting cop asked her for it), refusing to put out the cigarette she was smoking in her own car, or resisting arrest (let the nonsense of that excuse for an arrest settle in). After Bland is in handcuffs and other cops are present, you can even hear the cop who arrested her trying to work out, while on the phone with someone, a story to excuse his abuse of Bland.

As the cop escalated his physical attack, Bland yelled. Bland cursed. Bland insulted the policeman. She asked him repeatedly to give a logical justification, which never came, for his physical aggression against her.

If Bland continued to be upset and strongly communicated her anger during her confinement the next three days, how would that be anything but a normal, justified reaction? Why shouldn't she scream about the abuse of her rights and the pain inflicted on her? Why shouldn't she challenge the illogic and injustice of her captors' actions? Such is natural and to be expected in reaction to extreme harassment and physical abuse.

Bland is now dead, apparently from hanging in a jail cell after being forcibly confined for three days. She was a victim of an out-of-control police, prison, and prosecution system that allowed a cop to harass, attack, and arrest her illegitimately and then proceeded to keep her in jail. Did Bland kill herself, or was she murdered? Some of Bland's friends and family members dispute the suicide allegation. But, either way — suicide or murder — it is all but certain that the unjust system that created so much needless anguish for Bland in her final days, and individuals who carried out tasks to advance the injustice, are culpable for Bland's death.

August 12, 2015

Police Invincibility Melting Away in Dallas-Fort Worth Metroplex

It is not just ice cream melting off cones in the 100-plus degrees heat of the Dallas-Fort Worth Metroplex. The reactions of local police chiefs to two recent high-profile incidents of apparent police brutality and unjustified killing in the metroplex of around seven million people give hope that police invincibility for destructive and wrongful conduct is melting away as well.

We have heard the story many times. A cop assaults or kills an individual. The police leadership, as well as police union and government officials, immediately line up expressing great deference for the cop's action, while painting the injured or killed individual in the worst possible light. The cop, at most, is put on desk duty or on paid leave for a while. Even if evidence stacks up that the cop behaved wrongly, the local prosecutor decides not to seek an indictment of the cop or goes through a prosecutor-orchestrated grand jury circus designed to ensure no indictment is issued. Much later, the harmed individual or the family of the deceased may be able to settle for some monetary compensation, often with a stipulation of keeping quiet about the matter.

Police invincibility is real and powerful. But, with the increased recognition among the public that police have become a great danger to the safety police are supposedly charged with protecting, this invincibility is melting away here and there.

Two recent examples from the metroplex cities of Arlington and McKinney are illustrative.

The latest sign of the melting is the firing Tuesday of Arlington, Texas cop Brad Miller who is alleged to have shot dead Christian Taylor at a local automobile dealership at around 1:00 a.m. on Friday. While the standard cop-protecting narrative had started to run, it was cut short Tuesday when Arlington Police Chief Will Johnson announced Miller's firing for actions related to the shooting. Patrick McGee and Manny Fernandez explain in the New York Times:

> "Based on a preponderance of evidence available to me and facts revealed by the investigative team," Chief Johnson said, "I have decided to terminate Officer Miller's employment with the Arlington Police Department for exercising poor judgment."
>
> The chief's announcement represented a shift in the official police narrative of the events leading up to the shooting. Previously, Chief Johnson told reporters that Officer Miller and his training officer had a confrontation with Mr. Taylor inside the dealership as they tried to arrest him, and that led Officer Miller to fire his weapon. The chief had declined to describe that event, explaining that investigators had not determined "the nature of the confrontation."
>
> But in Tuesday's news conference, Chief Johnson offered a detailed account of the confrontation, saying that Mr. Taylor never made physical contact with any of the officers at the scene and indicating that Officer Miller's own actions had escalated the confrontation.
>
> The chief also said that the officers had said they saw a bulge in Mr. Taylor's pocket. It turned out to be a wallet and a cellphone. "It is reasonable that officers were concerned that a weapon may be present," Chief Johnson said. "This further underscores the questionable nature of Officer Miller's decision of entering the building alone and without an arrest plan."

In June, McKinney, Texas cop Eric Casebolt resigned four days after being caught on video in what appeared to many people, including Ron Paul Institute Advisory Board Member Andrew Napolitano, to be an illegal assault at a local pool party. And Casebolt may have resigned just moments before he would have otherwise been fired. As in Arlington, the official narrative in McKinney abruptly turned around as the facts came out and public interest grew. Sarah Mervosh relates the narrative transition in the Dallas Morning News:

> The officer's terse, two-word resignation did not include an apology or acknowledgment of wrongdoing, said McKinney Police Chief Greg Conley, who on Tuesday condemned Casebolt's actions as "indefensible" and "out of control."
>
> The chief distanced himself from his former employee on the same day his department dropped charges against the sole person arrested at the scene, signaling a swift shift in police's handling of the video-recorded encounter that went viral.

These relatively prompt decisions of two police chiefs to hold cops accountable for acts that brought pain and death to the local communities offer some reason for hope that the old narrative that ensures police invincibility and stands in the way of justice may be melting away — at least in this corner of America. Yet, melting requires heat, and, in this case, that heat must come from public pressure. It is notable that in both the Arlington and McKinney instances the cops' actions had been under widespread public examination. Such public scrutiny of police conduct is likely critical for putting to rest once and for all the old narrative that encourages police abuses and then sweeps those abuses under the rug.

37

September 1, 2015

Families Choose Homeschooling to Escape Draconian California Vaccination Mandates

There is an "out" for Californian parents and children dreading the July 2016 implementation of the state's recently adopted Senate Bill 277 — draconian legislation eliminating exemptions to child vaccination mandates. That out is homeschooling, and many Californian parents are spending this year exploring homeschooling and preparing for a homeschooling future.

While children attending government and private schools, as well as other entities including daycares, in the state will be mandated starting next summer to submit to a state-set vaccination schedule with virtually all exemption means eliminated, the new law does not apply to children in homeschool.

Californian father Davis Fairon says in a KGO-TV news story that the vaccination mandate is a threat to freedom. States Fairon, "we're not allowed to think for ourselves; we've got to do what the government tells us to do." Fairon and his wife have decided to homeschool and not to vaccinate their baby according the state's vaccination schedule.

Other parents in California will make the same decision. Anita Chabria provided in a Guardian article last week a window into some of the ways the state vaccination mandates are pushing California parents to opt for homeschooling. In her article, Chabria tells the stories of two mothers who are taking, or considering, the homeschooling leap because of their desire to protect their children from dangers related to the California state government's vaccination mandates:

> Lyn Elliott, a mother of a 20-month-old girl, says she is taking a serious look at home schooling because of the law. While her daughter Rebel is "mostly vaccinated," there are certain shots she feels are unnecessary "and that I feel have risks."
>
> Next summer she will have to face the choice of giving vaccinations she does not want, or lose access to daycare – where some of the vaccine requirements will also apply. A single parent after her husband died in a motorcycle accident, she says home schooling could mean a critical drop in her income, but it's a move she feels compelled to make.
>
> "For myself and my personal situation, school was something I was somewhat looking forward to," she

says. "I think it would actually be more beneficial for [Rebel] to be in public school but I am not willing to take that risk or let them make that decision for me just to make my life easier."

Nicole Arango, a 34-year-old mother of two, said she faced a similar choice and decided to move forward with home schooling now.

She recently moved from Oxnard, California, to Simi Valley with her son, Ryan, 13, and daughter, Juliet, 6. Because Ryan had an adverse vaccine reaction when he was young, Arango has chosen not to vaccinate further. Rather than put them in school in their new town for a year and have to pull them out when the law goes into effect, she is beginning home schooling this fall.

"I was already kind of on the fence about home schooling anyway but the vaccine law really pushed me over because that's not something I'm going to have shoved down my throat," she said. "I feel like I have no other alternative."

Homeschool supporters across America have often been effective in defending a homeschooling zone of liberty. Indeed, fear of taking on homeschool defenders appears to be a reason the California government has chosen not to subject homeschool children to the new law.

But, homeschooling families and their supporters becoming complacent could allow local, state, or national governments to impose new mandates — regarding vaccination or any of numerous other matters — on homeschooling families. Indeed, there is an organized effort to subject homeschooling to a multitude of authoritarian "reforms" in all states. Such reforms include government registration of homeschools, background checking of homeschool parents, standardized testing and portfolio reviewing of homeschool students, random home visits and additional testing for "flagged" homeschool families, and the same medical requirements (including vaccination mandates) for homeschool students as for students in government schools.

In other words, the effort is underway to obliterate all the freedom from government mandates that homeschooling offers and to even use homeschooling regulations as a means to create additional government intrusions into families and homes.

Can homeschooling families and their allies repel the "reform" onslaught and even remove some of the current government restrictions on homeschooling? For the sake of liberty, let us hope the answer is "yes."

38

September 19, 2015

Was Ahmed Mohamed's Arrest Really All About Religion and Race?

Many people are framing the arrest of student Ahmed Mohamed at MacArthur High School in Irving, Texas on Monday in terms of Mohamed's race and religion. The argument goes that a white and non-Muslim student would not have been arrested as was Mohamed for bringing to school a home-assembled clock that school workers and police say looks like a bomb.

Even if convincing evidence does come to light indicating Mohamed's race or religion was the determining factor leading to his arrest, which is not the case of yet, it is a mistake to think that other students are immune from such treatment because they are white or non-Muslim. Such thinking will also stand in the way of ending the systematic abuse of students that allowed Mohamed's arrest to occur.

The race and religion framing of Mohamed's abuse has been pushed much in the media since Mohamed was arrested, irrespective of whether there is any evidence supporting the characterization. For example, Council on American-Islamic Relations (CAIR) National Communications Director Ibrahim Hooper, in an MSNBC interview, asserted "the clear understanding that this would not have happened to somebody who wasn't named 'Ahmed Mohamed,' who didn't have brown skin, who wasn't of Sudanese heritage."

And what is the basis for this conclusion? A "gut level" understanding. Continues Hooper, "I mean, we just at a gut level understand that that would not have occurred the way it occurred if the circumstances or if his background had been different."

Nihad Awad, CAIR's executive director and co-founder, interviewed Thursday on the PBS Newshour, provided a prime example of the jump by many people to characterize Mohamed's abuse with the label "Islamophobia." In response to interviewer Hari Sreenivasen's first question of "So tell me about your contact with the family," Awad answers in part:

> When this happened to the family, the family contacted our office in Dallas, and we recognized that this was another case of unfortunate Islamophobia and targeting of young people just because of their faith tradition, not because of their deeds or their behavior.

This characterization is in line with CAIR's new 25-second promotional video that couples the popular hashtag #IStandWithAhmed and CAIR's islamophobia.org website.

CAIR has significantly contributed to disseminating information and opinion regarding Mohamed's abuse, even holding the Wednesday press conference featuring Mohamed, members of his family, and his lawyer on the front lawn of Mohamed's Irving home.

Writing in The Intercept, Glenn Greenwald made an effort to present some actual reasoning, instead of just hurled assertions, to support the belief that Mohamed's abuse, or at least some extent of his abuse, is due to some or all of his abusers' perception of Mohamed's religion. Greenwald presents the demonization of Muslims that has come with the United States government's wars in Muslim-majority countries across the world, as well as negative attitudes toward Muslims held by some Americans and, he suggests, by the mayor and some city council members of Irving, to support the contention that Mohamed was targeted because of Mohamed's religion.

Greenwald also offers support in the form of Mohamed's telling of a comment one cop made and how Mohamed felt after hearing the comment:

> When he was brought into the room to be questioned by the four police officers who had been dispatched to the school, one of them — who had never previously seen him — said: "Yup. That's who I thought it was." As a result, he "felt suddenly conscious of his brown skin and his name — one of the most common in the Muslim religion."

Maybe if Mohamed were not brown, not Muslim, or not either, he would not have been abused, or the abuse would have terminated earlier. Yet, the points Greenwald offers provide no more than reasons to investigate that possibility. The points are certainly not dispositive that even the tiniest fraction of the abuse Mohamed suffered is due to any perceptions of his religion or race.

Government high schools in Texas are generally overseen by elected school boards, not by city councils and mayors. Nevertheless, expressed views of politicians from around the school district's geographic area may indeed provide some reason to dig more for a religion or race-based motive for Mohamed's abuse. Similarly, the existence of anti-Muslim attitudes in America may provide reason to suspect that such attitudes played a role, even a major role, in Mohamed's abuse or in the extent of that abuse. But, in no way does the existence of such attitudes establish that those attitudes motivated the abuse of Mohamed or even that such attitudes were held in some degree by people who abused Mohamed.

Further, whether the cop's quoted comment has anything whatsoever to do with Mohamed's religion or race is not at all clear. That Mohamed interprets the comment as he does provides a window into Mohamed's thinking, not into the thinking of the quoted cop.

If people weren't stirring up fear and hatred to support the US government's seemingly unending wars across the world, and if those wars were ended so the threat of blowback could recede, it certainly makes sense that less students, like Mohamed, would be wrongfully arrested. Given that the pro-war talk often frames the enemy in terms of the Muslim religion and, as Greenwald notes, the US government "has spent decades waging various forms of war against predominantly Muslim countries — bombing seven of them in the last six years alone," it also seems reasonable to suspect that Muslim students are subjected to such abuse at a higher rate than are non-Muslim students. But, none of this general conjecture provides the slightest bit of evidence that any of the abuse Mohamed suffered is due to school officials' or cops' perceptions related to Mohamed's religion or race.

Many students who are white and non-Muslim are abused by school officials and cops for purported reasons just as preposterous as the reasons asserted for Mohamed's arrest. Rutherford Institute President John W. Whitehead persuasively presented the case this week that the abuse of students in America by school officials and cops is pervasive and destructive. Whitehead gives an overview of the problem, stretching across religious and racial lines, in his article "Public School Students Are the New Inmates in the American Police State," stating:

> From the moment a child enters one of the nation's 98,000 public schools to the moment she graduates, she will be exposed to a steady diet of draconian zero tolerance policies that criminalize childish behavior, overreaching anti-bullying statutes that criminalize speech, school resource officers (police) tasked with disciplining and/or arresting so-called "disorderly" students, standardized testing that emphasizes rote answers over critical thinking, politically correct mindsets that teach young people to censor themselves and those around them, and extensive biometric and surveillance systems that, coupled with the rest, acclimate young people to a world in which they have no freedom of thought, speech or movement.

By all means, people should look for credible evidence that

some or all of the abuse Mohamed suffered was motivated by people's perceptions of his religion or race. But, just to put his abuse in a racial or religious motivation box without credible evidence to support that conclusion is mistaken. Doing so also suggests the nonexistence of the very real systematic infringement of rights of students — both with and without any motivation related to perceptions of the students' religions or races — that occurs each day in schools across America.

It may make some people feel better to define, without basis, Mohamed's abuse as just a manifestation of religious or racial animus. But, such an approach does not address the fundamental problem. The approach disregards the systematic abuse of students — across religious and racial lines — and the entrenched policies and procedures supporting such abuse. Failing to take on the systematic problem directly will allow many more students like Mohamed to be similarly abused.

39

October 6, 2015

Senate Criminal Justice Reform Bill Would Create New Mandatory Minimum Sentences

No wonder Americans have such disdain for Congress. On Thursday, a bipartisan group of nine United States senators joined together to introduce the Sentencing Reform and Corrections Act. In a press release heralding the bill's introduction, sponsor Sen. Chuck Grassley (R-IA), who is chairman of the Senate Judiciary Committee, and several of the bill's cosponsors commend the bill as mitigating overly-harsh aspects of the US criminal justice system, including mandatory minimum sentences. Left unmentioned is the fact that the bill, should it become law, would actually create new mandatory minimum sentences while lengthening existing maximum sentences.

Say one thing and do another. The deception continues on Capitol Hill.

No doubt, most or all of the senators who signed on to the Sentencing Reform and Corrections Act are aware of shifts in public sentiment regarding incarceration and the drug war in which mandatory minimums have played a prominent role. Seeking to appease public demands for reductions in government power while surreptitiously increasing that power is an old trick in the Washington, DC chicanery book.

Reading the press release announcing the bill, we see the senators promoting their bill as a fulfillment the public's demand. Yet, reading the Sentencing Reform and Corrections Act, we see that the Senators are actually attempting to do something entirely different behind the scenes.

The press release's description of the Sentencing Reform and Corrections Act paints the bill as rolling back rigid and excessive components of the US sentencing law:

> The bill narrows the scope of mandatory minimum prison sentences to focus on the most serious drug offenders and violent criminals, while broadening and establishing new outlets for individuals with minimal non-felony criminal histories that may trigger mandatory minimum sentences under current law. The bill also reduces certain mandatory minimums, providing judges with greater discretion when determining appropriate sentences, and preserves cooperation incentives to aid law enforcement in tracking down kingpins.
>
> In addition to reducing prison terms for certain offenders through sentencing reform, qualifying inmates can earn reduced sentences through recidivism reduction programs outlined in the CORRECTIONS Act introduced by Cornyn and Whitehouse. The bill also makes retroactive the Fair Sentencing Act and certain statutory reforms that address inequities in drug sentences.

The Sentencing Reform and Corrections Act's creation of new mandatory minimum sentences and lengthening of maximum sentences are left unmentioned. Via this omission, the press release conveys the false impression that the reforms contained in the bill are all in line with reducing the rigid harshness of the US judicial system.

The press release's quotes from Sens. Dick Durbin (D-IL) and Mike Lee (R-UT) in particular contribute to the deception that the Sentencing Reform and Corrections Act would boldly roll back mandatory minimum sentences.

Says Durbin:

> This compromise represents more than three years of work on criminal justice reform. The United States incarcerates more of its citizens than any other country on earth. Mandatory minimum sentences were once seen as a strong deterrent. In reality they have too often been unfair, fiscally irresponsible and a threat to public safety. Given tight budgets and overcrowded prison cells, our country must reform these outdated and ineffective laws that have cost American taxpayers billions of dollars. This bipartisan group is committed to getting this done.

Says Lee:

> Since my time as a federal prosecutor, I have been concerned that federal sentencing laws too often require punishments that just don't fit the crime. These laws require many nonviolent offenders to spend years in prison, often with few opportunities for meaningful reform. Today's legislation addresses both of these problems by reducing mandatory minimums and by expanding opportunities for programs that have been proven to reduce recidivism. I am grateful for the close collaboration with senators from both parties that has made this important bill a reality today.

Look at the actual bill and you see that the Sentencing Reform and Corrections Act is far from the sweeping roll back of mandatory minimums suggested in the press release. In fact, the bill creates several new mandatory minimum sentences and extends the length of maximum sentences.

The Sentencing Reform and Corrections Act would create new mandatory minimum sentences for convictions related to:

- domestic violence;

- providing "controlled goods or services" to anyone named in a particular US Department of Treasury list, any organization the US designates as a "terrorist organization," or a "state sponsor of terrorism;"

- providing goods or services, "without a license or other written approval" from the US government, to anybody "in connection with a program or effort of a foreign country or foreign person to develop weapons of mass destruction;" and

- providing "defense articles or defensive services, without a license or other written approval of the Department of State, to, or for the use of, a country subject to an arms embargo by the United States."

Notably, much of the new mandatory minimums in the Sentencing Reform and Corrections Act are seemingly for the purpose of fighting the US government's Global War on Terrorism. The proliferation of mandatory minimums through the last few decades found much of its justification in the war on drugs. As the US government is slowly being forced to give up on aspects of that war, it is building up its new liberties suppressing vehicle — the war on terrorism — using the previous war as the model for the new war. The Sentencing Reform and Corrections Act is yet another part of this disturbing trend.

The US Department of Justice's role in the war on terrorism is largely consumed with creating "terrorists" via entrapment or sting operations instead of actually finding real terrorists for prosecution. What a handy tool it will be for Federal Bureau of

Investigation (FBI) agents to hang new mandatory minimum sentences over an individual alleged to have taken one action or made one comment that may be interpreted as a step toward aiding terrorism after months or years of a government employee or informant encouraging the individual to run afoul of US law.

The Sentencing Reform and Corrections Act also increases the current 10-year maximum penalty to 15 years for violation of any of a slew of prohibitions related to obtaining, possessing, or transferring a gun or ammunition. Beyond putting people in prison for years for doing something that harms nobody, such sentences create an additional deleterious consequence for many criminal defendants. Long sentences for gun law violations are used by prosecutors as leverage against drug and other crime defendants. Thus prosecutors can pressure defendants to plead guilty instead of demanding a trial. If you make potential sentences long enough, guilty individuals will reluctantly accept excessive sentences and innocent individuals will fold in hopes of leniency in lieu of taking their chances in court.

While some people up against the US judicial system would benefit from some of the reforms in the bill, other individuals will be caught up in the Sentencing Reform and Corrections Act's lengthening of prison sentences.

Cosponsor Sen. Patrick Leahy (D-VT) proclaims in the press release that the bill "marks a new chapter in criminal justice reform." Instead, the Sentencing Reform and Corrections Act is more of the same.

40

October 27, 2015

Niya Kenny is a Brave Young Lady

Sometimes parents exaggerate in praising their children. But the mother of Niya Kenny, an 18-year-old student at Spring Valley High School in Columbia, South Carolina, is spot-on when she describes as brave Kenny's actions in response to school cop Ben Fields on Monday roughing up and arresting a fellow student. "My child, and I'm not mad at her, she was brave enough to speak out against what was going on and didn't back down and it resulted in her being arrested," says Kenny's mother.

In militarized American schools, small discipline matters can quickly result in school-based or called-in cops roughing up and arresting students. Such was the case in Kenny's math class this week when Fields responded to a complaint of a student's failure to either participate or leave the class by yanking the student out of her seat and attached desk, hurling her across the classroom floor, and arresting her.

In a WLTX-TV story, Kenny says she was "in disbelief" and "screaming and crying like a baby" in reaction to what the cop did. Kenny relates that she filmed the cop's actions and complained about those actions. Fields' response? He arrested Kenny too, for a charge that comes nowhere near even approaching passing the laugh test — "disturbing school."

Kenny's mother is right. Kenny is a brave young lady. In this age of SWAT it is indeed brave for Kenny to exercise her rights to film the police and criticize their actions. It is also just such brave actions that many more people must undertake if we are to overcome the police-state mentality rampant in America.

41

November 6, 2015

Participating in Class? School Cops Can Arrest You for That Too

Some people came to the defense of school cop Ben Fieldes who last week yanked a student in a Spring Valley High School math class in South Carolina out of her seat and attached desk, hurled her across the classroom floor, and arrested her. They

said Fields' actions were justified because the student was oc-
cupied with her cell phone instead of participating in the class.
Now comes news from the College of DuPage in Illinois that
school cops can do pretty much the same thing to a student
who is participating in class.

Former DuPage student Jaclyn Pazera filed a lawsuit this
week against the college. The lawsuit is in response to two
school cops, caught on video, yanking her from her seat and
attached desk, pinning her to the ground, and handcuffing her
while she was attempting to participate in her philosophy class
at the college last year.

As reported by Justin Kmitch in the Daily Herald, Pazera
was charged with "obstructing a peace officer and resisting a
peace officer," both of which charges were dropped on Tuesday
of last week — the day the prosecution of Pazera was scheduled
for trial. Of course, the charges against Pazera were absurd from
the beginning. They are among the standard charges piled on
victims of police brutality in an attempt to defend the indefensi-
ble, shift the blame, and provide leverage to prevent the victims
from taking the kind of legal action Pazera took this week.

Even the charges' nomenclature reeks of dishonesty. "Peace
officer!" Give me a break!

Apparently, the police had been enraged by Pazera, shortly
before their attack on her, smoking in a place not designated as a
smoking area. In this upside-down age of SWAT, maybe Pazera
got off easy. In July, Sandra Bland ended up dead in a Texas jail
cell three days after her arrest in a traffic stop for failure to use a
turn signal when changing lanes. That traffic stop escalated into
a horror show of physical abuse and incarceration right after
Bland did not immediately comply with a cop's request that she
extinguish a cigarette she was smoking in her own car.

42

Will Oakland Raiders Linebacker Ray-Ray Armstrong Go to Prison for 'Taunting' a Police Dog?

It is not even a man bites dog story. Instead, it is just a man barks at dog story. Yet, for one National Football League (NFL) player it is a story that threatens to conclude with his incarceration.

Oakland Raiders Linebacker Ray-Ray Armstrong's alleged barking at a dog on Sunday may cost him thousands of dollars in fines and several years in prison. Why you ask? Because Armstrong is alleged to have barked at a police dog, and, in this age of SWAT, some dogs are protected by the law much more than are ordinary people.

You see, Armstrong was at the Pittsburgh Steelers' stadium just before a Raiders away game when, as Jacob Klinger relates the story at Penn Live, "Armstrong lifted his shirt, began pounding his chest and barking at an Allegheny County Sheriff Office bomb-sniffing dog." Most people would consider this action to be somewhere between harmless jest and a bit rude. But, in the state of Pennsylvania, Klinger notes, it is also a felony termed "taunting a police animal" and carrying a maximum punishment of a $15,000 fine plus seven years in prison.

43

Is There a War on Police or a War on Us?

There has been much talk about a "war on police" in 2015. The story goes that police in America are in great danger from a rise in violent attacks against them. It is suggested that the attacks are stirred up by criticisms and protests of police misconduct.

As the end of the year approaches, however, we find that the war on police is a myth, with deaths of police at near the record low. Instead, the war in America seems to be a war by — rather than on — police, with police killing about three people a day this year.

Radley Balko presents the numbers on shooting deaths of police in a Tuesday Washington Post article. Balko relays that, according to the National Law Enforcement Officers Memorial Fund, 38 cops have been shot dead in America this year. Balko further notes that this number includes "at least one suicide and two cases in which a cop was shot by another cop." The 2015 gun-related deaths of police, Balko relates, are among the least of any year from the last nearly 150 years of data.

There are occasions when a cop is killed just for being a cop. But, this is far rarer than many media reports and statements from police and politicians would suggest. For example, some people jumped to blame the killing of Fox Lake, Illinois cop Joseph Gliniewicz in September on a war on police. But, evidence was later made public indicating Gliniewicz, who was worried about potential repercussions for his misconduct including embezzlement, orchestrated his suicide to make it look like he had been murdered while investigating suspicious individuals.

A couple years earlier, Texas cop Adam Sowder was shot dead by Henry Magee when Sowder and eight other cops conducted a raid on Magee's home. A grand jury declined to indict Magee who had explained that he acted to defend his family from the cops who he thought were robbers.

Meanwhile, the Washington Post reported on December 26 an assessment that police shot dead nearly 1,000 people this year, and Mapping Police Violence calculated that, through December 15, police killed, at least 1,152 people this year in America. Among the killed individuals are people who were justifiably shot to end an immediate threat to kill or seriously injure others. But, the lives lost include also individuals who posed no such threat.

In 2015, people around America have been drawn to the stories of some of the individuals who police have killed without apparent justification. Consider the deaths of Noel Aguilar in Long Beach, California; Eric Garner in New York, New York; Freddie Gray in Baltimore, Maryland; Jeremy Mardis in Marksville, Louisiana; Laquan McDonald in Chicago, Illinois; Tamir Rice in Cleveland, Ohio; and Christian Taylor in Arlington, Texas. Then ask yourself this question: Is there a war on police or a war on us?

Part 3: Militarism

44

August 17, 2013

For the Back to School List — Military Recruiter Opt Out Form

While shopping for pens, notebooks, or a backpack, don't forget to consider adding one more item to your back to school list — a military recruiter opt out form. All government school systems and most private schools that receive education funding from the United Stated government are required to provide to military recruiters high school students' names, addresses, and telephone numbers, plus any additional information about the students provided to colleges or prospective employers. The only way to prevent the sharing of this information is for a student or parent to opt out of the disclosure.

The American Friends Service Committee (AFSC) has made your shopping for an opt out form easy by providing on its website an opt out form that can be printed, filled out, and signed in two minutes.

Do not wait for a school to inform you of your right to opt out. Though schools are required to provide notice of the right to opt out, the US Department of Education directs that such notice may be buried in "[a] single notice provided through a mailing, student handbook, or other method that is reasonably calculated to inform parents."

If you would like to do something more, check out AFSC's other suggestions on its "Five ways to counter military recruitment in your school district" web page. The suggestions relate to providing people with information — that they can opt out, that there are opportunity costs of high military spending, that there are options other than joining the military. Also, you can suggest to anyone who is considering enlisting in the military that he watch AFSC's 14-minute video "Before You Enlist" that describes aspects of military service that recruiters are unlikely to mention in their sales pitches.

45

February 19, 2014

Eric Cantor Evokes George Washington and Founders to Promote His War Agenda

Apparently trying to one-up President Barack Obama, who last month twisted American history and logic to equate US government mass spying with Paul Revere and other revolutionaries' actions to protect Americans from an oppressive government, House of Representatives Majority Leader Eric Cantor (R-VA) is claiming President George Washington and the American Founders would support Cantor's world-wide interventionist agenda.

Cantor made the laughable assertion a key theme of his "An America That Leads" speech Monday at the Virginia Military Institute. The agenda Cantor proposes in his speech, and that we can expect the Republican leadership of the House to push, can be summed up as war, war, and more war. Here are some ways Cantor proposes America "leads":

- Cantor laments any easing of sanctions on Iran and suggests imposing new sanctions, as well as employing the "credible threat of the use of military force" in diplomatic talks with Iran;

- Cantor laments that the US has forgone a military attack on Syria and calls on the US to take action to "change the balance of power on the ground" in Syria;

- Cantor laments that the US military may soon exit Afghanistan and calls for the military presence to continue;

- Cantor laments the easing of US intervention in Libya and calls for the US to "bolster the capabilities of the Libyan security forces and, as necessary, be willing to engage in and support counter-terrorism efforts;"

- Cantor laments that North Korea has, despite US sanctions, "yet to pay a meaningful price" and calls for increasing the sanctions and conducting joint military actions with "regional allies;"

- Cantor laments the US government's failure to more aggressively challenge China regarding sea lanes in the vicinity of China and several other nations and calls for the US to provide "guidance, security, and coordination" in Asia;

- Cantor calls for "equipping security forces" in countries around the world for use in those countries and in their respective regions;

- Cantor laments that "we cannot continue to blindly reduce defense spending" (throwing aside the reality of a decade-plus of huge increases in military, intelligence, and "homeland security" spending) because the US needs to "project adequate military power in any theater, be it the Middle East, Latin America or Asia;" and

- Cantor calls on the US to "invest" in a "more lethal military" — to "promote peace and stability," he says.

In the introduction of his speech, Cantor suggests that George Washington would support his foreign policy agenda:

Today, we celebrate our nation's first Command-

er-in-Chief George Washington. Since Washington led
our armed forces and this nation, America has relied
upon a strong military to defend our homeland and our
freedoms.

America's military strength, global leadership combined with a benevolent purpose helped spread the
promise of democracy to the oppressed, a message of
hope to the destitute, and the blessings of security to
the weak. In doing so, we have earned new allies, van-
quished old foes, and further secured our own nation.
But today, that formula that has served this nation and
the world so well is very much in doubt.

This assertion by Cantor is as ridiculous as Obama's assertion a month before, at the beginning of Obama's mass spying
speech, that the National Security Agency (NSA) bureaucrats
scooping up every bit of personal information they can find
about us are the same as Paul Revere riding through the countryside to warn that an invading army of "redcoats" are coming.
Today the NSA is the redcoats, exercising via intrusive, high-
tech means the general warrant powers that the British redcoats
used in a clunkier, old-fashioned manner in violation of liberty,
property, and privacy.

The NSA is the redcoats anew. And Cantor is espousing the
foreign interventionism that Washington terms in his farewell
address "European Ambition, Rivalship, Interest, Humour or
Caprice," the embrace of which Washington said would endan-
ger the "peace and prosperity" of the US.

Washington almost appears clairvoyant later in his farewell
address when he ponders that his warnings against foreign intervention will likely not count for much in the long term and
cautions against "Impostures of pretended patriotism" — a
spot-on description of Cantor's effort to turn Washington's foreign policy counsel on its head:

In offering to you, my Countrymen, these counsels
of an old and affectionate friend, I dare not hope
they will make the strong and lasting impression, I

could wish--that they will controul the usual current of the passions, or prevent our Nation from running the course which has hitherto marked the Destiny of Nations: But if I may even flatter myself, that they may be productive of some partial benefit, some occasional good; that they may now & then recur to moderate the fury of party spirit, to warn against the mischiefs of foreign Intriegue, to guard against the Impostures of pretended patriotism—this hope will be a full recompence for the solicitude for your welfare, by which they have been dictated.

Five years later, President Thomas Jefferson, in his first inaugural address, phrased the nonintervention maxim memorably with the succinct phrase "peace, commerce, and honest friendship with all nations, entangling alliances with none." Jefferson considered this principle so important that he included it in a short list of "the essential principles of our government, and consequently those which ought to shape its administration." This principle is diametrically opposed to just about everything Cantor's speech claims furthers the American Founders' foreign policy.

Cantor, in the conclusion of his speech, says:

> I strongly believe that if we champion the values this country was founded on and we embrace our role as a world leader, America won't just be a beacon of hope and freedom for the next 100 years, but for centuries to come.

Of course, the values Cantor champions in his speech are not the values of the founding. Rather, as explained by Washington and Jefferson, the founding values explicitly reject Cantor's interventionist values.

The Republican leadership in the House appears poised to push a foreign policy agenda aiming to eliminate the remnants of the American Founders' nonintervention principles. Yet, likely because this agenda is the opposite of what American public opinion supports, the leadership is advancing the agenda with a deceitful claim of sanction by the American Founders. Time will tell if modern day George Washingtons, Thomas Jeffersons, and Paul Reveres are able to alert the people and if a new revolution can reinstate values more in line with the peace and prosperity Washington endorsed in his farewell address.

46

Absolute Perversion of the Law in US Drone Killings

We see in the United States government's "targeted killings" program carried out by drones and other means a perversion of the law so extreme that it brings to mind the introductory paragraph of Frederic Bastiat's classic book The Law:

> The law perverted! The law — and, in its wake, all the collective forces of the nation — the law, I say, not only diverted from its proper direction, but made to pursue one entirely contrary! The law become the tool of every kind of avarice, instead of being its check! The law guilty of that very iniquity which it was its mission to punish! Truly, this is a serious fact, if it exists, and one to which I feel bound to call the attention of my fellow citizens.

As individuals we possess the, hopefully, rarely exercisable right to use lethal force to defend ourselves and others against people who threaten us with death or serious injury. Even then, in a court case regarding such a killing we are further called upon to prove that the killing is justified and rebut the presumption that the killing is wrongful.

Governments may rely on this individual defensive right as a justification for their exercise of killing power, terming the government's right to kill as an extension of individuals' right to kill in defense of themselves or others. In the targeted killings program, the Obama administration has perverted this reasoning beyond recognition so that in Bastiat's phrasing an "entirely contrary" direction — unjustified homicides — is pursued.

The legal perversion of the US government's targeted killings program is explained with dramatic details in a speech by Future of Freedom Foundation Policy Advisor James Bovard and a discussion of Ron Paul Institute Chairman and Founder Ron Paul with The Intercept writer Jeremy Scahill. The revelations in the speech and discussion give ample support for RPI Advisory Board Member Andrew Napolitano's declaration that the targeted killings are both illegal and unconstitutional.

Bovard answers two questions in his speech at the New Hampshire Liberty Forum last month to explain the legal perversion of the US government's targeted killings:

> How much evidence should the US government be obliged to show before it kills an American citizen? None, according to the Obama administration. And how much evidence should the government be obliged to possess of an American's wrongdoing before it officially targets him for killing? That's a secret according to Obama.

Bovard proceeds to explain that Obama's targeted killings program is both more active and more flagrant in lawlessness than the program Obama inherited from President George W. Bush:

> The Obama administration is pioneering these pretexts for presidential killings. The drone assassinations have increased more than 500 percent since Obama took office, and Obama is claiming openly and publicly rights that George W. Bush only claimed secretly.

The program's secretive application is illustrated by Bovard in the context of the judiciary supporting the Obama administration's refusal to tell the father of Anwar al-Awlaki the legal standards for including al-Awlaki on the targeted killings list, claiming protection from disclosure as state secrets. The US government later used a drone to kill al-Awlaki in Yemen.

As Bovard goes on to suggest, Obama may want to keep the reasoning behind targeted killings so secret because the reasoning is flimsy, based on conjectures such as that people present in a known terrorist area or carrying guns must be terrorists or up to no good.

Paul and Scahill's Ron Paul Channel discussion delves into the Obama administration's unaccountable use of drones to kill overseas. Scahill elaborates with one example how, in addition to covering up the reasoning behind drone killings, the US government can also cover up who is killed and even the fact that the US government is behind the killings:

> So, what happened very early on when Obama came to power is that he embraced some of the most dark forces within the US national security apparatus and began to give them wide-ranging authorities to wage war in countries where Congress had not actually declared war. And one of the places where he really started striking heavily was in Yemen.
>
> And, so, this scene that we saw relates to the first time that President Obama authorized a missile attack against Yemen. It was in December of 2009. They said that they were taking out an al-Qaeda training facility. It turns out that it was a village of Bedouins and 14 women were killed, 21 children. We have the names of all of them. And they have not been able to produce any actual al-Qaeda figures that were killed in that attack.
>
> And you'll of course remember, Ron, that, when this bombing happened, the Yemeni government took responsibility for it publicly, and the Obama administration allowed them to do it and in fact sent them a note of congratulations saying, "Wow, great job on striking against the terrorists." At the end of the day, this was General David Petraeus, President Obama, and the CIA and the Joint Special Operations Com-

mand conspiring to start a secret bombing campaign against Yemen.

In the complete interview, Scahill explains in more detail the growth of this executive branch power through the Bush and Obama administrations, and even back to the end of World War II. In particular, Scahill notes how Obama embraced "the life's work of Donald Rumsfeld and Dick Cheney ... essentially to enact a coup d'état in the United States where one branch of government — the executive branch — would essentially operate a dictatorship over what they broadly termed national security policy or counter-terrorism policy." Scahill elaborates:

> Under Bush and Cheney we had Murder Incorporated. There were no morals whatsoever. They waged war on the world. They sent thousands of young Americans to their deaths in these unnecessary wars. But, under Obama, he's actually trying to make an argument that the US not only has a right to do these assassination operations — though they call them targeted killing — but that the US is right to do it, and that it's lawful to do it, and that it's constitutional to do it.
>
> I don't understand how Mr. Nobel Peace Prize Winner, a constitutional lawyer, can actually with a straight face say that he can observe as the prosecutor, judge, jury, and executioner of an American citizen who has not been charged with a crime and is not on an active battlefield fighting against US forces or attacking US individuals. I don't understand how he, with a straight face, can say that to the American people.

Despite Obama's statement in his January State of the Union speech that he would follow "prudent limits" on the use of drones, the targeted killings program remains in full force. As the killings — directed by people thousands of miles away using secret reasoning — continue, it seems appropriate for people to consider Bastiat's explanation in The Law of the proper limits on government:

What is law? What ought it to be? What is its domain? What are its limits? Where, in fact, does the prerogative of the legislator stop?

I have no hesitation in answering, Law is common force organized to prevent injustice; — in short, Law is Justice.

It is not true that the legislator has absolute power over our persons and property, since they pre-exist, and his work is only to secure them from injury.

47

May 19, 2014

US House Considers Gold Medal for Shimon Peres, Bill Touts US-Israel 'Unbreakable Bond'

The United States House of Representatives is scheduled to consider today awarding a Congressional Gold Medal to Israel President Shimon Peres. Notably, the short bill, HR 2939, that authorizes the creation of the gold medal and its award to Peres touts Peres' "pivotal role in forging the strong and unbreakable bond between the United States and Israel" and states that "[b]y presenting the Congressional Gold Medal … Congress proclaims its unbreakable bond with Israel and reaffirms its continual support for Israel." Peres also previously served as prime minister of Israel, as well as in other high-level positions in the Israel government.

It would be appropriate today for members of the House to reflect on the words of the first person awarded a Congressional Gold Medal — President George Washington. In particular, they may read Washington's farewell address, in which Washington encouraged the United States government to follow a noninterventionist foreign policy. You cannot square Washington's recommendation with having an "unbreakable bond" with any foreign government. Unlike House Majority Leader Eric Cantor who twists Washington into a champion of a worldwide interventionist agenda, some House members may find wisdom in the reading.

Back in 2003, Congress approved awarding a Congressional Gold Medal to a leader of another foreign nation — Great Britain Prime Minister Tony Blair. The short bill, S 709, authorizing that medal also contained supportive language endorsing foreign intervention, declaring:

> The Speaker of the House of Representatives and the President Pro Tempore of the Senate shall make appropriate arrangements for the presentation, on behalf of Congress, of a gold medal of appropriate design, to Prime Minister Tony Blair, in recognition of his outstanding and enduring contributions to maintaining the security of all freedom-loving nations.

Ron Paul Institute Chairman and Founder Ron Paul, who was serving then in the House as a representative from Texas, plainly stated the message of that Congressional Gold Medal award:

> …Tony Blair is being given this medal for one reason: he provided political support when international allies were sought for America's attack on Iraq. Does this overtly political justification not cheapen both the medal itself and the achievements of those who have been awarded it previously?

Even if the Congress will not go so far as following Paul's advice that it stop awarding Congressional Gold Medals altogether, maybe more House and Senate members will at least stand up to the medals' use as a tool in promoting war and an interventionist foreign policy.

July 3, 2014

Ron Paul: US Threatening Greater Middle East War, Stock Market Crash, and Oil and Gold Rise

Over at the Ron Paul Channel, Ron Paul Institute Chairman and Founder Ron Paul is warning of consequences from the US government escalating its military involvement in Iraq. Paul concludes:

> Expect one day for this insanity of our foreign policy to translate into a much greater war in the region. When that comes, look for a stock market crash, oil prices to skyrocket and gold prices to soar.

Paul warns in his editorial that increasing US military involvement in Iraq shows that the US is "falling off a cliff into the quagmire of an ever-worsening civil war in Iraq."

In contrast, Rear Admiral John Kirby, the Pentagon press secretary, insists "[t]here's no mission creep," despite President Barack Obama sending at least 650 American troops to Iraq in the past two weeks.

Who should we believe?

Consider that in November of 2002 Department of Defense Secretary Donald Rumsfeld predicted the 2003 US war on Iraq would last "[f]ive days or five weeks or five months, but it certainly isn't going to last any longer than that."

In contrast, Paul, in the fall of 2002 explained that the proposed war against Iraq would be a continuation of the 1991 US invasion of Iraq and subsequent twelve years of US bombing of the country and warned that the US may become involved in decades of "nation-building" in Iraq after a 2003 invasion.

The US military wasn't largely out of Iraq until December of 2011, and then only because the Iraq government refused to agree to a US-pushed status of forces agreement that would give US military members immunity from prosecution in Iraq. In June, Kirby announced that the Iraq government had made the immunity promise. Now the US military is returning to Iraq, a hundred troops here and a hundred there.

Whether regarding war against the Philippines, Korea, Vietnam, Afghanistan, or Iraq, the American people have been promised that US military action would be limited in extent and short in duration. That promise has worn very thin.

49

August 4, 2014

No Dissent Heard as House and Senate Quickly Approve $225 million for Israel War

On Friday, the last day before the annual congressional August recess, new legislation (H.J.Res. 76) was introduced on the US Senate floor and rushed to passage in both the Senate and US House. The legislation gives the Israel government another $225 million dollars for the Iron Dome system Israel is using in the ongoing Israel-Palestine war.

On the Senate floor the speakers line-up of Senate Majority Leader Harry Reid (D-NV) and Minority Leader Mitch McConnell (R-KY), along with Senators Lindsey Graham (R-SC) and John McCain (R-AZ), lauded the legislation before it passed by a voice vote.

No opposition was voiced on the Senate floor.

In the House, the entire consideration of the legislation on the House floor consumed less than two minutes and included no substantive comments whatsoever regarding the legislation.

When the roll call vote occurred later in the evening, the legislation passed in the House by a vote of 395 to 8.

Reid began the non-debate on the Senate floor. He proposed that the new legislation be substituted for legislation that had been passed in the House over nine months earlier and since had absolutely no action in the Senate.

After speeches by Reid, McConnell, McCain, and Graham,

the new legislation passed in the Senate by unanimous consent, meaning no Senator blocked approval of the legislation's passage and that there is no recorded vote from which individual senators' approval or disapproval may be identified.

In the time between the introduction of the new legislation and its adoption in the Senate, not a negative word could be heard. Instead the Senate floor resounded with statements praising Senate bipartisanship and "friendship" between the US and Israel governments.

McConnell started off the good times and backslapping, stating, "this is a good example of our being able to put aside partisan considerations and work together to help our good friend Israel."

Advancing further the expressions of joint admiration on the Senate floor McConnell next said, "I particularly want to salute Senator Graham and Senator McCain, who have been absolutely relentless in their efforts to make sure we send this important signal to Israel at a very tough time for them."

Friendship was in the air as McConnell continued, "I think it is important for us to send a signal that the United States stands behind one of its best friends — if not its best friend — in the world."

Up next, McCain continued the bipartisan and intergovernmental friendship celebration, stating:

> I thank again our majority leader and the Republican leader for coming together on this most important signal. This isn't just about money. It is a signal from the American people and the American taxpayers that we are with the Israelis...

Then came Graham, who McCain introduced warmly by noting, "There has been no one more relentless in this effort than the Senator from South Carolina."

Graham did not disappoint in his relentless expression of unity across party and government lines. "It is so appropriate that today, of all days, the Senate speaks in one voice," said Graham early on in his comparatively long-winded comments. "I cannot thank Senator Reid enough for making this happen," continued Graham.

Then, when the subject shifted from the Senate to the Israel government, Graham's speech took a Churchillian turn:

> It is not only the missiles that matter; it is the message that goes with the missiles: We are with you. Here are the missiles. Use them to defend yourself. We will stand with you on the battlefield. We will stand with you in the court of public opinion, and we are going to push back against the United Nations, which is becoming more and more anti-Israeli. As dysfunctional as the Congress has been, this is one of our finer moments.

Graham concluded with a restating of the bipartisanship and intergovernmental friendship message:

> To our friends in Israel: There is more to come when it comes to standing by your side.

> I thank both leaders of the Senate for rising to the occasion.

Reid, though, got the better of his Republicans in the good vibes contest. After noting "there are times when partisanship does not exist" and confirming his "faith in this institution and our sticking by our friend," Reid noted that the US is not doing nearly enough for Israel. The two governments are friends after all.

Reid explained:

> The situation in Israel is grave. We think this Iron Dome protects Israel. It protects a lot of Israel. But Israel does not have enough Iron Domes — plural — to protect them. They need more. But this will certainly be a step in the right direction.

Reid then concluded with a flourish:

> I don't know of a bond of friendship that we have or ever had in world history better than this one, and so I will stand by Israel. I will stand by Israel for a lot of personal reasons but certainly for political reasons,

and I have no hesitation in declaring to the world that is how I feel.

With that said, the legislation immediately passed in the Senate by unanimous consent.

On the House floor, when the legislation had made its way across the Capitol building, the mood was much different. Instead of backslapping and boasts about bipartisanship and best-friends-ever governments, the House members on the floor moved with determined speed through introducing the legislation and calling a roll call vote.

There was no time in the House for rhetorical flourishes of any kind.

Were the House members afraid that some mood-killing party crasher might be running down a hall toward the House floor to scream "I object!"?

Whatever the motivation, the representatives on the House floor very quickly ran through the procedural motions to pass the legislation without even the slightest semblance of debate.

The entire House consideration of the legislation lasted less than two minutes and was composed of hurried procedural recitation.

An observer of the House floor action would likely not even understand that the Israel war funding legislation was being considered given that the legislation was only referred to using the old name of the bill the House passed in October rather than the name of the new substitute bill just passed in the Senate.

50

August 11, 2014

House and Senate Leaders Line Up Behind Obama on Bombing Iraq

President Barack Obama is encountering no opposition from the top four Democrat and Republican leaders in the

House and Senate as he escalates US military action in Iraq with new bombings.

US Senate Minority Leader Mitch McConnell (R-KY) has chosen not to comment regarding the matter, just as he did last year regarding a potential US military attack on Syria until he announced his opposition the same day Obama called off the planned attack. The other three top Republican and Democrat leaders in both chambers of Congress have all issued statements supporting the US military's ongoing bombings in Iraq.

In contrast, some Congress members are adamantly opposing the escalation. Rep. Alan Grayson (D-FL), for example, wrote an editorial in USA Today pleading, "We have to get past this bizarre notion that every time there's something in the world we don't like, we bomb it."

With Obama having started the bombings at the beginning of Congress' annual August recess and lined up the support — or silence in the case of McConnell — of the top party leaders in both congressional chambers, the military escalation will be old news by the time senators and representatives return to DC in September.

It is as if Obama and his congressional accomplices have learned their marketing lesson from last year when popular opposition caused Obama to rescind his request for a congressional vote to approve a US military attack on Syria.

Following are the statements issued by the Senate Majority Leader, US House of Representatives Speaker, and House Democratic Leader supporting the ongoing US bombings in Iraq:

Senate Majority Leader Harry Reid (D-NV):

I support President Obama's decision to send humanitarian air drops to the thousands of stranded Iraqi civilians who have been forced to flee their homes and are at risk of dying. I also support the President's decision to launch air strikes as long as no combat forces are on the ground. These air strikes are the correct action for our national security, they will protect American interests and save lives in Iraq.

I look forward to the Administration's continued close consultations with Congress.

House Speaker John Boehner (R-OH):

The president's authorization of airstrikes is appropriate, but like many Americans, I am dismayed by the ongoing absence of a strategy for countering the grave threat ISIS poses to the region. Vital national interests are at stake, yet the White House has remained disengaged despite warnings from Iraqi leaders, Congress, and even members of its own administration. Such parochial thinking only emboldens the enemy and squanders the sacrifices Americans have made. The president needs a long-term strategy – one that defines success as completing our mission, not keeping political promises – and he needs to build the public and congressional support to sustain it. If the president is willing to put forward such a strategy, I am ready to listen and work with him. For now, I wish Godspeed to all our men and women participating in these operations.

House Democratic Leader Nancy Pelosi (D-CA):

I support the President's leadership to avert a massacre of the Yazidi people and other religious minorities in Iraq. ISIS's brutal treatment, depriving Yazidis of food and water in 120 degree heat on the mountain and threatening to slaughter them if they descend, is outside the circle of civilized human behavior.

It is also appropriate that the President authorized air strikes against ISIS should they threaten U.S. personnel and other interests in Erbil or elsewhere in Iraq.

As the President reiterated, there is no American military solution to the situation in Iraq. Defeating ISIS will require Iraq's leaders to see beyond their divisions and come together to fight this common threat. These actions are the only way to achieve durable security and stability for all Iraqis.

I was pleased by the President's continued assurances that he will not send U.S. troops back into combat in Iraq. I appreciate the briefings provided in advance of the President's announcement. Congress looks forward to receiving additional information and intelligence on these humanitarian and military operations.

51

Here Comes Increased Deficit Spending to Fight ISIS

You might think that, with the US government debt increasing year after year and bloated US military spending nearly equal to the combined military spending of the rest of the world, the US government would try to find a way to fight the Islamic State (ISIS) without increasing spending. Supposing the US government proceeds with further escalating yet another Middle East war, couldn't President Barack Obama and Congress at least work together to pay the bill by transferring billions of spare dollars from elsewhere in the vast and wasteful US military and intelligence budgets? How about starting by canning the US government's mass spying program?

If you are asking these sorts of questions, you obviously do not have the qualifications to serve as a US House of Representatives committee chairman overseeing the distribution of largess to the military-industrial complex.

US House Armed Services Committee Chairman Howard P. "Buck" McKeon (R-CA) demonstrates in his Wednesday morning press release how to aid the "masters of war," declaring:

> First, ISIS is an urgent threat and a minimalist approach, that depends solely on [fiscal year 2015] funding or pinprick strikes that leave fragile forces in Iraq and Syria to do the hard fighting, is insufficient to protect our interests and guarantee our safety in time.

While you might want to hold on to your wallets, the days when doing that could stop government spending are long past. Obama, McKeon, and their fellow war conspirators in politics and business have the Federal Reserve to create more dollars for yet more war.

52

September 3, 2014

Remembering Eugene V. Debs' Imprisonment for Speaking Against War

Eugene V. Debs nearly 100 years ago was a political prisoner in the United States for the "crime" of opposing the United States government's participation in World War I and conscription of people to fight in that war. In March of 1919, the US Supreme Court, pointing to the Espionage Act of 1917 for justification, upheld Debs' conviction by a trial jury and ten-year prison sentence for making antiwar comments in a June 16, 1918 Canton, Ohio speech.

Justice Oliver Wendell Holmes, Jr. wrote the Supreme Court's short Debs v. United States opinion that upheld the conviction and ten-year prison sentence of Debs for two charges that Holmes described as follows:

> This is an indictment under the Espionage Act of June 15, 1917… It has been cut down to two counts, originally the third and fourth. The former of these alleges that on or about June 16, 1918, at Canton, Ohio, the defendant caused and incited and attempted to cause and incite insubordination, disloyalty, mutiny and refusal of duty in the military and naval forces of the United States and with intent so to do delivered, to an assembly of people, a public speech, set forth. The fourth count alleges that he obstructed and attempted to obstruct the recruiting and enlistment service of

the United States and to that end and with that intent delivered the same speech, again set forth.

In effect, Debs was incarcerated for exercising his right to free speech regarding two political matters — the US government choosing to participate in World War I and the US government using the draft to help fight that war. One may expect the justices to have reread the First Amendment to the US Constitution and promptly overturned Debs' conviction. However, Holmes explains that a prior Supreme Court decision had already settled the inapplicability of Debs' First Amendment defense.

The prior Supreme Court decision, announced just seven days earlier, was for the case Schenck v. United States. The Supreme Court's Schenck opinion allowed Holmes in the Debs opinion to bypass offering ridiculous contortions of logic to justify throwing a prominent labor and political leader in prison for criticizing the heart of the US government's war policy. Instead, Holmes could just summarily deem Debs' conviction and sentence constitutional and legitimate based on precedent. Here is how Holmes, again writing for the Supreme Court, argued in the court's Schenck opinion that a flier opposing the draft was not protected under the First Amendment:

> We admit that, in many places and in ordinary times, the defendants, in saying all that was said in the circular, would have been within their constitutional rights. But the character of every act depends upon the circumstances in which it is done. *Aikens v. Wisconsin,* 195 U.S. 194, 205, 206. The most stringent protection of free speech would not protect a man in falsely shouting fire in a theatre and causing a panic. It does not even protect a man from an injunction against uttering words that may have all the effect of force. *Gompers v. Bucks Stove & Range Co.,* 221 U.S. 418, 439. The question in every case is whether the words used are used in such circumstances and are of such a nature as to create a clear and present danger that they will bring about the substantive evils that Congress has a right to prevent. It is a question of proximity and de-

gree. When a nation is at war, many things that might be said in time of peace are such a hindrance to its effort that their utterance will not be endured so long as men fight, and that no Court could regard them as protected by any constitutional right.

So there you have it: the First Amendment protects your free speech so long as that speech cannot affect US government policy, or at least so long as your free speech cannot pose a serious threat to something the Supreme Court thinks it is very important to promote, such as the US government participating in World War I and forcing Americans to fight in that war.

Debs was an eloquent opponent of this war, and for that, coupled with his prominence in American labor and politics, he was imprisoned.

In addition to his labor union activities, Debs had run four times as the Socialist Party nominee for US president before his conviction, winning more votes each time. In his last pre-imprisonment run in 1912, Debs won over 900,000 votes — 6.0% nationwide.

In 1920, while serving his prison term, Debs again ran for president, winning a few thousand more votes than in 1912 and 3.4% nationwide.

Debs knew his June 16, 1918 Canton, Ohio speech — despite his care in presenting the speech such that it would comply with US government speech restrictions — could lead to his imprisonment. Indeed, in his speech, Debs talks of other individuals who had been imprisoned for the "crime" of exercising their right to free speech. Debs explains near the beginning of the speech why he spoke anyway:

> I realize that, in speaking to you this afternoon, there are certain limitations placed upon the right of free speech. I must be exceedingly careful, prudent, as to what I say, and even more careful and prudent as to how I say it. I may not be able to say all I think; but I am not going to say anything that I do not think. I would rather a thousand times be a free soul in jail than to be a sycophant and coward in the streets.

53

Obama Distorts Founders and Constitution to Promote War and Worldwide Domination

President Barack Obama, in his speech Wednesday to make the case for a United States war on ISIS, suggested merely talking with some Congress members is enough to legitimate the war and invoked the Founders as supporters of worldwide US domination. In contrast to Obama's assertions, the US Constitution places in Congress the war declaration power and the Founders largely prescribed a foreign policy centered on nonintervention.

Many people hoped in the early days of the United States that calls for war and foreign intervention would be squelched by the constitutional requirement that war not be pursued unless it is first declared by Congress. But, such declarations have become passé in the years since World War II as American presidents have tended to treat war as something solely within their own control.

Obama makes no mention in his speech of seeking a congressional declaration of war. Instead, he says that talking with a few members of Congress as he pursues the war is good enough to justify continuing and expanding the war. Obama states in his speech:

> So tonight, with a new Iraqi government in place, and following consultations with allies abroad and Congress at home, I can announce that America will lead a broad coalition to roll back this terrorist threat.

Given that finding congressional members who will state their outright opposition to war on ISIS is not an easy task and that the US House of Representatives and Senate leadership has long supported Obama's pursuit of the war, a congressional debate and vote on the war may place little restraint on Obama. Yet, even if the war were approved in House and Senate votes, the pre-vote debate would help the American people focus on the issues involved, and the vote would make pro-war Congress members take, instead of duck, responsibility for the war.

To meet, or at least approach, constitutional requirements, some Congress members are arguing that there needs to be a congressional war declaration, or even just an authorization, for Obama to continue to pursue or to escalate the war on ISIS. That is true as far as it goes; an embrace of the nonintervention is also needed.

As the US war on ISIS escalates, many Americans appear to have lost — even if only temporarily — their adherence to nonintervention. Obama's withdrawal of his planned attack on Syria last year in the face of widespread public opposition suggests that Americans had been increasingly embracing nonintervention. But, Obama and his accomplices in politics, media, and industry regrouped and came back with a new plan to overcome American opposition to war. It seems that the roots for opposing war and supporting nonintervention are not yet strong enough to withstand this onslaught of propaganda promoting war on ISIS, including, alas, war in Syria.

At least in the short term, the people are not shutting down this war. With time that may change.

We can see a dramatic example of the extent of the departure from nonintervention principles since the early days of the US by comparing how Obama describes in his speech the role of the US in the world with how John Quincy Adams, who later became the sixth president of the United States, addresses the topic in a July 4, 1821 speech. While some people may suggest departures from nonintervention even before 1821, the US was then far from the across-the-globe meddler it is today.

First, consider Obama's twisting of American Founders' support for freedom, justice, and dignity into an endorsement of US domination worldwide:

> America, our endless blessings bestow an enduring burden. But as Americans, we welcome our responsibility to lead. From Europe to Asia, from the far reaches of Africa to war-torn capitals of the Middle East, we

stand for freedom, for justice, for dignity. These are values that have guided our nation since its founding.

Tonight, I ask for your support in carrying that leadership forward. I do so as a Commander-in-Chief who could not be prouder of our men and women in uniform –- pilots who bravely fly in the face of danger above the Middle East, and servicemembers who support our partners on the ground.

Second, consider then-Secretary of State Adams' comments describing noninterventionist foreign policy as a component of how America had aided people around the world:

And now, friends and countrymen, if the wise and learned philosophers of the older world, the first observers of mutation and aberration, the discoverers of maddening ether and invisible planets, the inventors of Congreve rockets and shrapnel shells, should find their hearts disposed to inquire, what has America done for the benefit of mankind? let our answer be this–America, with the same voice which spoke herself into existence as a nation, proclaimed to mankind the inextinguishable rights of human nature, and the only lawful foundations of government. America, in the assembly of nations, since her admission among them, has invariably, though often fruitlessly, held forth to them the hand of honest friendship, of equal freedom, of generous reciprocity. She has uniformly spoken among them, though often to heedless and often to disdainful ears, the language of equal liberty, equal justice, and equal rights. She has, in the lapse of nearly half a century, without a single exception, respected the inde-pendence of other nations, while asserting and maintaining her own. She has abstained from interference in the concerns of others, even when the conflict has been for principles to which she clings, as to the last vital drop that visits the heart. She has seen that probably for centuries to come, all the contests of that Aceldama, the European World, will be contests between inveterate power, and emerging right. Wherever the standard of freedom and independence has been or shall be unfurled, there will her heart, her benedictions and her prayers be. But she goes not abroad in search of monsters to destroy. She is the well-wisher to the freedom and independence of all. She is the champion and vindicator only of her own. She will recommend the general cause, by the countenance of her voice, and the benignant sympathy of her example. She well knows that by once enlisting under other banners than her own, were they even the banners of foreign independence, she would involve herself, beyond the power of extrication, in all the wars of interest and intrigue, of individual avarice, envy, and ambition, which assume the colors and usurp the standard of freedom. The fundamental maxims of her policy would insensibly change from liberty to force. The frontlet upon her brows would no longer beam with the ineffable splendor of freedom and independence; but in its stead would soon be substituted an imperial diadem, flashing in false and tarnished lustre the murky radiance of dominion and power. She might become the dictatress of the world: she would be no longer the ruler of her own spirit.

When we again hear a US president or secretary of state speaking like Adams instead of like Obama — whether due to actual conviction or political expediency — it will most likely be because Americans' support for nonintervention has grown much stronger. Then, the task for the American people will be to make sure that the politicians follow through on the noninterventionist pronouncements.

September 29, 2014

Donald Rumsfeld: Barack Obama Lacks 'Clarity of Vision'

It is rich hearing Donald Rumsfeld, who made some outlandish statements to advance the 2003 Iraq War he helped instigate and manage as secretary of defense, fault US President Barack Obama for not providing "clarity of vision."

Rumsfeld, in a Friday interview with Rusty Humphries of the Washington Times, says:

> If there is one thing that we have seen, it's that this presidency has been exemplified by not providing the kind of clarity of vision that a leader must provide if in fact they want followers. So, if you don't decide what your mission is, where you're going, and give people confidence that you will go there and not back off and not move aside you're not going to get any followers.

Here are some examples of Rumsfeld's "clarity of vision" before and in the early days of the 2003 US invasion of Iraq:

> The Iraq War would last "[f]ive days or five weeks or five months, but it certainly isn't going to last any longer than that."

> *November 14, 2002 interview on Infinity Radio.*

And:

> Not at all. If you think — let me take that, both pieces — the area in the south and the west and the north that coalition forces control is substantial. It happens not to be the area where weapons of mass destruction were dispersed. We know where they are. They're in the area around Tikrit and Baghdad and east, west, south and north somewhat.

March 30, 2003 ABC's This Week with George Stephanopoulos.

It turns out Rumsfeld misled Americans in two of the key arguments for convincing many Americans to support the US invasion of Iraq — that the war would be short and that the war was needed to protect the American people from weapons of mass destruction (WMDs).

Later, this advocate of leaders providing "clarity of vision" denied ever saying that he expected a short war or that he knew where the purported Iraq weapons of mass destruction were hidden.

Obama's hyping the danger of ISIS to the American people and declaring that the war will be won with no US "boots on the ground" appears to demonstrate exactly the kind of "clarity of vision" Rumsfeld personifies. It also demonstrates the linguistic contortions to which presidential administrations will resort when propagandizing for war. Maybe in a few years Obama will, following Rumsfeld's lead, deny ever having made the claims.

55

September 30, 2014

Speaker John Boehner Says House Should Vote on ISIS War but Refuses to Allow Vote

While the United States Constitution says authority over declaring and funding war resides in the Congress, US House of Representatives Speaker John Boehner refuses to allow a House vote regarding congressional authorization of the war on ISIS. Boehner says he disagrees with how President Barack Obama is pursuing the war. Boehner also says the House should vote on the war. But instead of calling a vote on the war — something Boehner could have done any time during the war's escalation — Boehner just waits for the president to present him with a resolution that Boehner, like a diligent servant, promises to promptly put on the House floor for a vote.

Does Boehner not understand that he is the elected leader

of one of two bodies of the legislative branch in which constitutionally the war declaration and war funding powers reside?

Has Boehner failed to hear any of his fellow House members' appeals to him throughout the escalation of US military action against ISIS that the House should debate and vote the war up or down?

It seems incredibly unlikely that Boehner is so ignorant of the authority of the House and himself regarding the US government's war on ISIS. A more likely explanation of Boehner's decision to just go along with the president on the matter is that Boehner and other leaders in the House and Senate, who have long supported the war on ISIS, have no intention of taking any action that could in any way restrict Obama's pursuit of the war.

Boehner's deference to Obama regarding the war on ISIS is so great that Boehner expressed in an ABC interview with George Stephanopoulos aired Sunday that, while Boehner both thinks there should be a vote in the House and disagrees with how Obama is pursuing the war, Boehner will not bring the war issue to the House floor for a vote this year unless Obama presents him with the resolution to be considered. In fact, Boehner, who has refused to let the House vote on the war as it has escalated, says he would even call the House out of recess and back into session for a vote if Obama sends him a resolution authorizing the war.

Boehner sounds nothing like a leader in the branch of the US government charged with authorizing and funding wars in this exchange from the ABC interview:

Stephanopoulos: I know you've said that - assuming you're speaker next year - you'd want to have a vote on a resolution - why not now?

Boehner: I'd be happy to.

The president typically in a situation like this would call for an authorization vote and go sell that to the American people and send a resolution to the Hill. The president has not done that.

He believes he has authority under existing resolutions to do what he's done.

Stephanopoulos: You don't agree?

Boehner: I think he does have the authority to do it. But the point I'm making is this is a proposal that the Congress ought to consider.

Stephanopoulos: Our reporter Jeff Zeleny has talked to a couple sources on Capitol Hill - said you and other leaders actually warned that if it came up now it would splinter both parties and might not pass.

Boehner: I did not suggest that to anybody in my caucus, or to the president for that matter.

Stephanopoulos: So to be clear - if the president put a resolution forward now, you'd call Congress back?

Boehner: I'd bring the Congress back.

Boehner's inaction regarding a vote on the war on ISIS is particularly amazing considering that the war directly conflicts with a resolution the House passed in July in opposition to sustained US military action in Iraq. Rep. Jim McGovern (D-MA) explained this conflict succinctly in a September House floor speech:

> On July 25th, this House voted 370-to-40 -- 370 to 40 – in favor of my resolution to require specific Congressional authorization for "sustained combat" operations by U.S. Armed Forces in Iraq.

> Yet since August 8th, the U.S. Navy and Air Force have flown more than 2,700 missions against the Islamic State in Iraq, including 156 airstrikes. These airstrikes have occurred almost daily over the past 6 weeks. Last week the President announced that those operations will escalate and likely expand into Syria. This morning they expanded to targets near Baghdad. If that

doesn't qualify as "sustained combat," Mr. Speaker, I don't know what does.

So if this House is serious about what it said in July, then we should demand a vote on congressional authorization for U.S. military operations in Iraq and Syria.

While the Senate has failed to act on the resolution H. Con. Res. 105 to which McGovern refers, the language of the resolution expresses an opinion of the overwhelming majority of House members that is at odds with the ongoing US war against ISIS. Here is the text of the resolution:

CONCURRENT RESOLUTION

Prohibiting the President from deploying or maintaining United States Armed Forces in a sustained combat role in Iraq without specific, subsequent statutory authorization.

Resolved by the House of Representatives (the Senate concurring),

SECTION 1. PROHIBITION REGARDING UNITED STATES ARMED FORCES IN IRAQ.

The President shall not deploy or maintain United States Armed Forces in a sustained combat role in Iraq without specific statutory authorization for such use enacted after the date of the adoption of this concurrent resolution.

SEC. 2. RULE OF CONSTRUCTION.

Nothing in this concurrent resolution supersedes the requirements of the War Powers Resolution (50 U.S.C. 1541 et seq.).

Now, with both bodies of Congress in recess, Rep. Walter Jones (R-NC) has written Boehner requesting that Boehner at least allow a vote on the war when the House reconvenes in November. In the letter, Jones, a Ron Paul Institute Advisory Board member, notes that Boehner has, by not allowing a vote, ignored the counsel of Jones and other representatives, as well as disregarded James Madison's concise description of the congressional role in declaring US wars:

> On August 27, 2014, I joined Congressman Jim Mc-Govern and Congresswoman Barbara Lee in asking you to allow a debate and a vote on an authorization for the use of United States Armed Services in Iraq and Syria before Congress recessed at the end of September. I am disappointed we did not have a debate on such an authorization.

> Those of us in both parties who believe in the Constitution, believe that Congress must debate and declare war. As James Madison wrote, "THE POWER TO DECLARE WAR, INCLUDING THE POWER OF JUDGING THE CAUSES OF WAR, IS FULLY AND EXCLUSIVELY VESTED IN THE LEGISLATURE."

> Mr. Speaker I am asking you to allow a full debate and vote on an authorization for the use of United States Armed Forces in Iraq and Syria when Congress reconvenes in November. Many members are asking for this to take place before the end of the year.

Jones' plea is nothing more than that Boehner act in accord with what the Constitution and propriety demand — do what a House speaker should be expected to do without any prodding. With Boehner such pleas have so far fallen on deaf ears.

56

October 16, 2014

Defense Secretary Hagel to Congress: 'Give the Military More Money'!

While you might expect there would be a "peace dividend" with the winding down of the United States military occupations in Afghanistan and Iraq, Secretary of Defense Chuck Hagel is making the rounds over the congressional recess to project the message that the United States Congress must not dare reduce military spending — even via fake sequestration "spending cuts" that just cut the rate of spending growth.

The Hill reports Hagel delivered this message on Wednesday to an audience assembled by the Association of the United States Army. The audience must have been pleased with Hagel's call given the long list of military spending requests in the organization's legislative agenda.

Back in August, Ron Paul Institute Chairman and Founder Ron Paul predicted that the building ISIS War would ensure the disintegration of any hoped-for peace dividend. Paul noted that House of Representatives Armed Services Committee Chairman Buck McKeon (R-CA) was already calling for extra spending to fight ISIS. Problems caused by the new spending, Paul warned, would include more Federal Reserve money printing and increased ISIS recruitment.

Hagel, though, is not putting all his military golden eggs in one basket. He presents a long list of "threats" and "commitments" to justify always increasing the US government's military spending. From the US Department of Defense's press release concerning Hagel's speech:

> The defense secretary noted that while a another [sic] Iraq or Afghanistan-type campaign is unlikely, this does not mean that demand for the Army is diminishing, or that the Army's place in U.S. national security strategy is eroding.

> While there are no longer 150,000 soldiers engaged in ground wars in Iraq and Afghanistan, Hagel said, there are still almost as many soldiers either deployed or forward-stationed in nearly 150 locations around the world. This includes 80,000 soldiers in the U.S. Pacific Command area of responsibility and nearly 20,000 soldiers in South Korea standing ready to "fight tonight."

"There are also 40,000 soldiers under Central Command; 28,000 soldiers in Europe, and thousands more in both Africa and South America — some of whom I visited in Colombia last week," Hagel said. "The demands on the Army will only grow more diverse and complicated going forward. Threats from terrorists and insurgents will remain with us for a long time, but we also must deal with a revisionist Russia — with its modern and capable Army — on NATO's doorstep."

Not content with just the new costs of the ISIS war, estimated at $100 billion for this year alone, Hagel throws in the full spectrum of US military interventions, from the drug war operations in Latin America to the expanding US military involvement in Africa to the residual cold war and recently escalated military commitment in Europe to the US troops in South Korea due to a war begun over sixty years ago to a new cold (for now) war the US government is promoting against Russia.

One thing is for sure, the Obama administration and congressional leadership are lock-step in their support of exorbitant US military spending and the broad use of the US military around the world.

While many Americans want a peace dividend, their priorities differ from those of the politicians in leadership in the US executive and legislative branches.

57

House Majority Leader: Charlie Hebdo Killings Justify US Intervention Worldwide

If the statement issued Wednesday by US House Majority Leader Kevin McCarthy (R-CA) is an indication of how the US House and Senate — both now under Republican leadership — will respond legislatively to the killings in Paris last week, expect expanded authorization and funding for US military action and other intervention the world over.

As news of the killings at the Paris office of Charlie Hebdo was spreading, McCarthy issued the following statement:

> I condemn today's horrific terrorist attack in Paris. My thoughts and prayers are with the victims, their families, and the French people. This terrorist attack, like so many before it, is an assault on fundamental democratic principles that are essential to a free society. It is also a reminder that the war on terrorism is not over, that radical Islamic terrorist organizations have not been defeated, and that they continue to pose a threat at home and abroad. Whether it is ISIL in Iraq and Syria, the Taliban, Haqqani network, and al Qaeda in Afghanistan and Pakistan, Ansar al Sharia and other terrorists in Libya, Boko Haram in Nigeria, or al Qaeda affiliated groups in Yemen, Somalia, and Mali, free and moderate societies face a growing and determined terrorist enemy. We ignore this gathering danger at our peril. We must recommit to our common efforts against these violent enemies and stand with our friends around the world. For their sake and for our own, we must prevail in this fight against violent extremism.

There you have it: It is the opinion of the number two majority party leader in the House that the killings at Charlie Hebdo mean the US government should "recommit" to fighting its worldwide war on terrorism for the sake of Americans and "our friends around the world." Indeed, McCarthy includes among the "determined terrorist enemy" the US must recommit to fighting six named and an undefined number of unnamed groups in nine countries in the Middle East, Asia, and Africa.

McCarthy fails to mention the risk that the recommitment to the US government's Global War on Terror he endorses will inspire more blowback and thus *decrease* Americans' safety.

February 13, 2015

Don't Trust Obama's Rhetoric — His War Authorization Allows Fighting by US Ground Troops

The proposed Authorization for Use of Military Force (AUMF) that President Barack Obama submitted to Congress on Wednesday would allow United States ground troops to engage in battle around the world. No matter what aspirations Obama may declare regarding limiting the use of US ground troops, the proposed AUMF places little to no restraint on their use in the ISIS War.

Obama spoke truthfully in his statement announcing his AUMF proposal when he said, "The resolution we've submitted today does not call for the deployment of US ground combat forces to Iraq or Syria." Though truthful, Obama's comment is deceptive because it leaves out some important information. Left unsaid is the fact that the proposed AUMF authorizes Obama and the next US president to deploy ground troops worldwide at their discretion.

The proposed AUMF, should it become law, gives the president and his successor the broad power "to use the Armed Forces of the United States as the President determines to be necessary and appropriate against ISIL and associated persons or forces…" anywhere in the world for three years after the AUMF's enactment. The AUMF also contains one provision purportedly limiting the use of US ground troops. This provision states that the broad power given to the president "does not authorize the use of the United States Armed Forces in enduring offensive ground combat operations."

A quick, uncritical read of the proposed AUMF may suggest that the "enduring offensive ground combat operations" provision in the AUMF means the AUMF bars US ground troops from engaging in battle. However, further consideration reveals the AUMF may be used to justify unlimited use of US ground troops.

Consider the word "offensive" included in the supposed limitation on the use of ground troops. The US government has a long record of expansively defining its military actions as "defensive." The official story of the US government sending in the military as a last resort and only to defend the American people from attack endures despite a tradition of non-defensive US wars that span wars against American Indian nations, the Korean War, and the Iraq War. Recall that Obama justified the bombings in Iraq and Syria that escalated the ISIS War, in part, as needed to "defend" US government employees overseas.

Consider also the word "enduring." There is no limit whatsoever on even "offensive" ground combat operations so long as those operations are not "enduring."

As pointed out by Rep. Jim McGovern (D-MA), who is quoted in Roll Call on Wednesday, the "enduring offensive ground combat operations" language provides no limitation. Instead, it is just propaganda. Says McGovern, "What that is is language that's supposed to make people like me feel better.... In real terms, it doesn't mean anything."

Indeed, even Obama's spokesman has admitted that this language imposes little to no limitation on what Obama or the next president can do. A revealing video accompanying the Roll Call article features White House Press Secretary Josh Earnest saying that the ground troops language in the AUMF proposal submitted to Congress is "intentionally fuzzy" because "we believe it's important that there aren't overly burdensome constraints that are placed on the commander in chief who needs the flexibility to be able to respond to contingencies that emerge in a chaotic military conflict like this."

The ground troops limitation in Obama's proposed AUMF for the ISIS War may help Obama make his case to the American people for yet more war. It also may provide cover for Congress members who do not want to appear as if they are supporting more endless war. But, it is in fact a limitation in name only. Judge Andrew Napolitano, a Ron Paul Institute Advisory Board member, starkly explains the situation in an interview with Fox News host Shepard Smith. Napolitano advises that, unless Congress adopts an AUMF that includes language expressly saying "you may not use ground troops," which Napolitano assures us Congress will not do, "the president has the discretion to use ground troops on his own."

59

Will Reading of George Washington's Farewell Address Influence Senate Warmongers?

Per longstanding United States Senate tradition, on Monday afternoon a senator — this year Sen. John Hoeven (R-ND) — will read President George Washington's farewell address on the Senate floor. The Senate website declares that no Senate tradition "has been more steadfastly maintained," noting the first reading of the speech on the Senate floor occurred in 1862 and that "[e]very year since 1896, the Senate has observed Washington's Birthday by selecting one of its members, alternating parties, to read the 7,641-word statement in legislative session."

With the Senate for so many years promoting, financing, and allowing the executive branch to unilaterally pursue overt and covert interventions across the globe, one question comes to mind: Will the reading of Washington's farewell address, with its hard-hitting noninterventionist foreign policy admonitions, have any influence on the many warmongers and war facilitators in the Senate?

We can hope that the words will resonate with at least one of these senators. Maybe the speech will lead a senator or two to rethink imposing sanctions, funding foreign governments, supporting coups, waging wars, or feeding the military-industrial complex. Certainly, though, even a senator who reads the speech aloud does not automatically transform thereby into a noninterventionist. Uber interventionist Sen. John McCain (R-AZ), for example, delivered the speech on the Senate floor in

1987 — his first year in the Senate.

If the annual reading of Washington's farewell address is just a well-trodden farce for the Senators, it still may yield some benefit. Some people watching the delivery of the speech on C-SPAN 2 may be prompted to thought and further research when they hear Hoeven repeat the following foreign policy observations of George Washington:

> Observe good faith & justice towds all Nations.
> Cultivate peace & harmony with all--Religion &
> morality enjoin this conduct; and can it be that good
> policy does not equally enjoin it? It will be worthy of
> a free, enlightened, and, at no distant period, a great
> Nation, to give to mankind the magnanimous and
> too novel example of a People always guided by an
> exalted justice & benevolence. Who can doubt that in
> the course of time and things the fruits of such a plan
> would richly repay any temporary advantages wch
> might be lost by a steady adherence to it? Can it be,
> that Providence has not connected the permanent
> felicity of a Nation with its virtue? The experiment,
> at least, is recommended by every sentiment which
> ennobles human Nature. Alas! is it rendered impossi-
> ble by its vices?

> In the execution of such a plan nothing is more essen-
> tial than that permanent inveterate antipathies against
> particular Nations and passionate attachments for oth-
> ers should be excluded; and that in place of them just
> & amicable feelings towards all should be cultivated.
> The Nation, which indulges towards another an habit-
> ual hatred, or an habitual fondness, is in some degree
> a slave. It is a slave to its animosity or to its affection,
> either of which is sufficient to lead it astray from its
> duty and its interest. Antipathy in one Nation against
> another--disposes each more readily to offer insult
> and injury, to lay hold of slight causes of umbrage,
> and to be haughty and intractable, when accidental
> or trifling occasions of dispute occur. Hence frequent

collisions, obstinate envenomed and bloody contests. The Nation, prompted by ill will & resentment sometimes impels to War the Government, contrary to the best calculations of policy. The Government sometimes participates in the national propensity, and adopts through passion what reason would reject; at other times, it makes the animosity of the Nation subservient to projects of hostility instigated by pride, ambition and other sinister & pernicious motives. The peace often, sometimes perhaps the Liberty, of Nations has been the victim.

So likewise, a passionate attachment of one Nation for another produces a variety of evils. Sympathy for the favourite nation, facilitating the illusion of an imaginary common interest, in cases where no real common interest exists, and infusing into one the enmities of the other, betrays the former into a participation in the quarrels & Wars of the latter, without adequate inducement or justification: It leads also to concessions to the favourite Nation of priviledges denied to others, which is apt doubly to injure the Nation making the concessions--by unnecessarily parting with what ought to have been retained--& by exciting jealousy, ill will, and a disposition to retaliate, in the parties from whom eql priviledges are withheld: And it gives to ambitious, corrupted, or deluded citizens (who devote themselves to the favourite Nation) facility to betray, or sacrifice the interests of their own country, without odium, sometimes even with popularity; gilding with the appearances of a virtuous sense of obligation a commendable deference for public opinion, or a laudable zeal for public good, the base or foolish compliances of ambition corruption or infatuation.

As avenues to foreign influence in innumerable ways, such attachments are particularly alarming to the truly enlightened and independent Patriot. How many opportunities do they afford to tamper with domestic factions, to practice the arts of seduction, to mislead public opinion, to influence or awe the public Councils! Such an attachment of a small or weak, towards a great & powerful Nation, dooms the former to be the satellite of the latter.

Against the insidious wiles of foreign influence, (I conjure you to believe me fellow citizens,), the jealousy of a free people ought to be constantly awake; since history and experience prove that foreign influence is one of the most baneful foes of Republican Government. But that jealousy to be useful must be impartial; else it becomes the instrument of the very influence to be avoided, instead of a defence against it. Excessive partiality for one foreign nation and excessive dislike of another, cause those whom they actuate to see danger only on one side, and serve to veil and even second the arts of influence on the other. Real Patriots, who may resist the intriegues of the favourite, are liable to become suspected and odious; while its tools and dupes usurp the applause & confidence of the people, to surrender their interests.

The Great rule of conduct for us, in regard to foreign Nations is in extending our comercial relations to have with them as little political connection as possible. So far as we have already formed engagements let them be fulfilled, with perfect good faith. Here let us stop.

60

House Votes to Keep Paying for ISIS War It Neither Debated Nor Authorized

The US House of Representatives on Friday again voted to pay for war on the Islamic State (ISIS) without ever having a debate and vote on the authorization of the war. This result is par for the course given the House leadership is well practiced in manipulating House rules to scuttle efforts by Reps. Walter Jones (R-NC) and Jim McGovern (D-MA), as well as by other House members, to ensure that the legislative branch fulfills its constitutional responsibility to decide when the US government uses military force.

By barring war debates and votes, the House leadership ensures the continued legislative rubber-stamping of the wars the executive branch unilaterally pursues.

The authorization of funding for the ISIS War that the House approved Friday is included in the massive National Defense Authorization Act (NDAA) for Fiscal Year 2016 (HR 1735) that covers funding authorization for the Department of Defense generally. This leaves any representative who voted for the legislation with the ability to deny responsibility for the ISIS War by saying he voted for the NDAA just to advance some combination on other provisions in the bill.

Over at the Huffington Post, Jennifer Bendery tells the sad tale of how House leadership suppressed efforts to bring a debate and vote on the war to the House floor during consideration of the NDAA. Bendery explains:

> The House passed legislation Friday that clears the path for spending tens of billions of dollars on overseas wars, including the one against Islamic State militants that Congress still hasn't authorized.
>
> Lawmakers voted 269-151 to pass the fiscal 2016 National Defense Authorization Act, which would, among other things, permit Congress to spend $89.2 billion on war funding. Republicans allowed 135 amendments to the bill, which covered topics ranging from immigration to remotely piloted aircraft to fire hoses being exempt from certain purchasing requirements.
>
> But they shut out any debate on the need for an Authorization for Use of Military Force to put limits on the months-long war against the Islamic State. At

the same time, the defense bill authorizes spending billions more fighting the group also known as ISIS. A handful of lawmakers tried to attach AUMF amendments to the legislation, but were denied.

"Last night, the Rules Committee voted down an amendment I offered to the NDAA in the form of a limited and narrow authorization against ISIS," Rep. Adam Schiff (D-Calif.) said Thursday. "The majority's objection was that the defense bill was not the place to debate the war. Perhaps not, but if not here, where?"

All of this should be of little surprise in an institution whose top officer — House Speaker John Boehner (R-OH) — has been saying for well over half a year that the House should vote the ISIS War up or down but refuses to ever allow a debate and vote to occur on the matter.

61

May 31, 2015

Speaker John Boehner's Endless Excuses for Blocking an ISIS War Debate and Vote

US Speaker of the House John Boehner (R-OH) is like the fellow you ask over for dinner time and again who always has a reason to decline the invitation. He says, in turn, that he has to work late, has to deal with a family emergency, needs to feed the neighbor's cat, and is too tired. The excuses pile up, and you finally get the message: The guy won't come over, but he lacks the backbone to just say "no."

For nearly a year, Boehner has been proclaiming his desire for the House to debate and vote on the Islamic State (ISIS) War that the executive branch has been pursuing. But, instead of scheduling a vote, something the House Republican leadership does regularly for all kinds of legislation, Boehner keeps coming up with new excuses for letting the war proceed without any House consideration.

The responsibility for inaction resides with Boehner and the House Republican leadership. They could have put a declaration of war, or just an authorization for use of military force (AUMF), on the House floor anytime on their own. To insist, as Boehner has repeatedly during the ongoing US military action in Iraq and Syria, that the House can only work from a proposed AUMF from President Barack Obama is just a way to duck responsibility.

Boehner proclaimed on May 19 his newest excuse for blocking a House debate and vote on the war. Boehner now says the proposed AUMF legislation for the ISIS War that President Barack Obama sent to the House over three months ago is not quite right. Therefore, Boehner says, Obama should start over, writing a new proposed AUMF and sending that to the House. Boehner returned to the matter in a Tuesday press conference in which he complained that the proposed AUMF Obama sent to Congress in February is not "a robust authorization that will allow the president to use the tools at his command to actually go out and fight and win this war."

Boehner's critique of Obama's proposed AUMF does not even square with reality. Boehner is criticizing Obama's proposed AUMF as too weak. However, Obama's proposed AUMF that has been sitting in the House since February is actually so broad and elastic that it allows for extensive worldwide US military action, including fighting by US ground troops, irrespective of nebulous assurances of restraint contained in the proposed AUMF.

Further, Boehner had his opportunity to advise Obama regarding what should be in a proposed AUMF and refused to do so. Asked in a December 4 press conference if Obama should include "American troops on the ground leading that fight" in a proposed AUMF, Boehner answers, "I'm not going to speculate on what the president should suggest to the Congress in terms of what that authorization should look like."

Hold on a minute there. Boehner is actually saying that, while Obama's proposed AUMF from February is not right and the president should send the House a new proposed AUMF that is right, Boehner will not say what should be in a proposed AUMF to make sure it is right.

Unless Obama can read Boehner's mind, Boehner's request for a new proposed AUMF is an invitation for months more of continued House inaction. Reviewing some of Boehner's previous statements and deeds regarding House consideration of the ISIS War it is hard to conclude otherwise than that the House Republican leadership desires such inaction.

The reality is that Boehner has been playing a game with the ISIS War authorization issue all along. While Boehner talks big, the last thing he has wanted to do is have a debate and vote on the House floor.

In a January 21 press conference Boehner declared that Obama sending the House a proposed AUMF would lead, "surely" by the spring of this year, to the House completing hearings, as well as holding a floor debate and vote. On February 11, Obama sent the House his proposed AUMF. Yet, nothing is happening; House Republican leadership continues to block a House floor debate and vote on the ISIS War. Spring ends June 21. Tick tock.

Four months earlier, Boehner had expressed an even more urgent desire to take action on an AUMF. In September, he told George Stephanopoulos in an ABC interview that Boehner would bring the House back from recess to consider an AUMF should Obama propose one. Yet, once Obama did in February offer a proposed AUMF, there was no follow-through in the House. Since Obama offered a proposed AUMF, over three months have passed — including five recesses totaling six weeks. After all this time, the only action Boehner can muster is to send the proposed AUMF back to the president for a redo.

A Wednesday press release from Rep. Walter Jones (R-NC), who has been publicly hounding Boehner for months to just schedule a vote, relates the frustrating way that Boehner says he wants to hold a debate and vote on the ISIS War yet continues to block any debate and vote. Jones' press release notes:

> On September 25, 2014, Speaker Boehner told The
> New York Times that he wanted to wait until 2015

to bring an AUMF to the House floor for a debate and a vote to avoid bringing it up during a lame duck session. On December 6, 2014, Speaker Boehner said that House Republicans would work with the president to get an AUMF request approved if the president sent one to Congress. On February 11, 2015, President Obama sent his AUMF request to Congress. In over three months, the House has failed to act on the president's request, or any alternative.

The press release from Jones, a Ron Paul Institute for Peace and Prosperity Advisory Board member, proceeds to chronicle some of the many actions, all fruitless, taken by Jones and other House members to bring about of a full debate and vote in the House regarding the ISIS War:

On February 6, 2015 in anticipation of President Obama sending an AUMF request to Congress, Congressman Jones and Congressman McGovern sent a letter to Speaker Boehner urging him to schedule a full debate on the president's AUMF request.

On February 23, 2015, Congressman Jones led a coalition urging Speaker Boehner to follow regular order on President Obama's AUMF request so that the House could make changes to it and have an open debate and a vote on it.

Last September, when the president started conducting airstrikes against ISIS and arming Syrian rebels, Congressman Jones sent a letter to Speaker Boehner asking for a full debate on an authorization for the use of military force in the region.

Last July, Congressman Jones introduced H. Con. Res. 105 to prohibit the deployment of U.S. armed forces in a sustained combat role in Iraq without congressional authorization. The resolution passed with 370 votes.

Last August, Congressman Jones, Congressman McGovern, and Congresswoman Lee formed a bipartisan coalition to urge the House Foreign Relations Committee to draft an authorization regarding Iraq and Syria. They also urged Speaker Boehner to bring up the authorization for a debate and a vote before Congress recessed at the end of September.

That list is just a beginning. Unmentioned in the list, for example, is that the House Republican leadership in May prevented consideration of House members' amendments to the National Defense Authorization Act (NDAA) that would have brought to the House floor at least some debate and a vote related to the ISIS War.

Back in a May 1 C-SPAN interview, Rep. Jim McGovern (D-MA) succinctly pinned blame on Congress members for ducking their responsibility regarding the ISIS War:

> Congress is basically abrogating its responsibility. And you can't have it both ways. You can't sit back and criticize the president for committing troops into another war in Iraq and in Syria, but then say: "But I don't want to do my job. I don't want to vote yes or no on it." It's too easy for congress to just kind of stand back and let it all happen, because, if it goes bad you can say "I told you it was going to go bad" and if it goes good you can say "well, I was with them all the way."

Boehner is Exhibit A in this two-faced abrogation of responsibility.

62

December 17, 2015

'Leaders' McConnell and Ryan Support Unlimited War Power for Obama and Next President

US Senate Majority Leader Mitch McConnell (R-KY) and House Speaker Paul Ryan (R-WI) like to portray themselves as strong leaders who act to protect congressional authority against Obama administration power grabs. But, in regard to the ISIS War, both congressional leaders are happy to cede — year after year — power without limit to President Barack Obama and whoever the next president may be.

McConnell told Roll Call on Friday that he opposes the Senate voting on an authorization of the ISIS War until, if ever, sometime after the January of 2017 inauguration of a new president. Just let Obama conduct the ISIS War however he pleases for the remainder of his term, and do not dare impose any limits on the next president either: That is McConnell's position.

Meanwhile, Ryan is expressing willingness to hold a House debate and vote on an Authorization for Use of Military Force (AUMF) for the ISIS War, but only so long as it is assured the AUMF in no way restricts what Obama or a future president may do.

Niels Lesniewski reports on the AUMF discussion in Roll Call's interview with McConnell:

> "The president obviously feels he has the authority now to do what he's doing," McConnell said. "And the discussions with Democrats on AUMF make it clear that the only kind of AUMF they would support is one that would include such micromanagement of the military exercise as how many troops you could have, how long they could stay, and all of this.
>
> "I would not want to saddle the next president with a prescriptive AUMF. We're going to have a new president a year from now," McConnell continued. "He or she may have a different view about the way to deal with ISIS and that part of the world. I don't think we ought to be passing an AUMF as the president exits the stage when he already thinks he has the authority to do what he's willing to do now."

There you have it: McConnell opposes an ISIS War debate and vote because he wants to preserve unlimited war-waging power in the presidency.

So absent from this so-called leader is any gumption to lead on this matter the US Constitution squarely puts in the hands of Congress members that he does not even express his own opinion about whether Obama or the next president even has actual authority to pursue the ISIS War. Look at the "weasel words" he throws out: "[t]he president obviously feels he has the authority now to do what he's doing." Well, the president is either right or wrong about that. What do you think, Mr. Leader?

As long as McConnell does not say what he thinks about the war and continues to block a debate and vote on the war, he can take advantage of an old trick in the Washington, DC chicanery book — claim credit for the ISIS War should it prove popular in public opinion or blame the war on someone else should it prove unpopular.

In refusing to schedule a debate and vote on the ISIS War, McConnell is ceding to Obama and the next president (whoever that will be) the ability to pursue war without limit and without the constitutionally required congressional declaration.

At least McConnell is now upfront enough to say that he has decided to duck his responsibility, unlike the recently-resigned House Speaker John Boehner (R-OH) who misleadingly spoke month after month about his desire to have an ISIS War debate and vote in the House that never materialized.

Ryan, Boehner's successor as speaker, similarly speaks aspirationally about the House someday debating and voting on the ISIS War. Do not mistake Ryan for an advocate of peace or of following the Constitution regarding war powers, however. Ryan says he both believes Obama has the authority to proceed in the ISIS War without any congressional action and opposes moving forward with any AUMF Obama would reject or that would "handcuff the next president."

McConnell and Ryan's announced positions are of little surprise given the lack of opposition to the ISIS War from any of the top Republican and Democrat leaders in the US House and Senate since the Obama administration began pursuing the war, without any congressional debate or vote, last year.

Either the McConnell or Ryan way, ducking responsibility is the ignoble path followed by the so-called congressional leadership.

Part 4: Surveillance

63

June 16, 2013

US Mass Spying Loses Obama's 'Shoddy Coat of Legitimacy'

Declan McCullagh at cnet.com reports on Rep. Jerrold Nadler's revelation that the United States executive branch has admitted in a secret briefing to Members of the US House of Representatives that a US government analyst can listen to phone calls at his own discretion without any warrant or other authorization. McCullagh's dense article, well worth a close read, proceeds to explain that this means "thousands of low-ranking analysts" probably can unilaterally decide to snoop on the contents of email, text, and instant messages as well. McCullagh also addresses the enormity of the mass spying operation and its capabilities.

Nadler's revelation directly contradicts President Barack Obama's emphatic denials earlier this month:

> When it comes to telephone calls, nobody is listening to your telephone calls. That's not what this program is about. As was indicated, what the intelligence community is doing is looking at phone numbers and durations of calls. They are not looking at people's names, and they're not looking at content. But by sifting through this so-called metadata, they may identify

potential leads with respect to folks who might engage in terrorism. If these folks -- if the intelligence community then actually wants to listen to a phone call, they've got to go back to a federal judge, just like they would in a criminal investigation.

So I want to be very clear -- some of the hype that we've been hearing over the last day or so -- nobody is listening to the content of people's phone calls. This program, by the way, is fully overseen not just by Congress, but by the FISA Court -- a court specially put together to evaluate classified programs to make sure that the executive branch, or government generally, is not abusing them, and that it's being carried out consistent with the Constitution and rule of law.

And so, not only does that court authorize the initial gathering of data, but -- I want to repeat -- if anybody in government wanted to go further than just that top-line data and want to, for example, listen to Jackie Calmes' phone call, they would have to go back to a federal judge and indicate why, in fact, they were doing further probing.

Now, with respect to the Internet and emails -- this does not apply to U.S. citizens and it does not apply to people living in the United States. And again, in this instance, not only is Congress fully apprised of it, but what is also true is that the FISA Court has to authorize it.

Obama's claims that only metadata was collected, that the program was fully overseen by Congress, and that content of phone calls and internet communications could only be obtained via FISA court authorization was repeated approvingly by ardent defenders of the mass spying program.

Even if Obama's claims had been true, they provided little assurance that the spying program is not dramatically infringing on our privacy.

First, metadata of our phone calls and internet communications, rather than being trivial, does provide very detailed information about our personal lives. Jay Stanley and Ben Wizner's concise article at Reuters laying out the revealing nature of metadata begins with the following observation:

> In the wake of The Guardian's remarkable revelation Wednesday that the National Security Agency is collecting phone records from millions of Americans, defenders of this dragnet surveillance program are insisting that the intelligence agency isn't eavesdropping on the calls – it's just scooping up "metadata." The implication is that civil liberties complaints about Orwellian surveillance tactics are overblown.

> But any suggestion that Americans have nothing to worry about from this dragnet collection of communications metadata is wrong. Even without intercepting the content of communications, the government can use metadata to learn our most intimate secrets – anything from whether we have a drinking problem to whether we're gay or straight. The suggestion that metadata is "no big deal" – a view that, regrettably, is still reflected in the law – is entirely out of step with the reality of modern communications.

Second, keeping Congress apprised of the mass spying program provides little extra protection. As Nadler's revelation indicates, not all members of Congress had been fully informed about the mass spying program. Indeed, Director of National Intelligence James R. Clapper even claimed, in response to a question from Sen. Ron Wyden, that the National Security Agency (NSA) was not intentionally collecting any kind of data on millions or hundreds of millions of Americans. Yet, even if all members of Congress had been fully informed of the program, that would provide little consolation. Congress is capable of supporting bad programs and doing so for decades. In fact, the highest ranking Democrat and Republican Senators on the Senate Select Committee on Intelligence reacted to the revelation of the FISA court order for Verizon to give over to the US government information concerning its millions of customers' phone conversations by quickly preparing a joint press conference to unequivocally defend the mass spying program.

Third, while Nadler's revelation indicates FISA court approval is not required to snoop on the contents of Americans' private communications, requiring such approval would likely provide little to no protection. The secretive FISA court last year failed to deny any of 1,789 applications for monitoring electronic communications.

The US government's mass spying program would be a horrendous abuse of power even if it were draped in a shoddy coat of legitimacy as President Obama described it. Nadler's new revelation confirms the suspicions of critical observers and the warnings of whistle-blowers that the program is even worse.

64

June 18, 2013

House Intel Committee's Sham Hearing on Mass Spying

Today the Permanent Select Committee on Intelligence in the United States House of Representatives is holding a hearing designed to cheer the US government's secret mass spying programs. The committee leadership's one-sided agenda is highlighted by the title of this morning's hearing — How Disclosed NSA Programs Protect Americans, and Why Disclosure Aids Our Adversaries — and the hearing's witness list, composed entirely of high-level managers and lawyers in government entities administering the programs:

General Keith Alexander, Director of the National Security Agency (NSA)

James Cole, Deputy Attorney General

Sean Joyce, Deputy Director of the Federal Bureau of Investigation (FBI)

Robert Litt, General Counsel, Office of the Director of National Intelligence

65

Surveillance State: We Are One Step Away from Glass Houses

In Yevgeny Zamyatin's dystopian novel We, the people of One State live in transparent apartments with curtains required to be open nearly all the time so police and informants may view the residents' every action. Listening to George Washington University Law School Professor Jeffrey Rosen's interview last week on The Take Away, it becomes disturbingly clear that Americans are one step away from this level of government snooping on our activities.

Rosen details how police can use facial recognition software combined with abundant cameras to track and catalog our activities. As Rosen explains, the snooping is not limited to attempting to catch suspected criminals. Rather, police may use the technology to follow the daily activities of any person whose photo is contained in vast photo databases, such as anyone with a driver license.

The US government is working with states to expand quickly the use of facial recognition surveillance. Jennifer Lynch of the Electronic Frontier Foundation warned last year:

> Recently-released documents show that the FBI has been working since late 2011 with four states—Michigan, Hawaii, Maryland, and possibly Oregon—to ramp up the Next Generation Identification (NGI) Facial Recognition Program. When the program is fully

deployed in 2014, the FBI expects its facial recognition
database will contain at least 12 million "searchable
frontal photos."

The database will quickly grow much larger. Lynch explains
that agreements between the FBI and states in the pilot program allow the states to add just about anyone's photo to the
database, including data dumps of driver license photos.

In addition to expanding the photo database, the US government is working on significantly improving the cameras and
facial recognition software police use. For example, Gene Healy
of the Cato Institute describes some efforts of the US Department of Homeland Security (DHS). First, DHS "has awarded
a $5.2 million federal contract to the defense firm Electronic
Warfare Associates to develop facial recognition technology
allowing video cameras to pick 'watch-listed' suspects out of
crowds at distances of up to 100 meters." Second, DHS is considering using, inside the US, Gorgon Stare, "a drone-mount-
ed camera array under development by the Air Force that can
watch whole cities at a time." As we have seen again and again,
military equipment and tactics developed in US wars abroad
are later used domestically.

How can we evade the snooping? Maybe we can wear
masks to regain some of our lost privacy from prying government eyes. But, the government will likely respond by outlaw-
ing wearing masks. In fact, last year the Canadian government
made wearing a mask or otherwise concealing your identity at
a "riot or unlawful assembly" a crime punishable by up to 10
years in prison.

At least we can stay in our homes with the curtains closed
— until the US government takes the next step toward One
State.

Canada Joins US in the Hot Seat for Industrial Espionage

Brazil President Dilma Rousseff, after condemning US government mass spying on Brazilian companies in her speech last month before the United Nations General Assembly, is now singling out the Canada government for engaging in industrial espionage targeting Brazil's mines and energy ministry. The Associated Press reports on Rousseff's concerns, as well as the Brazil foreign minister's discussion of the spying with Canada's ambassador to Brazil at a meeting Monday:

> Brazil has demanded clarifications from the Canadian government about allegations that its spies targeted Brazil's mines and energy ministry, in what the Brazilian president, Dilma Rousseff, said appeared to be an act of industrial espionage.

> The foreign minister, Luiz Alberto Figueiredo, summoned the Canadian ambassador to "transmit the indignation of the Brazilian government and demand explanations," the foreign ministry said in a statement following the revelations, broadcast on Sunday night on Brazil's Globo network.

> The report said the metadata of phone calls and emails to and from the ministry were targeted by Canada's Communications Security Establishment (CSE). It did not indicate if emails were read or phone calls listened to.

> The report was based on documents leaked by former National Security Agency contractor Edward Snowden and follows revelations that the US and the UK had also targeted Brazil.

> During Monday's meeting, Figueiredo's statement ex-

pressed "the government's repudiation of this serious and unacceptable violation of national sovereignty and the rights of people and companies".

As noted in the Globe and Mail, whistle-blower Edward Snowden's revelation of Canada's involvement in the spying included releasing a slide presentation by a member of the Canada government intelligence agency Communications Security Establishment Canada (CSEC) at a June 2012 meeting of the Five Eyes — a spying cooperation and sharing organization of the governments of Australia, Canada, Great Britain, New Zealand, and the United States. As the Globe and Mail article explains, the slides reveal the Brazilian ministry was targeted for snooping:

> Using a program called Olympia, CSEC took aim at Brazil's Ministry of Mines and Energy, describing it as a "new target to develop" despite "limited access/target knowledge."

Nevertheless, in the US, President Barack Obama and some of the legislators charged with overseeing the US mass spying program continue to assure us the program's focus is on counter-terrorism.

There is no reason to believe US intelligence agencies are somehow immune from the lobbying and revolving doors that create huge payoffs for private companies seeking profits through government connections instead of competition. In fact, the secretiveness of intelligence budgets and operations — secure from regular oversight and public scrutiny — make intelligence programs more, not less, subject to corruption.

From lucrative weapons contracts in the Department of Defense to regulatory capture in the Food and Drug Administration (FDA), the US government is the road to easy money for well-connected companies. In varying ways, companies around the world use close ties with other governments — including the Five Eyes governments — to create profits.

While connected companies can benefit from the US government mass spying program, the program also threatens

American companies' business prospects in the international marketplace. RT reports on the example of German companies' increasingly negative attitude toward the US:

> The number of German companies considering the US as a high-risk for industrial espionage and data theft has quadrupled in 2 years, according to an Ernst and Young study. The US left Russia behind, as the Snowden revelations ate into America's profile.

> The portion of German managers, IT and security professionals, saying the US was a dangerous place for industrial espionage grew to 26% in 2013 from just 6% two years earlier, according to the survey conducted by Ernst and Young (EY).

> "Until now [German companies] mostly identified China and Russia as the location of [potential] attackers. Now companies realise that western intelligence agencies also employ very comprehensive surveillance measures," Bodo Meseke, executive director of fraud investigation and dispute services at EY, said.

> In the latest survey, that covered 400 companies across Germany, 28% said China was the riskiest place, Financial Times (FT) reports. Russia was ranked third with 12% concerned about a threat it poses, the Financial Times (FT) reports.

Trust is critical in business relationships, and the US government mass spying program seems to be eroding trust and creating an anti-US business bias. Trust may also be eroding for companies associated with other governments, from the Five Eyes governments to Israel, that are cooperating with the US mass spying program. Ending the mass spying could advance commerce by helping rebuild trust with Brazilians, Germans, and other people around the world.

October 21, 2013

US Mass Spying Targets Mexico Presidents to Advance the Drug War

In contrast to the counter-terrorism narrative used to defend the US government's mass spying program, unfolding revelations suggest the program's Latin America efforts are focused on much besides terrorism. First, evidence arose that the US spying program, alone and in coordination with spying programs of other nations, is engaging in industrial espionage against Brazilian companies and the Brazil government's mines and energy ministry. Now, new revelations suggest that the US spying program targeted current and former Mexican presidents, along with other high level Mexican government officials, for surveillance to advance the war on drugs.

Jens Glüsing, Laura Poitras, Marcel Rosenbach, and Holger Stark provide the new revelations regarding Mexico today in a Der Spiegel article, including that the US National Security Agency (NSA), working with the US Central Intelligence Agency (CIA), has since at least May 2010 snooped on the email communications of high level Mexican government officials including Presidents Felipe Calderón and Enrique Peña Nieto, as well as cabinet members. The article goes on to explain that another spying operation the NSA called "whitetamale" focused on a Mexican government department conducting Mexico's drug war:

> In August 2009, according to internal documents,
> the agency gained access to the emails of various
> high-ranking officials in Mexico's Public Security
> Secretariat that combats the drug trade and human
> trafficking. This hacking operation allowed the NSA
> not only to obtain information on several drug cartels,
> but also to gain access to "diplomatic talking-points."

In the space of a single year, according to the internal documents, this operation produced 260 classified reports that allowed US politicians to conduct successful talks on political issues and to plan international investments.

It may be more than a coincidence that August 2009 is also when the Mexican government enacted legislation decriminalizing the possession of small amounts of various drugs including marijuana, cocaine, heroin, ecstasy, and methamphetamine.

In the summer of 2012, the NSA added on to its Mexico agenda targeted spying on the communications of then-presidential candidate Peña Nieto as well as people closely and remotely connected to him. The Der Spiegel article suggests a motivation for the spying arose from Peña Nieto's campaign promise to change the Mexico government's drug war policy:

> First and foremost, though, Peña Nieto promised voters he would change Mexico's strategy in the war on drugs, announcing he would withdraw the military from the fight against the drug cartels as soon as possible and invest more money in social programs instead. Yet at the same time, he assured Washington there would be no U-turn in Mexico's strategy regarding the cartels. So what were Peña Nieto's true thoughts at the time? What were his advisers telling him?

> The NSA's intelligence agents in Texas must have been asking themselves such questions when they authorized an unusual type of operation known as structural surveillance. For two weeks in the early summer of 2012, the NSA unit responsible for monitoring the Mexican government analyzed data that included the cell phone communications of Peña Nieto and "nine of his close associates," as an internal presentation from June 2012 shows. Analysts used software to connect this data into a network, shown in a graphic that resembles a swarm of bees. The software then filtered out Peña Nieto's most relevant contacts and entered

them into a databank called "DishFire." From then on, these individuals' cell phones were singled out for surveillance.

According to the internal documents, this led to the agency intercepting 85,489 text messages, some sent by Peña Nieto himself and some by his associates. This technology "might find a needle in a haystack," the analysts noted, adding that it could do so "in a repeatable and efficient way."

It would not be surprising to see evidence emerge that the US government conducts similar spying on political officials and candidates in other countries where dissatisfaction with the international war on drugs is growing. This is, after all, a war the United States government has spent over one trillion dollars and over 40 years fighting.

68

November 15, 2013

Cisco blames NSA Spying for Reduced Sales

Cisco Systems executives, whose company's stock price fell Thursday in percentage terms the most since February of 2011, are pointing to US National Security Agency (NSA) spying as a cause of the reduced sales of its products including networking equipment.

Cisco Systems Chief Executive Officer John Chambers suggested in the company's earnings conference call with analysts on Wednesday that concerns about NSA spying contributed to Cisco's decreased sales in China. Invezz expands on the spying's impact on Cisco sales with comments from Cisco's chief financial officer and figures for reduced product orders in Russia and Brazil:

Chief financial officer Frank Calderone said that the

projected revenue decline was partially due to the recent revelations about internet surveillance by the US National Security Agency, which prompted "a level of uncertainty or concern" among customers internationally. In the last quarter new orders dropped 12 percent in the developing world, with Brazil down 25 percent and Russia off 30 percent.

Russia and Brazil are two countries where US government spying may be expected to especially cause reduced sales by American companies The Russian government provided NSA whistle-blower Edward Snowden with temporary asylum despite US government objections, while Brazil Prime Minister Dilma Rouseff condemned before the United Nations General Assembly the US mass spying program in general and US spying on Brazilian companies in particular.

US government spying is hitting both personal liberty and American companies' bottom lines.

69

January 23, 2014

Judge Napolitano: Obama's NSA Proposals Maintain Totalitarian Hallmarks

Speaking Tuesday with host Steve Doocy on Fox News, Judge Andrew Napolitano, a Ron Paul Institute Advisory Board member, concludes that the mass spying program reform proposed in President Barack Obama's Friday speech maintains the program's "hallmarks of a totalitarian government." Napolitano explains:

> The president's new proposals do not change the fundamental principal that the government on a massive scale is violating the fundamental right to privacy that every American has, and the specifically guaranteed right to privacy in the Constitution. The Constitution

doesn't say all spying is illegal. It says spying on all of us is illegal. So, if the government wants to spy on a conversation you and I are having, it goes to a judge and explains to the judge why in that conversation it will probably learn of some criminal activity. But, that doesn't give the government the right to get a warrant or the judge the right to issue a warrant to spy on everybody in the state of New Jersey or Bergen County in order to capture just you and me.

Indeed, the United States government's mass spying program in many ways goes far beyond the methods of surveillance imposed by past governments inclined toward exercising total control over the people subject to those governments' power.

The Transportation Security Administration (TSA) and US Customs and Border Protection (CBP), along with police employing stop and frisk, routinely harass people with the long popular authoritarian demand, "Let me see your papers." However, much of the US government's privacy invasion activities have moved into the creation and use of massive, searchable databases of information, including regarding our private conversations and financial transactions.

The US mass spying program also snoops on and records our physical movements via cell phone location information, surveillance cameras, license plate readers, financial transaction tracking, and other means. With the click of a computer mouse, a government bureaucrat can see much more information about us than an agent of a totalitarian government of old could read on required "papers" stuffed in our pockets or collect from spies' and informants' reports.

John W. Whitehead of the Rutherford Institute reports in detail earlier this month a multitude of ways the US government harnesses the powers of modern surveillance against the American people. Whitehead applies to the surveillance system the unfortunately apt appellation "the electronic concentration camp."

A totalitarian aspiration is to move the doctrines of prison administration beyond the prison walls. In prison there is little privacy. Cell bars not only restrict prisoners' movement, they also eliminate the privacy a solid door would afforded. A prisoner's body can also be denied privacy. Strip searching prisoners and requiring public showering, urinating, and defecating can reinforce a prison doctrine that the prisoner has no self-ownership. This particular comparison may seem peculiar except that the US government has already routinely subjected people traveling through American airports to scanners producing naked photographs through their clothes and full body "pat-downs" — treatment analogous to strip searches and frisks in prison. The "electronic concentration camp," reinforced by the TSA, CBP, and other police, appears to be on the rise.

Whitehead includes in his report an important question for all Americans, "The question now is: will we take a stand and fight to remain free or will we go gently into the concentration camp?" Hopefully Obama's deceptive speech will be ineffective in lulling many Americans into choosing totalitarianism over freedom.

70

May 21, 2014

Toothless USA FREEDOM Act Losing Support

The USA FREEDOM Act (HR 3361), which is supposedly designed to thwart the US government's mass spying program, appears to be confirming Ron Paul Institute Executive Director Daniel McAdams' warning from September: "beware NSA spying and beware the PATRIOT Act and beware FISA reauthorizations. But most of all...keep your eyes on the reformers!"

The stench from the USA FREEDOM Act has grown so obvious that privacy-related interest groups are renouncing their support of the bill after the bill, which had already passed through the committee approval process, was revised Tuesday to gain the Obama administration's support. It is becoming harder by the day to have faith the legislation is even a small step toward greater respect for freedom.

Even before the revisions this week, it was easy to be suspicious of the legislation's strength to control government spying just from the fact that it passed unanimously in both the Judiciary and Intelligence Committees of the United States House of Representatives. Together, the committees have fifty-nine members.

We are familiar with House Intelligence Committee Chairman Mike Rogers (R-MI) as the fellow who joked with former National Security Agency (NSA) and Central Intelligence Agency (CIA) Director Michael Hayden about working together to kill NSA whistle-blower Edward Snowden. Rogers also claimed French people should have been "applauding and popping champagne corks" when they learned of the US government's monitoring of tens of millions of French telephone calls.

Former Judiciary Committee Chairman Rep. Jim Sensenbrenner (R-WI) who is famed for his sponsorship of the USA PATRIOT Act, is the sponsor of the eerily similarly named USA FREEDOM Act. Channeling Captain Renault's line from Casablanca that "I'm shocked, shocked to find that gambling is going on in here!" Sensenbrenner sponsored the USA FREEDOM Act after exclaiming he was shocked to discover his USA PATRIOT Act had been used to justify mass spying. Sensenbrenner remains a member of the Judiciary Committee.

Maybe a little over ten years from now Sensenbrenner will throw up his hands in shock and say that he cannot believe the government is using the USA FREEDOM Act to violate people's rights. Then he can sponsor, with Rogers' support, the USA JUSTICE Act.

Rep. Zoe Lofgren: USA FREEDOM Act Secretly 'Altered in Worrisome Ways'

On Wednesday — the day before the United States House of Representatives voted to approve the USA FREEDOM Act (HR 3361) — Rep. Zoe Lofgren (D-CA) explained on the House floor that back-room machinations changed the bill between the votes approving it in the House Judiciary and Intelligence Committees and the bill's consideration on the House floor. These shenanigans outside the routine committee process, Lofgren explains, made meaningless some restraints on US government mass spying contained in the bill. Lofgren states:

> After [the USA Freedom Act] was reported out unanimously by the House Judiciary Committee, certain key elements of this bill were changed. I think it's ironic that a bill that was intended to increase transparency was secretly changed between the committee markup and floor consideration, and it was altered in worrisome ways.

Lofgren proceeds to explain that, under the bill, mass spying may be justifiable in multiple geographic areas including areas as large as an entire state or even the southern or eastern United States, meaning the bill does not stop the mass spying from continuing throughout the entire United States.

Lofgren also notes that all nine of her amendments were ruled out of order. In fact, no amendments at all were considered during the House floor debate.

Many people, including many individuals in the American majority who oppose the mass spying program, would concur with Lofgren's final words in her speech: "We should insist that we do better than this, Mr. Speaker."

Back in 2011, House Speaker John Boehner assured us the

House would do better, saying upon assuming the speaker position:

> The people voted to end business as usual, and today we begin carrying out their instructions.
>
> …
>
> After all, this is the people's House. This is their Congress. It's about them, not us. What they want is a government that is honest, accountable and responsive to their needs. A government that respects individual liberty, honors our heritage, and bows before the public it serves.
>
> Let's start with the rules package the House will consider today. If passed, it will change how this institution operates, with an emphasis on real transparency, greater accountability, and a renewed focus on the Constitution. Our aim will be to give government back to the people. In seeking this goal, we will part with some of the rituals that have come to characterize this institution under majorities Republican and Democratic alike. We will dispense with the conventional wisdom that bigger bills are always better; that fast legislating is good legislating; that allowing additional amendments and open debate makes the legislative process 'less efficient' than our forefathers intended.
>
> These misconceptions have been the basis for the rituals of modern Washington. The American people have not been well served by them. Today, mindful of the lessons of the past, we open a new chapter.
>
> Legislators and the public will have three days to read bills before they come to a vote. Legislation will be more focused, properly scrutinized, and constitutionally sound. Committees, once bloated, will be smaller, with a renewed mission, including oversight….

That was the promise. The reality is the USA FREEDOM Act — a complex bill concerning extensive US government violations of individual rights that is rewritten behind closed doors to override the committee hearings and markup process two days before the full House votes on the bill upon completion of a House floor debate in which no amendments from House members may be considered.

72

June 6, 2014

Have You Reset the Net?

Suppose your neighborhood experienced a dramatic increase in home break-ins. What might you and your neighbors do in response?

Some residents may join together in a neighborhood watch. Many residents will review their home security precautions. Some people will put new locks on their doors. Other neighbors will build or improve fences, close their curtains more often, install security lights or an alarm system, acquire a guard dog, or keep a gun at the ready.

It has been a year since the publication of the first revelations on the United States government's mass spying program based on documents obtained by whistle-blower Edward Snowden. Yet, many people have not undertaken additional precautions in response.

A broad range of organizations launched on Thursday, under the title "Reset the Net," a campaign to encourage people to take steps to protect private communication from government break-ins. Reset the Net describes its message in a promotional video:

> The call is simple. Find some territory of the internet that you can protect from prying eyes. Seize it and hold it.

The express goal of the Reset the Net coalition sounds reasonable — much like the steps neighbors would take in response to home break-ins.

The coalition includes "good neighbor" members such as the American Civil Liberties Union that has fought the US government's mass spying program. It also includes members whose intentions should be looked at with greater concern — Google, for example.

Just like with criminals who break into homes, there is no sure way to defend yourself from the US government's snooping — especially if you are specifically targeted. But, many people taking an extra step or two of precaution may significantly reduce the mass spying's effectiveness. One place to start exploring options is the Electronic Frontier Foundation article "Ten Steps You Can Take Right Now Against Internet Surveillance."

73

May 14, 2015

Sen. Bob Corker Thinks the NSA Is Collecting Too Little of Our Private Information!

United States Sen. Bob Corker (R-TN) made news on Wednesday with his astounding comment that he is "shocked" by "how little data" the National Security Agency (NSA) is collecting via the US government's mass surveillance program and with his advocacy that the program "needs to be ramped up hugely." Considering the vast scope of the spying program, Corker's plea for yet more snooping appears to be a call for God-like omniscience. Indeed, Corker is all but calling for the US government to seek the kind of all-seeing power Jesus described God as possessing when Jesus told the disciples that God has numbered the individual hairs on a person's head and knows when a sparrow falls to the ground.

In a video address released today, Ron Paul Institute Advisory Board Member Andrew Napolitano spells out the great reach of the US government's mass surveillance program that Corker wants expanded. Napolitano, the senior judicial analyst at Fox News and a former judge, explains:

> We now know that for the past 13 years the government of the United States of America has been capturing the content of every telephone call, every text message, every email, every monthly bank statement, every utility bill, and every credit card bill of everybody in the United States of America.

Napolitano further explains in his video address that the Constitution was written "to prevent the government from being able to look at every word and every document and explore every one of our thoughts without getting a search warrant as required in the Constitution." Yet, the US government has proceeded year-after-year as if it has the authority to exercise such God-like power, pointing to the PATRIOT Act as its legislative permission slip.

Desperate to keep and expand this power, politicians like Corker are scurrying to extend the provisions of the PATRIOT Act that give legal cover for the snooping and other extraconstitutional powers before those provisions' June 1 expiration date. Once people gain God-like powers over others, they often do not choose to relinquish those powers readily. Instead, like Corker, they often seek to expand those powers ad infinitum.

74

May 28, 2015

Judge Andrew Napolitano: Mass Surveillance Will Continue Even Without PATRIOT Act Section 215

Privacy advocates looking forward to an end of the Unites States government's mass surveillance program due to the looming sunset of PATRIOT Act section 215 may do well to shelve their Champagne bottles. Judge Andrew Napolitano, in a Fox News interview on Wednesday, presented his grim assessment that the US National Security Agency (NSA) snooping would continue even absent the section 215 authority.

Napolitano, a Ron Paul Institute Advisory Board member, says in the interview that the US government is lying to the American people with the claim that the mass surveillance would be suspended upon the expiration of the PATRIOT Act provision used to justify the mass surveillance program. Instead, Napolitano explains the snooping will continue reliant on two other legal justifications. Napolitano states:

> There are two other provisions in the law that the NSA relies on which will cause it to continue to spy on Americans even if section 215 of the PATRIOT Act does expire. One of those is a section of the FISA law called section 702, and one of them is a still-existing executive order signed by President George W. Bush in the fall or 2001, which has not been tinkered with, interfered with, or rescinded.

Meanwhile, the potential of section 215 of the PATRIOT Act expiring is being used to push through the US Congress the USA FREEDOM Act that will give the mass surveillance program a new legal framework just as the old legal framework provided in the PATRIOT Act is coming under greater judicial scrutiny.

The "reform" USA FREEDOM Act (act two of PATRIOT Act sponsor Rep. Jim Sensenbrenner (R-WI)) has passed in the House and is available for consideration in the Senate. But, the failure of the new bill to end or even significantly restrict the mass spying program has become increasingly evident. If Congress does not send to President Barack Obama the USA FREEDOM Act in its current form or a simple extension of set to expire PATRIOT Act provisions soon, expect an effort to quickly push through Congress a "new and improved" USA FREEDOM Act.

There will be much bluster about an "improved" USA FREEDOM ACT — a pig with lipstick — striking the right balance to protect both liberty and security. But, as with the PATRIOT Act 14 years ago, national security state special interests will control the tinkering behind the scenes, and the American people will learn what was wrought only after the bill passes.

75

New Hampshire Library Stands Up to US Government, Reinstates Tor Relay

The board of trustees overseeing the Kilton Public Library in West Lebanon, New Hampshire, on Tuesday decided, despite pushback from the United States Department of Homeland Security, to reinstate a Tor relay the board had approved in an effort to enhance privacy on the internet. The library board drew the attention of Homeland Security when the board decided in June to make the Kilton Public Library the first library in America to install a Tor relay. After Homeland Security promptly responded by telling state and local government officials that the Tor relay may aid criminals, the board had suspended the relay.

Vocal support in the community aided the library board in its decision to reinstate the Tor relay. Nora Doyle-Burr reports in the Concord Monitor that "a full room of about 50 residents and other interested members of the public expressed their support for Lebanon's participation in the [Tor] system" at the board's Tuesday meeting.

Similarly, vocal public support buttressed local California politicians in the Bay Area and Davis in their efforts to reject armored vehicles the US government provides to local police. And vocal public support has been key for state and local governments across America moving away from participating in the war on marijuana.

While Americans may often feel there is no hope against oppressive government, occurrences such as with the Kilton Public Library this week show that determined local action can successfully counter the US government leviathan.

December 1, 2015

Despite What You May Have Heard, Mass Surveillance Continues

Many news reports are heralding that the expiration this week of Section 215 of the PATRIOT Act authority has ended the United States government's mass surveillance program. Meanwhile, in a Fox News interview, Judge Andrew Napolitano throws cold water on such claims.

Napolitano bluntly declares that the expiration of Section 215 authorization in no way prevents the US government from continuing its mass surveillance program. Napolitano explains that the National Security Agency (NSA) can continue to "gather phone calls, transcripts of phone calls, transcripts of emails, in real time" from all or nearly all Americans irrespective of the expiration of Section 215 authorization.

In addition to the President George W. Bush executive order Napolitano mentions in the interview, the US government can also turn to the supposedly anti-mass surveillance USA FREEDOM Act, signed into law in June, for support as it continues the mass surveillance program. The US FREEDOM Act, typical of "reform" in the US government, masquerades as doing one thing when in fact it does the opposite.

As Ron Paul Institute Chairman and Founder Ron Paul wrote on May 3 — about a month before the bill made it through Congress — "a look at the USA FREEDOM Act's details, as opposed to the press releases of its supporters, shows that the act leaves the government's mass surveillance powers virtually untouched."

Indeed, shortly after President Barack Obama signed the bill, former NSA Director Michael Hayden proclaimed it "cool!" that the USA FREEDOM act would allow the mass surveillance program to continue unhindered.

Throughout the corrupt legislative process through which the USA FREEDOM Act moved, levers were pulled behind the scenes to ensure that any "reform" that reached the president would not threaten the continuation of the mass surveillance program. From starting with a crummy bill sponsored by the man who had introduced the PATRIOT Act in the House years before to employing exceptional shenanigans, including rewriting the bill after it had been approved by committee and then refusing to allow any amendments during House floor consideration, every effort was taken to make the bill unthreatening to the mass surveillance program. Compounding this subterfuge, the legislation was at the same time promoted loudly in a public relations campaign as a victory against overly intrusive government.

As Napolitano, a Ron Paul Institute Advisory Board member, explained around the time the USA FREEDOM Act was signed into law, the so-called gain for liberty accomplished by the legislation amounts to some government snoopers doing their snooping remotely instead of on-site at telecommunications companies.

The USA FREEDOM Act ruse should have come as no surprise. As Paul noted in the summer of 2013 regarding a failed amendment offered on the House floor by Rep. Justin Amash (R-MI) in opposition to the mass surveillance program that whistle-blower Edward Snowden had recently exposed, the Republican and Democratic leadership in the House voted against Amash's amendment and "for the police state." In a year's time that leadership was back, with help from the Obama administration and surveillance-state businesses, to ensure the continuation of the mass surveillance program via the USA FREEDOM Act bamboozlement.

Enough with the reforms that provide cover for continuing liberty violations. Instead, American politicians should follow the advice Paul has vigorously expressed since soon after Snowden's first revelations: End the mass surveillance program and "get rid of the NSA."

Part 5: Guns

77

July 18, 2013

Adam Kokesh and the Drugs and Guns Prosecution Trap

Podcast host Adam Kokesh appears to have joined the long list of victims of the US government's drugs and guns prosecution trap. After a US Park Police raid on his Virginia residence last week, media reported Monday that Kokesh was charged with possession of a Schedule I or II drug under the federal Controlled Substances Act while in possession of a gun. After his arrest, a judge ruled that Kokesh is prohibited from owning or possessing a firearm through the end of his prosecution.

In the drugs and guns prosecution trap, when a defendant merely possesses a gun while allegedly in violation of the Controlled Substances Act, the government seeks to impose additional penalties for the gun possession. These penalties may be imposed even if the defendant did not use a gun in any violent activity or even in any activity related to drugs.

The drugs and guns prosecution trap can be used to pressure a defendant to plead guilty in return for a reduced penalty instead of exercising his right to a trial. As explained by Eric Stern, counsel to former Montana Governor Brian Schweitzer, the top US government prosecutor in Montana used gun possession charges "pervasively" as part of a strategy to intimidate

Montanans who possessed marijuana in compliance with state medical marijuana laws into pleading guilty in plea-bargains. Stern elaborates:

> And some of the government's tactics in Montana were simply over the top. Charges were piled on high and thick, basic federal items like "possession with intent to distribute" or "conspiracy to manufacture," carrying enormous penalties and designed to give the defendant little choice but to say "uncle," and plea-bargain for a lesser sentence.

> And one charge, used pervasively, was almost laughable if you know anything about Montana: "use of a firearm in furtherance of a drug crime," by which was meant that a defendant kept a shotgun in his greenhouse, or in his truck that he used to transport seed and fertilizer, or that he carried a sidearm. Montanans commonly keep guns on their person, in their vehicles, at their homes, at their ranches, and at their place of business and especially if they have valuable wares on the premises. They require no permits. But the gun charge gave prosecutors powerful leverage because it carries mandatory prison time under federal rules.

Chris Williams is one of the few Montana medical marijuana defendants who went to trial instead of taking a plea deal. Reason writer Jacob Sullum relates how Williams, a partner in Montana Cannabis, was found guilty at a trial in which he was not allowed to even mention the state's medical marijuana law. Sullum explains how the gun charges accounted for 80 years of Williams' effective life sentence:

> What explains this astonishing range of penalties, from zero prison time to nearly a century? Mandatory minimums. Specifically, prosecutors charged Williams, after he turned down a series of plea deals, with four counts of using firearms in furtherance of a drug crime, based on pistols and shotguns kept at the Helena grow operation where he worked. Fed-

eral law prescribes a five-year mandatory minimum penalty for the first such offense and 25 years for each subsequent offense. Furthermore, the sentences must be served consecutively. Hence Williams, who was convicted of all four gun charges, will get at least 80 years when he is sentenced in January, even though he was not charged with wielding the guns, let alone hurting anyone with them. In fact, having the guns around would have been perfectly legal had he not been growing marijuana.

After Williams' arrest, incarceration, and rigged trial for trying to provide people with medical marijuana in compliance with state law, Williams was offered a second chance at a plea-bargain. This time, Williams agreed to drop his appeal in return for the prosecutor dropping three of Williams' four gun charges and three of his four drug charges. As a result, the judge sentenced Williams to five years in prison for the first gun charge and 130 days of time already served for the remaining drug charge. Stern suggests that the prosecutor's willingness to offer Williams a second chance at a plea-bargain was due to Williams having become "something of a cause célèbre" with "websites devoted to freeing him." Williams explains that the primary factor behind his acceptance of the "very rare post-verdict compromise" was that the top US prosecutor in Montana "threatened to use legal maneuvering" to take away Williams' ability to appeal.

The accounts of Kokesh's housemates and colleagues in various news reports and on his podcast website relate a brutal, SWAT-style raid on their home and uncomfortable conditions in jail for Kokesh. This may be just the beginning of Kokesh's problems now, as he is facing effectively limitless prosecution resources while caught in the drugs and guns prosecution trap.

July 23, 2013

NRA vs Medical Associations: Guess Who Wants You in the Government Database?

A conflict may be emerging between the National Rifle Association (NRA) and several large national medical and mental health associations regarding the expansion of US and state government mental health databases. Medical Daily reported last week that four national medical and mental health associations have sent letters to the US Department of Health and Human Services (HHS) expressing concern about a proposed rule to increase the flow of mental health records into the FBI's National Instant Criminal Background Check System (NICS). The NICS database holds a vast amount of information about Americans — including people who have no intention of ever buying firearms — to be checked whenever anyone attempts to purchase a gun from a US licensed firearms dealer.

The American Medical Association, the American Psychiatric Association, the American Psychological Association, and the National Association of State Mental Health Program Directors are, in sending the letter, expressing direct opposition to the NRA's multi-year effort to enhance government restrictions of gun ownership and possession by creating a US government mental health database and encouraging the flow of information into that database.

Recently, the NRA lobbied the Florida legislature to pass and governor to sign legislation that increases the flow of mental health records from Florida to the NICS database. The legislation also expands the prohibition on Floridians purchasing guns or qualifying for concealed carry permits to include not just those involuntarily committed by courts to mental institutions, but also those who at one time voluntarily sought mental treatment after being threatened with involuntary commitment. Florida Governor Rick Scott signed that bill into law on June 28.

In its letter to HHS, the American Psychiatric Association opposes such expansions of gun purchase restrictions to people who voluntarily seek mental health care, stating:

> We cannot support attempts by states to broaden mental health disqualifications (e.g., by including voluntary hospitalizations). An individual's confidence in the privacy he or she will be afforded when seeking medical care, particularly mental health care, often singularly determines whether or not that individual will agree to receive health care treatment.

Additionally, those who agree to mental health care under the threat of involuntary commitment may not even believe they have a mental condition. They may agree simply to avoid the cost, time, and turmoil of opposing an involuntary commitment process. Or, they may prefer having some control over where and how their mental health care is conducted.

Mistaken identity is another serious problem with this expansion of federal government mental health databases. For example, under New York's state mental health database program, two unfortunate New Yorkers had their guns confiscated. Neither of them met the mental health prerequisites for confiscation, but they did share the same name and approximate age. Buffalo News reporter Lou Michel explains:

> When state police received only a name and approximate age, [New York State Police Superintendent Joseph] D'Amico said, his staff checked handgun permits statewide and found two men of about the same age and same name of David Lewis. The state police then contacted the Erie County clerk and another county clerk elsewhere in the state where those people lived.
>
> The outcome was not good for either "David Lewis." Both had their licenses suspended and guns temporarily removed, though it was eventually determined neither had mental health issues.

With the New York State Police receiving hundreds of reports a day for inclusion in the state's mental health database, there will be plenty of opportunities for similar mistakes.

It is reassuring to privacy advocates that large national medical and mental health associations are expressing concern about the US mental health database. But stopping or reversing the growth of the US database, along with similar state databases, will require taking on the multi-year NRA effort to expand them. It will also go against the inclination governments have shown to know everything about our private lives, whether that be our phone and internet conversations, where we drive, or our mental health histories.

79

September 22, 2014

Andrew Napolitano: US Using Gun Transfer Forms to Violate Free Speech and Privacy

Ron Paul Institute Advisory Board Member Andrew Napolitano, speaking with Elisabeth Hasselbeck on Fox News regarding race and ethnicity questions people are required to answer to purchase a gun from a US government-licensed firearms dealer, explained that mandating answering questions on any form whatsoever violates speech and privacy rights. In short, Napolitano concludes, "It's none of the government's business who has guns."

Napolitano, a former New Jersey state judge, explains that the right to keep and bear arms "is an extension of the natural right to defend yourself."

In addition to violating privacy rights and the gun rights recognized in the Second Amendment, Napolitano details how the required completion of the Bureau of Alcohol, Tobacco, Firearms and Explosives (ATF) form 4473 violates the right of speech recognized in the First Amendment. Napolitano says:

This is called forced speech. The First Amendment

says Congress can't infringe speech. The courts have interpreted that to mean Congress can't also compel you to speak. So, the government can't say, "Hey, Hasselbeck, what's your race, what's your ethnicity, and why do you want that gun?" The government doesn't have the lawful, moral authority to do that. But, yet, that is what it is trying to do with these forms.

While not addressed by Napolitano explicitly in the Fox News interview, the mandated completion of ATF form 4473 also violates the Fifth Amendment-recognized right against self-incrimination by making individuals provide information about themselves to the US government in order to complete a purchase.

Additionally, the required answering of the form's questions is a violation of the Tenth Amendment given that the Constitution nowhere delegates to the US government the power to impose the mandate.

Because of the ATF form 4473 mandate, the US government respects some constitutional rights less for a person who tries to buy a gun from a US government-licensed firearms dealer than for a person who the government alleges committed a crime. The alleged criminal can assert and often have respected through the entire criminal investigation and prosecution process the right to remain silent.

Rep. Diane Black (R-TN) introduced in the US House of Representatives on Thursday the FIREARM Act that seeks to prevent the US government from requiring "any person to disclose the race or ethnicity of the person in connection with the transfer of a firearm to the person."

Black's legislation only eliminates the mandate to answer the race and ethnicity questions. Therefore, even should the bill become law, people will still be required to answer many other questions in order to buy a gun from a US government-licensed firearms dealer. That means gun buyers will be required to submit to the violation of their rights protected under the First, Second, Fifth, and Tenth Amendments. In fact, a gun buyer would still be subject to 24 personal questions, plus a request for the individual's social security number that the form says is "optional" but "will help prevent misidentification." Among the 24 questions, buyers are required to answer whether they use illegal drugs, have been committed to a mental institution, have been convicted of a domestic violence misdemeanor, or have been dishonorably discharged from the US military.

On top of purchasers' mandated answers, sellers would, even with Black's legislation becoming law, still be required to provide on the form additional information about each buyer and the particular guns purchased. This information includes a description of identification documents provided as well as a detailed inventory, including even serial numbers, of all firearms purchased.

The collection of ATF form 4473 information in violation of rights protected under at least four amendments of the Bill of Rights is particularly disturbing in the age of US government mass spying. People who fill out the form should also be concerned about the National Rifle Association (NRA)-supported effort to expand both government databases of people's private information and legal prohibitions on who may purchase and own guns.

For the time being, people can still under the "gun show loophole" buy guns, at least in some parts of the US, from individuals not licensed by the US government as firearms dealers and thus without completing ATF form 4473. That, though, pretty much means not buying from the local gun store that is required to be licensed as a precondition of selling guns. It sure is disturbing that you need to use a "loophole" to protect yourself from the US government violating the rights the Constitution requires the government to respect.

October 23, 2014

35,000 People and Counting on New York's New 'No Guns List'

The US government has demonstrated with its No Fly and Selectee Lists, in operation for over a decade, how to deny respect for tens of thousands of individuals' travel and privacy rights without even the slightest nod to due process protections. Over the last 19 months, the New York government has followed a similar course, using a new "No Guns List" to deny respect for tens of thousands of individuals' right to keep and bear arms.

New York Times writer Anemona Hartocollis explains in a Sunday Times article that New York state's 2013 gun control law the Secure Ammunition and Firearms Enforcement (SAFE) Act is facilitating the prohibition of gun ownership and possession for many New Yorkers by compelling physicians, psychologists, registered nurses, and licensed clinical social workers to report to the government the identities of any patients they think are "likely to engage in conduct that would result in serious harm to self or others."

Hartocollis notes that the vast majority of people thus reported, due to the idiosyncratic determination of a medical worker, are then put on the state's new No Guns List. In just the 19 months since the implementation of this SAFE Act provision, nearly 35,000 individuals have thereby been added to the list.

The only thing standing in the way of someone reported on being placed on a growing list of people barred for mental health reasons from owning or possessing a gun is a county bureaucrat who can review the report before a name is sent on to the state government.

But, as explained in the Times article, the county government review is often cursory or nonexistent:

New York's law gives county officials the responsibility

of reviewing the reports from mental health workers, ostensibly providing an added layer of oversight. But several said in interviews that they had little capacity to independently confirm whether the finding that a patient was dangerous was justified.

The way the law has played out, local officials said, frontline mental health workers feel compelled to routinely report mentally ill patients brought to an emergency room by the police or ambulances. County health officials are then supposed to vet each case before it is sent to Albany. But so many names are funneled to county health authorities through the system — about 500 per week statewide — that they have become, in effect, clerical workers, rubber-stamping the decisions, they said. From when the reporting requirement took effect on March 16, 2013 until Oct. 3, 41,427 reports have been made on people who have been flagged as potentially dangerous. Among these, 40,678 — all but a few hundred cases — were passed to Albany by county officials, according to the data obtained by The Times.

As of Saturday, the state updated the database to 42,900 reports, and said that roughly 34,500 of those were unique individuals. The rest of the names were duplicates because people had been reported more than once.

Kenneth M. Glatt, commissioner of mental hygiene for Dutchess County, said that at first, he had carefully scrutinized every name sent to him through the Safe Act. But then he realized that he was just "a middleman," and that it was unlikely he would ever meet or examine any of the patients. So he began simply checking off the online boxes, sometimes without even reviewing the narrative about a patient.

"Every so often I read one just to be sure," Dr. Glatt, a psychologist, said. "I am not going to second guess. I don't see the patient. I don't know the patient." He said it would be more efficient — and more honest — for therapists to report names directly to the Division of Criminal Justice Services, which checks them against gun permit applications.

Not even a conscientious and thorough review by a team of well-qualified government workers would be a sufficient protection for someone faced with the deprivation of his property and means of defense. Where in the process is a trial or even any of the due process protections expected for an American criminal defendant? Nowhere.

The SAFE Act's reporting on patients provision, codified in New York Mental Hygiene Law Section 9.46, says that the state will use the reports it receives from medical workers to help determine "whether a [firearms] license issued pursuant to section 400.00 of the penal law should be suspended or revoked, or for determining whether a person is ineligible for a license issued pursuant to section 400.00 of the penal law, or is no longer permitted under state or federal law to possess a firearm."

This suggests some bureaucrats in Albany can use the reported information to decide on their own, and based on whatever criteria they find relevant, whether reported individuals may keep and bear arms. But the reality seems to be that the Albany bureaucrats are handling their part of the process the same way so many of their county counterparts are. It is made clear in the mental health frequently asked questions section of the governor office's web pages dedicated to the SAFE Act that restrictions on gun ownership and possession are automatically imposed upon the reporting of an individual to the state level:

> **Q:** What information will a local [director of community services] report to [the New York State Division of Criminal Justice Services], and what can DCJS do with such information?
>
> **A:** A local DCS may only disclose a patient's name and other non-clinical identifying information (e.g., date of birth, race, sex, SSN, address) to DCJS, and that

information can be used by DJCS to determine if the patient has a firearms license.

If the patient has a firearms license, State Police will report that information to the local firearms licensing official, who must either suspend or revoke the license. The information may also be used in connection with a determination of firearms license eligibility should the subject of the report apply for a firearms license in the subsequent five years.

In the implementation of the mental health law provision of the SAFE Act we see the liberty-suppressing potential of a mandated "if you see something, say something" informant program combined with a government database and a routine bureaucratic process.

Whether or not you live in New York, own a gun, or have been subjected to a mental health evaluation, the development and use of New York's new No Guns Database should be of concern. Weeks, months, or years from now a new government database may be put into action — with your name in it.

The experience in New York is in line with prior Ron Paul Institute for Peace and Prosperity reports concerning the movement on the state and US government level to expand the size and use of government mental health databases in the name of gun control.

81

April 22, 2015

VA Sending Veterans' Mental Health Information to the FBI to Aid Gun Restrictions

A February 2012 memorandum of understanding between the United States Department of Veterans Affairs (VA) and the Federal Bureau of Investigation (FBI) lays out a process pursuant to which the VA has been regularly sending to the FBI mental health information about VA patients. So reports Patrick Howley at the Daily Caller on Tuesday. The mental health information transferred is intended to aid the FBI in adding individuals to the National Instant Criminal Background Check System (NICS) list of individuals restricted from owning or possessing guns.

The Daily Caller article quotes an astonishingly cavalier statement the VA provided in response to the article's disclosure:

> "The Department of Veterans Affairs' policy to inform veterans of their rights regarding the Brady Act has not changed," VA told TheDC in a statement. "As has been policy for multiple administrations, VA acts in accordance with federal law and works with the Department of Justice to properly maintain the NICS database. VA notifies any veteran who may be deemed by VA to be mentally incapable of managing his or her own funds of the opportunity to contest this determination and also to seek relief from the reporting requirements under the Brady Act, as required by law."

The VA's stated justification for its actions leads to many discomforting questions.

What of the long-respected American legal protection of doctor-patient confidentiality? Is it, and all other privacy protections, just a phantom of the past in this age of US government mass surveillance?

How can the VA claim that its actions are justified because it informs patients of the privacy-violating, rights-restricting policy it uses against patients? These veterans, many of whom are seeking help necessitated by their work in the military, often have the only other option of seeking outside help on their own dime — something the government told them they would not have to do. Patients may logically choose to waive confidentiality to some degree in some instances, but this seems far from a fair waiver situation. It looks more like duress.

Where is the due process? You do not meet due process by summarily depriving someone of the ability to exercise his rights without even a court adjudication and then "generously" allowing him to go through a long, confusing, and expensive process of attempting to prove the deprivation was not justified. That turns due process on its head. Examples of VA determinations of mental health in the Daily Caller article suggest that in some cases the determinations go far beyond lacking due process and descend into the realm of total nonsense.

Where is the recognition that the rights at issue here are explicitly protected in the Second Amendment of the United States Constitution? It seems the VA values a vague reference to "policy for multiple administrations" above the Constitution.

The VA's actions, like other government actions discussed in several Ron Paul Institute reports, are part of the ongoing expansion of the scope of mental health databases and of the databases' use by the US and state governments to prevent people from exercising gun rights.

82

April 24, 2015

Kansas One-Ups Texas by Adopting Concealed Carry without Classes, Fees, or a Surveillance Database

Many people perceive Texas as a bastion of rugged individualism and minimal government. Kansas not so much so. This month both states' governments are moving toward implementing laws removing some restrictions on people carrying handguns. Yet only Kansas is doing so without requiring an individual to take a course, pay a fee, and put his personal information into a government database — perfect for facilitating surveillance — before being able to legally carry a handgun.

On April 2, Kansas Governor Sam Brownback signed into law SB 45. The bill legalizes the carrying of concealed handguns by many people in Kansas without the requirement that they first pay a fee, take a class, obtain a permit, or provide personal information for inclusion in a government database.

Brownback is quoted in the Kansas City Star the day he approved the legislation:

> Asked why he did not think training should be required if it is valuable, Brownback said carrying a gun is a constitutional right.

> "We're saying that if you want to do that in this state, then you don't have to get the permission slip from the government," Brownback said. "It is a constitutional right, and we're removing a barrier to that right."

The Kansas state government had already recognized a legal right to open carry a gun without a government permission slip.

Alongside the "constitutional carry," Kansas will also continue to maintain the preexisting concealed carry system with required permits, fees, courses, and database submissions. People may choose to go through this permitting process so they can obtain recognition of their right to carry a gun in other states under reciprocity.

Over in Austin, Texas, the state House of Representatives passed HB 910 on April 20 that would allow concealed carry permit holders to also choose to legally open carry a modern handgun. The House bill is similar to a bill (SB 17) the state Senate approved on March 17.

Current Texas law allows modern handguns to be carried only by people with Texas concealed carry licenses and only if the handguns are concealed.

Texas Governor Greg Abbott pledged in his February State of the State speech to sign into law an open carry bill, and he is expected to approve this year an open carry bill after both the Texas House and Senate pass identical legislation. But, with both bills that have passed so far including permit, fee, training, and database inclusion requirements, it is all but certain that the final bill that becomes law will include these requirements as well.

In Texas, a government permission slip, along with associated fee, course, and database submission requirements (including the submission of fingerprints), appears set to be a prerequisite for legally exercising the right to carry a modern handgun either concealed or openly. The only other Texas carry options are to openly carry a long gun or an antiquated black powder gun — options many individuals often find impractical.

The saying goes that everything is bigger in Texas. Well, the Texas governor certainly has some big talk about liberty. In his February State of the State speech Abbott boasted:

> Let me briefly follow up on a word I mentioned a moment ago – liberty. In a single word, it encapsulates what this country stands for, what Texas symbolizes. I will expand liberty in Texas by signing a law that makes Texas the 45th state to allow Open Carry.

But, on this issue, Abbot should set aside his boasting for a moment and pay attention to how Brownback and the Kansas legislature have one-upped their Texas counterparts.

83

July 20, 2015

On Social Security? Obama Wants Your Gun!

In a move that Alan Zarembo of the Los Angeles Times reports could result in the US government barring millions of Americans from owning guns, President Barack Obama's administration has been quietly planning to have the Social Security Administration report the private information of Social Security recipients to the National Instant Criminal Background Check System (NICS).

Among the millions of people who may, as a result, be deprived of the ability to legally possess guns are, Zarembo notes, about 1.5 million Social Security recipients who "have their finances handled by others for a variety of reasons" and about 2.7 million people who receive Social Security disability payments due to mental health problems.

The Obama administration's planned Social Security program is similar to an ongoing Department of Veterans Affairs (VA) program for reporting private mental health and other information to the Federal Bureau of Investigation (FBI) for inclusion in NICS. My April 22 Ron Paul Institute article "VA Sending Veterans' Mental Health Information to the FBI to Aid Gun Restrictions" provides details and analysis regarding the VA program. The RPI article also puts the VA program in the context of the "ongoing expansion of the scope of mental health databases and of the databases' use by the US and state governments to prevent people from exercising gun rights."

As with the VA program, the planned Social Security program baselessly equates a person's inability or disinclination to handle some or all of his financial activities or decisions with the person posing a danger to others. Zarembo writes:

> Though such a ban would keep at least some people who pose a danger to themselves or others from owning guns, the strategy undoubtedly would also include numerous people who may just have a bad memory or difficulty balancing a checkbook, the critics argue.
>
> "Someone can be incapable of managing their funds but not be dangerous, violent or unsafe," said Dr. Marc Rosen, a Yale psychiatrist who has studied how veterans with mental health problems manage their money. "They are very different determinations."

While National Rifle Association (NRA) chief lobbyist Chris W. Cox's quote in the Zarembo article suggests the NRA opposes the planned Social Security program, there is reason for skepticism. The NRA has worked over the years to create government mental health databases, to encourage the addition of more information in those databases, and to promote using such databases to restrict gun ownership.

December 6, 2015

'No Gun for You!': Obama's 'Soup Nazi' Gun Control Proposal

The Soup Nazi character in the Seinfeld television show sells, at his take-out restaurant, soup that some people consider the best in New York City. But, there is a catch. Customers placing their orders at the restaurant's counter are in fear that one mistake in phrasing or some other minor misstep will draw the ire of the Soup Nazi along with his decree "No soup for you!"

In a CBS television interview the day of the killings in San Bernardino, California, President Barack Obama effectively proposed giving an unknown number of nameless bureaucrats arbitrary "Soup Nazi" power to decide which individuals in America may or may not possess or obtain guns. If Obama's proposal becomes law, one bureaucrat, based on the flimsiest of reason or an outright mistake, could summarily decree an individual barred from gun ownership. "No gun for you!"

Here is what Obama, in his own words, recommends in the Wednesday interview:

> And for those who are concerned about terrorism, some may be aware of the fact that we have a no-fly list where people can't get on planes, but those same people who we don't allow to fly could go into a store right now in the United States and buy a firearm and there's nothing that we can do to stop them. That's a law that needs to be changed.

The next day, a vote was held in the US Senate regarding an amendment offered by Sen. Dianne Feinstein (D-CA) that would, in line with Obama's recommendation, allow the US government to decree that individuals with some supposed connection to a terrorism threat are barred from accessing guns. By a 54 to 45 vote, senators voted not to move forward with the amendment.

Obama's proposal may seem reasonable to many people. But, the apparent reasonableness arises from the assumption that the No Fly List is composed of people who have been objectively determined to be terrorists through an exhaustive, fastidious, and transparent process that is consistent with US constitutional principles.

That assumption could hardly be further from the truth. As I examined in my article "The Abominable No Fly List" in October of last year, the operation of the No Fly List is both arbitrary and an absolute menace to liberty.

That article provides an introduction to the Kafkaesque horror of the No Fly List. Here are a few of the major points. People's names are put on the No Fly List through an entirely secret process that allows a person to be included and retained indefinitely on the list without any evidence whatsoever that the person has any connection to terrorism. Indeed, a person can even be included on the list via clerical error. In its own internal review, the US government even determined in 2007 that tens of thousands of names were improperly included on the No Fly List. Further, the list is operated without even the slightest regard for the due process rights of the people put on the list. The government does not even tell people they have been put on the list. Instead, a person who just wants to travel from point A to point B is told "No flight for you!" — likely after a long interrogation — and turned away without further explanation. Want to find out if you are on the No Fly List and to try to regain the US government's respect for your right to fly? Here is what you do: Hire some lawyers; sue the US government; proceed through a long, expensive, and arduous court case (maybe held largely in secret to protect "state secrets"); and cross your fingers.

New York state's 2013 Secure Ammunition and Firearms Enforcement (SAFE) Act provides a preview for what Obama's proposal may look like if implemented. Under the state law, tens of thousands of individuals have been put on a "No Guns List" resulting in the disavowal of their right to keep and bear arms. The purported purpose is to keep guns out of the hands of people with mental problems, not terrorists. But, the result is large-ly the same — the arbitrary restriction of the liberty of peo-ple based on bureaucrats' whims and rote paperwork moving. County government officials rubber-stamp the reports received from health care workers asserting people's mental problems. In turn, state employees routinely dump the reported individuals into the state's No Guns List.

Meanwhile, the United States Department of Veterans Administration (VA) has been operating a program similar to the New York "No Guns List." The VA reports veterans' mental health information that the FBI then uses to add people to the gun-possession-barring National Instant Criminal Background Check System (NICS) list. True to the No Fly List model, this is all done without the slightest respect being given to the veterans' rights, including the right to due process.

Underlying both the ongoing mental health and the proposed terrorism-based prohibitions on the exercise of gun rights is the notion that it is legitimate for the government to outlaw the exercise of individual rights absolutely, indefinitely, and without a due process and innocent-until-proven-guilty-respecting fair adjudication of the particular facts related to the individual affected. This can only be considered justice in a perverted sense of, say, precrime justice, Star Chamber justice, or street justice. It is not the kind of justice contemplated in the Bill of Rights of the US Constitution.

You may feel slighted if the Soup Nazi shouts out at you with disdain "No soup for you!" But, it's New York City after all; you can pick up a sandwich or a pizza slice a few doors over, and a good enough soup is available at the diner around the corner. In contrast, when the US government says "No gun for you!" you are left with only bad options — accept the deprivation of your ability to possess guns or break the law and risk suffering the legal consequences, including prison time, should you be caught.

85

Don't Believe the Hype About Gun Shootings in the US

Since the San Bernardino killings last week, many statements of politicians and stories in the media are painting a picture of "gun violence" in America that, on a closer look, appears to be far from reality.

These are some of the messages we hear in constant rotation: Be afraid of your neighbor who has a few guns and some boxes of ammunition; he must be planning a violent attack. Panic about the mass murders epidemic. Dread the explosion of violent crimes of recent years.

The barrage is deafening. But, should it be believed?

It is true people use guns to kill other people, including in mass murders. But, it is also important to not fall for exaggerated claims related to guns and mass murder.

Below are a few observations on guns and mass murder that should be considered when evaluating the fear-building messages that seem to be favored by many individuals in politics and the media:

- The Nation writer Jon Wiener reports in a Friday article that the "arsenal" of guns and ammunition Syed Farook and Tashfeen Malik owned is within the norm for millions of Americans. Contrary to what many stories in the media suggest, the fact that people possess such guns and ammunition in no way means they are planning to engage in a mass killing or terrorist act.

- Mark Follman, the national affairs editor at Mother Jones, writes in a Thursday New York Times op-ed that so far this year there have been four mass shootings, not the 355 claimed in the Washington Post or similar numbers asserted elsewhere in the media. The inflated numbers many media report, Follman explains, are created by broadening the definition of mass shooting far beyond the historical categorization focused on the indiscriminate-killing-motivated murder of four or more people in a public venue that Follman and his Mother Jones colleagues employ.

- John R. Lott, Jr., in his Fox News column on Thursday tallies the public shootings of four or more people — excluding those "that might be better classified as struggles over sovereignty" — in the United States and Europe. He concludes that, during the period from 2009 through the middle of June of this year, the US ranks, after adjustment for the respective countries' population sizes, eighth for the mass public shooting death rate and ninth for the frequency of attacks.

- Heritage Foundation Policy Analyst Jason Snead relays in a November 12 commentary Federal Bureau of Investigation (FBI) statistics indicating a 37 percent drop in violent crimes and 39 percent drop in murders over the twenty years from 1994 to 2013. Snead further relays Department of Justice numbers indicating that over the years spanning from 1993 to 2011 there was a 39 percent reduction in firearm-related homicides.

- Radley Balko notes in a July of 2014 Washington Post article that, in 2013, "47.3 percent of those convicted for federal gun crimes were black — a racial disparity larger than any other class of federal crimes, including drug crimes." Balko proceeds to mention a United States Sentencing Commission finding that black people are more likely than white people to be subjected to US gun crime mandatory minimum sentences and weapon possession "enhancement" penalties. This may come as a surprise to many individuals who are pushing for new gun laws and stricter enforcement of existing gun laws. Ominously, criminal justice reform legislation with powerful bipartisan backing in the

US Congress proposes increasing maximum criminal penalties related to guns.

Be cautious of tales spread in times of heightened fear. These tales are often spun for the purpose of converting fear into support for expansions of government powers that the communicators have long supported but could not implement in calmer times. Though it may be difficult when fear is burning all around you, give a try to stepping back, taking a breath, asking questions, and looking for alternative viewpoints. You just may find that the people promoting the fear are the ones who pose the greatest danger.

Part 6: Government Chicanery

86

James Comey Won't Improve the FBI

Expect business as usual at the Federal Bureau of Investigation (FBI) after Monday's Senate confirmation of James B. Comey, Jr. to be the Bureau's new director. Comey had previously served as George W. Bush's Deputy Attorney General. Every indication is that Comey will lead the FBI in the same trajectory it has traveled under Director Robert S. Mueller's leadership since September 2001 — a trajectory the American Civil Liberties Union (ACLU) outlines as dangerous to liberty in the succinct report "The Ten Most Disturbing Things You Should Know About the FBI Since 9/11."

Mueller, a Bush appointee, so impressed Obama that Obama extended Mueller's term an extra two years, making Mueller the second longest serving FBI director after J. Edgar Hoover. In support of the extended term, Obama praised Mueller in May 2011, stating:

> In his ten years at the FBI, Bob Mueller has set the gold standard for leading the Bureau. Given the ongoing threats facing the United States, as well as the leadership transitions at other agencies like the Defense Department and Central Intelligence Agency, I believe continuity and stability at the FBI is critical

at this time. Bob transformed the FBI after September 11, 2001 into a pre-eminent counterterrorism agency, he has shown extraordinary leadership and effectiveness at protecting our country every day since. He has impeccable law enforcement and national security credentials, a relentless commitment to the rule of law, unquestionable integrity and independence, and a steady hand that has guided the Bureau as it confronts our most serious threats. I am grateful for his leadership, and ask Democrats and Republicans in Congress to join together in extending that leadership for the sake of our nation's safety and security.

At the June 21 White House announcement of Comey's nomination, Obama and Comey effusively praised outgoing FBI Director Mueller's job performance and promised Comey would carry on Mueller's work. Mueller, also at the announcement, praised Comey and endorsed Comey's selection for FBI director. Obama stated:

> And, Bob, I can't tell you how personally grateful I am to you and to Ann for your service. I know that everyone here joins me in saying that you will be remembered as one of the finest directors in the history of the FBI, and one of the most admired public servants of our time. And I have to say just personally not only has it been a pleasure to work with Bob, but I know very few people in public life who have shown more integrity more consistently under more pressure than Bob Mueller. (Applause.)

> I think Bob will agree with me when I say that we have the perfect person to carry on this work in Jim Comey — a man who stands very tall for justice and the rule of law.

To make it clear that Mueller agreed with Obama's selection of Comey, Mueller commented:

> And, finally, I want to commend the President for the choice of Jim Comey as the next Director of the FBI.

I have had the opportunity to work with Jim for a number of years in the Department of Justice, and I have found him to be a man of honesty, dedication and integrity. His experience, his judgment, and his strong sense of duty will benefit not only the Bureau, but the country as a whole.

Comey also praised Mueller before promising Obama and Mueller that he would "honor and protect" Mueller's legacy at the FBI:

I must be out of my mind to be following Bob Mueller. (Laughter.) I don't know whether I can fill those shoes. But I know that however I do, I will be standing truly on the shoulders of a giant, someone who has made a remarkable difference in the life of this country. I can promise you, Mr. President and Mr. Director, that I will do my very best to honor and protect that legacy.

The FBI appears to be one more place where Obama's promise of "Hope and Change" has been replaced with "More of the Same."

87

October 24, 2013

House Republicans' Hollow 'Local Control of Education' Rhetoric

By guiding HR 2083, the Protecting Students from Sexual and Violent Predators Act, to the Floor Tuesday for passage by a voice vote, the House Republican leadership demonstrated the hollowness of the praise it heaped on local control of education when HR 5, the Student Success Act, passed in the House three months earlier.

The nice sounding but ominous in consequences Protecting Students from Sexual and Violent Predators Act presents serious federalism, constitutional, and individual liberty concerns. The legislation standardizes nationwide — and expands — school-related background check policies that states have implemented. In particular, HR 2083 mandates fingerprinting, as well as state and FBI criminal background checking, of millions of school and local or state educational agency employees. The requirements also apply to all persons who, because they work for private entities or public agencies with a school contract or agreement, have "unsupervised access" to students.

HR 2083 provides no opt-out provision for states, school districts, or any current or potential employees. Refusal to submit to any of the fingerprinting or background checks will result in being fired or refused employment. The legislation also disqualifies people who have been convicted for any of a list of crimes from the opportunity to work in any of the covered jobs despite the fact that they have served their entire court imposed punishments. This effectively creates an *ex post facto* punishment prohibited under the US Constitution.

Funneling all these fingerprints and background checks to the US government also helps build the databases supporting the US government's mass spying program.

HR 2083 passed by voice vote after a chorus of praise from several representatives, and some moderated concern expressed by Rep. Keith Ellison (D-MN) in the House floor debate. Indeed, the Hill writer Pete Kasperowics identified HR 2083 as part of a package of legislation "just about everyone agrees on" that House Republican leadership had scheduled for consideration after "weeks of bitter partisan fighting about spending and the debt ceiling."

As with the PATRIOT Act and other legislation designed to expand police powers in the US and suppress local political control, HR 2083 is cleverly named to put any legislator who opposes it immediately on the defensive. "Why don't you want to protect the children from murderers and sexual predators?" media and constituents would ask any legislator who dares to oppose the bill.

On July 19, when HR 5, the Student Success Act, passed in

the House, many Republicans were singing the praise of local control of schools. Yet the Republican leadership, with the consent of the Democrat leadership, this week put HR 2083, with its one-size-fits-all US government mandates, on the House floor for passage by voice vote.

To understand the apparent shift in the Republican House leadership's education policy goals over the last three months, it is helpful to consider what Republicans responsible for moving education legislation in the House said when HR 5 passed on July 19.

Here is what Speaker of the House John Boehner (R-OH) said in a press release regarding the Student Success Act the day that legislation passed in the House:

> [The Student Success Act] protects local schools
> from new requirements and red tape, and lets school
> districts identify, recruit, and keep the best teachers
> possible.

Similarly, the Republican House leadership's number two, Majority Leader Eric Cantor (R-VA), issued a statement that day praising the Student Success Act for removing "mandates on our local schools."

Boehner and Cantor were outdone by their fellow Republican House members Reps. John Kline (R-MN) and Todd Rokita (R-IN), chairmen respectively of the Education and the Workforce Committee and that committee's Subcommittee on Early Childhood, Elementary, and Secondary Education. Both HR 2083 and HR 5 proceeded to the House floor via the committee. Kline (the sponsor of HR 5) and Rokita said, also on July 19, the following in their press release trumpeting the passage of the Student Success Act:

> "For the first time in more than a decade, the House
> has approved legislation to revamp K-12 education
> law. This is a monumental step forward in the fight
> to improve the nation's education system and ensure
> a brighter future for our children," Chairman Kline
> said. "The Student Success Act will tear down barriers

to progress and grant states and districts the freedom and flexibility they need to think bigger, innovate, and take whatever steps are necessary to raise the bar in our schools."

"No Washington bureaucrat cares more about a child than a parent does. And no one in Washington knows what is better for an Indiana school than Indiana families do. That is why the Student Success Act puts an end to the administration's National School Board by putting state and local school districts back in charge of their own schools," said Rep. Rokita. "Many Hoosiers will also be pleased to know that the Student Success Act prohibits the Secretary of Education from coercing states into adopting Common Core, again returning accountability and standards to state and local school districts, where it belongs."

This praise for local control in education is in sharp contrast to the talking points repeated by Republican and Democrat representatives on the House floor on Tuesday — they said HR 2083 is needed to make employee hiring and retention decisions uniform nationwide. Yet, Subcommittee Chairman Rokita made the motion to suspend the rules that began debate on HR 2083. Then, in his House floor speech during the debate, Rokita praised HR 2083 for moving education decisions from local school districts and private employers to the US government — the exact opposite of what he praised HR 5 for doing:

Despite the fact that States have varying policies intended to protect children from sexual predators in schools, the GAO determined the policies were largely inconsistent and insufficient. According to the report, States don't consistently perform preemployment background checks, and when they do conduct these checks, they are not always fingerprinted or connected to the national criminal database.

There is widespread agreement on both sides of this aisle that more must be done to protect students. We

have worked with our colleagues to advance legislation that will ensure that every school employee--from
the cafeteria workers, Mr. Speaker, to the administrators, to the janitors, to the teachers, principals,
and librarians--that everyone is subject to a complete
background check that includes the FBI fingerprint
identification system and the National Sex Offender
Registry.

Why did Rokita and other Republicans responsible for
moving education legislation through the House reverse their
position on local control of education between July 19 and October 22? The answer is that they actually did not reverse their
position, despite the fact that anyone looking at their comments
logically would conclude that they had. The Republican leaders'
position on local control has remained the same: cloudy and
inconsistent. They just change their rhetoric to defend the legislation they are pushing at the moment.

Rokita let the truth spill out in his House floor speech in
favor of HR 2083, when he noted that a key requirement of the
local control eliminating HR 2083 was also contained in HR 5
that he had heralded as enhancing local control:

H.R. 2083 will require States that receive funds under
the Elementary and Secondary Education Act to have
policies and practices in place that ensure each school
employee is subject to a complete national criminal
background check. Mr. Speaker, a similar provision
was offered by two of my colleagues and good friends,
both from Pennsylvania, Mr. Fitzpatrick and Mr. Mee-
han. That provision was included in the House-passed
Student Success Act from last month.

The truth is HR 5 never was a bill to ensure local control
over education. That was just a talking point for Republicans to
use when boasting about the legislation that passed the House
without any Democrat "yes" votes. HR 5 was a large, ideolog-
ically-muddled bill containing a mish-mash of changes in US
government education policy, many driven by special interests

in search of easy financial gain.

Among its provisions limiting local control of education, HR 5 consolidated US government power over schools to benefit the military-industrial complex. As explained in a memorandum produced by the Republican majority of Kline's House Education and the Workforce Committee for the HR 5 floor debate, "The [Student Success Act] improves the military recruiting provisions in current law by ensuring recruiters have the same access to high schools as colleges and universities."

HR 5 has been referred to the US Senate where it can be ignored. Now the House leadership, Republican and Democrat, have stepped away from partisan theatrics to advance their shared education agenda, exemplified by HR 2083, that can gain passage in the Senate and acceptance from President Barack Obama. That agenda is not concerned with rhetorical flourishes about local control. Instead, it is focused on goals including strengthening and expanding the police, surveillance, and military interventionist activities of the US government.

88

April 30, 2014

Following Bundy Ranch Raid, Congress Moves to Transfer Tortoise Habitat to US Military

With the US House of Representatives back in session this week after the standoff between the US Bureau of Land Management (BLM) on one side and the Bundy family and protestors on the other, the House Committee on Natural Resources held a hearing regarding the BLM.

What did the hearing concern? Investigating the use of force by US government agents who raided the Bundy ranch, destroyed ranch property, and seized and killed ranch cattle? Reviewing the decades-long policy of arming more and more US government employees? Devising a plan to divest the US government of ownership of vast amounts of land, especially in western states?

No, no, and no!

The committee instead considered legislation — the Naval Air Weapons Station China Lake Security Enhancement Act (HR 4458) — that Rep. Kevin McCarthy (R-CA) said in his testimony before the committee would make permanent the transfer of over one million acres of BLM land to the Department of Defense!

Like the Bundy ranch land, the land subject to permanent transfer in McCarthy's legislation is home to the desert tortoise. This creature, that the BLM website says the bureau is "taking actions to conserve and recover," gained recognition in the Bundy ranch standoff.

McCarthy, the House majority whip, suggests in his testimony the tortoises will be safe in the expanded military installation. Maybe that will be the case, though the Department of Defense does not have the best record on protecting the environment.

The important question many people want answered is this: When will congressional committees hold hearings to investigate, and when will Congress pass legislation to remedy, the US government problems evidenced in the Bundy ranch raid?

89

July 17, 2014

House Procedure in Action: Pro-Drug War Amendment OK, Pro-Gun Rights Amendment Prohibited

US House of Representatives rules were strictly enforced Tuesday to prevent a full House vote on a pro-gun rights amendment offered by Rep. Thomas Massie (R-KY) despite the earlier incorporation into the bill of a pro-drug war amendment that would also appear to be barred by a strict application of the procedural rule.

Massie's attempt on the US House of Representatives floor to protect gun rights in the District of Columbia through offering an amendment to the Financial Services and General Government Appropriations Act (HR 5016) was ruled out of order by Rep. Brad Wenstrup (R-OH), the floor debate chairman, who ruled:

> The Chair finds that this amendment includes language requiring a new determination by the District of Columbia as to the state of Federal firearms law. The gentleman has not shown that this determination is already required.
>
> The amendment, therefore, constitutes legislation in violation of clause 2 of rule XXI.

While supporters of Massie's amendment may shrug their shoulders and declare "oh well, rules are rules," in the US House the rules appear to be quite flexible depending on what type of legislating an amendment proposes.

Just 21 days earlier, the House Committee on Appropriations added to the bill a pro-drug war amendment via a nearly party-line vote, with Rep. Henry Cuellar of Texas the only Democrat to join all 27 voting Republican committee members in voting "yes" on the amendment.

The drug war amendment — now part of the House passed bill — would prevent the DC government from spending money to enact or carry out any reductions of penalties related to possessing, using, or distributing for recreational purposes drugs, including marijuana, listed in schedule one of the US government's Controlled Substances Act. The restriction appears to be largely intended to oppose the DC government's recently passed marijuana decriminalization legislation though the broad restriction reaches farther.

The procedurally blocked gun rights amendment would prevent the DC government from spending money to enforce DC's legislative restrictions related to guns that go beyond US government restrictions.

Why is legislating in favor of the drug war in DC through the appropriations bill acceptable while legislating for gun rights in DC is not?

That is essentially the question Massie posed just before Wenstrup's ruling and in answer to the assertion of Rep. José E. Serrano (D-NY) on the House floor that the gun amendment is out of order because it "constitutes legislation in an appropriation bill" and imposes additional duties on DC by "requiring law enforcement or the DC council to determine what is prohibited by federal law."

Massie argues:

> [T]he underlying bill already contains language that is virtually identical in form to the amendment that I have offered. For instance, section 809 states that "none of the Federal funds contained in this Act may be used to enact or carry out any law, rule, or regulation to legalize or otherwise reduce penalties associated with the possession, use, or distribution of any schedule I substance under the Controlled Substance Act."
>
> There are multiple examples in the underlying bill where the structure of those portions of the bill are identical to my amendment and require knowledge of law.

Maybe more revealing of how the House operates is what happened right after Massie's appeal of Wenstrup's ruling and someone's immediately following motion to table the appeal. Within a few seconds you can hear someone say "This forces a vote right now that we don't have" with anything else said inaudible due to a microphone being turned off. Then we have an over seven minutes pause in all legislative activity. During this extended pause, Wenstrup stands at the podium, twice punctuating the silence by starting to resume consideration of the appeal and motion presented to him, only to stop mid-sentence.

The long pause ends right after we see a woman who

had been standing in a group of people near Wenstrup rush offscreen for a moment and then back onscreen and up some steps to next to Wenstrup's podium where she says something to a man with whom Wenstrup has been speaking for much of the pause. That man waves his hand and Wenstrup finally speaks a full sentence, quickly calling a vote on the appeal of his procedural ruling, which is then upheld on a voice vote. Nothing more is said about the motion to table the appeal, and its existence is not even recorded in the Congressional Record.

Read here the pro-drug war amendment that has been incorporated into the appropriations legislation:

> Sec. 809. (a) None of the Federal funds contained in this Act may be used to enact or carry out any law, rule, or regulation to legalize or otherwise reduce penalties associated with the possession, use, or distribution of any schedule I substance under the Controlled Substances Act (21 U.S.C. 801 et seq.) or any tetrahydrocannabinols derivative for any purpose.
>
> (b) None of the funds contained in this Act may be used to enact or carry out any law, rule, or regulation to legalize or otherwise reduce penalties associated with the possession, use, or distribution of any schedule I substance under the Controlled Substances Act (21 U.S.C. 801 et seq.) or any tetrahydrocannabinols derivative for recreational purposes.

Read here the pro-gun rights amendment that was procedurally denied a vote on the House floor:

> Sec. __. None of the funds made available by this Act, including amounts made available under titles IV or VIII, may be used by any authority of the government of the District of Columbia to prohibit the ability of any person to possess, acquire, use, sell, or transport a firearm except to the extent such activity is prohibited by Federal law.

Read here House Rule XXI, clause 2 that was used to rule that the full House could not vote on Massie's amendment:

(b) A provision changing existing law may not be reported in a general appropriation bill, including a provision making the availability of funds contingent on the receipt or possession of information not required by existing law for the period of the appropriation, except germane provisions that retrench expenditures by the reduction of amounts of money covered by the bill (which may include those recommended to the Committee on Appropriations by direction of a legislative committee having jurisdiction over the subject matter) and except rescissions of appropriations contained in appropriation Acts.

90

August 2, 2014

Eric Cantor Leaving US House for Wall Street Millions?

Did former US House of Representatives Majority Leader Eric Cantor (R-VA) announce his resignation from the House so he can speed up private negotiations to make the big bucks in the financial industry? That is the suggestion of a new Politico article.

The Politico article also indicates that Wall Street is already knocking on Cantor's door and quotes a "headhunter" who says Cantor has "relevant talents":

> Cantor has not made any public comments about what he will do next or if he has already decided his next move.
>
> However, GOP insiders said Cantor has already been approached by a number of K Street lobby shops, companies and Wall Street firms, but has not engaged in any serious negotiations with any of these potential suitors at this point, according to several sources

familiar with the conversations.

"He will have opportunities in the traditional Washington political world," said Nels Olson, a top headhunter at Korn Ferry. "I think he could have Wall Street, investment banks or private equity firms interested given his relevant talents."

While Cantor would be widely sought after in Washington, he is more seriously considering potential hedge fund, private equity or big bank opportunities, according to sources familiar with his post-Congress thinking.

Rep. Kevin McCarthy (R-CA) — who replaced Cantor as House Majority Leader and who Cantor described in his Thursday House floor farewell speech as "my closest confidant and my good friend" — pipes up in the article that Cantor "knows financial markets well."

When and how did Cantor gain this knowledge that the Politico article suggests will help him land a million dollars-plus salary on Wall Street?

An answer to that question is not apparent. But, any Wall Street firm or firms that hire Cantor will not have to provide a justification that satisfies curious onlookers.

Likely, Cantor's greatest asset for certain financial industry companies, as well as military-industrial complex entities that may throw him an additional hundred thousand here and there, was summed up by David Stockman in his article bidding "good riddance" to Cantor upon the representative's defeat in the June 10 Virginia Republican primary:

> In short, the [Federal Reserve] has turned Wall Street into a dangerous gambling casino and Washington into ceaseless fiscal auction. And that's where Cantor's real sin comes into play. Not once after the financial crisis did Cantor or the so-called establishment GOP leadership take on the elephant in the room. Never did he even remotely recognize that the monetary politburo ensconced in the Eccles Building has accomplished

what amounts to an economic coup d tat.

Stated differently, financial repression, ZIRP, QE, wealth effects and the Greenspan/Bernanke/Yellen "put" under the stock market and risk assets generally are not just a major policy mistake; they are a full-throttle assault on the heart and soul of conservative economics.

… [Cantor] has been an unabashed servant of the Washington War Party during his entire career. Time and time again, he helped whip the GOP rank and file into a frenzy of militaristic bombast about imaginary threats to America's security in places all over the globe which are none of our business. That absolute nonsense of sanctions and unrelenting hostility to the regime in Tehran is perhaps the most egregious example.

So Eric Cantor made a career of milking the Warfare State and pandering to Wall Street. This brought him nearly to the top of the Washington heap. But in the end, it did not fool his constituents. And most certainly it set back the conservative cause immeasurably.

As a former House member and majority leader, Cantor will continue to enjoy special access and influence in the US government that may be particularly valuable for prospective employers.

Indeed, immediately following Cantor's farewell speech, House Minority Leader Steny Hoyer (D-MD) immediately took the podium to speak regarding Cantor, largely focusing on the continuing influence and access Cantor will have in the US government. Hoyer stated:

I know that he will not be leaving the public community — the public square, that his voice will still be a voice of influence, and he will make a difference in whatever area he pursues. He will remain always a member of this body. He will visit us from time to time. We will welcome him back.

September 3, 2014

Mr. Cantor Goes to Wall Street

Hightailing it out of the United States House of Representatives after losing his reelection effort in the Republican Party primary is paying off well for uber war advocate and former House Majority Leader Eric Cantor (R-VA). With four months remaining in the House term he left early, Cantor is already literally raking in his Wall Street millions.

The New York Times reports the lucrative figures of Cantor's new job at a "Wall Street boutique investment bank":

> Mr. Cantor will be joining Moelis & Company as vice chairman and a director on its board, the firm said on Tuesday. He is expected to serve as a senior adviser to the firm's clients on strategic matters.
>
> Moelis & Company will pay Mr. Cantor a base salary of $400,000, along with an additional cash payout of $400,000 and $1 million in restricted stock that will vest over five years.
>
> Next year, the investment bank will give him a minimum incentive payout of $1.2 million in cash and $400,000 in restricted stock.

As David Stockman explained upon Cantor's primary defeat, Cantor has already done so much for "Wall Street." Here is one example:

> The fraught moment came on October 3, 2008 when [Eric Cantor] helped Hank Paulson, the Goldman Sachs plenipotentiary then occupying the 3rd floor of the Treasury Building, force the House GOP rank-and-file into a catastrophic retreat. That is, after properly rebuking the White House demand to bail-out the Wall Street gambling houses by voting "no" on the first TARP consideration, House Republicans were forced

into a shameful about face on the second vote.

The politically-connected portions of the financial industry know their current friends in Washington are watching how things work out for this former friend in Washington. So far so good for Cantor.

92

Speaker Vote Highlights US House's Unchecked Procedural Corruption

It seems unlikely that the current members of the United States House of Representatives will effectively rise up against their Democrat and Republican leaders to require that the House be run in a fair and honest manner. Yet, the potential of more Republican members opposing on Tuesday the reelection of Rep. John Boehner (R-OH) as speaker of the House than the 12 Republican representatives who chose not to vote for Boehner in 2013 is helping bring to light the crooked process by which "the people's House" so frequently operates.

Rep. Thomas Massie (R-KY) on Saturday lifted the veil some on corrupt House process, explaining in a press release why he will join other Republican House members in voting against Boehner's reelection as speaker. Massie, who joined the House in November of 2012, states:

> During my first two years as a congressman I discovered a significant source of the dysfunction. I watched the House Leadership:
>
> • Schedule a fiscal crisis in a lame duck session on the last legislative day before Christmas to get maximum leverage over rank and file members,
>
> • Mislead members into thinking that a vote on an

unpopular bill was postponed, only to then conduct a rushed voice vote on the $10 billion unfunded spending measure with fewer than a dozen members present,

- Give members less than 72 hours to read bills over 1,000 pages long, and

- Remove members from committees simply because they voted for the principles upon which they campaigned.

Massie thus presents a disturbing though incomplete list of instances of procedural corruption. Other recent examples include:

- Quickly passing by a voice vote on December 11 expansive legislation escalating US conflict with Russia and increasing US military and economic involvement in Ukraine after the conclusion of legislative business for the day, when almost all members of the House were away from the House floor, so that nobody was present to demand a debate and recorded vote,

- Altering a bill regarding the US government's mass spying program in secret after committee approval of the legislation and then preventing consideration of any amendments to the bill on the House floor in May,

- Applying House rules to favor or disfavor particular political agendas, for example, allowing an appropriations bill to restrict Washington, DC from reducing penalties related to marijuana while barring Massie from seeking in July to amend the bill on the House floor to restrict DC's enforcement of its firearms-related prohibitions, and

- Boehner declaring for months that the House should vote the ongoing war on ISIS in Iraq and Syria up or down, while all the while refusing to schedule a vote on the matter.

The list goes on. And the procedural shenanigans are nothing new. For example, back on November 22, 2003 a 15-minute vote — called in the middle of the night when constituents were sleeping — regarding approval of a pharmaceuticals industry-backed Medicare bill was held open for about three hours as leadership twisted arms until enough votes were switched to pass the bill. Rep. Dennis Hastert (R-IL) was the speaker then.

Neither are Democrat leaders blame free. Much of Speaker Boehner and other Republican leaders' process manipulation would go nowhere without the support or acquiescence of the Democrat leadership. Plus, we should expect a new Democrat speaker and assorted leaders to behave in much the same way Republican leaders have with a majority over the last four years. As Ron Paul Institute for Peace and Prosperity Chairman and former Republican Representative from Texas Ron Paul commented regarding the transition to a Republican majority in the US Senate, "it doesn't make a whole lot of difference." Paul elaborates that leaders like Boehner in the House and outgoing Senate Majority Leader Harry Reid (D-NV) are "bipartisan on the wicked things" including military interventions.

Whether the "R" or "D" team wins control of the House or Senate, as well as who are named as the leaders, is ultimately not of great importance in the quest for ensuring respect for individual rights and promoting peace. As Paul has explained on many occasions, positive change in American politics can arise only with expanded education of the people in the "ideas of liberty." When that education crosses the threshold where a core of people are firmly committed to advancing liberty and the majority of people are open to that transition, Paul explains, dramatic changes can occur.

As Paul says, "an idea whose time has come cannot be stopped by any army or any government." Neither can it be stopped by politicians like Boehner and Reid, or the out-of-view special interests with whom they work.

Part 7: Ron Paul and Libertarianism

93

June 14, 2013

Bill Kristol's Cato Crush

William Kristol is promoting at the Weekly Standard an article by "two of America's leading libertarian legal thinkers, no friends to intrusive government," to support Kristol's assertion that the National Security Agency (NSA) mass secret spying program is a "legitimate use of government power to protect the nation from our enemies abroad."

The defense of the NSA program by these two authors is of particular note because of the authors' affiliation with the Cato Institute that describes itself as "dedicated to the principles of individual liberty, limited government, free markets and peace" and having a "strict respect for civil liberties and skepticism about the benefits of both the welfare state and foreign military adventurism." The authors' article is providing valuable cover for the advocates of the mass spying program.

The authors of the article Kristol is promoting are Cato Institute Center for Constitutional Studies President Roger Pilon and Cato Institute Adjunct Scholar Richard A. Epstein who wrote an attempted sweeping exculpation of the NSA and all the branches of the US government for the NSA's mass spying on phone calls. Here is a portion of the authors' defense:

> Legally, the president is on secure footing under the

Patriot Act, which Congress passed shortly after 9/11
and has since reauthorized by large bipartisan majorities. As he stressed, the program has enjoyed the
continued support of all three branches of the federal
government. It has been free of political abuse since
its inception. And as he rightly added, this nation has
real problems if its people, at least here, can't trust the
combined actions of the executive branch and the
Congress, backstopped by federal judges sworn to
protect our individual liberties secured by the Bill of
Rights.

President Obama's conclusion, as characterized approvingly by the authors, is the exact opposite of the conclusion warranted. The United States has real problems if Americans do
not question and challenge US government actions. Pointing
to the agreement of the US government's three branches on a
program and the reauthorizing of the PATRIOT Act by large
bipartisan congressional majorities is an illogical defense. First,
the defense lacks basis given that the secrecy of the spying has
prevented courts from deciding cases challenging the spying.
Second, the three branches of the US government have agreed
plenty of times on bad programs; the popularity of a government program among a group of politicians is not determina-
tive of the program's merit.

The suggestion that the spying has been free of "political
abuse" is particularly bizarre. The nature of the mass spying is
itself an abuse by the government of people's privacy. But, maybe the authors mean by "political abuse" the use of the spying
to benefit or harm a particular political party or candidate, or
to treat people differently based on their political views. If that
is what the authors mean, how do they have the information
to know there has been no political abuse? In a secret multibil-
lion-dollars-a-year program the logical assumption would be
that somewhere, somehow the program has been used for that
kind of political abuse. Indeed, it would be expected that the
secrecy of the program would embolden some people to use it
for such purposes.

The authors proceed with the following history of the PATRIOT Act:

> That deference is especially appropriate now that Congress, through the Patriot Act, has set a delicate balance that enables the executive branch to carry out its basic duty to protect us from another 9/11 while respecting our privacy as much as possible. Obviously, reasonable people can have reasonable differences over how that balance is struck. But on this question, political deliberation has done its job, because everyone on both sides of the aisle is seeking the right constitutional balance.

Reality is much messier. Many people on "both sides of the aisle" were not seeking the right constitutional balance, and the PATRIOT Act does not set up a "delicate balance... respecting our privacy as much as possible."

For, an analysis of these issues that seems more in line with the espoused principles of the Cato Institute (and is not being promoted by William Kristol), check out "In Its Bubble of Secrecy, the National Security Bureaucracy Redefined Privacy for Its Own Purposes," a Jun 10 article by Jim Harper, the director of Information Policy Studies at the Cato Institute.

94

May 13, 2014

Is Today 'Lie about Ron Paul in Headlines Day'?

Looking at the Washington Post and Rare, one has to wonder if today is Lie about Ron Paul in Headlines Day.

First, the Washington Post published an article with the headline "Ron Paul thinks drug use is rampant inside prisons. He's wrong." That is a rather provocative claim. But, the claim is not at all backed up by the article. Paul, who is the chairman and founder of the Ron Paul Institute, is quoted in the article's first sentence:

> In his final speech on the floor of the House of Rep-
> resentatives, Ron Paul opined that reducing access to
> drugs in society was hopeless because "the authorities
> can't even keep drugs out of prison."

Of course, saying that drugs cannot be kept out of prison is
not the same as saying drug use is rampant in prison.

The article presents statistics suggesting people dramatically reduce their drug use while in prison. Yet, the article fails
to mention an obvious reason for any reduction in drug use in
prison: Drugs cost money, and people tend to have less access
to money to pay for drugs while they are in prison.

Prisoners may also seek out creative alternatives to alter
their consciousness in prison that both are more affordable
than the drugs they would be able to purchase should they have
income and are not discoverable in prison drug tests.

Next, Rare published an article today titled, "Ron Paul had
the best plan to save the kidnapped Nigerian schoolgirls." That
is intriguing. What is Paul's plan? If you read the article, you
find out that it is the article's author W. James Antle III — not
Paul — who has the supposed best plan.

After mentioning Paul's US House of Representatives bill
HR 3037 from October of 2001 that would have authorized issuing letters of marque and reprisal targeted in response to attacks in the United States a month earlier, Antle opines that the
marque and reprisal approach "may be more appropriate to the
situation in Nigeria" even though Antle concedes Boko Haram
does not even "directly threaten U.S. vital interests." Stepping
things up, Antle promotes the US government also use marque
and reprisal against other groups around the world as well. Here
is Antle's proposal in his own words:

> Letters of marque and reprisal are clearly insufficient
> for dealing with state-sponsored terrorism or acts of
> war carried out by nations. But they could be a solu-
> tion to dealing with criminal bands like Boko Haram.
> And with any luck, they could strike a blow against

smaller groups of terrorists and pirates at a fraction of the cost of war.

Despite what people may infer from the misleading headline, Paul, who is known for supporting a noninterventionist foreign policy, has not endorsed Antle's proposal.

95

Is Ron Paul the San Antonio Spurs of American Politics?

Many basketball fans are marveling at the San Antonio Spurs winning on Sunday night the team's fifth nonconsecutive National Basketball Association (NBA) championship. Cato Institute Executive Vice President David Boaz suggests at his institute's website that people should also marvel at Ron Paul Institute Chairman and Founder Ron Paul's similar, and unmatched, United States House of Representatives electoral accomplishments. Boaz explains:

> [Ron Paul] first won in a special election for an open seat. He then lost his seat and won it back two years later, defeating the incumbent. After two more terms he left his seat to run unsuccessfully for the U.S. Senate (and thereby did his greatest disservice to the American Republic, as his seat was won by Tom DeLay). Twelve years later, in 1996, after some redistricting, he ran again for Congress, again defeating an incumbent, this time in the Republican primary. Some political scientist should study the political skills it takes to win election to Congress without the benefit of incumbency — three times.

Paul's final return to the House in 1996 was a particularly arduous task. First, Paul won more votes in the Republican primary than Jim Deats who was the Republican nominee two years earlier. Second, Paul beat in the primary runoff Greg Laughlin, the incumbent four-term representative who had served as a Democrat but was running for reelection as a Republican with the support of virtually the entire Republican political establishment. Finally, Paul defeated in the general election his Democratic Party opponent Charles "Lefty" Morris in the district long represented by a Democrat.

Making things even more challenging for Paul, the district he won in 1996 was much different than the area he had represented in the late 1970s and early 1980s. The new district extended from the Gulf Coast to the edge of Austin in Central Texas. Paul previously represented a much smaller district hugging the Gulf Coast and Houston.

96

June 27, 2014

Ron Paul, the CIA, and Dr. Zhivago

It is no secret that Boris Pasternak's 1957 novel Dr. Zhivago influenced Ron Paul Institute Chairman and Founder Ron Paul. Indeed, Dr. Zhivago and Ayn Rand's Atlas Shrugged are the only two works of fiction included in the list of 48 books at the end of Paul's The Revolution: A Manifesto that Paul says influenced him over the years. What has long been a secret, though, is that the United States Central Intelligence Agency (CIA) played a significant role in helping promote the Pasternak novel.

A peek at the influence Dr. Zhivago had on Paul may be found in ABC News and National Public Radio profiles of Paul from 2011 that report on how Paul reading in his 20s a copy of Dr. Zhivago that his mother had given him put Paul on course reading many other books that helped him develop his understanding of libertarian ideas. This reading led directly to Paul first running for Congress in 1974 and continuing to communicate regarding political topics to this day. As Paul has explained many times, his runs for political office have been motivated largely by a desire to share ideas related to freedom with a larger audience.

Might Paul's mother not have given him Dr. Zhivago if the CIA had not boosted the book's popularity? Without reading the book, may Paul not have proceeded in the study that led him to help build support for liberty and nonintervention in the US and abroad?

In their book The Zhivago Affair: The Kremlin, the CIA, and the Battle Over a Forbidden Book, authors Peter Finn and Petra Couvee report how the CIA played a significant role in boosting Dr. Zhivago's popularity around the world. Interviewed by guest host Tom Gjelten on June 17 on the Diane Rehm Show, the authors explain that, after Pasternak's novel was published first in Italian translation in Italy, the CIA obtained a copy of the book in the original Russian, published it, and facilitated its smuggling into the Soviet Union. Finn suggests in the interview that the smuggling of the book into the Soviet Union provided a significant boost to the book's popularity:

Gjelten: So, Peter, you mentioned — this is the part that is really interesting to me — the book already was a bestseller before the CIA got involved, and, nevertheless, you write that in your judgment it would have had only a small elite readership…were it not for the fact that the Soviet Union got so upset about this. But, how do we know…one, what the reaction to this book would have been if the Soviet Union, the Soviet authorities had not gotten so upset; and, two, how do we know what the reaction would have been if the CIA had not gotten involved?

Finn: Well, on the first I think it is an educated guess. Russian literature — epic Russian literature — generally were not bestsellers at that time. And publishers love the word "banned" and, you know, this book was trumpeted in much of the news coverage as something that was banned in the USSR. And, therefore, people became intrigued. It was also an intellectual, sometimes difficult, book to read. But, the amount of coverage, the positive reviews led people to buy it in numbers they might not have. And the Soviet Union at various times did consider a small print run. If they had done that, we might have a different history today.

Later in the interview, Gjelten quotes from a July 9, 1958 memorandum by John Maury, the CIA Soviet Russia Division Chief, explaining the message of Dr. Zhivago:

> Pasternak's humanistic message — that every person is entitled to a private life and deserves respect as a human being, irrespective of the extent of his political loyalty or contribution to the state — poses a fundamental challenge to the Soviet ethic of sacrifice of the individual to the Communist system.

Paul and other discerning readers understood that this message applies beyond the borders of the Soviet Union as well.

It is interesting to ponder the possibility that this CIA covert operation may have helped start the extensive political education of one of the CIA's most prominent opponents — Ron Paul, who has over several decades exposed the dangers the CIA poses.

In his September 19, 1984 US House of Representatives floor speech "Some Observations on Four Terms in Congress" Paul explained the unconstitutional use of the CIA to thwart the people's will:

> If covert aid to a nation is voted down, the CIA and the administration in power can find the means to finance whatever is desired. Emergencies are declared, finances are hidden, discretionary funds are found, foreign governments are used, and policy as desired is carried out, regardless of the will of the people expressed by Congress.

Upon returning to the House in 1997, Paul continued to shine a light on the CIA's destructive activities, explaining in his House floor speech "America's Foreign Policy" on July 15, 1997 that "[i]t is not a hidden fact that our own CIA follows our international corporate interests around the globe, engaging in corporate espionage and installing dictators when they serve these special interests."

While unintended consequences of government actions are usually thought of as harmful, a CIA covert operation contributing to the emergence of Ron Paul's political activity would be a noteworthy instance of an unintended and very positive consequence.

97

July 25, 2014

'Hard-Core Libertarian' Austin Petersen's Advice for 'Soviet' Ron Paul

Austin Petersen, who describes himself in the introduction to his Freedom Report Podcast as a "hard-core libertarian" who cares about "pure freedom," is upset that Ron Paul wrote an editorial expressing skepticism regarding the US government's and media's line on the downing of a Malaysia Airlines flight in Ukraine.

Petersen, indeed, provides in his Wednesday podcast some advice for Paul: No more of that saying what you think stuff. If you do that, you might make some people uncomfortable, and the media might even run negative headlines!

Petersen's advice brings to mind former New York City Mayor Rudy Giuliani challenging Paul to "withdraw that comment and tell us that he didn't really mean it," when Paul discussed "blowback" from US foreign intervention during a 2007 presidential debate. By answering Giuliani with more education about the history of US foreign interventions and blowback instead of backing down, Paul, then a US House of Representatives member from Texas, took the limelight of the debate in a manner that strengthened his campaign and expanded his educational reach.

Petersen says Paul "sounds like he hates America" because — get this — an article concerning Paul's editorial was published with the headline "Ron Paul Defends Russia After Malaysian Plane Crash." That gives you an idea of the lack of logic involved in Petersen's presentation. Just to be crystal clear, Paul wrote neither that headline nor the article it accompanies.

Defending Russia is synonymous with hating America only among the people who relentlessly try to depict Russia as an enemy of the United States, not among libertarians who value peace, communication, and commerce internationally.

Also, there is no reason to conclude from Paul's editorial, or even from the headline of the article concerning the editorial, that Paul endorses everything the Russia government does.

Petersen in his podcast even presents an absurd discussion of how media cannot get away with publishing misleading headlines. The reality, as Paul knows from experience, is that, when media decides to attack you, media can mischaracterize you in multiple headlines in a single day. Petersen, not apparently willing to let reality interfere with making a point, says this does not happen.

Petersen, who touts his experience "in the media" to encourage people to accept the nonsense he is proclaiming, gives Paul's famous "blowback" confrontation with Giuliani as an example of how Paul sometimes makes counterproductive statements. Of course this confrontation in which Paul forcefully and succinctly explains that people want to attack America because of the US government's foreign interventions was a huge boost to Paul's presidential campaign, the spreading of Paul's message, and the creating and motivating of activists for nonintervention and respect for liberty.

Elsewhere in the podcast Petersen lets slip that his disagreement with Paul regarding Paul's "blowback" debate within a debate with Giuliani is not just based on a "message marketing strategy" difference of opinion. Instead, Petersen in fact takes Giuliani's side in the debate. Petersen explains:

> ...people probably hate us around the world not

because of our arrogance necessarily, although that may be part of it. The people probably hate us because they're a bunch of socialist backwaterers and they're jealous of our success. Now, people uh libertarians one of their favorite things is to make fun of the statement that George Bush made about "oh, they hate us for our freedoms." And it's funny, you know it sounds jingoistic and sounds just overly simplistic, but, the more you delve into the foreign policy history of the United States and into the war on terror specifically and the actors in the war on terror, the more you realize that there are actually people who do despise us for our freedoms.

Petersen proceeds along this line of thought further, never giving any credit to Paul's side of the debate.

People seeking more information regarding US foreign intervention and blowback can read some or all of the books Paul recommended to Secretary of State John Kerry in March, including Robert Pape's Dying to Win that provides an analysis of the motivation for suicide attacks.

Petersen also complains that Paul is using the same rhetoric as did "Soviet apparatchiks." Oh no — rhetoric cooties!

If we abandon every form of argumentation Vladimir Lenin — just one Soviet political leader — used in his voluminous communications, we may well be left with little means of arguing at all.

The only real point of Petersen's complaint is to associate with Paul through proximity the disconcerting term "Soviet apparatchik." Petersen's Soviet smear is just a "gotcha" turn of phrase; it is not an exercise in logic.

The "Soviet apparatchik" non-argument is a deceptive twofer for Petersen. At the same time it illogically smears a champion of freedom with endorsing the defunct Soviet Union, it similarly equates in people's minds the current Russian government with that of the defunct Soviet Union. The low-grade trick even seems to work on Petersen in his own presentation, with him having to correct himself after referring to Russia as the

Soviet Union.

Maybe it is too charitable, however, to refer to Petersen's Russia-Soviet Union misstatement as just a slip-up induced by his smear. Because Petersen is disturbed that Paul supposedly sounds like "a real America-hating socialist liberal," you might expect Petersen to make a greater effort not to sound like a devoted cold warrior who believes that Russia is the "evil empire" in new clothing still intent on invading the world to impose global communism. Yet, Petersen remarks in his podcast:

> The thing is that I worry sometimes that libertarians when they say, when they make these sorts of jokes about foreign policy, "oh, they hated us for our freedoms, ha, ha" it betrays a lack of full understanding of the true nature of what we are against. Now, just because I am a noninterventionist libertarian, it doesn't mean that I don't believe that there are threats around the world. And it also means that I think that we should acknowledge those threats, Russia being one of those primary threats.

Examining Petersen's allegation that Paul is using the "Soviet apparatchik" argument form, we find that there is no truth to the allegation — no matter how unimportant the allegation is in the first place. Here is Petersen's description of the "Soviet apparatchik" argument form along with his description of the argument form Paul uses:

> This is the concept called "Whataboutism." And I'm going to read this — you have to apologize for you — I'm going to read this to you from Wikipedia because I think it's got the best definition of what "Whataboutism" is:

> "Whataboutism is a term for the Tu quoque logical fallacy popularized by The Economist for describing the use of the fallacy by the Soviet Union in its dealings with the Western world during the Cold War. The tactic was used when criticisms were leveled at the Soviet Union, wherein the response would be 'What about...'

followed by the naming of an event in the Western
world loosely similar to the original item of criticism."

So, what I'm saying here is that every time something
wrong happens overseas or every time a big government does some evil thing overseas Ron Paul comes
out and says "Well what about the United States? What
about the United States?" in order to show the hypoc-
risy of the American government for making a stance
on that.

Yes, you read that right. In Petersen's sloppy attempt to
smear Paul by repeatedly saying Paul is like a "Soviet apparatchik," a "Soviet apologist," and a person "nostalgic for the Soviet
Union," Petersen lets slip the truth that the argument Paul is
making is just about the opposite of the one Petersen is smear-
ing Paul for allegedly presenting.

As presented by Petersen, a person would use the "Soviet
apparatchik" argument form to defend his own country's government by noting that other governments do bad things too.
In contrast, Petersen admits in passing before continuing with
his rhetorical trickery that the argument form Petersen dislikes
Paul using is Paul comparing actions by foreign actors with
those of Paul's own United States government to "show the hy-
pocrisy of the American government."

If Paul and other advocates for nonintervention overseas
and respect for liberty at home follow Petersen's urging and
stop presenting Paul's form of argument, they would be giving
up on a powerful means of educating people and exposing government wrongdoing.

After using the word "Soviet" repeatedly while never presenting the slightest logical argument to back the smear and
even illustrating for attentive listeners that the comparison is totally erroneous, Petersen proceeds to say that Paul, a prominent
champion of free markets, sounds like "a real America-hating
socialist liberal." This is just nonsense piled on nonsense.

Petersen's new assertion seems to rely on blind acceptance
of a left-right political spectrum that says liberals are America-hating and conservatives are America-loving.

While Petersen says in his podcast introduction "I'm not a conservative," his advice is that libertarians just shut up about areas where their philosophy leads them to conclusions that may be seen as anti-American, socialist, or liberal from a political orientation heavily biased toward an interventionist conservative perspective.

Petersen's advice to libertarians can thus be summed up as keep your libertarianism to yourself — at least to the extent it conflicts with interventionist conservatism. Following this advice also shuts the door on libertarians working with people "on the left" on important matters where they agree and can and do make a difference, from preventing a US military attack on Syria to rolling back the drug war.

All this nonsense from someone who does not describe himself as a "hard-core libertarian" who cares about "pure freedom" could just be laughed off. But, when presented by someone who claims to be on the same side as Paul on the issues, the nonsense should be addressed. Otherwise, people not familiar with libertarian ideas including nonintervention and respect for liberty may hear the unanswered nonsense and think that the libertarian philosophy is just as messed up and contradictory as the political views of many of the people working to grow the military-police-surveillance state.

98

August 8, 2014

NY Times Truncated Ron Paul History Puts Libertarians in Republican Box

As libertarians participate in a trans-ideological and trans-partisan effort that may overturn the warfare-police-surveillance state, the old media leaders seem to be taking on a mission to tame libertarianism's adherents by defining them as mainly a subgroup in the Republican Party.

First, the Associated Press and Washington Post ran articles, respectively, in June and July absurdly portraying Libertarian Party candidates as "spoilers" for Republican candidates — as if Republican candidates have an automatic claim to the votes of people who desire to support libertarian ideas.

With August upon us, the New York Times takes its turn, publishing Thursday an article "Has the 'Libertarian Moment' Finally Arrived?"

The Times article is open enough in its presentation of this supposed libertarian-Republican natural bond that it mentions briefly US House of Representatives Republican leadership's consideration in 2010 of denying then-Rep. Ron Paul (R-TX) the chairmanship of a monetary policy subcommittee in which Paul had served as ranking member under Democrat control of the House. But the article's sanitized retelling leaves out entirely the history of the Republican leadership's earlier successful actions to twice — in 2003 and 2005 — deny Paul a monetary policy subcommittee chairmanship.

This historical truncation related to the former libertarian representative and current Ron Paul Institute chairman conveniently makes more palatable the article's message that libertarians support the Republican Party. Here, the article briefly states that message:

> But not since the days of the Vietnam War and Nixon's imperial presidency have libertarians seen much profit in an alliance with the big-government Democrats. Instead, ever since a newly inaugurated President Reagan declared, "Government is the problem," politically practical libertarians have been more apt to cast their lot with the G.O.P.

This characterization of libertarians as bound to supporting Republican Party candidates permeates the entire article. For example, seven of the most talked about potential Republican presidential candidates are presented as potentially appealing to libertarian voters. Meanwhile, the article names no potential candidate outside of that purported libertarian electoral "home" as having any appeal to libertarians.

Like the AP and Washington Post articles, the Times article provides no real evidence to support its grand assertion. The Times and its counterparts seem to be following the tried-and-true course of repeatedly stating a false message to make it become conventional wisdom. With the rise of alternative news sources and the internet, this is a strategy that should with time be less and less successful.

The reality obvious to people familiar with Paul's House campaigns, terms in the House, and presidential campaigns is that that the Republican Party leadership often acted to stifle Paul's political efforts — from opposing Paul's campaign to return to the House in 1996, to denying Paul his seniority for time served in the House in the 1970s and 80s after he won that 1996 election, to suppressing Paul presidential nomination votes at the Republican National Convention.

The Times article sanitizes this history of Republican leadership's opposition to Paul. Instead of noting actions Republican leadership took to restrict Paul, the article mentions only how the House Republican leadership considered in 2010 denying Paul a chairmanship. As the Times article tells the story, it was just a brief bit of tenseness followed by the Republican leadership giving Paul what he wanted:

> Despite the fact that Ron Paul served nearly two decades in the House and established seniority on the Financial Services Committee, in late 2010 the incoming speaker, John Boehner, reportedly sought to deny Paul a subcommittee chairmanship (owing to Paul's views on monetary policy) before eventually buckling to the outcries of Paul supporters.

The real story is much different than the one suggested by the Times article. Unmentioned by the Times is how the Republican Party leadership went to extraordinary lengths in 2003, and again in 2005, to successfully deny Paul a monetary policy subcommittee chairmanship.

Also unmentioned is that in 2010 Paul had more seniority than Rep. Spencer Bachus (R-AL), who became chairman of the full Financial Services Committee — if you count Paul's

1970s and 80s terms that Republican leadership selectively disregarded.

Only after the Democrats then gained a majority in the House was Paul able to first obtain a subcommittee leadership position as a ranking member — the top minority party member.

During a 2009 House Financial Services Committee meeting, the committee chairman, then-Rep. Barney Frank (D-MA), explained some of the methods the Republican leadership used to twice block Paul from a subcommittee chairmanship. Frank also alludes to how Frank, after becoming chairman of the committee, made room for Paul to be a subcommittee ranking member by reestablishing the domestic monetary policy subcommittee the Republican leadership had eliminated:

> **Frank:** … First of all, a little history is in order. Despite partisan consensus for fixing the Fed developed after the Republicans lost power, the gentleman from Texas introduced this ["Audit the Fed"] bill in 1983 and got precious little support from anybody for much of the time.
>
> I do want to claim credit, as the chairman of the committee, for being the first one in 26 years who gave the gentleman from Texas a chance to operate this legislation.
>
> In fact, the gentleman from Texas has acknowledged that in 2003, under Republican majorityship, he was in line to be the chairman of the Domestic Monetary Policy Subcommittee, which promptly disappeared. It was merged into the International Monetary Policy Subcommittee for the sole reason of denying the gentleman from Texas the chairmanship.
>
> Two years later, when they figured they couldn't merge it into another committee, they dragooned the gentlewoman from Ohio, Ms. [Deborah D.] Pryce, who had been on leave from the committee to come back and assume a chairmanship of that combined subcommit-

tee, once again to preempt Ron Paul who said to me quite presciently at that time, "I guess I'll have to wait for you to be chairman to get anywhere on this." Well, I am the chairman and he's getting somewhere.

Now, that doesn't mean we are in complete agreement. I will yield to the beneficiary of my chairmanship.

Paul: I thank the chairman for yielding, and I want to say that you are claiming some credit, and you deserve this credit....

99

October 11, 2014

Celebrating Ron Paul's Forty Years in the Political Arena

Forty years ago this month, Ron Paul was in the final weeks of his first campaign for the United States House of Representatives. Paul, a Texas obstetrician who had never before run for political office, was the Republican nominee challenging Rep. Robert R. Casey, the eight-term Democrat incumbent. Casey won that race. But, a year and a half later Paul won the House seat in a special election after the seat had become vacant due to Casey's appointment to the Federal Maritime Commission.

Paul ran for office in 1974 and through the years in large part so he could have a platform for educating people with a consistent pro-liberty message.

In all, Paul won election to the House 12 times over a span of five decades. Paul's wins include the unmatched record of being elected three times to the House as a non-incumbent — once in his 1976 special election victory and twice (in 1978 and 1996) in victories against incumbents. Paul had some losses as well — in 1974 and a squeaker House reelection loss in the 1976 general election, as well as in his 1984 US Senate and

1988, 2008, and 2012 presidential races. Yet, Paul's lost races were fruitful in advancing his educational mission.

Paul left the House in January of 2013 after choosing not to seek reelection. While he is no longer in political office, Paul is focused as much as ever on education. His platform now, including as chairman and founder of the Ron Paul Institute for Peace and Prosperity, is greater than it was through much of his years in political office, allowing Paul to continue his work on building a powerful movement in support of liberty.

Some people disparage Paul for standing by his principles instead of jettisoning his principles in an effort to obtain political power. But, an important lesson of Paul's forty years and counting in the political arena is that being principled and consistent can yield a very important success — waking up people in America and around the world to the pro-liberty message.

100

February 23, 2015

The Washington Post's Gross Mischaracterization of Ron Paul's Message

Irrespective of the commonly held view that the Washington Post is the newspaper of record of America or at least of United States politics, David A. Fahrenthold's January 25 Washington Post article purporting to report on Ron Paul's participation the previous day at a Ludwig von Mises Institute event provides anything but an accurate record. Instead, Fahrenthold's article presents a gross mischaracterization of Paul's message.

Before the widespread use of the internet, people could be more easily hoodwinked by distortions such as those in the Washington Post article. Unless other major media contested the hogwash, there would be little chance that many people would encounter a response that sets the record straight. In contrast, today people can often protect themselves from such

disinformation by viewing on the internet material that discloses the truth — in this case the video of Paul's speech posted on
the Mises Institute website and the January 8 editorial by Paul
quoted in the Post article.

If you were to rely on the Washington Post for your understanding of Paul's message and his Mises Institute speech,
here is some of the impression you would be given. First, should
you search for "Ron Paul" on the Washington Post website, you
will see that the brief promotion for the article declares Paul's
"gloom and doom." Next, when you click through the link to
the article, you will see at the top of the article a photograph
of Paul with a caption proclaiming "Ron Paul's pessimistic attitudes." Then, reading Fahrenthold's article, you will come
across Fahrenthold's claim that Paul "has embraced a role as
libertarianism's prophet of doom."

Fahrenthold later in the article attributes to Paul, the founder and chairman of the Ron Paul Institute for Peace and Prosperity, the following:

> Ron Paul's solution, it appears, is to invite more calam-
> ity so that Americans are forced realize [sic] that the
> system is broken.

It would be interesting to see Fahrenthold try to back this
assertion. Instead he just immediately follows the assertion
with listing some predictions in Paul's January 8 editorial and
relating two quotes from the editorial: "Sanity will not return to
US leaders until our financial system collapses — an event for
which they are feverishly working," and "Before we can actually
restore our liberties, we most likely will have to become a lot
less free and much poorer."

Someone reading through the Washington Post article
quickly without the great skepticism merited would assume
that these Paul quotes back Fahrenthold's bold assertion that
Paul's solution is "to invite more calamity" and that the calamity
Paul wants to make happen includes the financial system collapsing and people becoming "a lot less free and much poorer."
The quotes, however, show in no way that Paul is advocating
making any of these problems occur. Instead, Paul is explaining

that the course is set for these problems to occur. Regarding the financial system collapse, Paul even says in the brief Post article quotes that it is other people, not Paul, who are "feverishly working" toward that eventuality.

No evidence is presented to back the Washington Post article's assertion that Paul's message is defined by doom, gloom, and pessimism. Neither is any evidence offered to back the article's assertion that Paul invites "more calamity" nor the assertion that Paul "has embraced a role as libertarianism's prophet of doom."

Paul does discuss in his January 8 editorial disturbing and dangerous conditions, but he does so in an effort to turn those conditions around. Indeed, Paul regularly expresses optimism in his writings, speeches, and interviews that the trend will be reversed so that in the future there will be more peace, prosperity, and liberty.

The Washington Post's twisting of Paul's message is like portraying the weatherman as the creator and controller of a hurricane because he warns it is coming.

It is as if Fahrenthold and the Washington Post believe they can in the internet age get away with putting out any claptrap smears they can concoct and have the smears accepted by the public. To some extent that belief is right. Fahrenthold's article was widely circulated on the internet. But, also, the internet makes it easier to fact-check the media and to disseminate fact-checking material that can be used to erode the influence of deceptive media stories.

Looking at Paul's January 8 editorial, which is quoted in — but not linked from — the Washington Post article, the Post's deception is quickly apparent. The first clue is the title of the Paul's editorial: "Inner City Turmoil and Other Crises: My Predictions for 2015." True to the title, Paul proceeds in the editorial to present some of his predictions regarding various crises in the new year. Paul's editorial clearly communicates Paul's desire that these crises not continue, grow, or arise in 2015. Paul, though, believes that they will.

Paul explores in his editorial, as Paul does in many other

writings, speeches, and interviews, the reality that there are many problems in America and the world, and that government actions often contribute significantly to the creation, continuation, and growth of problems. Paul, as usual, also explains that he opposes these harmful government actions. Conflating a person's description of problems with the assertion that the person supports the problems, as the Washington Post article does, demonstrates a severe lack of something, be it logical reasoning, reading skills, or fealty to truth.

Paul makes crystal-clear in his editorial's concluding paragraphs — about which Fahrenthold is silent — that Paul's outlook is very optimistic. Did Fahrenthold make it this far in his reading or just copy and paste into his article a couple quotes that sounded particularly alarming and call it a day?

Here is Paul speaking for himself in the last two paragraphs of his editorial:

> The real problem of course is that too many "stupid people" are IN our government and have high visibility on the major TV networks. There will be plenty of people, not officially associated with government, who will rebel against various governments around the world. The sentiments supporting secession, jury nullification, nullification of federal laws by state legislatures, and a drive for more independence from larger governments will continue.
>
> We should not be discouraged. Enlightenment is not nearly as difficult to achieve as it was before the breakthrough with Internet communications occurred. Besides we must remember that "an idea whose time has come" cannot be stopped by armies, demagogues, politicians, or even Fox News or MSNBC. The time has come for the ideas of liberty to prevail. I smell progress. Let's make 2015 a fun year for LIBERTY.

Paul's editorial unmistakably demonstrates that the characterization of Paul in the Washington Post article is rubbish. Thus, it comes as little surprise that the Post article provides no link when it briefly quotes the editorial.

In addition to reading — instead of just quoting — Paul's editorial, Fahrenthold had a second opportunity to learn first-hand Paul's views. As Fahrenthold reports in his Washington Post article, Fahrenthold attended the Mises Institute's January 24 conference in Houston, Texas at which Paul spoke. In fact the conference plays a central role in Fahrenthold's article.

Anyone watching Paul's speech at the Mises Institute conference can easily discern that Paul explains his message as being very different from the message Fahrenthold attributes to Paul. As Paul tends to do in his writings, speeches, and interviews, Paul explains in the speech that he is describing current and future crises that are caused in large part by Paul's political opponents who are advancing the growth of government power at the expense of peace, prosperity, and liberty. Paul also explains in the speech, as he does regularly in presentations of various forms, that Paul is optimistic that a peaceful revolution is building that will counter the crises and implement changes benefiting liberty and bringing about much more peace and prosperity.

In short, Paul explains in his speech, which Fahrenthold had the opportunity to hear at the Houston conference, that Paul opposes the doom, gloom, and calamity Fahrenthold suggests Paul supports.

Is it possible Fahrenthold skipped out on Paul's speech without even disclosing this in the Washington Post article? That would be an incredibly misleading omission given the clear impression conveyed in the article that Fahrenthold was at the conference to report on Paul. (The Post article does include a paragraph describing Paul's speech.) Such a failure to disclose would be consistent with the overall deceptive nature of the article.

Let's suppose Fahrenthold was present for Paul's speech. In that case, Fahrenthold would have had numerous opportunities to hear Paul explain Paul's optimistic attitude and opposition to crises and suffering facing Americans and people around the word. Yet, Fahrenthold neglected reporting the message Paul actually delivered at the conference, choosing instead to label Paul as communicating the opposite message.

Gone are the days when untrustworthy reporting in the Washington Post was the only ready way to obtain information about what is said in many speeches. Now you often can just watch a speech on your computer, tablet, or phone. If you do so with Paul's Mises Institute speech, you will witness Paul delivering a message totally at odds with the impression Fahrenthold presents. Rather than speaking like someone who Fahrenthold says "has embraced a role as libertarianism's prophet of doom," Paul indisputably communicates a message of hope in the speech.

In contrast to Fahrenthold's sour distortion of Paul's message, Paul starts his speech off gleefully pronouncing "good news." Here is how Paul begins his presentation:

> Thank you very much everybody. So, I would like to start off by talking about the subject, and the subject of course is secession and nullification, the breaking up of government. And the good news is it's gonna happen, it's happening.

The remainder of the first three minutes of Paul's speech further gives the lie to the Washington Post's characterization of Paul. Paul, in the first minute, discusses the "total failure" of communism, Nazism, and fascism in the 20th century. Paul notes Austrian economist Ludwig von Mises, for whom Paul has great respect, predicted in 1912 that communism would fail. In the second minute of his speech, Paul comments that the failure of these authoritarian systems is "very, very good news." Instead of prophesying doom, Paul proceeds in the remainder of the second minute to state that he believes "we live in an age, which I consider an end of an era, an end of an era that has made all these trials and tribulations." In his third minute. Paul explains that advocates of liberty, such as Paul, want to progress beyond tyranny that "has been around for a long time." Regarding tyranny, Paul says he thinks that it is "over and done with."

Maybe Fahrenthold did not hear the first three minutes of Paul's speech. But, Paul's speech continued for another 31 minutes. If Fahrenthold could manage to listen for just a few of those minutes, he could hear Paul make clear that Paul seeks to end the crises Paul describes and that Paul is optimistic about the future. In short, Fahrenthold would have heard Paul contradict entirely the gross mischaracterization Fahrenthold made of Paul's message in the Washington Post article.

Supposing that by 12 minutes into Paul's speech Fahrenthold was paying attention, shouldn't Fahrenthold have thrown out the distorted representation of Paul planned for the Washington Post article after hearing Paul then discuss war? Paul states:

> Unfortunately, all this mess depends on the propagandists, and that's where it is very, very tough. But, it is also the place where we are making inroads because there's more than three major networks on television. There are a lot of people outside of the three majors that are available — whether it's the internet or whatever — that a lot of people are waking up, especially the young people of this country, that this is enough of this killing, it's time that we change our foreign policy.

If Fahrenthold were daydreaming during that part of the speech, maybe he heard Paul saying the following a few minutes later:

> But, you know, I have argued the case that there is no reason we can't move in a better direction. The failure of the economic system. The failure of the foreign policy. Why can't civilization advance — advance in the understanding of peace?
>
> You say, "Well, there's going to be wars and rumors of wars for ever and ever, and that's the way it's been." But why is it that it has to be that way? I mean … recorded history isn't all that old. And, if you look at the history of freedom, it's just hundreds of years old. We have our ups and downs, but generally it's better understood now than it was thousands of years ago.
>
> So there's this effort to understand and move in this

> direction. But, so many people don't quite under-
> stand the importance of what we do. I believe if you
> took technology and, instead of using it to advance
> the weapons of war, take technology and advance the
> ability to promote peace and understanding, that is
> what we really need. And I think the tools are there. I
> think the internet and technology is there to spread a
> different message.

If those comments flew by Fahrenthold unnoticed, maybe he was jarred to attention when Paul then proceeded to say that "we can change the human condition" and advance peace. As support for this proposition, Paul then related inspirational stories of troops in World War I and World War II resisting the charge to kill and following instead what Paul terms "the natural tendency ... for the soldiers not to fight."

Giving Fahrenthold yet more reason to refrain from his deceptive caricaturing of Paul, Paul then explains that evil motivation, as well as ignorance buttressed by propaganda, supports the "war is the answer" view that causes "harm and injury." To anyone paying attention, this statement, like so many others in the speech, makes clear that Paul opposes the troubles about which he talks. Paul makes those observations 24 minutes into his speech, but maybe Fahrenthold had not settled in to listen yet.

Having clearly stated he believes that other people have created the problems of which he talks in his speech, Paul proceeds to offer a solution. Regarding war in particular, Paul says "a few individuals can't do it; you have to have a whole understanding by a people that we reject the notion of war." Speaking about solving a broader array of problems, Paul says:

> Our concern of course is based on our concept of
> liberty. I'm convinced that we can solve so many of
> our problems, whether economics or foreign policy,
> by just a better understanding of liberty. I believe our
> Founders understood this.

Paul then notes that he is "hopeful" because he sees "a lot

of enthusiasm" among young people at college campuses where he speaks. Paul suggests that the young people need to "hear there is enough support" so they will feel they can resist policies — including policies related to the Federal Reserve and foreign intervention — that are creating problems.

Later in Paul's Mises Institute speech, Fahrenthold was given yet another chance to realize the absurdness of the picture the Washington Post article Fahrenthold was planning would paint of Paul. Paul enters the concluding portion of his Mises Institute speech with a discussion of how the ideas of liberty can overcome the problems created by the promotion of war and oppression. This powerful analysis is very similar to comments Paul made in a speech two months earlier at a Mises Institute event in Costa Mesa, California.

Maybe Fahrenthold zoned out for, or just skipped out on, the speech he presented himself as reporting on for the Washington Post. Maybe Fahrenthold also failed to read the Paul editorial he quoted in the Post article. In any case, it would take "giving the benefit of the doubt" to preposterous length to excuse the gross mischaracterization of Paul's message in the supposed paper of record.

101

February 27, 2015

Former NSA and CIA Boss Michael Hayden Calls Himself an 'Unrelenting Libertarian'

Michael Hayden, who served in turn as director of the National Security Agency (NSA), principal deputy director of National Intelligence, and director of the Central Intelligence Agency (CIA) from 1999 through 2009, elicited laughs and a loud jeer of "No you're not!" in response to his assertion Friday morning during a Conservative Political Action Conference (CPAC) debate that he is an "unrelenting libertarian."

It is hard to imagine a more preposterous assertion from Hayden who defends the United States government's extensive torture program, many of the revolting details of which were recently revealed in a partially-released Senate Intelligence Committee report, and oversaw the NSA mass spying program. Libertarians, of course, oppose such violations of individual rights.

If Hayden had changed his mind and become an opponent of the massive rights violations that intelligence agencies committed under his oversight, his "unrelenting libertarian" claim might not be so ridiculous. However, Hayden is instead a steadfast defender of the violations. After NSA whistle-blower Edward Snowden revealed information about the US government's mass spying program, "unrelenting libertarian" Hayden "joked" about putting Snowden on President Barack Obama's targeted killings list. And, when Sen. Dianne Feinstein (D-CA), who then chaired the Senate Intelligence Committee, started making some critical comments about the torture program, the "unrelenting libertarian" dismissed Feinstein's concerns as the senator just being "emotional."

Hayden continues to defend US government encroachments of individual rights. In fact, that was the purpose of his participation in the CPAC debate in which he presented his astounding self-characterization. Hayden was debating Andrew Napolitano, the Fox News senior judicial analyst and a Ron Paul Institute Advisory Board member, regarding the US government's mass spying program. Hayden, as expected, presented a blanket defense of the program. At the beginning of the debate, Hayden drew applause and cheers from the audience for calling Napolitano "an unrelenting libertarian." Hayden then followed up with the comment "so am I," resulting in a very different audience reaction.

Part 8: This and That

102

January 14, 2014

A Tipping Point For Liberty Against Leviathan

Continuing revelations of the extensive scope of the US government's mass spying program, piled on top of decades of foreign intervention and liberty suppression at home, can lead Americans to question if they should give up their work for peace and liberty. Nevertheless, there is reason for hope that pursuing this work will yield success.

Speaking with host Neil Cavuto on Fox Business, Ron Paul Institute Advisory Board Member Andrew Napolitano warns that the US government has established a mass spying program so invasive that "we are close to a generation of Americans who will not even know what privacy means because they will grow up in a society in which everything they do from the moment of their birth — no matter how intimate or private the moment — will be monitored by the government, and they will accept that."

Napolitano explains that even when the crisis used to justify the government intrusion passes, "the freedom doesn't come back or, if it does, it doesn't come back all the way, and then that surrender is used by future generations of government as precedent for asking for more surrender of freedom."

The mass spying program thus appears to be another example of the process described by RPI Academic Board Member Robert Higgs whereby the government uses a crisis, in this case terrorism, to justify expanding government power at the expense of liberty. Higgs explains this process:

> How do once-free people lose their liberty? The formula may be stated succinctly: crisis and leviathan. Alternatively, and somewhat more fully stated, the procedure for the government officials and their supporters who hope to gain by quashing the people's liberties is (1) cause a serious crisis, thereby heightening the public's fears, and (2) blame others for the crisis, pose as the people's savior, and thereby justify the seizure of new powers allegedly necessary to remedy the crisis and to prevent the recurrence of such crises in the future. This gambit is as old as the hills, yet, given the right ideological preconditions, it works every time. Strange to say, the people never learn (in part because these experiences produce ideological change that fortifies the fiscal and institutional changes the government makes during the crisis).

Watching the government repeatedly using crises to grow larger at the expense of peace and liberty can be disheartening, especially considering that the government even creates many of the crises. For example, the US government's wars, foreign aid, and sanctions motivate violent acts against Americans.

The intentional operation of this process was rather famously explained by Rahm Emanuel in the context of a 2008 economic crisis. Gerald F. Seib reports in the Wall Street Journal:

> This opportunity isn't lost on the new president and his team. "You never want a serious crisis to go to waste," Rahm Emanuel, Mr. Obama's new chief of staff, told a Wall Street Journal conference of top corporate chief executives this week.
>
> He elaborated: "Things that we had postponed for too long, that were long-term, are now immediate and

must be dealt with. This crisis provides the opportunity for us to do things that you could not do before."

Yet, there is hope for reversing the growth of government threats to liberty and peace through the crisis and leviathan process.

In the Fox Business interview, Napolitano points to a statement the National Security Agency (NSA) issued in reaction to a question US Sen. Bernie Sanders (I-VT) submitted to the agency. Napolitano believes the NSA's statement clarifying that the NSA spies on members of Congress the same as the agency spies on other Americans may provide the impetus for Congress to use the "power of the purse" to curtail the spying.

Additionally, politicians should take heed of the apparent movement of public opinion in the US toward supporting a noninterventionist foreign policy and fearing big government. Indeed, last year public opposition helped prevent a US government attack on Syria and helped encourage the US House to nearly pass an amendment to significantly undercut the NSA's mass spying. This happened despite the Obama administration and bipartisan congressional leadership lining up on the opposing side in both instances.

Meanwhile, state and local governments are going their own way on marijuana policy, chopping away at the war on drugs — a decades long travesty the US government uses to expand its power, enrich special interests, and trample liberty.

Are we approaching a tipping point where the US government reverses course and substantially increases its respect for civil liberties at home and peace with other nations? While it can be disheartening to witness the US government leviathan with its multiple simultaneous wars, mass spying, rise of SWAT, and record-setting incarceration rate, rather sudden changes can occur in political systems that seem nearly omnipotent.

Whether a tipping point is near or far, people who value respect for liberty at home and a noninterventionist foreign policy can continue their educational efforts to lay the groundwork for change. Then, should an opportunity arise for radical change in one policy area or many, that change will more likely be towards greater respect for liberty and peace.

We can look again to Higgs for some valuable advice about taking on the government leviathan. Higgs writes in his June 1 Independent Institute article "State Power and How It Might Be Undermined":

> State power is the most dangerous force in modern life. State rulers, seeking their own aggrandizement and enrichment, employ this power systematically to plunder and abuse their subjects. Of course, they cannot act in this way without the assistance of many others, among whom some assist willingly, some in return for adequate compensation, and many only under duress.
>
> To maintain their grip on power, state rulers (1) bamboozle as many subjects as possible; (2) co-opt those whose cooperation or support is essential by bribing them with various sorts of payoffs; (3) intimidate those who are not essential and not fooled by threatening them with fines, imprisonment, and other punishments; and (4) kill those who are not essential, are not fooled, and will not bend to intimidation.
>
> Anyone who seeks to stymie or overturn state power must block these state actions or render them less effective. Resisters therefore have many options.
>
> First, they may work to reduce the number of people who succumb to the rulers' bamboozlement by exposing the rulers' lies, spreading truthful information, and revealing the rulers' venality and cynical disregard of the people's natural rights and the general public interest. People may withdraw their children from government schools and teach them at home; they may spread truthful information about the horrors of the state and the glories of freedom by means of the Internet and the World Wide Web. In short, people may use the word processor that is mightier than the Predator drone (formerly the pen that is mightier than

the sword) as well as face-to-face communication to reeducate those who have been taught, conditioned, and forced to drink's the rulers' Kool-Aid.

There are many ways individuals can take part in advancing peace and liberty against crisis and leviathan. And there is reason for hope. Some encouragement may be gained from reflecting on the concluding sentences of Malcolm Gladwell's intriguing book The Tipping Point: How Little Things Can Make a Big Difference:

> In the end, Tipping Points are a reaffirmation of the potential for change and the power of intelligent action, Look at the world around you. It may seem like an immovable, implacable place. It is not. With the slightest push -- in just the right place — it can be tipped.

103

Media Blaming Libertarians for Republican Candidates' Losses Four Months Before Election

The media is not waiting until after the November general election to blame Libertarian Party candidates for Republican Party candidates' upcoming losses. Indeed, Libertarian candidates are already being blamed for the Republicans' potential failure to gain a majority in of the United States Senate. The Washington Post on Sunday published an article suggesting that Libertarian candidates could "spoil" Republicans' chances of winning Senate races in eleven or more states, as well as some governor races.

Following an Associated Press article last month that erroneously suggested Libertarian governor candidate Ed Thompson caused the Republican incumbent Wisconsin governor to lose to the Democrat challenger in 2002, the Washington Post article points to Republican losses in the Virginia 2013 governor race and the 2006 and 2012 Montana US Senate races to support the assertion that Libertarian candidates are spoilers for Republicans.

What proof does the Washington Post article offer to advance this empirical argument? The Libertarian candidate received more votes than the number of votes by which the Democrat beat the Republican in each of those three races. That's it — an underwhelming "argument" to say the least. The article seems to trust that readers believe the baseless, though widely repeated, characterization of libertarianism as a subset of conservatism.

Of course, not every person who voted for the Libertarian candidates in the Virginia and Montana races would have voted for the Republican in the respective races had there been no Libertarian option. The Washington Post does not give reason to suppose that even a majority of the Libertarian candidate supporters would have done so. Some of these voters would have voted for the Republican and others for the Democrat. A significant number may have chosen not to vote at all on election day or to vote on other matters on the ballot but not in the particular race.

Even an individual who votes for a Libertarian candidate and views the Republican in the race as the second-best option may not be counted on as a voter for the Republican if the favored candidate were not in the race. For some people, a candidate being marginally better is not good enough. If there is no candidate that meets a certain threshold, then no candidate will earn the vote.

Other voters who like a Libertarian or other "third party" candidate the most may nonetheless vote for the Republican or Democrat candidate who the voters determine is "good enough." In these cases, voters choose to forego making a statement about who the best candidate is in order to try to play a part in deciding which candidate will win the immediate race or to send a message to the "major parties" regarding what kind of candidate can earn their votes.

Another group of voters will always or almost always choose a Republican or Democrat, viewing making any other choice as a "wasted vote."

On the other end of the spectrum, other people will only show up at an election if there is a rare candidate who inspires them and then only vote for that candidate, leaving other races with blank or write-in votes.

The fundamental issue is that third party candidates, be they Libertarians, Greens, or whatever, are not stealing votes from Republican or Democrat candidates. The votes were never the property of one party or candidate to begin with. Votes, like cash, may be spent however a person subjectively determines is best. Excepting instances of illegal election tampering, success in elections depends on marketing a product people are willing to choose over other available choices.

My recent article "A Tipping Point For Liberty Against Leviathan" explores some issues that are likely to be important for many voters in the November elections:

> Additionally, politicians should take heed of the apparent movement of public opinion in the US toward supporting a noninterventionist foreign policy and fearing big government. Indeed, last year public opposition helped prevent a US government attack on Syria and helped encourage the US House to nearly pass an amendment to significantly undercut the NSA's mass spying. This happened despite the Obama administration and bipartisan congressional leadership lining up on the opposing side in both instances.

Maybe, if some "third party" campaigns do better in the November elections than in past years, it will be because some voters see these campaigns as resonating with this movement in public opinion. If that is the case, "major party" candidates could better spend their time learning from their competitors' success than blaming them.

April 11, 2015

Gov. Charlie Baker Applauds US Government Circumventing State Law to Execute Dzhokhar Tsarnaev

Massachusetts does not have a death penalty. It has not had one for over thirty years — since the Massachusetts Supreme Judicial Court ruled in 1984 that the state's death penalty violated the state constitution. Yet, we have the spectacle of Charlie Baker, the state's Republican governor, proclaiming on Wednesday that Dzhokhar Tsarnaev, who a United States district court trial jury had that day found guilty of counts related to the Boston Marathon bombing, should be executed in contravention of Massachusetts law.

Executing Tsarnaev is an option only because the United States Department of Justice decided to prosecute him in the US court system. Had that decision to intervene not been made, prosecution would have surely been pursued in the Massachusetts state court system where Tsarnaev would face incarceration upon a guilty verdict, but not execution.

It is bad enough that US government politicians and bureaucrats routinely stomp on state and local decisions to restrict the exercise of government power via criminal law, as seen in the ongoing conflict between the US government enforcing US drug laws and state and local governments rolling back various aspects of the drug war. Must we also endure governors like Baker cheering the US government crushing their own states' limits on government power, including the power to terminate a person's life?

Boston attorney and Three Felonies a Day author Harvey Silverglate sums up the problem with the US government seeking the death penalty in the Tsarnaev case. Silverglate wrote in a Wednesday Boston Globe editorial, "Regardless of the jury's sentencing decision, this trial has starkly illustrated a decline in Massachusetts' state sovereignty in deciding — literally — life-or-death matters."

The US government's circumvention of the Massachusetts death penalty prohibition is a disturbing contravention of American states' historic dominion over criminal law matters, including murder trials. Years back people used to say, "Don't make a federal case out of it!" You do not hear that phrase much anymore. The expansion in recent decades of both the US criminal code and prosecutions in the US court system has made the phrase become virtually meaningless. The US government can make a federal case out of just about anything now and thus uproot state and local governments from their historic role in administering criminal cases and defining procedures and punishments. This abrogation often happens, as it has in the Tsarnaev case, with state politicians failing to defend their states' limits on government power. Sometimes, as with Baker, state politicians even applaud the US government's toppling of those limits.

105

June 24, 2015

If You Want to Get Rid of 'Racist Flags,' How About Starting with the American Flag?

It looks like open season has been declared on the battle flag of the Army of Northern Virginia, which is commonly referred to as the Confederate battle flag. But, if you are looking for a flag to ban as racist, you might as well start with the American flag.

After all, the American flag is associated with the United States government that sanctioned slavery from the enactment of the US Constitution in 1789 to the addition of the 13th Amendment to the Constitution in December of 1865 — months after the end of the war with the Confederate States. The CS government, in comparison, existed for less than five years, with slavery legal the entire time.

The American flag flies now for a government whose drug

war and larger law enforcement system is responsible for black Americans being harassed, arrested, and incarcerated in extraordinary numbers. Remember the 13th Amendment to the US Constitution makes an exception to allow slavery as "a punishment for crime." This is an exception that has been employed much in America recently, with the number of people incarcerated in prisons and jails growing five-fold in the last thirty years.

Of course, the Confederate battle flag opponents come out every four years to yell out "gotcha, you're a racist!" at any presidential candidate who refuses to recite that the South Carolina government should remove the "racist" Confederate battle flag from the grounds of the state capitol building. This occurs again and again despite the fact that the flag's presence is a state matter over which the US president has no role in deciding.

The killing of several people at a church in Charleston, South Carolina last week has helped inflame the quadrennial attacks on the Confederate battle flag.

Some people even believe the root cause of the killings resides in a statewide hatred of back people that is interwoven with the fabric of that Confederate battle flag flying on the state capitol grounds.

It is not too surprising to see film director Michael Moore's vehement comments calling for someone to tear down the Confederate battle flag on the South Carolina capitol grounds and relating the flag's presence to the killings. His comments are one sample of the torrent of similar comments being made since the killings.

Over at The Intercept, Jon Schwarz does not want to stop at taking down one flag. Schwarz writes that taking down the Confederate battle flag at the South Carolina capitol grounds "seems like a good start, but maybe not the place to end." Schwarz lists six additional cultural items to purge from the state — three statues, the name of a street in Charleston, the Charleston city seal, and the South Carolina state flag. He doesn't claim that any of these cultural items say anything explicitly racist. Rather, he says they all have some connection to slavery.

Schwarz sees this purge of his listed cultural items as just a start. Indeed, he is seeking suggestions for expanding the purge list:

> I'm sure there's much more that could be added to this list. If you're from South Carolina and would like to make some suggestions, please get in touch. (Also please get in touch if you have any ideas for getting Andrew Jackson off our money.)

As alluded to in the Andrew Jackson reference, Schwarz's desired purge goes far beyond South Carolina. As he says, "every other place in America also celebrates the ugliest parts of our past."

It is doubtful that a very high percentage of people looking at a twenty dollar bill or one of the statues Schwarz wants removed from South Carolina are celebrating the most inhumane things the individuals represented, did, or may be associated with. Some people take in the aesthetic and leave it at that. Some people ponder the times during which the individuals represented lived. Some people curse or celebrate the individuals represented. Different strokes for different folks.

The call for a widespread elimination of cultural items that may cause some people discomfort because of a relationship to slavery — and potentially a much longer list of verboten people, occurrences, and beliefs — brings to mind the destruction of cultural items in war. Addressing the intentional destruction of cultural items by the Islamic State (ISIS), Sturt W. Manning, the director of the Cornell Institute of Archaeology and Material Studies and professor of classical architecture at Cornell University, explains:

> All attacks on archaeological sites and artifacts are brutal assaults on our collective human memory. They deprive us of the evidence of human endeavors and achievements.
>
> The destruction eloquently speaks of the human folly and senseless violence that drives ISIS. The terror group is destroying the evidence of the great history of

Iraq; it has to, as this history attests to a rich alternative to its barbaric nihilism.

While the sought purge of cultural items in South Carolina and throughout America is different in many ways from the destruction of cultural items pursued by ISIS, Manning's observations suggest some important similarities. In America such cultural cleansing similarly threatens to obliterate Americans' "memories" and the evidence of history. The whitewashing also attempts to alter the American narrative to remove the alternatives, with their both good and bad aspects, that may be suggested by the purged cultural items.

The German government's attack on "degenerate art" in the 1930s and '40s is an illustrative example of the systematic destruction of cultural items.

Many people will find more surprising than Moore and Schwarz's comments the articles by writers identified with libertarianism who single out the Confederate battle flag as universally conveying a predominantly or solely racist message.

Cato Institute Executive Vice President David Boaz wrote in 2001 that the Mississippi state flag should be altered because "the Confederate emblem in the state flag can't be separated from slavery." But of course it can, just like the American flag can be separated from slavery.

The governments of both the US and CS recognized the legality of slavery in their respective jurisdictions throughout their war. As the war proceeded, the US began eliminating slavery in conquered territory, but slavery remained legal and enforced in states that had not seceded from the US. Still, today many of the people singing the national anthem while looking at the US flag at any given sporting event are not seeing the American flag as a symbol of slavery. Many of these people look past the decades of slavery and slave trade under US government protection. They also look past the Fugitive Slave Act that denied slaves their freedom even if they could escape to a state that outlawed slavery, as well as the fact that the US Constitution guaranteed through the year 1808 the legal continuation of the importation of slaves.

Boaz's conclusion derives from defining the Confederate States War as being about one thing: the Confederate States desire to protect slavery. This is a conclusion with which many people disagree. And even people who agree with Boaz's conclusion about the war can still revere the Confederate battle flag while opposing slavery and racism.

Why is this so hard for so many people to understand? All sorts of Americans revere the American flag even though they don't agree with everything the US government has done. An American Indian may cherish the American flag, not defining it as a representation of a government that slaughtered his ancestors and drove them from the land on which they lived. A liberal may cherish the American flag, not defining it as a representation of a government that does not guarantee single-payer health care, a $15 an hour minimum wage, and gay marriage. A conservative may cherish the American flag, not defining it as a representation of a government that imposes too much taxes, is soft on illegal immigration, and allows abortions. A libertarian may cherish the American flag, not defining it as a representation of a government that engages in endless offensive wars, mass surveillance, and the war on drugs.

Steve Chapman is emphatic in a Monday article at Reason that the Confederate battle flag has a universal racist message. Chapman states:

> In 2015, anyone displaying that flag knows what it means to viewers, particularly black ones. It's an expression of hostility, not only toward black people, but to broader ideals of how the nation should come to terms with the legacy of racism.

Yet, in the same article, Chapman discloses that in 1972 he displayed a Confederate battle flag from his dorm room window at college. And he says he did so for reasons that had nothing to do with expressing racism. Chapman explains:

> Like a lot of people below the Mason-Dixon Line — white people, anyway — I saw the emblem as a token of regional pride. I didn't revere slavery and Jim Crow.

283

> But I thought there was much about the South to love.
>
> And if the flag annoyed the Yankees a little, that was OK. They were not as noble and blameless as they pretended to be. They were not going to make me repudiate my native region.

Chapman provides no explanation in his article why someone, like himself, could revere and display the Confederate flag without any racist motivation in 1972 while, in 2015, displaying the flag with a motivation like he had as a college student is impossible. It is hard to imagine what sort of tortured reasoning would be used to argue that point.

In 2011, Byron Thomas, a student at the University of South Carolina Beaufort, did just what Chapman did nearly forty years earlier. Thomas hung a Confederate battle flag in his dorm room window. Thomas even stood up to university administrators who demanded he take the flag down. As reported in a 2011 Associate Press article, Thomas presented an explanation for his action that is very similar to how Chapman describes Chapman's motivations as a college student. Says Thomas: "When I look at this flag, I don't see racism. I see respect, Southern pride." This week, Thomas discussed in a CNN interview his reasons for his continuing reverence for and display of the Confederate battle flag.

Chapman and Thomas also serve as an example that people's views regarding the Confederate battle flag are not determined by their race. Chapman is white. Thomas is black. Yet, as college students they both displayed the Confederate battle flag and did not view their doing so as an expression of racism.

Many people who would heap scorn on Chapman or Thomas for displaying the "racist" Confederate battle flag would praise someone for displaying the American flag. Yet, the American flag is associated with a government that has done much wrong, including to black people.

The "racist" label can be affixed to the American flag just as it can to the Confederate battle flag. The histories of the governments associated with both flags provide plenty of ground for arguments supporting the label's applicability. Yet, each flag is cherished both by people who abhor racism and by people who embrace racism. If the Confederate battle flag must be taken down because of the history of the government with which it is associated, then why not take down the American flag as well?

About the Author:

Adam Dick is a senior fellow at the Ron Paul Institute for Peace and Prosperity. His writings, speeches, and interviews may be found at the Ron Paul Institute's website and AdamDick.com.

Mr. Dick worked from 2003 through 2013 as a legislative aide for US Rep. Ron Paul, responsible for correspondence related to all policy issues and serving as Rep. Paul's primary aide for the issues of drug prohibition, gun rights, property rights, free speech, religion, and the District of Columbia.

Before working for Rep. Paul, Mr. Dick was co-manager of Ed Thompson's 2002 Wisconsin governor campaign. By winning over 10 percent in the governor race, Mr. Thompson earned the state Libertarian Party an appointee on the Wisconsin State Board of Elections. Mr. Dick was the first board member selected by the state party chairman.

Mr. Dick worked previously as a lawyer in New York and Connecticut. He lives with his wife and son in Dallas, Texas.

www.ingramcontent.com/pod-product-compliance
Lightning Source LLC
Chambersburg PA
CBHW031147270326
41931CB00006B/178